CSCE DECISION-MAKING:
the Madrid Experience

CSCE DECISION-MAKING: the Madrid Experience

by

Jan Sizoo

and

Rudolf Th. Jurrjens

1984 **Martinus Nijhoff Publishers**
a member of the KLUWER ACADEMIC PUBLISHERS GROUP
THE HAGUE / BOSTON / LANCASTER

Distributors

for the United States and Canada: Kluwer Academic Publishers, 190 Old Derby Street, Hingham, MA 02043, USA
for the UK and Ireland: Kluwer Academic Publishers, MTP Press Limited, Falcon House, Queen Square, Lancaster LA1 1RN, England
for all other countries: Kluwer Academic Publishers Group, Distribution Center, P.O. Box 322, 3300 AH Dordrecht, The Netherlands

Library of Congress Cataloging in Publication Data

Sizoo, Jan, 1937-
CSCE decision-making.

Bibliography: p.
Includes index.
1. Conference on Security and Co-operation in Europe.
I. Jurrjens, Rudolph Th., 1938- . II. Title.
III. Title: C.S.C.E. decision-making.
JX1393.C65S59 1984 327.1'7'094 84-10196
ISBN 90-247-2989-0

ISBN 90-247-2989-0

Copyright

PRINTED IN THE NETHERLANDS

PREFACE

This study is the combined effort of a theorist and a practitioner. Both obtained doctorates in Political Science at the *Vrije Universiteit* [Free University] in Amsterdam. Rudolf Jurrjens (1938) has taught international relations at this university since 1968, with a break in 1975/76 when he was a visiting scholar at the Research Institute on International Change of Columbia University; his doctoral dissertation was entitled *THE FREE FLOW: People, Ideas and Information in Soviet Ideology and Politics*, and he has published several articles on East-West relations. Jan Sizoo (1937) was a permanent member of the Netherlands delegation to the CSCE meeting in Madrid. Previous experiences in his career as a Dutch diplomat include membership of the Netherlands delegation to NATO when he specialized in the preparations for the Helsinki consultations and the MBFR negotiations. The texts of the chapters on the organization and course of the Madrid Meeting in the present study came, in the first instance, from his pen. His doctoral thesis was on rightist political movements in Europe since the French Revolution and was entitled *INZAKE RECHTS* [*Concerning Right*], and he has also published several articles on international affairs.

The authors would like to express their thanks to various members of delegations in Madrid who were kind enough to read the first draft of the book and to give their comments upon it and who also supplied additional information which has enriched the text. Thanks are also due to members of the Madrid Executive Secretariat who did their utmost to make available all the documents that were required and who provided Annex 5 of the book.

The authors are particularly grateful to their translator, Christine Thirlway whose collaboration in bringing this book to birth was invaluable. Her personal interest in the book extended further than merely rendering it into correct English.

Finally, acknowledgements go to two people from the Amsterdam Free University: to Ronald Smallenburg who, as student at the Department of International Relations, prepared the Index, the list of Abbreviations and Selected Bibliography, and to Ingrid Vernie who, in typing the manuscript, managed to decipher successfully the handwriting of three different people.

The text of this book, its political and other opinions as well as its shortcomings are wholly the personal responsibility of the authors.

October 1983

Jan Sizoo
Rudolf Th. Jurrjens

CONTENTS

PREFACE 5
ABBREVIATIONS 13
TABLES AND FIGURES 15
INTRODUCTION 17

I. OPTIONS FOR A CSCE 23

1. Introduction 23
2. Agenda Options 24
3. Institutional Options 33
   3.1. The Alliance-Based Approach 33
   3.2. The UN-Linked Approach 34
   3.3. The Independent Approach 39
4. Procedural Options 41

II. CHOICES MADE FOR THE CSCE 49

1. Introduction 49
2. The CSCE Agenda 50
3. The CSCE Follow-up System 53
4. The CSCE Rules of Procedure 56
   4.1. The Rule of Consensus 57
   4.2. Reservations and Interpretative Statements 60
   4.3. Rotation of the Chairmanship 63
   4.4. Working Methods 65
   4.5. The Executive Secretary 66
   4.6. Languages 67
   4.7. Records of the Meetings, Publicity 67
5. Points for Consideration 68

III. THE PARTICIPATING STATES AND THEIR OBJECTIVES 77

1. Introduction 77
2. The Participating States 77
3. The Non-Participating Mediterranean States 81
4. Objectives of the Participating States 84
   4.1. Western Objectives 84
   4.2. East European Objectives 88
   4.3. NNA Objectives 90
5. The Proposals 91
   5.1. Western Proposals 94
   5.2. East European Proposals 97

5.3. NNA Proposals 102
5.4. Other Proposals 106

IV. THE REPRESENTATIVES AT MADRID 109

1. Introduction 109

2. The Delegates 109

3. Instructions and Reports 112

4. Relations with the Press 117

5. Relations with Pressure Groups 119

6. Personality versus Political Power 123

7. National Delegations 126

V. THE FORMAL SETTING OF THE DECISION-MAKING PROCESS 131

1. Introduction 131

2. The Purple Book 131

2.1. Agenda 133
2.2. "Optical Division" 136
2.3. "Cut-Off" 138
2.4. Time Schedule 138
2.5. Final Closing Date 139
2.6. Follow-up 140
2.7. Consensus 141

3. Working Methods 143

4. The Plenary 143

5. The Subsidiary Working Bodies 145

6. Drafting Groups 149

7. Working Bodies Created by the Plenary 150

VI. THE ACTUAL SETTING OF THE DECISION-MAKING PROCESS 153

1. Introduction 153

2. Contact Groups 153

3. Coffee Groups 159

4. Structured Informal Negotiations 161

5. Sherry Groups 161

6. Mini Groups 163

7. Government-to-Government Appeals 164

8. Caucuses 167

VII. THE RESULTS OF THE DECISION-MAKING PROCESS AND THEIR LIMITS .. 176

1. Introduction 176

2. Limits of the Final Act 176

3. Limits of the Review of Implementation 184

4. Limits of the Madrid Concluding Document 185

VIII. THE DECISION-MAKING PROCESS: PROCEDURE AS ISSUE 193

1. Introduction 193

2. 11 November 1980: The Stopped Clock 194

3. 9 February 1982: The Polish Chairman 197

4. 5 March 1982: The Night of Silences 203

5. Consensus on Procedures 208

IX. THE DECISION-MAKING PROCESS: SUBSTANCE AS ISSUE 212

1. Introduction 212

2. From Proposal to Provision 212

3. Drafting Techniques 216

4. Aspects of Negotiation 220

4.1. The Demandeur 220
4.2. Roles to be Played 223

5. The Process in Phases 228

5.1. Phase II (27 January - 10 April 1981): Examination of Proposals 230
5.2. Phase III (5 May - 27 July 1981): Drafting the Document 233
5.3. Phase IV (27 October - 18 December 1981): Search for Solutions 234
5.4. Phase V (9 February - 12 March 1982): Review of Implementation Once Again 236
5.5. Phase VI (4 November - 17 December 1982): New Western Proposals 237
5.6. Phase VII (8 February - 25 March 1983): Preparing the End-Game? 239
5.7. Phase VIII (19 April - 15 July 1983): The End-Game 240
5.8. The Malta Phase (15 July - 6 September 1983) 242

X. THE MADRID RESULTS 247

1. Introduction 247

2. The Review of Implementation 247

2.1. Themes Discussed 248
2.2. Basket Discussions 251
2.3. Détente and Implementation 253

3. The Madrid Concluding Document 255

3.1. First and Third Basket 255
3.2. Second Basket 258
3.3. Follow-up to Madrid 259
3.4. Reservations and Interpretative Statements 261
3.5. The Madrid Concluding Document: a Catalogue of Contemporary Problems 265

XI. CONCLUSIONS AND RECOMMENDATIONS 266
1. Introduction 266
2. The Madrid Conditions 266
3. The Madrid Experience 269
4. Recommendations 275

ANNEXES 285
1. Blue Book: Chapter 6 Rules of Procedure 285
2. Final Act: Chapter on Follow-up to the Conference 288
3. The Purple Book: Decisions 290
4. The Madrid Concluding Document 296
5. Manning Table of the Executive Secretariat 318

SELECTED BIBLIOGRAPHY 322

INDEX 328

ABBREVIATIONS

BBC	British Broadcasting Corporation
CBM	Confidence Building Measure
CDE	Conference on Disarmament in Europe
CES	Conference on European Security
CMEA	Council for Mutual Economic Assistance (also known as COMECON)
CPSU	Communist Party of the Soviet Union
CSBM	Confidence and Security Building Measure
CSCE	Conference on Security and Co-operation in Europe
EC	European Communities
ECE	Economic Commission for Europe
EEC	European Economic Community
EPC	European Political Co-operation
ESC	European Security Conference
DG	Drafting Group
FRG	Federal Republic of Germany
GATT	General Agreement on Tariffs and Trade
GDR	German Democratic Republic
ICNT	Informal Composite Negotiating Text
IM(C)O	Inter-Governmental Maritime (Consultative) Organization
IMF	International Monetary Fund
INF	Intermediate range Nuclear Forces
IRA	Irish Republican Army
ISNT	Informal Single Negotiating Text
ITU	International Telecommunication Union
MBFR	Mutual and Balanced Force Reductions
MPT	Multilateral Preparatory Talks
NATO	North Atlantic Treaty Organization
NNA	Neutral and Non-Aligned (countries)
OECD	Organization for Economic Co-operation and Development
PLO	Palestine Liberation Organization
RM	*Reunión de Madrid* [Follow-up Meeting of Madrid]
RSNT	Revised Single Negotiating Text

SALT	Strategic Arms Limitation Talks
SCEWER	Standing Commission on East-West Relations
START	Strategic Arms Reduction Talks
SU	Soviet Union
SWB	Subsidiary Working Body
UIC	*Union Internationale des Chemins de Fer* [International Railway Union]
UN(O)	United Nations (Organization)
UNCLOS (III)	(Third) United Nations Conference on the Law of the Sea
UNEP	United Nations Environment Programme
UNESCO	United Nations Educational, Scientific and Cultural Organization
UK	United Kingdom
US(A)	United States (of America)
USSR	Union of Socialist Soviet Republics
WEU	West European Union
WHO	World Health Organization
WP	Warsaw Pact

TABLES AND FIGURES

Tables:

3-1 The Proposals for a Concluding Document 92
9-1 The Negotiating Process in Phases 226/7

Figures:

5-1 The Formal and Actual Setting of the Decision-Making Process in Phases 132
5-2 The Formal Setting of the Decision-Making Process (1981) 142
6-1 The Informal Setting of the Decision-Making Process (1981) 154
6-2 The Informal Setting of the Decision-Making Process (1982) 162
6-3 The Informal Setting of the Decision-Making Process (1983) 164
9-1 The Course of a Proposal for the Third Basket 214

INTRODUCTION

In 1985 Helsinki will be the scene of a commemoration of the tenth anniversary of the conclusion of the Conference on Security and Co-operation in Europe, the CSCE, an occasion marked by the solemn signature of the Final Act by "the High Representatives" of the 35 participating states. This event, which took place on 1 August 1975, was regarded at the time as a milestone in human history. After years of consultation and negotiation a document had been produced which not only established a set of important principles to serve as guide for the participating states in their mutual relations but also contained a series of concrete provisions to enable those countries and their citizens to draw closer together.

An important element in what was laid down in the chapter of the Final Act on the follow-up to the conference was the provision that diplomats should be able to meet together regularly to discuss progress in implementation of the Final Act and at the same time have the opportunity to take new initiatives that might lead to improvement in mutual co-operation. The first of these follow-up meetings took place in Belgrade from 4 October 1977 to 9 March 1978. It was for many a disappointing experience. There was very little shared opinion in discussions on fulfilment of the Final Act particularly when it came to human rights conditions and implementation of provisions from the part of the Final Act concerned to promote freer exchange between the states both of persons and of information.

If up to then the Helsinki Act had led to little in the way of concrete policy guidance, in Belgrade, equally, the absence of any unanimity on what might be done to improve relations in Europe in the future ruled out any hopes of a substantial concluding document to that end, in spite of some hundred proposals put forward for inclusion in such a document. What was decided in Belgrade was that the process should continue with three expert meetings on specific subjects and a second follow-up meeting to be held in 1980 in Madrid.

It was widely feared that the Madrid Meeting would produce little more result than its forerunner in Belgrade. Nonetheless, in the Madrid preparatory phase the basis was laid for an effort to bring the meeting to its conclusion in March 1981, once more with a concluding document which, it was hoped, would have more breadth and content than that of Belgrade. Finally, after a conference of unanticipated duration, cramned with debates that bristled with bitterly enunciated accusations and inculpations, the desired result was achieved three years later in September 1983. The atmosphere of the final session when the 35 foreign ministers adopted the concluding document reflected the increased tension between the participating states, which had already played so drastic a role throughout the conference.

It comes therefore as no surprise to find that although the Madrid Concluding Document does have as concrete result the pushing forward of the CSCE process in a further series of meetings mandated in the document, the text is largely limited to setting out a catalogue of the problems that exist without prescribing authoritatively how they should be solved. It may be asked whether, with or without the increased tension between the participants, it might have been possible to reach a similar outcome in a more efficient way, or even perhaps whether a different approach to negotiations that were of such magnitude might not have led to markedly better results. The personal feelings of relief experienced by more than one Madrid diplomat when the final consensus was reached deserve every sympathy. What had seemed to be a never-ending litany could at last be rounded off with an "Amen" even if one that was less than hearty, but for the future, they hoped that never again would they have to go through such an experience: Madrid never again.

This study is concerned with the problems that reared their heads in the conference chamber. It examines the conditions of the Madrid Meeting with regard to agenda, institutional framework and rules of procedure and the way these conditions affected the organization, course and results of the meeting in Madrid. On the basis of the Madrid experience on these points it then becomes possible to make an attempt to recommend modifications of an organizational and procedural nature which may lead to greater efficiency in the decision-making process of future meetings and also, we take leave to hope, to the achievement of results of higher political value.

If the political relevance of the present study relates to the recommendations formulated in its concluding chapter, its theoretical interest lies in the fact that it presents a highly detailed case study on the general problem of the impact of rules of procedure on multilateral diplomacy. The analysis of the role of delegates and the negotiating aspect of the decision-making process touches upon several hypotheses from recent theoretical writing which are discussed in this context.

The basic problem can now be more precisely formulated as follows:

> What conditions concerning agenda, institutional framework and rules of procedure determined the organization, course and results of the Madrid Meeting and - in view of the aims of the CSCE as laid down in the Helsinki Act - what modifications of these conditions would be acceptable to the 35 participating states in order to increase the efficiency of decision-making at future meetings?

A set of three questions has been derived from this problem:

1. What conditions for the organization of a negotiating platform on security and co-operation in Europe were chosen for the CSCE?
2. In what way did these conditions affect:
   (a) the organization of the Madrid Meeting (the participating states and their representatives as well as the formal and actual organizational framework);
   (b) the decision-making process in Madrid (the limits imposed and the effects on content: matters of procedure and substance);
   (c) the results of the Madrid Meeting?
3. Given the Madrid experience, what modifications can be recommended for future meetings?

These three questions are basic to the structure of the book. The first is covered in the first two chapters. Chapter I discusses the options for agenda, institutional framework and rules of procedure for the CSCE as these were suggested in the period before the CSCE process started with the organisation of the Helsinki Consultations in November 1972. The choices that were actually made for the CSCE and therefore for the Madrid Meeting, are outlined in Chapter II. At the end of this chapter some points are singled out for consideration and provide the basis for the recommendations made in the concluding chapter.

The first part of the second question, the effect of the conditions on the organization of the Madrid Meeting, is dealt with in the following four chapters. Chapter III is concerned with the states participating in the meeting and their aims in connection with the implementation debate, and then with the proposals for provisions in a concluding document. Chapter IV is a study of the negotiators themselves, their relations with Ministries at home, with the press and with pressure groups, their personal role in negotiations and their position within their own national delegations. Chapter V looks at the setting of the meeting as result of the formal conditions - Agenda, Time Schedule and Working Methods - leaving it to Chapter VI to describe and explain the actual setting; policy development can only come to fruition in an environment more informal that that provided by the formal organs prescribed by the rules.

The second part of the second question, the effect of the rules on the decision-making process, occupies the next three chapters. Chapter VII considers the limits imposed on the process by the rules, both in the phase of implementation discussions (when the substantive limits of the Final Act itself play a crucial part), and during the drafting of the concluding document. In Chapter VIII the central theme is the application of the rules to the procedure seen at three critical moments when they were pushed to or beyond their limits, while in Chapter IX it is matters of substance that are under scrutiny. It traces the course followed by a proposal on a substantive matter from its formulation in the capital city of the participating state up to its final appearance as a provision in the concluding document. The negotiating aspect of the process is seen against a background which includes the condition of consensus and the roles that the participants necessarily play. Finally, an attempt is made to analyse the decision-making process in terms of turning-points and phases.

The effects of the rules on the organization and course of the meeting having been dealt with in the preceding chapters, Chapter X tackles the last part of the second question: the effect of the rules on the results of the Madrid Meeting. In the light of the aims of the participating states as they were explained in the third chapter, how can these results be characterised?

The concluding Chapter summarizes the findings of the previous chapters and attempts to answer the third and last question following the conclusion drawn from the chapters on the Madrid conditions and the Madrid experience and makes recommendations aimed at modifying conditions for future CSCE meetings.

The authors are aware of certain necessary and inevitable limitations inherent in the set-up of the present study. First of all the authors' personal points of view will unavoidably play a role in some, although not all descriptions, explanations, conclusions or recommendations: they have perceived things from the view-point of a Western participant.

It should be added here that no attempt is made to put the Madrid Meeting into historical perspective. This book is obviously a contemporary account of events and in twenty years' time, and with the advantage of hindsight, clearly certain elements at "Madrid" will appear in a different light.

Furthermore this is a study of the Madrid Meeting. Even though external facts are brought in when they can be seen to have had direct influence on the meeting, the main subject is always declared policy. Unacknowledged objectives and the domestic processes that made up the background of the policies followed by the participating states are outside the compass of the study. The same is true of the reciprocal question of the impact of the meeting on political reality, and in particular of the actual implementation of the Helsinki Act. What happened in the reality that lay outside the conference chamber as a result of what happened inside it, it is not this book's business to tell.

Finally, the theoretical object of this study is to show the effect of certain conditions on the organization, course and results of the *Madrid* Meeting. The extent to which particular conclusions apply in general to international decision-making lies outside the scope of the study. It should always be remembered that as a specimen of multilateral diplomacy the CSCE process is a process *sui generis*.

As far as the political objective of this study is concerned, the recommendations for future meetings take into account not only the desirability but also the acceptability of the modifications they propose. However, acceptability is ultimately a question of political choice, where irrational elements and sensibilities also play their role and these are notoriously unpredictable.

Moreover, unpredictable incidents anywhere in the world can have a drastic and instantaneous impact on the climate of the CSCE, as was shown by the Korean airliner tragedy at the time of the closing session of the Madrid Meeting. A similar incident just before the next follow-up meeting in Vienna would undoubtedly affect any chances of implementing whatever recommendations may be envisaged. Nevertheless, both authors in their separate capacities as practitioner and theorist, are of the opinion that the proposed modifications resulting from their common effort, would be beneficial to the CSCE process as such, and should therefore be considered to be in the interest of all participating states, to whatever political grouping they may belong.

I. OPTIONS FOR A CSCE

1. Introduction

The politicians, diplomats, scientists and commentators, who in the period before 1973 set themselves to think about the actual form a multilateral negotiating platform on security and co-operation in Europe should take, were certainly not the first to do so. Numerous predecessors had submitted their so-called "peace plans" in many previous centuries, even before 1648, the year of the Peace of Westphalia with its recognition of the idea of the modern nation-state. Famous names that spring to mind include William Penn, the Abbé de Saint-Pierre, Jean Jacques Rousseau, Jeremy Bentham and Immanuel Kant (1).

Understandably, the main concern of all plans was the question of war and peace. As European security organizations, the proposed institutions were to preserve the territorial *status quo* and to provide a basis for the settlement of disputes. Most of the plans contained as central institution an assembly of representatives or agents of the sovereigns, meeting periodically (Penn recommended meeting annually or at least every two of three years) or in permanent session. Many writers suggested one vote for each sovereignty and adhered to the principle of majority rule.

In a nutshell, three elements are touched upon here: agenda, institutional framework and rules of procedure. Before discussing more specifically in the next Chapter the choices made for the CSCE with respect to these three elements, the present Chapter will examine in three sections the respective options as these were put forward in the years before the CSCE actually started. Items for the agenda that were proposed in this period embraced virtually every aspect of East-West relations: security, disarmament and arms control; economic, trade and financial questions; energy, transport and communication, environment, science and technology; education, culture and tourism (2). Since these items are all to be found in the Final Act itself, it seemed more useful to limit the first section of the present Chapter to the actual political developments which led to the holding of a CSCE, insofar as these developments were related to the agenda which found ultimate approval. The second and third sections can then be devoted to the expressed options for the institutional framework and rules of procedure respectively.

As has already been said, the next Chapter will deal with the choices actually made for CSCE, choices for the agenda, institutional framework and rules of procedure which therefore also guided the Madrid Meeting. It is at the end of that Chapter that some points will be brought forward for consideration in order to help us tackle the question of efficiency of decision-making at future meetings. These points will provide the framework for formulating recommendations in this respect in the concluding chapter of the present study.

2. Agenda Options

When in the late sixties and early seventies of this century the climate of "détente" made it possible to consider new efforts that, it was hoped, might be more successful than previous ones, to find a more acceptable *modus vivendi* between East and West, a quarter of a century had already passed since the end of the Second World War. In the beginning great mutual distrust had blocked every effort to come to better terms on the European continent in this post-war period, known as the period of "Cold War". It was the Cuba missile crisis of October 1962 in particular when the two nuclear superpowers - USA and USSR - were in eyeball to eyeball confrontation, which is generally thought to have been the turning point which led to the period of more relaxation between East and West which ultimately enabled the organization of a multilateral forum to discuss and negotiate matters of security and co--operation in Europe.

It was, however, still to be another few years before the process which led to the holding of a CSCE actually started (3). This process developed in the form of a dialogue between the two military alliances - NATO and the Warsaw Pact - in the period from 1966 till 1972, when the Helsinki Consultations started in preparation for the CSCE. In this communiqué dialogue the parties signified their wishes for a security conference on one side and for talks about force reductions in Europe on the other. This indirect dialogue was more or less institutionalized by the NATO countries' foreign ministers in their Rome Declaration of

May 1970, in which they directed the Italian Foreign Minister "to transmit this Declaration on their behalf through diplomatic channels to all other interested parties, including neutral and non-aligned governments". This declaration also concerned Mutual and Balanced Force Reductions (MBFR). A month later in Budapest the Warsaw Pact countries' foreign ministers issued a declaration on the CSCE (June 1970), announcing that this document, likewise, would be "conveyed to the governments of all the states concerned". This became normal diplomatic practice. After that time innumerable diplomatic bilateral contacts took place between all European countries, on levels from Prime Minister down to Counsellor, with the object of obtaining further insight into each other's point of view, as expressed in the communiqués, concerning the agenda and other methods of procedure of both conferences. As mentioned in the introduction to the present Chapter the following account covers points selected out of the communiqué dialogue between the two alliances on the basis of the importance they later proved to have in relation to the CSCE agenda.

After some preliminary steps, such as the speech of the Polish foreign minister Rapacki before the UN General Assembly in December 1964 and the mention of a conference of European states by the Consultative Committee of the Warsaw Pact in January 1965, the process in question was set in motion when in July 1966 the Warsaw Pact published its "Bucharest Declaration". This "Declaration on Strengthening Peace and Security in Europe", as it was called, developed seven "main directions", in which measures for the strengthening of security on the European continent were to be taken. The final point recommended the "convocation of a general European conference to discuss the questions of ensuring security in Europe and organizing general European co-operation". This conference, characterized as "an important landmark in the contemporary history of Europe" was expected to contribute not only to the establishment of a system of collective security in Europe but also to the all-round development of economic, scientific, technical, and cultural relations. The proposal was endorsed in April 1967 by the European Communist and Workers Parties which met in Karlovy Vary.

The reaction of NATO to the Warsaw Pact initiative was cautious and deliberate. The final communiqué of the ministerial meeting of the North Atlantic Council in Reykjavik in June 1968 discussed the follow-up to the Report on the Future Tasks of the Alliance (the so-called "Harmel Report", approved in December 1967) in the following terms: "The study noted that in certain respects improvements in East-West relations had taken place. It concluded that, while further improvements could be favourable, opportunities for rapid progress towards general détente should not be over-rated". The same cautious approach was clearly expressed in the annex to the communiqué, which signalled preparedness to explore negotiations on balanced and mutual force reductions. In this "Reykjavik Declaration" it said: "Ministers recognised that the unresolved issues which still divide the European Continent must be settled by peaceful means, and are convinced that the ultimate goal of a lasting, peaceful order in Europe requires an atmosphere of trust and confidence and can only be reached by a step-by-step process".

A message "to all European countries" sent from Budapest in March 1969 formed the next step taken by the Warsaw Treaty member countries. This message reaffirmed the Bucharest proposals of 1966, summoned "all the countries of Europe with a call for co-operation in convening a general European conference", and made an additional suggestion "as a practical step towards strengthening European security" of a "meeting, at the earliest possible date, of representatives of all interested European states, to establish by mutual agreement the procedure for calling the conference and also to determine the items on the agenda".

Three years after the Warsaw Pact countries' Bucharest Conference, the NATO ministers, meeting in Washington in April 1969, let it be known that they had instructed their permanent representatives in Brussels to draft a list of issues which would lend themselves to fruitful negotiation with the Soviet Union and other countries of Eastern Europe. This task took up a good two years and was carried out by senior diplomats from the fifteen NATO countries in Brussels, who regularly met together for this purpose in a special committee. The results of this extensive study, discussion and negotiation appeared in subsequent NATO communiqués.

With less circumspection the Warsaw Pact countries continued their campaign. In October 1969, meeting this time in Prague, they now put forward two brief but lucidly formulated items for an agenda:

1. the ensuring of European security and renunciation of the use of force or threat of its use in the mutual relations among states in Europe;
2. expansion of trade, economic, scientific and technical relations on the principle of equal rights, aimed at the development of political co-operation among European states.

These two items contain the seeds of what were later to become baskets I and II respectively of the agenda of the Helsinki Final Act, although in the first basket various other principles were also deposited, e.g., respect for human rights.

Two months later, in December 1969, the NATO ministers in Brussels reacted with a Declaration of which paragraph 11 read: "Allied governments consider that not only economic and technical but also cultural exchanges between interested countries can bring mutual benefit and understanding. In those fields more could be achieved by freer movement of people, ideas and information between the countries of East and West". The second sentence consciously introduced a new idea, designed to counterbalance the East European proposals which mentioned improvement of co-operation between states. The idea behind the proposal concerning "freer movement of people, ideas and information" which was later seen by the East European countries only as a propaganda stunt on the part of the West, was that peace and security in Europe would not be promoted only by improving the relationships between states, as proposed by the East European countries, but also and more particularly by the development of understanding between their individual inhabitants, and that for this purpose it was necessary to increase the exchange of information about the conditions of life in these countries. In short: détente was to embrace more than simply a *rapprochement* among states. The Iron Curtain would have to become permeable. The expression "freer movement of people, ideas and information" later became one of the concepts basic to Western proposals for the third basket.

Following paragraph 11 of the NATO Declaration of December 1969 which added the single "freer movement" notion to the agenda proposed by the Warsaw Pact countries in Prague, paragraph 12 introduced two more areas of possible co-operation between East and West: "the field of human environment" and "the more specialized field of oceanography". The first of these found itself in the second basket but has never become of great significance. Co-operation between the European states in environmental studies, in the context of the ECE and other competent organizations, is already satisfactory enough to require no fresh stimulus from the CSCE.

Six months later, in its spring communiqué of May 1970, NATO put forward two agenda points, clearly defined:

1. the principles which should govern relations between States, including the renunciation of force;
2. the development of international relations with a view to contributing to the freer movement of people, ideas and information and to developing co-operation in the cultural, economic, technical and scientific fields as well as in the field of human environment.

The first of the Prague items had been more or less carried over into the first point here which, however, extended it in general terms to "principles which should govern relations between states", which could include other principles; in the end, ten principles were included in the Final Act. In the second agenda point the proposal concerning "freer movement" was not yet treated as a separate item. Co-operation in the fields of culture and environment now appeared officially and was additional to the second Prague item. The ministers of the Warsaw Pact countries, meeting a month later in Budapest (June 1970) expressed their agreement with this amplification. Their memorandum stated: "They believe that questions of the environment might be discussed within the framework of the second item of the agenda proposed in Prague, which could also be broadened to include a clause about the development of cultural relations".

In their communiqué of May 1970 the NATO ministers had also touched upon the organizational aspect of the negotiations. Having taken note of the Report on the Procedures for Negotiation which they had commissioned from the Permanent Council, they stated that they were ready to multiply exploratory conversations with all interested parties on all questions affecting peace. The communiqué then continues:

> In so far as progress is recorded as a result of these talks and in the on-going talks - in particular on Germany and Berlin - the Allied Governments state that they would be ready to enter into multilateral contacts with all interested governments. One of the main purposes of such contacts would be to explore when it will be possible to convene a conference, or a series of conferences on

> European Security and Co-operation. The establishment of a permanent body could be envisaged as one means, among others, of embarking upon multilateral negotiations in due course.

In December 1969 the British Labour Government had proposed the establishment of a standing commission on East-West relations (SCEWER) which might function in any one of three ways: as a preparatory mechanism for a conference, as a permanent follow-up institution to a conference or as an alternative to a conference. However, within NATO agreement had not yet been reached about what should happen after a CSCE. Fears were great that in a CSCE established in the form of a permanent institution, the balance might lie too much in favour of the Soviet Union. Three perceptible Soviet aims played a particular role here, i.e., the attempts by the SU to loosen the ties between Western Europe and the United States, to prevent further West-European integration, and to acquire a *droit de regard* in Western Europe (4).

In the organizational area the Warsaw Pact countries reacted promptly to the NATO suggestions. Their communiqué of June 1970 now proposed a new item for the agenda: "Establishment at the all-European conference of an organ for questions of security and co-operation in Europe". In November 1970, however, NATO Secretary-General Manlio Brosio made clear that the permanent body proposed by the NATO ministers was not necessarily the same as the organ proposed by the Warsaw Pact. The new agenda point in the Warsaw Pact communiqué nevertheless led half a decade later to the inception of the last chapter of the Final Act under the title "Follow-up to the Conference".

After a short period of rest during which neither of the two alliances made any new proposals, the NATO ministers issued a communiqué in December 1971 revealing the results of its commission set up 2½ years before: on possible subjects for discussion with the Soviet Union and other East European countries:

> This report examined four areas of discussion at such a conference: (A) Questions of Security, including Principles Governing Relations between States and certain military aspects of security; (B) Freer Movement of People, Information and Ideas, and Cultural Relations; (C) Co-operation in the Fields of Economics, Applied Science and Technology and Pure Science; and (D) Co-operation to improve the Human Environment.

The first of these agenda items distinguished clearly for the first time between what was later called the "non-military aspects of security" or the "Principles", and the "military aspects of security", which was later to include the so-called Confidence Building Measures (CBMs). Further to be remarked is that the proposal concerning "freer movement" had here become a separate agenda item; the more this proposal was discussed within NATO the more importance it acquired, so that the ideas expressed became of such weight that it was realized that bracketing the proposal with the agenda item concerning economic co-operation would not allow enough scope to the philosophy behind it. Some NATO countries also thought it important to treat the problems in the area of the environment as a separate agenda item, since this subject had received by far the lion's share of public interest in recent years. As has been remarked before, the subject of "environment" was in the end included in the Final Act if not as a separate agenda item at least as a discrete section of the second basket.

Six weeks after this meeting of the NATO ministers, the Warsaw Pact ministers re-assembled in Prague at the end of January 1972 and published a "Declaration on Peace, Security and Co-operation in Europe" in which it was implicitly recognized that refraining from the use of force was not the only principle of importance in the relations between European states, as had been suggested two years before in Prague. This time seven "fundamental principles" were proposed for recognition and to be put into practice, namely: inviolability of frontiers; non-use of force; peaceful coexistence; foundations of good neighbourly relations and co-operation in the interest of peace; mutually advantageous contacts among States; disarmament, and support for the United Nations.

In this Declaration however, no attention was paid to the NATO proposals for effective measures for military security, nor to the NATO proposal for "freer movement". On the first of these points the NATO communiqué which was published four months later at the end of May 1972, in Bonn, was once more explicit: "Ministers considered that, in the interest of security, the examination at a CSCE of appropriate measures including certain military measures, aimed at strengthening confidence and increasing stability would contribute to the process of reducing the dangers of military confrontation". Already, within NATO, these measures were known as CBMs.

It took several years, during which the climate of international politics improved, to bring each party to accept the other's proposals on the holding of the conference. As we have seen from the communiqué of May 1970 NATO had made the actual beginning of the multilateral preparation of the conference dependent on sufficient progress in East-West negotiations. These negotiations were the talks between the two parts of Germany, the negotiations which the FRG carried on separately with the USSR and with Poland, the four-Power talks on Berlin, and SALT.

New perspectives for settling the German problem and for an East-West *rapprochement* were created because of the change in policy initiated by the "Grand Coalition" in the Federal Republic, which became known as *"Neue Ostpolitik"* [New East Policy]. In the future Bonn would no longer consider steps towards the unification of Germany as a pre-condition for striving towards any settlement on a European scale, but would see a unified Germany rather as something to be achieved as the result of a process of détente between East and West. This policy change by the Kiesinger-Brandt government, endorsed by President Johnson, led to the signature of the two renunciation-of-force treaties between the FRG and the USSR and the FRG and Poland in August and December 1970 respectively.

The four-Power talks on Berlin took more time. The NATO communiqué published in Brussels in December 1970 made the conditions for a multi-lateral preparation of the conference more stringent: instead of "progress" (still the term used with respect to SALT and the bilateral inter-German talks) it was now a "satisfactory solution" to the Berlin talks that was required and this was not achieved until June 1972. One month earlier the required progress in SALT had been confirmed by the signature of the SALT-I documents when President Nixon visited Moscow in May 1972. The treaty between the two German states was to follow in November 1972.

One final important problem remained still to be solved: that of the relationship between the preparatory talks on the CSCE - as favorite element in Warsaw Pact policy - and the exploratory talks on MBFR which NATO, ever since the "Reykjavik Signal" of 1968, had consistently given such high priority. Were the MBFR talks to be part of the CSCE? If not, were they to be held separately but in parallel? Which of the two conferences should begin first? Should the link between the two be constituted by getting the CSCE to adopt a declaration about the principles which should govern the MBFR talks, or should the MBFR report to the CSCE? The two military alliances held differing opinions on the subject of linkage between the conferences. The Warsaw Pact countries, in their Budapest memorandum of June 1970, had proposed discussing the question of the reduction of foreign armed forces in an organ to be established at the all-European conference, thus *following* a CSCE. The Bonn communiqué of May 1972 contained the NATO countries' counter proposal "that multilateral explorations on mutual and balanced force reductions be undertaken as soon as practicable, either *before* or in parallel with multilateral preparatory talks on a Conference on Security and Co-operation in Europe".

A few months after this NATO communiqué, on 14 September 1972, when Henry Kissinger visited Moscow, party-leader Leonid Brezhnev put forward a time table which showed the staggered arrangement of CSCE and MBFR as proposed by the NATO countries, but according to which the CSCE would begin first, thus inclining more towards the Warsaw Pact position on this point. No mention was made of any organic link between the two conferences although nothing in the timetable of the two conferences precluded the possibility of the CSCE, which would be the first to get off the ground, itself initiating such a link (which never in fact happened). From the point of view of the USSR and the USA there was no need of an organic link however desirable this might seem for some of the smaller European countries. Neither of the superpowers felt any obligation to discuss their security interests in Central Europe in a forum of 35 countries where they would be on an equal footing with such states as Liechtenstein, Malta and Monaco.

Brezhnev's proposal of 14 September was for the multilateral preparatory talks preceding the CSCE to begin on 22 November of that year (as had previously been proposed officially to all interested states by the Finnish government) followed by the MBFR multilateral exploration "by the end of January 1973". It would then be possible to open the actual CSCE "by the end of June 1973" and to have the formal opening of the conference on MBFR "in September or October 1973". After consultations in the NATO council the American government was able to reply to the Soviet government that the NATO countries agreed to the dates for starting the preparatory talks for the CSCE and the exploratory talks for the MBFR. They considered the dates proposed for both main conferences "reasonable", a term which was used because the NATO countries did not wish to bind themselves to fixed closing dates for the two sets of initial talks. These preparatory talks would themselves have to show that it would be worthwhile launching the main CSCE and MBFR.

With regard to the options for the agenda of the CSCE the conclusion can be drawn here that this forum was envisaged as covering virtually every aspect of security and co-operation in Europe.

3. Institutional Options

As we have seen above, the three alternative forms of the standing commission on East-West relations proposed by the British Labour Government in December 1969, comprised a preparatory mechanism for a conference, a permanent follow-up institution to a conference, or an alternative to a conference. In a study on the CSCE follow-up meeting in Madrid when proposals made in the period before the Helsinki consultations are being considered, it is only those in respect of the last two forms that are relevant. As far as the idea of building institutions in an East-West context goes, three approaches can be distinguished. In the first the security dimension of the East-West negotiations would be taken care of in an organization based on the two alliances - NATO and the Warsaw Pact (the alliance-based approach). In the second an institutional framework with organizational and procedural links with the United Nations is proposed (the UN-linked approach), while the third approach proposes the same framework but without the UN link (the independent approach).

3.1. The Alliance-Based Approach

In January 1968, in the United States, Zbigniew Brzezinski, in an article in *Foreign Affairs*, made several suggestions for new institutions as part of a framework for East-West reconciliation (5). He discerned economic, cultural, political and security aspects in the process of growing together of East and West and, in a different way, of the two Germanies, which would "eventually require an institutionalized multilateral framework". His first suggestion in this respect concerned the creation of a special East-West economic assembly, perhaps sponsored by OECD, ECE, and CMEA, fostering East-West ventures, communication and technological co-operation. In these areas he thought of studies on multilateral co-operation between market and state economies, and the development of all-European projects such as a Lisbon--Moscow superhighway, and envisaged migration of surplus labor from East to West, association of the East European countries and the Soviet Union with GATT or IMF, preferential agreements with the EEC and broader East--West convertibility.

A second suggestion concerned the creation of an East-West Political Assembly "in which direct and continuing discussions could be held", be it initially as a rather informal body for off-the-record discussions comparable to the Bilderberg meetings. After a gradual involvement of the communist states in the specialized functions of the Council of Europe, this organization itself might perhaps be transformed into the assembly in question.

Finally Brzezinski suggested "perhaps by the early 1970's" the creation of a European Security Commission, based on the two alliances. "Its more specific purpose would be to monitor troop movements in Central Europe and make periodic inspections of troop postures. It might also advance other schemes designed to moderate the military confrontation...".

Two and a half years later, in October 1970, Brzezinski repeated in another article in the same journal his suggestion for institutionalization (6). His items for the Western agenda for negotiations included "the creation of a joint NATO-Warsaw Pact commission or a European security commission, to monitor eventual security arrangements and perhaps even to initiate others [i.e., for the specific purposes mentioned above], especially in the nuclear field, matching thereby progress in the bilateral American-Soviet talks" and "the creation of permanent consultative East-West political machinery, for example at deputy foreign ministerial level".

3.2. The UN-Linked Approach

As we have seen from their communiqué of June 1970 the Warsaw Pact countries proposed as an item for the agenda of the CSCE the establishment of an organ for questions of security and co-operation in Europe. It may be presumed that this organ was somehow envisaged as constituting part of the system of collective security in Europe, to which they had already committed themselves in the Warsaw Treaty itself. In this "Treaty of Friendship, Co-operation and Mutual Assistance", concluded on 14th May, 1955, the second paragraph of Article 11 reads:

> Should a system of collective security be established in Europe, and a General European Treaty of Collective Security concluded for this purpose, for which the Contracting Parties will unswervingly strive, the present Treaty shall cease to be operative from the day the General European Treaty enters into force.

This system of collective security has been put forward in East European writings on numerous occasions ever since, as a superior alternative to the system based on the two defense alliances. These writings are, however, less explicit as to how exactly the system would work in practice. Some illustration of the ideas the Soviet thinkers had more specifically in mind in the period before the Helsinki Consultations can be derived from a discussion organized by the Editorial Board of the monthly *International Affairs* in September 1971 (7). Among the contributions from the eleven prominent Soviet participants S.I. Beglov's tackled the question of the juridical embodiment and concrete content of the security system. According to Beglov the agenda-proposals of the Warsaw Pact countries went "directly to the heart of the most essential elements of a future security system, namely, repudiation of the threat or use of force, equitable co-operation, and the establishment of an agency for security and co-operation". To the author one thing was clear: a regional all-European agreement had to be equipped with an effective mechanism for settling disputes by peaceful means, while there should also be a consultation procedure which in the event of threatening situations could be resorted to by the signatories as the shortest way of taking concerted action.

Beglov noted, however, that for the time being no short answer could be given to the question whether the European security system would be confined to a proclamation of the binding rules of peaceful coexistence (i.e., repudiation of the threat or use of force and peaceful settlement of disputes) or whether the question of a formula for mutual assistance and also for sanctions against potential violators of peace would also arise. In this respect all would depend on the final and agreed interpretation of the collective security system by the participating countries. As a point in favour of a system which would embrace more than simply the proclamation of rules Beglov referred to the UN Charter which provides for effective collective measures to prevent or eliminate threats to peace and to suppress acts of aggression or other breaches of the peace. (Articles 33, 37 and the Articles 52, 53 and 54 of Chapter VIII, "Regional Arrangements".)

In this context Beglov also pointed to the principle of collective action as a basic provision in the Draft of a General European Treaty of Collective Security in Europe (8). This Treaty, submitted by the Soviet delegation at the Berlin Four-Power Conference of Foreign ministers in 1954, was open to all European powers, including the two German states as equal participants "pending the creation of a united, peace-loving and democratic German State". Article 8 of this treaty dealt with the organizational aspect:

> 8. With the purpose of holding consultations between the Signatories to this Treaty as provided for in this Treaty and of discussing the problems arising out of the task of ensuring security in Europe, provisions shall be made for:
> a) periodic and, when necessary, special consultations at which each Signatory State shall be represented by a member of Government or other specially authorised representative;
> b) the creation of a Standing Consultative Political Committee, whose duty shall be to prepare the appropriate recommendations to the Governments of the Signatories to this Treaty;
> c) the creation of a military consultative organ, whose competence shall be specified additionally.

It is further interesting to note that the article following this one, "recognizing the special responsibility borne by the Permanent Members of the UN Security Council for the maintenance of international peace and security" invited the governments of the USA and the Chinese People's Republic (!) to send representatives to these bodies as observers. The official link with the UN was made in Article 6, which prescribed, in conformity with the UN Charter, the immediate communication to the Security Council of information on action that the Signatories to the Treaty have taken or intend to take in fulfilment of the right to self-defence or for the purpose of maintaining peace and security in Europe.

Beglov once more reminded his audience that under Article 53 of the UN Charter regional agencies may take enforcement action only with the authorisation of the Security Council: any formula for regional mutual assistance and enforcement sanctions must be in accordance with the UN Charter and the prerogatives of the Security Council. This last point, however, which underlines the implied right of veto of the permanent Council members, provided one of the sources of scepticism in comments outside the Soviet bloc. Given the sad record of the Security Council in the fulfilment of its main task of keeping and restoring world peace, was there any reason to suppose that in a system for European security in which four out of the five permanent members of the Council participated, the same controversies would not arise in a regional context, or that a European system would work better than the universal system? (9)

Among West European efforts to design East-West institutionalized frameworks Frans Alting von Geusau's model for a "Standing European Conference" provided an example which can also be reckoned under the heading of the second approach. This model is based on two principles:

> (1) An eventual machinery should be broad enough to enable coordinated negotiations on all relevant issues and flexible enough to enable negotiations between some states directly concerned on certain issues;
> (2) It should be related to the United Nations and its relevant specialized agencies as a "regional arrangement" according to the UN Charter (10).

The central place in the model is occupied by the European Regional Conference in which NATO and Warsaw Pact countries are joined by four neutral countries and one non-aligned, namely: Austria, Finland, Sweden, Switzerland and Yugoslavia. This conference, in the model graphically linked to the UN General Assembly and Security Council, is scheduled to meet once in two or three years while its tasks are to be executed in four commissions with a more limited membership:

1. A European Arms-Control Commission with a membership of fourteen: six NATO, six Warsaw Pact, and one neutral and one non-aligned country: Sweden and Yugoslavia. This commission is linked to the - existing - Conference of the Committee of Disarmament and a - new - European Arms--Control Agency. The agency is created to supervise compliance with agreements and has links with the - existing - International Atomic

Energy Agency and the new Secretariat. The task of the commission itself is drafting agreements on arms-control and disarmament and supervising the agency.

2. A European crisis-management and Peaceful Settlement of Disputes Commission with ten members: four NATO, four Warsaw Pact and the same neutral and non-aligned countries. This commission's tasks include inquiries, good offices, mediation and conciliation. In the three regional subcommittees for Northern-, Central-, and Southern Europe and the Mediterranean the membership is expanded with additional members from the region, an organizational pattern which could also be followed with regard to the Arms-Control Commission.

3. A European Commission on the German Questions consisting of ten members: the four former occupying powers, the two German states and two neighbouring Warsaw Pact countries. This commission would provide a forum for consultation on Berlin and German questions.

4. The Economic Commission for Europe with the GDR as additional member and allotted additional tasks.

Finally, ECE and UNESCO are linked to a new permanent organ: a Clearing House for industrial, technological and cultural relations.

Many of the suggested frameworks for an organization for security and co-operation in Europe, which originated in the Western academic community, came close to the model described here. Although there were variations in the names of the organs or their competence, most of the frameworks envisaged a link, often ill-defined, with the United Nations organization. For instance, among the ideas put forward in the *Bulletin of Peace Proposals* Johan Galtung formulated as one of his seven theses on the European Security Conference: "Any European security system should be tied to the UN" (11). Equally explicit on this point were "Some Institutional Suggestions for a System of Security and Co-operation in Europe", made by a working group on European Co-operation and Security:

> It is envisaged that the new system would at the earliest possible juncture be brought into formal relationship with the United Nations and, more particularly, the Security Council, under Articles 52 and 53 of the Charter. Appropriate links, in the form of inter-agency and inter-secretariat agreements and arrangements, would also be established with the organs and the UN Specialized Agencies more particularly concerned, providing for systematic participation of the UN system and its secretariats in the activities of the proposed Conference (12).

3.3. The Independent Approach

Not all theorists, however, endorsed the idea of a UN-linked approach. In an article in *Review of International Affairs* Tomislav Mitrović discussed three international legal systems (13). The first concerns the universal system of security of the UN, which was never fully developed because of disagreement between the great powers. The second concerns the bloc-inspired system of security on the sub-regional level of a divided Europe. Since this system had proved increasingly obstructive to any positive change in relations between the European states, Mitrović claimed that a third international legal system was required, combining elements of the two previous systems with novel features corresponding to the present aims and interests of the states. Although his suggested scheme included a "UN Committee of Observers" which might grow into an organ corresponding to his projected All--European Conference, Mitrović's framework nevertheless constitutes what may be called an independent approach. The discussion in the *Bulletin of Peace Proposals* records objections made by Jeanne Laux and Michael Palmer to the UN link in the framework suggested by the Working Group on European Co-operation and Security. In their opinion:

> The conception of collective security embodied in the UN Security Council is utterly inimical to the conception of a future pan-European system implicit in the paper ... What is to be gained for Europe - for the Europe preferred by the authors - by resurrecting the Security Council of 1945? To rely on a Security Commission for Europe linked to the UN Security Council is to abandon the legal equality of sovereignty even before we have begun the process of working out mechanisms to minimize the consequences of real power inequalities between states. One need not go so far as some Yugoslavs (in seeing all great powers as hegemonial) nor as far as the Albanians (in viewing the European conference itself as a joint machination between the Superpowers) in order to question the logic - *if* the goal is to shift away from hierarchical patterns of European interstate relations - of typing the SCE to the UN Security Council (14).

It will come as no surprise that the approach which does not incorporate the UN link can be exemplified by the framework of an East--West Standing Commission, which was suggested by Michael Palmer. The autonomous commission is kept independent of UN control for two reasons.

Firstly, at the time Palmer was writing neither of the two parts of Germany was a member of the United Nations, and secondly there was a fear that a regional organ of the UN dealing with security issues could fall foul of vetoes expressed in the Security Council to thwart the adoption of "small country measures". Since neither Western nor Eastern states would be prepared to allow others to interfere in their sub--regional affairs a regional juridical mechanism for the peaceful settlement of disputes under Articles 52-54 of the UN Charter would be a difficult affair to implement.

Palmer suggested that a Ministerial Council "meeting once or twice a year and chaired by participating countries in rotation" would be the most appropriate governing body of a commission, with a Council at Permanent Representative level meeting between Ministerial sessions. A Secretary General would be assisted by an International Secretariat. According to the role the Commission played this secretariat could range from a skeleton staff of national civil servants whose functions would be limited to the preparation of agendas and the recording of decisions, to a strong central secretariat vested with powers of initiative.

Three organs are offered as optional in Palmer's framework: a Parliamentary Assembly, an Office of the Clerk of the Assembly (modelled on those of the Assemblies of the Council of Europe and WEU) and an Agency for the control of armaments in the form of a permanent secretariat. An alternative to the latter would be the use of the existing WEU Agency, matched by a specially created equivalent agency in Eastern Europe.

Finally the standing commission might delegate work to a series of committees of governmental experts that would meet regularly and report back to the commission. Palmer mentions the following examples:

> (a) Committee on European security; (b) Committee on European economic contacts - working closely with the ECE, which should remain the executive agency for East-West economic co-operation; (c) Committee on European environmental problems; (d) Committee on European scientific and technological co-operation - also working closely with the ECE; (e) Committee on European cultural contacts (15).

It later transpired that even the framework suggested by Palmer was too ambitious as far as its level of institutionalization was concerned. The CSCE decided on a framework with more built-in flexibility.

4. Procedural Options

As we have seen above Michael Palmer mentioned the possibility of rotation of the chairmanship for an East-West commission. On the question of the system of decision-making in general, Palmer gave as his opinion:

> Majority decisions must be ruled out in view both of the nature of a conference and also of the numerical imbalance between the NATO and Warsaw Pact countries. Decisions would therefore have to be reached by consensus or, if formal votes were to be held, by unanimity based on each country casting one vote: consensus would obviously be more flexible (16).

Because of the crucial importance of the consensus procedure as an alternative to voting, this aspect will be elaborated here in more detail. Although prior to the sixties the term consensus was not in use in international law as a formal description of the procedure in question, some form of decision-making by the no-objection method and without recourse to voting was familiar to several international fora. However, in the mid-sixties C. Wilfred Jenks could note in this regard:

> We appear to be entering upon a new phase in which the keynote is no longer either unanimity or majority decision but consensus. The wheel has not come, and will not come, full circle, but there has been a marked shift of emphasis from the desire to ensure that decisions are no longer blocked by a requirement of unanimity or a veto to the desire to ensure that they reflect a sufficiently wide consensus to make them effective in practice (17).

An authoritative and satisfying definition of consensus, "this hybrid phenomenon of contemporary multilateral diplomacy, which is primarily aimed at avoiding confrontations" appeared to be a complicated affair (18). One could say that as a procedure of decision-making, consensus makes it possible to achieve effective results in multilateral diplomacy by avoiding both the sterile dictatorship of the automatic majority and the paralyzing autocracy of the unanimity-blocking minority. Those who do not express objections against the consensus-compromise are bound by it, unless they expressly indicate not having participated in it. In addition to the possibility of expressing a reservation, there is also that of recording one's own interpretation.

Furthermore, one could say that the consensus-procedure strives to bring together the positive dimensions of the three principles that can be distinguished as "competing elements in shaping the approach to international decision-making", as Inis L. Claude, Jr., put it (19): the equalitarianism of traditional law, the majoritarianism of democratic philosophy, and the elitism of European great power diplomacy. At the same time the consensus-procedure can mitigate the negative aspects of the principles consequent on voting behavior resulting from the support of respectively the requirement of unanimity, the principle of majority rule, or the special status for great powers expressed in the right to veto.

The United Nations Charter adheres to the rule of the simple or special majority with the exception of the power to veto substantive decisions of the Security Council vested in its five permanent members. Notwithstanding the principle (laid down in Article 27 of the Charter) that a party to a dispute shall abstain from voting on decisions with regard to the pacific settlement of disputes or the accepted practice whereby an abstention by a permanent member on a substantive proposal is not regarded as a veto, the privileged position of the powerful has often been the object of severe criticism especially from those who see the excessive use, provoked or not, of the right to veto, as an abuse of power which paralyzes the Security Council, an organ designed to be of central importance for the management of the vital interests of the international community. The "Uniting for Peace" resolution of (1950) was a device to enable the General Assembly - with its majority rule - to take over the central position.

More recently, however, the criticism has lost some of its sharpness. It was realized that without the co-operation of the powerful veto-holders a clear and firm verdict would not be effective in solving the problem or conflict in question. In addition, the analogy drawn by Claude seemed appropriate: the threat to the United Nations constituted by excessive use of the veto as a monkey wrench, may be counterbalanced by its operation - albeit imperfectly - as a safety device, a fuse in the circuit of international decision-making. His advice was that "a stalemate in the Council was an inconvenience but a showdown would be a disaster" (20).

While the big powers came to see a common interest in keeping up the importance of the council as central arena and came to understand that voting cannot be a substitute for negotiation, the increase of UN membership meant an automatic majority in the General Assembly for the group of the less powerful. Also here the danger of a clear and firm verdict turning into a empty gesture was to lead to efforts directed at more fruitful compromise.

Within the framework of the United Nations the need for formalization of the procedure of consensus has become especially apparent in view of the tremendous proliferation of multilateral negotiations in recent times, negotiations which have involved an ever greater number of participating states and an ever greater number of issues of increasing complexity. In this respect a prominent place is occupied by the Third United Nations Conference on the Law of the Sea (UNCLOS III). A first point of interest concerns the "Gentleman's Agreement" on consensus, which was approved by the UN General Assembly in November 1973. This agreement was incorporated in a declaration made by the President and endorsed by the Conference during the following summer. The declaration, taken up as Appendix in the UNCLOS III Rules of Procedure, stipulates that "the Conference should make every effort to reach agreement on substantive matters by way of consensus and there should be no voting on such matters until all efforts at consensus have been exhausted" (21). In the Chapter on decision-making of the UNCLOS III rules of procedure Rule (37) provides an extensive mechanism to guarantee that all efforts at reaching general agreement will have been exhausted before a matter of substance is put to the vote.

From the viewpoint of innovation in multilateral diplomacy the UNCLOS III experiment is even more interesting because of what was labelled by Barry Buzan as "active" consensus procedure: the set of techniques evolved at UNCLOS in order to push the process of consensus formation. This procedure is distinguished from "passive" consensus procedure which indicates the mere substitution of consensus for voting as a way of making decisions (22). With an almost universal participation (in 1974 out of the 149 UN states 137 reacted positively to the invitation to participate in UNCLOS) and so many technically complex and politically delicate issues of such great economic interest, international policy formation becomes an extremely cumbersome affair. Since the passive consensus procedures did not provide enough incentives to initiate compromise, a proposal was adopted (by consensus) in 1975 to mandate the chairmen of the three main committees to produce Informal Single Negotiating Texts (ISNT's). Later in the UNCLOS III process these texts were revised in a similar way (leading to so-called RSNT's) and put together as an Informal Composite Negotiating Text (ICNT). It appeared that notwithstanding occasional tensions, this procedure did increase efficiency in policy-formation, provided that the committee chairmen remained primarily chairmen and did not become simply text drafters.

Even if the actual term "consensus" was not used in the UNCLOS III rules of procedure themselves, it does appear in the recent "Draft Standard Rules of Procedure for United Nations Conferences" submitted by the Secretary General at the request of the General Assembly in its 35th session (23). Rule (51) mentions under the heading "consensus":

> 1. The Conference shall make every effort to ensure that all its substantive decisions are taken by consensus or general agreement.
> 2. Notwithstanding any measures that may be taken in compliance with paragraph 1, a proposal or motion before the Conference shall be voted on if a representative so requests.

Rule (53) stipulates that all matters of substance shall be decided by a two-thirds majority, all matters of procedure by a simple majority, while the question whether a matter is one of procedure or of substance is decided by a majority. All decisions are taken by majorities of "representatives present and voting", meaning representatives casting an affirmative or negative vote: representatives who abstain from voting are regarded as not voting.

These provisions also underline the important fact that in general for all decision-making in a United Nations framework the possibility of voting remains on the cards: this will necessarily play a role during negotiations. It is in an organization such as, for instance, NATO - where no votes are taken, even unofficially, and where up till recently reservations on agreed provisions were never aired outside the discussion chambers - that one can meet a consensus procedure in its purest form, operating in a multilateral forum. The CSCE provides another example as we shall see.

NOTES:

1. See Harold K. Jacobson, Networks of Interdependence; International Organizations and the Global Political System (New York: Alfred A. Knopf, 1979), pp. 23 ff., with reference to Sylvester John Hemleben, Plans for World Peace Through Six Centuries (Chicago: The University of Chicago Press, 1943).

2. See for instance, appendix I "Examples of items for all-European security and co-operation" from the report by the Working Group on European Co-operation and Security, "Some Institutional Suggestions for a System of Security and Co-operation in Europe", Bulletin of Peace Proposals, vol. 3, no. 1, 1972, pp. 85 ff.

3. For studies which analyse the developments of the period before the Helsinki-conference see, for instance, Karl E. Birnbaum, Peace in Europe; East-West Relations 1966-1968 and the Prospects for a European Settlement (London: Oxford University Press, 1970); Timothy Stanley and Darnell Whitt, Détente Diplomacy: United States and European Security in the 1970's (New York: Dunellen, 1970); Hans--Peter Schwarz and Helga Haftendorn (eds.), Europäische Sicherheitskonferenz [European Security Conference], (Opladen: Leske Verlag, 1970); Michael Palmer, The Prospects for a European Security Conference (London: Chatham House, PEP, 1971). For an extensive overview, including the various national points of view, see Hans--Adolf Jacobsen, Wolfgang Mallmann, and Christian Meier, (eds.) Sicherheit und Zusammenarbeit in Europa (KSZE); Analyse und Dokumentation [Security and Co-operation in Europe (CSCE); Analysis and Documentation], (Cologne: Verlag Wissenschaft und Politik, 1973). Among more recent publications mention can be made of Ljubivoje Aćimović, Problems of Security and Co-operation in Europe (Alphen aan den Rijn: Sijthoff & Noordhoff, 1981), (Parts one and two).

4. Compare for instance the two following perceptions:

   > Any such conference [i.e., a European Security Conference] would undoubtedly see the Russians striving to attain a triple objective: (1) to hasten American withdrawal from Europe; (2) to gain formal acceptance of the status quo in Eastern Europe; and (3) once again to inhibit further European integration, especially in the field of defense.

   Anthony Hartley, "Europe between the Superpowers", Foreign Affairs, vol. 49, no. 2, January 1971, p. 277.

   > Unquestionably, Russia and her allies have been the prime movers for an ESC. Soviet motives are probably a combination of the following: (a) to legitimize the European territorial and ideological status quo by a multilateral renunciation-of-force agreement; (b) to forestall or delay West European political--military integration by decreasing perceived security threats and freezing current institutional arrangements with a treaty; (c) to increase trade and technology exchanges with Western Europe, which may be impossible without corresponding improvements in all aspects of East-West relations; (d) to secure its Western flank in the event of Chinese hostilities; (e) to divorce Western Europe from the United States in various aspects of economic,

political and military affairs, perhaps by weakening or dissolving NATO.

Benjamin S. Rosenthal, "America's Move", Foreign Affairs, vol. 51, no. 2, January 1973, pp. 380-381.

5. See Zbigniew Brzezinski, "The Framework of East-West Reconciliation", Foreign Affairs, vol. 46, no. 2, January 1968, pp. 256-275.

6. See Zbigniew Brzezinski, "America and Europe", Foreign Affairs, vol. 49, no. 1, October 1970, pp. 11-30.

7. See "European Security System: Content and Ways of Ensuring It", International Affairs (Moscow), November 1971, pp. 64-88.

8. For the text of the Draft see Milestones of Soviet Foreign Policy, 1917-1967 (Moscow: Progress Publishers, 1967), pp. 146-148.

9. See for instance Hanspeter Neuhold, "Die neutralen Staaten Europas und die Konferenz über Sicherheit und Zusammen-arbeit in Europa" [The Neutral States of Europe and the Conference on Security and Co--operation in Europe], Europa Archiv 13/1973, also taken up in Hermann Volle and Wolfgang Wagner (eds.), KSZE, Beiträge and Dokumente aus dem Europa Archiv [CSCE, Contributions and Documents from Europa Archiv] (Bonn: Verlag für Internationale Politik GMBH, 1976), p. 61.

10. See his statement in Conference on European Security, Hearings before the Subcommittee on Europe of the Committee on Foreign Affairs, House of Representatives, Ninety-Second Congress, Second Session (Washington D.C.: US Government Printing Office, 1972), p. 183. See also his own contribution to F.A.M. Alting von Geusau (ed.), NATO and Security in the Seventies (Leyden: A.W. Sijthoff, 1971), pp. 103 ff.

11. Johan Galtung, "Seven Theses on the European Security Conference", Bulletin of Peace Proposals, vol. 1, no. 1, 1970, p. 77. See also his contribution to Johan Galtung (ed.), Co-operation in Europe (New York: Humanities Press, Inc., 1970), p. 99.

12. Working Group on European Co-operation and Security, op. cit., p. 78.

13. Tomislav Mitrović, "Institutionalization of European Security and Co--operation", Review of International Affairs, no. 501, February 20, 1971, pp. 26-28.

14. Jeanne Laux and Michael Palmer, "A Rejoinder to 'Some Institutional Suggestions for a System of Security and Co-operation in Europe'", Bulletin of Peace Proposals, vol. 3, no. 2, 1973, pp. 185-186. In his contribution to the discussion Pierre Hassner favored the link with the UN system, although he shared the preoccupations of those to whom the Security Council means precisely the Great Power primacy we are trying to get away from: "I don't think the veto of the permanent members of the Council is a problem, since in the European System every state would, in effect, have a veto". Pierre Hassner, "Remarks on 'Some institutional Suggestions for a System of Security and Co--operation in Europe'", Bulletin of Peace Proposals, vol. 3, no. 2, 1972, p. 192. Differences in opinion with regard to a possible UN link

can also be found in the summary of proceedings of the conference which was held in Vienna on March 10-22, 1972. See "Organization of Security and Co-operation in Europe; The Vienna Proceedings", Bulletin of Peace Proposals, vol. 3, no. 2, 1972, pp. 179-180. Hanna Newcombe, while distinguishing between compatible and incompatible regionalism, favoured a global system in which the Security Council deals with inter-regional conflicts and functions as an instance of appeal for intra-regional conflicts which a Regional Security Commission could not settle. Unlike Galtung's views in Co-operations in Europe she preferred the exclusion rather than the inclusion of both superpowers in the Security Commission for Europe. Hanna Newcombe, "United Nations Regional Security Commissions: A Proposal", Bulletin of Peace Proposals, vol. 3, no. 3, 1972, pp. 274-279.

15. Michael Palmer, op. cit., p. 60.

16. Michael Palmer, "A European Conference: Preparation and Procedure", The World Today, vol. 28, no. 1, January 1972, pp. 36-46; an excerpt from this article is included in Conference on European Security, the Hearings report mentioned in note 10 above, pp. 170-174.

17. C. Wilfred Jenks, LL.D., "Unanimity, The Veto, Weighted Voting, Special and Simple Majorities and Consensus as Modes of Decision in International Organisations", Cambridge Essays in International Law, Essays in Honour of Lord McNair (London: Stevens & Sons, 1965), p. 48.

18. Eric Suy, "The Meaning of Consensus in Multilateral Diplomacy", Robert J. Akkerman et al. (eds.), Declarations on Principles; A Quest for Universal Peace (Leyden: Sijthoff, 1977), p. 272.

19. Inis L. Claude, Jr., Swords into Plowshares; The Problems and Progress of International Organization, 4th edition, (New York, Random House, Inc., 1971), pp. 118 ff.

20. Ibid., p. 157.

21. UN Doc. A/CONF. 62/30/Rev. 1 (1974). For a history of the gentleman's agreement see, for instance, Louis B. Sohn, "Voting Procedure in United Nations Conferences for the Codification of International Law", American Journal of International Law, April 1975, vol. 69, no. 2, pp. 333 ff.

22. Barry Buzan, "Negotiating by Consensus: Developments in Technique at the United Nations Conference on The Law of The Sea", American Journal of International Law, April 1981, vol. 75, no. 2, pp. 328 ff. For reviews of the UNCLOS process of earlier date, see, for instance, Robert D. Eustis, "Procedures and Techniques of Multinational Negotiation: The LOS III Model", Virginia Journal of International Law, Winter 1977, vol. 17, no. 2; and the volume "Restructuring Ocean Regimes" of International Organization, Spring 1977, vol. 31, no. 2, in particular Edward Miles, "The Structure and Effect of the Decision Process in The Seabed Committee and the Third United Nations Conference on The Law of The Sea", pp. 159-234.

23. UN Doc. A/37/163.

II. CHOICES MADE FOR THE CSCE

1. Introduction

The basic choices with respect to agenda, institutional framework and rules of procedure which guided the Madrid Meeting, were made during the so-called "Helsinki Consultations". These Consultations, which were held from 22 November 1972 until June 8, 1973, were usually called "Multilateral Preparatory Talks" (MPT) and this is still their current designation in Western and Eastern European literature: the word "multilateral" served to differentiate them from the innumerable bilateral consultations which had gone before in preparation for the CSCE; by the term "preparatory" the Western countries wished to convey that the object of the consultations was to establish the conditions for such a conference; finally the word "talks" indicated that, given the preparatory nature of the negotiations, there was as yet no question either of a conference or a meeting. The whole designation Multilateral Preparatory Talks thus reflected the cautious and reserved demeanour of the Western countries as they approached Helsinki.

Nevertheless, it is interesting to note that the most important decisions in the field of procedure in the CSCE were taken as early as within the first week of the Helsinki Consultations (22-28 November 1972) when the ambassadors of the countries invited by the Finnish Government met together to prepare for the Conference (1). At that time the principle of consensus was established, not only for substantive matters but also with application to the laying-down and amendment of rules of procedure. At the same time the principle of rotating the chairmanship was laid down. Furthermore the possibility of setting up working bodies on special subjects was thrown open, such bodies being envisaged as "open-ended" or open to participation by any delegation. These and other subjects have been selected to be dealt with in the section "rules of procedure" of the present Chapter.

The procedures agreed were laid down in the "Final Recommendations of the Helsinki Consultations" to which the participants expressed their collective agreement on 8 June 1973. In particular Chapter VI, called

"Rules of Procedure", of these Recommendations* proved to be of paramount importance and these rules have become the basic operating procedures guiding not only the activities of the three stages of the Conference particularly during the second stage in Geneva, but also all other meetings organized as a follow-up to the Conference. The complete "Final Recommendations of the Helsinki Consultations" is known as the "Blue Book" from the colour of the cover chosen at its publication. Since then the two other CSCE documents about procedural modalities have also become popularly known by the colour of their covers. The Yellow Book, containing the agenda for the Belgrade Meeting, and the Purple Book containing that for Madrid** both stipulate: "The rules of procedure, the working methods and the scale of distribution for the expenses of the Conference will, *mutatis mutandis*, be applied to the Meeting". This reference to "the rules of procedure ... of the Conference" meant that the Blue Book, which applied to the Conference, would also apply to the Belgrade and Madrid Meetings.

The rules of procedure formed only one item on the list of conditions for convening a conference which the participants in the Helsinki Consultations recommended to their governments. Other conditions specified in the Blue Book concerned its organization, agenda and related instructions, participation, date, place and financial arrangements. In view of the previous Chapter's extensive report on the agenda-related developments before the Helsinki Consultations, the Blue Book recommendations on the agenda will be touched upon below only briefly.

The last point of the Blue Book agenda, which focused on the follow-up to the conference, contained only one paragraph. In order to find out the institutional conditions for the Madrid Meeting it is necessary to examine the respective Chapter in the Final Act itself, as we shall see.

2. The CSCE Agenda

It was in the Blue Book that the conference found its definitive name, the Conference on Security and Co-operation in Europe. The Warsaw Pact countries, from the time of their 1966 Bucharest Declaration, had

---

* see Annex no. 1
** see Annex no. 3

appealed for the convening of an "all-European Conference" which would discuss both security and co-operation. They were consistent in their use of the adjective "all-European" and of the words "security" and "co-operation". Sometimes they spoke of "European co-operation", sometimes of "co-operation in Europe" or "peaceful co-operation in Europe". The most frequent phrase was "an all-European conference on the question of security and co-operation in Europe". Western countries never took up the term "all-European" because this could have been interpreted to exclude the US and Canada. For the same reasons, from about 1970, the use of the term "European co-operation" was consciously avoided by the West because co-operation with the North American states was equally important within the framework of the proposed Conference. The NATO communiqué of December 1970 is the first to speak clearly about "a conference, or a series of conferences, on security and co-operation in Europe". The year before, in their Declaration of December 1969, the NATO ministers had mentioned references by East European countries to "an early Conference on European Security" (CES), a term which continued for a long time in daily use, together with the much-used title: "European Security Conference" (ESC). After the Helsinki Final Act had become widely known, the Conference and its follow-up Meetings at Belgrade and Madrid were referred to in the Western press mostly as "The Helsinki Conference", or the "Human Rights Conference" or the "Security Conference". Both the latter names do the CSCE and the Final Act an injustice because they describe a part instead of the whole. The Final Act does not deal only with security, nor is it limited solely to human rights, but also covers other matters.

Inherent in the name of the conference is the idea of balance; the Conference on Security and Co-operation and its follow-up Meetings were concerned with co-operation as well as security in various fields. This equilibrium is reflected in the Final Act, clearly signifying that in the movement towards the reduction of tension co-operation is just as important as security. The way the different parts of the Final Act stand in relation to each other represents the achievement of long hours of negotiation but also within each Chapter of the Act great effort was put into finding a balance. Security in one scale must act as a counterweight to co-operation in economic and humanitarian fields in the other. The first Chapter itself does not deal exclusively with the military aspects of security (the so-called confidence-building measures) but also with the non-military approaches expressed in the ten principles "guiding relations between participating states" under which are included not only principles dealing with the inviolability of frontiers and the rights inherent in sovereignty of states, but also those which define and recognise the rights of the human individual.

Chapter II of the Blue Book gives an outline of the agenda for the second stage in Geneva and thereby sketches in the outline of the Final Act with which negotiations in Geneva were to conclude. The word agenda is used in the present book in various different ways because it is recognised as having a variety of meanings. In general an agenda is a list of items of business to be considered at a meeting. It does not necessarily follow, however, that these items must be dealt with in the order in which they appear on the agenda. However this may be, the Warsaw Pact as well as the NATO countries, in the course of their communiqué dialogue between 1966 and 1972, proposed a number of agenda items which they thought should be included for treatment at the Conference. All these proposed agenda items finally ended up in five Chapters of the Final Act, each in its turn comprising a large number of subjects. The most important of these Chapters acquired the label *basket* (2), of which the meaning is: a collection of subjects which have something in common. The five Chapters of the Final Act are as follows:

I. Questions relating to Security in Europe, consisting of two sections, namely: (1) a Declaration on Principles Guiding Relations between Participating States and (2) a Document on confidence--building measures, known as the military aspects of security; these two sections together, thus the whole of the first Chapter, are called the first basket.

II. Co-operation in the field of Economics, of Science and Technology and of the Environment; this whole Chapter is known as the second basket.

III. Questions relating to Security and Co-operation in the Mediterranean.

IV. Co-operation in Humanitarian and Other Fields; this Chapter is distinguished as the third basket.

V. Follow-up to the Conference; this Chapter is sometimes but not often called the fourth basket.

As has already been mentioned, Chapters I, II, IV and V originate in proposals made by the Warsaw Pact and NATO countries in their Communiqués or Declarations between 1966 and 1972. Six years of communiqué dialogue and thus six years of study within each of the two alliances, preceded the commencement of the Helsinki Consultations on 22 November 1972.

Oral negotiations between Western and Eastern European countries and those European nations which belonged neither to the Warsaw Pact nor to NATO, then continued from November 1972 until July 1975, followed by the signing of the Final Act on 1 August 1975. The Final Act therefore, was the result of nearly a decade of studies, discussions and negotiations within and between all participating States, which is to say within and between 35 sovereign states.

3. The CSCE Follow-Up System

The short paragraph of the Blue Book on the question how to proceed after the Conference provides a clear indication that the reticent view on institutionalization held by the Western countries had prevailed over the more ambitious views held by the Neutral and Non--aligned (NNA) countries and the countries of the Warsaw Pact. Decisions on how to proceed after the Conference were made dependent on progress made at the Conference itself. The paragraph (53) of the Blue Book reads in full:

> The Co-ordinating Committee shall consider, on the basis of the progress made at the Conference such measures as may be required to give effect to the decisions of the Conference and to further the process of improving security and developing co-operation in Europe. Having considered proposals to this effect, including proposals of an organizational nature, it shall make any recommendation which it deems necessary. In examining the follow-up of the Conference, the Committee shall also consider the contributions which it believes could be asked from existing international organizations.

During the second stage of the CSCE in Geneva (1973-'75) the two viewpoints came closer to each other. Several proposals played a role in these negotiations (3). A Czechoslovakian proposal which had East European support, aimed at a consultative commission with permanent status. Proposals put forward by NNA countries and Romania ranged from a permanent co-ordination commission to a series of periodical conferences. In the end, the proposal from the EC countries, submitted by Denmark in April 1974, provided the main basis for the negotiations which resulted in the text of the Chapter in the Final Act on "Follow-up to the Conference"*. This proposal followed the same line of reasoning as the text of the Blue Book. It preferred to leave decisions on how to continue the multilateral follow-up process to a meeting (the Belgrade Meeting) at which they could be taken in the light of an analysis of how implementation of the Final Act had developed in the interim period.

According to the Final Act this implementation is to take place on unilateral, bilateral and multilateral levels. For the last level a clear distinction is made between *conference* and *meetings* (4). The first and only "Conference" to date, on Security and Co-operation in Europe, took place in three stages which were held respectively in:

- Helsinki, from 3-7 July 1973
- Geneva, from 18 September 1973 - 21 July 1975 and once more
- Helsinki, from 30 July - 1 August 1975.

In addition to the conference two sorts of "meetings" are recognized. The first of these is "meetings of experts of the participating States", of which there have been three. Besides these, and more important, are the meetings "at the level of representatives appointed by the Ministers of Foreign Affairs", two of which have taken place, the Belgrade Meeting and the Madrid Meeting. By analogy with the Belgrade Meeting of 1977, the Madrid Meeting was officially entitled: "The Madrid Meeting 1980 of Representatives of the Participating States of the Conference on Security and Co-operation in Europe, held on the basis of the provisions of the Final Act relating to the Follow-up to the Conference". Although what took place in Madrid was thus a follow-up "Meeting", in the present book this "Meeting" is generally referred to as the "conference" in Madrid because its actual nature was that of an intergovernmental conference (5).

The Final Act announced as first of this type of meetings the meeting to be held at Belgrade in 1977. It was to be preceded by a preparatory meeting that "will decide on the date, duration, agenda and other modalities of the meeting of representatives appointed by the

---

* see Annex no. 2

Ministers of Foreign Affairs". The only institutional link between the successive meetings of the type of Belgrade and Madrid of which the Final Act makes mention is expressed in the following sentence: "This meeting will define the appropriate modalities for the holding of other meetings which could include further similar meetings and the possibility of a new Conference".

As regards the tasks of this type of follow-up meeting the second paragraph of the chapter's operative section starts out by stating that the participating States declare their resolve to continue the multilateral process initiated by the Conference:

> (a) by proceeding to a thorough exchange of view on the implementation of the provisions of the Final Act and of the tasks defined by the Conference, as well as, in the context of the questions dealt with by the latter, on the deepening of their mutual relations, the improvement of security and the development of co-operation in Europe, and the development of the process of détente in the future.

This sentence is of evident importance with respect to making up the agenda taken in the sense of the order of conduct of business during the follow-up meetings. In Madrid the sentence led to hot debates, as we shall see in Chapter V.

Finally, the last paragraph of the follow-up Chapter of the Final Act furnished the sentence - already discussed in the context of the Yellow and Purple Books in the introduction to the present Chapter - on rules of procedure, working methods and scale of distribution for the expenses of the Conference, which will, *mutatis mutandis*, be applied to all the envisaged meetings. This provision implied that, for instance, the rule of consensus among CSCE-participants might also apply to questions relating to the implementation of CSCE decisions within the framework of international organizations, such as the ECE and UNESCO. Both these organizations are explicitly mentioned in connection with multilateral implementation efforts. The question of individual CSCE-states or the organizations themselves reporting to the CSCE, was left open: in practice ECE and UNESCO were allowed to deliver contributions to the follow-up meeting, but these speeches did not take the form of official implementation reports.

The last two sentences of the same paragraph introduce the

principle of rotation with regard to the location of all the envisaged meetings, and stipulate that the services of a technical secretariat will be provided by the host country.

It is clear from the Chapter of the Final Act on follow-up to the Conference, that the outcome of the negotiations on this text lay closer to Western preferences than to those expressed by NNA or Warsaw Pact countries.

4. The CSCE Rules of Procedure

The first paragraph of Chapter VI, "Rules of Procedure", of the Blue Book, states the basic principle of the CSCE: "All States participating in the Conference shall do so as sovereign and independent States and in conditions of full equality. The Conference shall take place outside military alliances".

The principle of sovereign equality of all participants was proposed by the Finnish delegation presiding over the meeting, in the very first days of the Helsinki Consultations, and met with no opposition. Romania brought in an amendment to define even further the equality and independence of the states, proposing that these conditions should hold for the states "independent of their belonging or not to a Military Alliance", a form of words which raised objections from the Soviet delegation and which finally resulted in the second of the sentences already quoted.

Acceptance of the principle of equality altered the pattern of the East-West dialogue which, up to the time of the Consultations, had been carried on between military blocs via their communiqués. At the same time it ruled out the possibility either of an Executive Board or permanent Presidency shared between the USSR and the US. Henceforth, in theory, the smallest state would have as much say as the largest, a neutral country as much as an aligned one.

The ultimate consequence of the equality principle, the consensus rule, was adopted in the same week: here the right of veto was extended to every participant and ceased to be the prerogative of the most powerful: an end was put to the possibility of imposing the will of the majority and to predictable majority alignments in the decision-making process. The principle of equality also gave rise to the idea of rotating the chairmanship, both in the plenary assemblies and any working groups. Finally, the same principle ensured that all such working groups should be "open-ended" with free access for every state. It is for this reason that in the CSCE there are no formal committees whose membership is confined to an elite.

The idea of equality of participating states was also included explicitly in the Final Act itself, at the insistence of the Romanians in Geneva; it appears in the text of Principle IX of the Ten Principles governing relations between participating states. Entitled "Co-operation among States", this principle states that in developing their co-operation each of the states will make its contribution "in conditions of full equality". This can be interpreted as imposing an obligation to apply the consensus rule throughout the subsequent practice and application of what is agreed multilaterally and bilaterally in the framework of the CSCE.

4.1. The Rule of Consensus

In theory, all participating states are equal. The Blue Book lays down in Chapter VI, "Rules of Procedure", rule (69):

> Decisions of the Conference shall be taken by consensus. Consensus shall be understood to mean the absence of any objection expressed by a Representative and submitted by him as constituting an obstacle to the taking of the decision in question.

Further references will be made to the, at times, grotesque consequences of the consensus rule, in Chapter VIII where the negotiating process in Madrid is described, but the following remarks would seem appropriate here.

Before the Helsinki Consultations started, experts in Western capitals examined the implications of various possible voting procedures in the CSCE (6). At that time, although no-one supposed that any agreements the conference might reach in the future would be legally binding treaties, great political weight was nevertheless expected to be attached to them. Now, it could not be supposed that any state, small or great, would allow itself to be politically bound by a number of rules, either concerning international law or human rights, or of military significance, for which it had not itself voted; nor was it reasonable to assume that the great powers would be ready to bow to a majority decision, especially if it concerned security interests vital to them. Therefore, inside NATO, even before the Helsinki Consultations began, the general feeling was that the consensus rule would have to apply in general, but only to matters of some substance. For the conclusion had also been reached in Western capitals that for certain sorts of questions, for example in the field of procedure, the possibility of departing from the consensus rule must remain open; otherwise any one of the participants alone would be able to block the progress or even conclusion of the negotiations. But East European countries would not hear of any departure from the consensus rule at all. Romania, especially, held unrelentingly to the principle of full equality of all the participating states, and thus to the application of the consensus rule to every subject.

If one of the consequences of the consensus rule was that the big powers were not subjected to majority decisions in which they had no share, for smaller countries it was equally a safeguard. In their case it was also an actual stimulus to taking part in the debate for they knew that their consent would be necessary to the final decision. On the other hand the consensus rule paved the way for the use, or misuse, of the right of veto that each participating state, large or small, had been granted regardless of its importance. This right could also be used to threaten a decision with a veto in order to get agreement for another decision on a different subject.

Malta's representative provided examples of this which, because of their exceptional character, have a certain notoriety in CSCE history. The consensus rule was used by Malta in such a way that on one occasion in Geneva, in the course of an all-night deliberation, a despairing delegate from the Soviet Union actually went so far as to propose departing from the rule in certain cases.

This was in June 1973 when the Helsinki Consultations could not be concluded because Malta's delegate was determined first to get his own way in matters of special interest to Malta. The proposal was to invite the Arab Mediterranean States to participate in the Conference, and was met with modified rapture from the other participating states. The Maltese vote in the consensus necessary for adoption of the collective proposals and for the closure of the Consultations, was only "bought" by granting the Mediterranean States special status as "non-participating

States", with the right to be consulted on the subject of various agenda items. Earlier in the Consultations, this idea had been rejected by those taking part, for fear that the Middle East problem might be introduced into the CSCE.

The same strategy was used by Malta at the end of stage II of the Conference, in Geneva, when those negotiating were about to close their negotiations so as to obtain the signatures of their heads of state to the Final Act before the summer of 1975. Once more Malta temporarily opposed the consensus on the closure of negotiations until she finally obtained satisfaction with respect to her proposals concerning parts of the Chapter of the Final Act: "Questions relating to Security and Co-operation in the Mediterranean", notably its penultimate paragraph where the states declare their intention of "reducing armed forces in the region". In Belgrade, three years later, history repeated itself when the Maltese delegate was able to hold up the closure of the Meeting for four days until the other participating states had been driven to agree to the provision in the Belgrade Concluding Document which read: "Questions relating to security [in the Mediterranean] will be discussed at the Madrid Meeting". This subject which, by those means, found its way on to the Madrid agenda, was the only item fixed before the Madrid Meeting began. But this use of the consensus rule, when carried to such an extreme degree, becomes pointless if political reality is left too far behind. There are few participating states really interested in the CSCE's dealing with questions relating to security in the Mediterranean. The "contributions" from the non-participating Mediterranean States were therefore given a courteous hearing in Madrid but aroused no discussion.

It was, of course, a right not confined to the smaller states to withhold consent to a certain decision in order to obtain their wishes in another area. Larger countries were just as much entitled to declare: "I shall not accept your proposal unless you accept mine". In these cases the question was that of a delegation's refusal to co-operate in a certain decision because it did not receive support for another decision on a different subject. None of the cases concerned objections to the content of the proposed decision in itself. One may wonder whether this use of the rule conforms to what the authors had in mind when they wrote in the Blue Book: "Consensus shall be understood to mean the absence of any objection expressed by a Representative and submitted by him as constituting an obstacle to the taking of the decision in question". This wording passes over whether the objection should relate directly to the content of that decision itself. Although the impression given at first glance may be that it should.

Naturally the consensus rule is also used to prevent a decision where a delegation is unable to agree to its actual content. This might be called the proper use of the rule. Here its force lies in its preventive action and in this sense it dominates the whole process of negotiating the text of a decision from the first step onwards. All parties know from the beginning that the decision can only be adopted if no-one has any objection to it. This inevitably leads to compromises, vague wording and escape clauses because the alternative is no text at all. This situation is described in detail in Chapter VII.

Yet once a decision has been reached by consensus it has more moral force than if it had been taken by majority vote. The CSCE is neither a national parliament nor an international court both of which have a well-defined legal capacity which also lays down that a majority decision is binding on all those concerned including those in the minority who are of a different opinion. As an international conference the CSCE enjoys no legal competence whatsoever; its 35 participants are separate sovereign states. The Final Act derives its value and its force from the fact that it was collectively approved by these 35 countries, none of whom can deny responsibility because every one of them was involved in the process of bringing it to birth. In consequence all the 35 countries are to a greater degree answerable for their failures to fulfil their commitments than would have been the case if the various parts of the Act had been passed by separate majority votes. Because the Final Act was established by consensus, the 35 participating states who signed it have a mutual obligation, if not legal then moral, to fulfil its provisions down to the last jot and tittle.

4.2. Reservations and Interpretative Statements

In order to mitigate the most extreme consequences of the consensus rule and to provide a way out when the difficulties in the way of a decision threatened to become insuperable, the drafters of the Blue Book introduced three ways of taking a decision by consensus even when it did not have the *positive* approval of all the parties. However, little use has ever been made of these possibilities and they had no influence on the course of negotiations in Geneva or Belgrade. Consensus is not merely a procedure laid down in a number of rules but an ideal which shapes the whole spirit of a conference.

The first mitigation of the Blue Book's rule of consensus arises from its *negative* approach: "Consensus shall be understood to mean the absence of any objection ... to the taking of the decision". No positive approval is required; silence means consensus. The Vatican representative made it clear during the Helsinki Consultations that his silence was not to be interpreted as agreement but rather as an effort not to stand in the way of the consensus.

A second qualification of the rule of consensus is contained in the provision that the objection to the decision must be submitted by the delegation as "constituting an obstacle to the taking of the decision in question". In other words the delegation can let its objections to a decision be known and yet have no objection to the decision being taken. The delegation concerned wishes it to be known that it is less than enthusiastic about the proposed decision but will not stand in the way of its adoption. In fact any delegation which expresses itself in this way is simply pointing out its own readiness to make concessions, bowing to the majority in this case.

The third and more explicit mitigation of the consensus rule is found in paragraph (79) of the Rules of Procedure which reads:

> Representatives of States participating in the Conference may ask for their formal reservations or interpretative statements concerning given decisions to be duly registered by the Executive Secretary and circulated to the participating States. Such statements must be submitted in writing to the Executive Secretary.

This offers no sort of guarantee that the reservations and interpretative statements were to enjoy the same status as the decision itself. The official publications of the Final Act and subsequent concluding documents do not extend to reservations and interpretative statements so that only specialized CSCE experts know anything about them. It is true that they have to be duly registered and circulated by the Executive Secretary to the participating states. They appear therefore in print in the "journals" of the particular sessions but this registration is of little relevance since there is no permanent secretariat but only one which changes with each host country and, in fact, none at all in the interim periods between follow-up Meetings, so that the final result is that after a number of years these "journals" become difficult to get hold of and only an assiduous librarian would be capable of tracking them down.

With the help of members of the Spanish Executive Secretariat we were ultimately able to consult all the Geneva and Helsinki journals and thus acquaint ourselves with the reservations and interpretative statements registered in connection with the Final Act. At the start it had proved impossible for the Spanish Executive Secretariat to produce a single document either from Helsinki, Geneva or Belgrade and when requests had been made to the various governments only the Finnish administration turned out to be able to provide photocopies of all the documents required. The net result from all these documents was as follows.

There is only one official reservation concerning the whole of the Final Act on the basis of rule (79), made by Turkey. This reservation is political in character and neither withholds approval nor condemns the content of the Final Act. The Turkish delegation in Helsinki simply registered the statement, repeated in Belgrade and later Madrid, that the provisions of the Final Act would not be applied by Turkey in her relations with Cyprus "until such time that a government legitimately representing the two communites is established in Cyprus". To this, Cyprus' standard reaction, always supported by Greece, was that such a unilateral reservation was in conflict with the political commitment of all participating states to implement fully, unilaterally, bilaterally and multilaterally all the provisions of the Final Act.

In Helsinki, Belgrade (and later Madrid) the US delegation similarly made a political reservation but this was never presented as a reservation according to rule (79) such as would have had to be registered and distributed by the Executive Secretary, nor did he in fact do this. The US reserved her position with regard to the "illegal incorporation, by force of arms, of the States of Latvia, Lithuania, and Estonia by the Soviet Union". According to the US government the statement in Principle IV of the Final Act that no occupation or acquisition of territory in contravention of international law will be recognized as legal, is applicable to the Baltic states (7).

In Geneva, there were six cases where delegations accepted a certain provision while furnishing it with their own interpretative statement in the sense of rule (79) of the Blue Book. On a single occasion a Chairman's statement was registered encountering no opposition. A further interpretative statement concerned a translation problem. All these cases were concerned with first basket provisions. In two further cases, two delegations declared their objections to a text but did not wish to stand in the way of its adoption (8). There were approximately twenty cases of provisional registration of a provision where delegations declared themselves in agreement with this registration on condition that agreement would also be reached in a manner satisfactory to them on a further text on the same subject. Should this fail to occur then the delegation reserved the right to return later to the provisionally registered text. Such reservations as these, which were an element in the tactics of negotiation, were naturally assumed to cease to apply as soon as all provisions had been definitively approved.

4.3. Rotation of the Chairmanship

The most important rule of procedure of the CSCE, after the consensus rule, is the principle of rotation whereby the occupant of the chair changes at each new session, in alphabetical order. This gave every state an equal part in chairing all the conference sessions. During the Helsinki Consultations it was the Romanian delegation which insisted on this system even though other delegations feared that the work of the conference would suffer in consequence. For the Romanians it was yet another method of preventing a bloc-to-bloc configuration within the CSCE. In Helsinki, Geneva and Belgrade the difficulties arising from rotation and foreseen by the other delegations were eventually solved by converting the formal committees into informal "mini-groups" under a fixed chairman supplied by one of the NNA countries and known as the "co-ordinator".

Rotation of the chairmanship is laid down in rules (70) and (71) of the Rules of Procedure in the Blue Book. Rule (70) was important during the Conference's first stage at ministerial level (3 - 7 July 1973) when it was necessary to draw lots in order to decide the order of rotation. Rule (71) governed the rotation of the chairmanship in working bodies of the conference during the second stage (Geneva, 18 September 1973 - 21 July 1975). For the most important working body, the Co-ordinating Committee, daily rotation was the rule but for other work groups: "(b) The Chairmen of Sub-Committees and of other subsidiary bodies of the Conference shall be designated on a basis of rotation in accordance with practical arrangements to be established at the appropriate time by the bodies in question". It was assumed that work requirements in particular sectors could derive advantage from a more spaced-out rhythm of rotation (9).

In fact, in Geneva, *daily* rotation became the rule in *all* formal work groups. This principle was once more clearly stated in the Yellow Book for the Belgrade Follow-up Meeting: "The Chair at the opening and closing plenary meetings shall be taken by the Representative of Yugoslavia. After the opening meeting the Chair shall be taken in daily rotation, in French alphabetical order, starting with the Representative of the Federal Republic of Germany". The FRG had been appointed by lot as first occupant of the chair after the host country. French alphabetical order is not only followed for the subsequent order of rotation of the chairmanship, it is also the order followed when delegations sit round the table (10).

The importance attached to rotation of the chairmanship gives some indication of the role which chairmen were expected to play. In theory and practice it was a restrained one for although it is the chairman who grants permission to speak he is not supposed to push the meeting actively along lines of his own choosing. Most chairmen stuck to their passive role but this did not mean that there was no distinction among chairmen: some were more successful than others either because of their personalities or their own particular insight into what was required in a given situation.

A question of some importance is whether the chairmanship shall be rotated daily or meeting by meeting. Rules (70) and (71) speak respectively of meeting by meeting and daily rotation (11). The controversy is about what ought to happen at midnight if the meeting overruns. In Geneva and Belgrade it was sometimes decided by silent assent to allow the current chairman to see the meeting out but sometimes a consensus decision would be taken to bring in the following day's chairman as soon as midnight struck. In Madrid this question led to argument which sometimes became acrimonious, as we shall see in Chapter VIII.

4.4. Working Methods

During the Helsinki Consultations it was decided, in spite of initial opposition from the Soviet Union, to set up "working bodies of the Conference"; these were committees and sub-committees which could in turn set up further working groups. Rule (68) stipulates that "The working bodies and working groups of the Conference shall be open to all the participating States". The open-endedness of these bodies is a consequence of the consensus rule because all participants must be granted the opportunity of making known their objections to no matter what decision of whatever committee. However, during the last stage of negotiations in Belgrade, the principle was breached by the informal arrangement according to which the NNA countries only decided on and invited to negotiations a certain number of representatives from the caucuses, but these informal discussions were in fact well outside the official negotiation framework of the CSCE.

At the institution of committees during the Helsinki Consultations the West envisaged an inductive working method which, in the context, meant that a final communiqué would be drafted from the bottom upwards. Any particular text would first be exhaustively discussed by a sub--committee of experts and only if the dispute could not be settled would it be taken up at a politically higher level, i.e., at the level of heads of mission. This method became the rule in the CSCE.

The fact that it became the practice in the CSCE to use the inductive or "bottom-up" method which focuses from the beginning, at expert level, on details of the national proposals, is in contrast to the dominating role allotted by the Blue Book and later the Yellow and Purple Books, to the bodies which were eventually bound to take the final decisions at the highest political level, the three Geneva "Committees", and the Plenaries in Belgrade and Madrid. According to the Blue Book (rules 16, 30 and 42) the "Committees" in Geneva were to "be assisted by the appropriate Sub-Committees" but were to formulate the final document themselves. The Plenaries in Belgrade and Madrid were commissioned "to guide" their Subsidiary Working Bodies in their work and then to carry out the drafting work themselves only "assisted by" the Drafting Groups.

It could thus be assumed that the Committees and Plenaries would provide their working groups with political guidelines and assign to them the task of embodying these in concrete texts for a concluding document. As political bodies at the highest level they would then have performed the function of laying down and directing policy. But, as a consequence of the inability of these high-level, political bodies to confine the course of the actual negotiations in the subsidiary organs within the boundaries of a strict policy, these organs at expert level in fact enjoyed an extensive autonomy.

4.5. The Executive Secretary

The CSCE has retained its conference character and never been turned into an organization; there is thus no permanent secretariat but each follow-up meeting acquires an *ad hoc* Executive Secretary appointed by the host country. The Rules of Procedure in the Blue Book grant him authority in only one instance when they designate him "responsible for the recruitment of his staff". The other relevant rules (74, 75, 76) do little else but limit his powers. "He is designated by the host country subject to agreement by the participating States". Even here the idea of consensus is not absent. Up to this time appointments of Executive Secretaries by host governments have been uncontroversial. He is conceived as fulfilling a neutral role as appears from his title "the Executive Secretary for technical matters" who is expected to work "under the authority of the Conference".

In practice the Executive Secretariat has provided a service indispensable to the conference. In Geneva it had a staff of 350 (12) and in Madrid it started with 164, two thirds of whom were language staff including a large number of interpreters and translators*. The cost of the executive secretariat is spread over the participating states by means of an agreed scale of distribution.

The provision that the Executive Secretary is himself "responsible for the recruitment of his staff" worked very well in practice. As "a national of the host country" he was in a position to recruit his assistants from among his own compatriots and this position was never

---

* see Annex no. 5

challenged. This made it unnecessary for him to observe the principle of geographic distribution which obtains in, for example, UN organisations and is capable of producing an administrative secretariat of quite unreasonable proportions.

4.6. Languages

The Rules of Procedure (81, 82) in the Blue Book stipulate that: "The working languages of the Conference and of its working bodies shall be: English, French, German, Italian, Russian and Spanish. Speeches made in any of the working languages shall be interpreted into the other working languages". This means that at any meeting of any committee a team of twelve interpreters is necessary for simultaneous interpretation of the language in use into the five other languages. In Madrid in the first period there were two or three meetings taking place at the same time which meant that the secretariat had to have at least 36 interpreters at its disposal.

Originally the Finns proposed the use of only three languages, English, French and Russian. Halfway through 1972 German was added as the language spoken in five CSCE countries: the FRG, the GDR, Austria, Switzerland and Liechtenstein. Even before the beginning of the Helsinki Consultations this led to demands from Italy at first (13) and then from Spain for their languages to be made official languages of the conference as well. Italian is spoken in four CSCE countries: Italy, San Marino, Switzerland and the Holy See. When Italian had been accepted Spain argued that Spanish could not possibly be left out as it was one of the working languages of the UN.

At a later stage of the Helsinki Consultations an attempt was made to reduce the number of languages to one or two but it proved impossible to get a consensus for this. In fact, English swiftly became the most important working language for the informal bodies. From the beginning texts were prepared in English in the first instance, and subsequently translated by the secretariat into the five other languages. For this task in Madrid the Secretariat employed a pool of 12 to 24 translators.

4.7. Records of the Meetings, Publicity

In accordance with the relevant recommendations in the Blue Book it became the custom to make unclassified verbatim records of the public sessions of the Plenary, in other words the opening and closing sessions. Other sessions of the plenary and committees are, in principle, not open unless the participants decide otherwise, which they seldom have done. "Journals" are made of the closed sessions and these are available for public inspection, just like the verbatim records, but are of little importance. The only enduring interest of these journals is their registration of official decisions by the Plenary (for instance, that the conference would adjourn for a number of months) and of interpretative statements and reservations.

This does not mean that journalists need ever feel frustrated for lack of information because after each meeting the diplomats who attended the meeting are usually quite willing to give an account of their recent experiences. One of the functions of the CSCE for all concerned was to be a propaganda forum so publicity was never shunned.

The fact that CSCE negotiations are not secret is for instance borne out by the books written on these negotiations. They give highly detailed accounts of daily negotiations complete with national points of view, draft texts and proposed amendments. The CSCE is an open book.

5. Points for Consideration

Now that the options that were open for the agenda, follow-up system and rules of procedure of the CSCE, and the choices that were made, have become familiar, it should be possible to single out certain points that may have had a deleterious effect on the efficiency of the Conference as a decision-making process and to use these as a basis for suggesting improvements that might usefully be introduced at future CSCE meetings.

a. the CSCE agenda

The Final Act covers virtually all conceivable aspects of security and co-operation in Europe and yet not all the items can be considered as of equal importance in discussions and negotiations at follow-up meetings. The question may be raised whether striving for a "substantial and balanced" concluding document at such meetings will not inevitably lead to a certain unjustifiable loss of efficiency because of the multiplicity of proposals, all of which may be desirable with an eye to the national home front, but many of which are of minor importance for significant international decision-making. The final result is liable to be either no substantial document at all or one that, while substantial, cannot be considered as an improvement on the Final Act. One of the first questions is how to avoid this situation.

b. the follow-up system

1. It may be useful to look at the *level of institutionalization* of the Conference by comparing the latter with international organizations, whether governmental or non-governmental, on the basis of three characteristics. First of all, such institutions normally hold regularly scheduled meetings of member representatives whereas CSCE meetings take place only as agreed at a previous meeting. Secondly, they have specified procedures for decision-making whereas CSCE rules of procedure and working methods are applied *mutatis mutandis* and decisions on date, duration, agenda and other modalities are left to preparatory meetings. Thirdly, international organizations usually have a permanent secretariat while CSCE rules provide only for a technical secretariat supplied for each separate meeting by the country of its location. It must be asked whether such a low level of institutionalization will not result in much time and energy being wasted, especially during the preparatory stages of the follow-up meeting, and whether it would not therefore be advisable to increase the degree of institutionalization of the follow-up meetings.

2. As a basis for considering the *programme of business* of follow--up meetings one might consider what types of decision international organizations are able to make in general and how many of these are actually relevant to the CSCE. Five major categories can be distinguished:

a) *informational decisions* involving the gathering, analysis, exchange and dissemination of data and point of view;

b) *normative decisions* involving the definition and declaration of standards: what is meant here are proclamations that are designed to affect the milieu in which domestic and world politics are conducted;

c) *rule-creating decisions*, similarly involving definition and declaration of standards but with the purpose here of framing instruments that can have a legally binding effect whether or not this would necessitate implementatory action by member states;

d) *rule-supervisory decisions* involving measures taken to insure compliance with rules in force by those subject to them. The successive steps in this process range from ways of detecting evidence that a violation has occurred, through verification of that evidence to the imposition of sanctions;

e) *operational decisions* involving the use of resources at the organization's disposal (14).

It is clear from the development of the CSCE process that the rule-creating and operational types of decision need not be considered in the present context at least for the time being or in the near future. For all three other types a mandate can be derived from the second paragraph of the operational part of the Final Act's Follow-up Chapter, which indicates the agenda of follow-up meetings. However, because of the underlying ideological East-West split and the forum aspect of the follow-up meetings, it must be assumed that informational and rule-supervisory activities will necessarily dominate these meetings. If these are the facts of the case it is open to question whether continuing with the traditionally-composed agendas of follow-up meetings can be justified in view of the fact that they fail to take account of which sorts of decision are inevitably going to be of paramount importance, and therefore do not provide a tight structure of discussions reflecting the reality of the situation. Would it be an improvement to allow a more flexible interpretation of the agendas prescribed for the meetings, in particular with respect to the strict separation of review of implementation from introduction and examination of new proposals, or if more use were made of the possibility of organizing separate expert meetings and of international organizations or other multilateral fora, for discussion or negotiation?

c. the rules of procedure

1. In the CSCE the *consensus* procedure was made applicable to procedural as well as substantive matters. If the consensus rule is applied to decision-making on procedural issues it seems more than probable that it will result in considerable time-wasting because it is

likely to be employed at times for sheer tactical reasons with no reasonable substantive justification. If this is so would it be advisable to replace the rule of consensus in procedural matters with some kind of voting system? With regard to the consensus rule's application to substantive matters, it is a moot point whether policy formation by this method, when there are so many participants, can possibly be efficient at all as a decision-making process. In this case should some kind of voting procedure for substantive matters be recommended, or at least some sort of "active" consensus procedure, comparable, for instance, to the ones recently adopted for the UNCLOS III negotiations?

2. The working of the mechanisms of *formal reservations and interpretative statements* gives rise to the query whether since these escape mechanisms do not appear to have played a significant role in the CSCE they should be replaced by more attractive mechanisms which would be guaranteed a more prominent place in the decision-making process.

3. On the subject of *rotation of the chairmanship* it may be asked whether the inexorable application of this rule (daily rotation in all organs) will not always be inefficient because each new chairman must spend some time acquainting himself with the subject in hand and is precluded from carrying out a long-term chairing policy. Should the Conference therefore be urged to mitigate the rule of daily rotation of chairmanship in all organs?

4. With respect to *working methods* the question may be raised whether the "bottom-up" approach in policy formation will not always prove to be inefficient because the Plenary or central organ in the formally prescribed procedure, although bound to take the final decision, is not sufficiently implicated from the beginning. If this is so would anything be gained by practical as well as theoretical recognition of the Plenary as the central organ for guiding the process of policy formation? As far as the informal organs are concerned, which were created to facilitate the process of policy formation, the question seems to be whether, in view of the fact that they were found both necessary and useful they should, in future, be used more intensively and at an earlier stage, and whether adhering strictly to the formal procedure, on the other hand, would not be inefficient in comparison.

5. With respect to the *Executive Secretary* it may well be asked whether the limited terms of reference allotted to him do not impose too

great a restriction on his capacity for action before, during and after follow-up meetings, and whether it would therefore be advisable to broaden his competence.

6. Does the recognition of six working *languages* of the CSCE produce so great a volume of work and require such a number of translators and interpreters as seriously to reduce the efficiency of the decision-making? Would it be possible and helpful to distinguish between official and working languages and at least limit the number of the last category (preferably to English alone)?

7. Is it efficient to continue the publication of journals such as *Records of the Meeting* in view of their limited importance, or would it be better either to abolish them altogether or to give them a more prominent role?

8. Regarding CSCE *publicity rules* the question is whether the policy of restricted access to the plenaries does not have the effect of adding unduly to the burden of the participants by making it necessary for them to recount what happens in the Plenary for the benefit of those who are not permitted to attend in person (journalists and others). Would it be better instead to make the plenaries more accessible to the public?

NOTES:

1. See Luigi Vittorio Ferraris (ed.), Report on a Negotiation, Helsinki-Geneva-Helsinki 1972-1975 (Alphen aan den Rijn: Sijthoff & Noordhoff International Publishers BV, 1979), pp. 9-14.

2. Historical footnote: In January 1973 during the Helsinki Consultations the numerous proposals on different subjects had to be put in order even before the agenda items were fixed. An ideal put forward by the Netherlands and Switzerland now bore fruit. The Swiss delegation formulated as it were four imaginary baskets, into which everyone was invited to put their proposals as they saw fit. The Swiss delegation would then empty these baskets and channel their contents into a working document. The Swiss delegation numbered and then labelled the baskets as follows: basket I security; basket II economics and environment; basket III human contacts, information and cultural co--operation; basket IV follow-up.
In Luigi Vittorio Ferraris (ed.), op. cit., p. 13, it is claimed that it was the Dutch delegate who first put forward the idea of "putting the various proposals of each delegation into a basket" and so introduced the word "basket". The Netherlands representative apparently referred to, the late Jhr. B.E. Quarles van Ufford, did in fact confess to his friends that he had used the word - in a moment of inspiration - but in its French form. He had seen in his mind's eye four baskets standing on the platform and cried out: "On jette toutes les propositions dans un panier". Later on the French word in use became "corbeille" instead of "panier".

3. For report and analysis of the negotiations on the follow-up see Luigi Vittorio Ferraris (ed.), op. cit., Chapter XII and Ljubivoje Aćimović, op. cit., Part Three, Chapter III-11.

4. The French, Italian and German texts of the Final Act make use of three terms rather than two; their middle term is somewhat wider in meaning than the third; French: la Conférence, des rencontres, des réunions; Italian: Conferenza, incontri, riunioni; German: Konferenz, Zusammenkünfte, Treffen. The threefold division was used in paragraph 2 (b) of the Chapter "Follow-up": the "rencontres", "incontri" and "Zusammenkünfte" in the Follow-up to the Conference were not only to include meetings at the level of representatives appointed by the Ministers of Foreign Affairs but also any other meetings. The distinction became irrelevant in the end because in Belgrade what the West wanted was a second follow-up meeting of representatives.

5. As defined by Johan Kaufmann in Conference Diplomacy (Leyden: A.W. Sijthoff, 1970), pp. 21-22.

6. See also Luigi Vittorio Ferraris (ed.), op. cit., p. 67.

7. For the Turkish reservation see document Helsinki CSCE/III/I, dated 31 July 1975; the American reservation is included in the statement by Warren Zimmerman, deputy chairman of the US delegation, Madrid, December 15, 1980, in: "Negotiating with the Soviets in Madrid, World Affairs, vol. 144, no. 4, Spring 1982, pp. 361-362.

8. The six interpretative statements were registered (or re-registered) in Geneva on 19 and 20 July 1975; five of them concerned the section entitled "Principles" and one the Document on Confidence-Building Measures, both in the first basket.

a) When the second paragraph of Principle VI: "They will accordingly refrain from any form of armed intervention or threat of such intervention against another participating State" was accepted, the Romanian representative declared that the concept "armed intervention" meant, by definition, an unlawful act and that this text was linked to the preceding paragraph;

b) With reference to the adoption of the text of Principle VII on "Respect for human rights and fundamental freedoms" and the statement it contained that: "They confirm the right of the individual to know and act upon his rights and duties in this field", the FRG representative made the following statement: "We understand the words 'duties in this field' to refer to the limitations which are placed upon the exercise of human rights under the Universal Declaration of 1948 and the two United Nations Conventions of 1966, and of which the individual should be aware when exercising his rights";

c) The Italian representative, joined by the representatives of Canada and the USA, stated that he was "aware of the discrepancy existing in the formulation of the Tenth Principle between the expression 'obligations under international law' in the first paragraph and the expression 'legal obligations under international law' in the second paragraph". Because the Italian Government's view was that "any obligation under International Law is automatically a legal obligation", Italy's representative stated: "We therefore interpret the two expressions at present existing side by side in the formulation of the Tenth Principle as entirely equivalent to one another in their political and juridical substance, notwithstanding the difference in wording";

d) The representatives of Spain, Sweden and Romania, joined by those of Cyprus and Portugal, made an interpretative statement on the phrase in the Final Clauses of the Declaration containing the ten Principles, which says that: "the present Declaration does not affect their rights and obligations, nor the corresponding treaties and other agreements and arrangements". The three representatives claimed that this phrase referred to rights, obligations, treaties, agreements and arrangements that were "in conformity with international law" (thus excluding the so-called Brezhnev doctrine). The Swedish delegation stated in addition that these were rights, obligations, treaties, agreements, and arrangements which were in force at the time of the adoption of the Final Act;

e) Greece's representative, joined by the representative from Cyprus, referred to the second operative clause of the section in the first basket on "Matters related to giving effect to certain of the above Principles", stating that "the two cases envisaged at the end of this paragraph (invasion or attack) are not exhaustive, but are mentioned only by way of example";

f) The representative of the USA made a statement with respect to the second paragraph under "Prior notification of major military manoeuvres" to the effect that none of the provisions of that paragraph should be considered to apply to independent naval manoeuvres, independent air manoeuvres, or manoeuvres involving only naval and air forces, operating together. The US delegate also made a statement with respect to the two paragraphs under "Prior notification of other military manoeuvres" to the effect that the two provisions of those paragraphs should not be considered to apply outside of the area described in the third paragraph under "Prior notification of major military manoeuvres". The USSR delegation confirmed that it was on both questions of the same view.

The registered statement by the Chairman, which encountered no opposition, stated that in the Preamble to the ten Principles the reference to the Charter of the United Nations should be taken to imply a reference to the UN declaration known as the UN Friendly Relations Declaration.

The interpretative statement on the translation problem concerned a statement from the UK delegation, joined by eight other Western delegations declaring that they accepted the text of Principle VII "on the assumption that the word 'viera' in the Russian text has the same broad meaning as the word 'belief', or its equivalent, as it appears in the English and all the other texts of the third paragraph and in Article 18 of the International Convenant on Civil and Political Rights". The representative of the USSR and three other East European delegations declared it necessary on this subject "to inform all members of Committee I that the Russian word 'viera' fully and precisely corresponds to the English word 'belief' in the context of the third paragraph of the Seventh Principle ...".

Liechtenstein's representative registered a statement in the journal asking for a reservation regarding the text of the provision in the section "Human Contacts" of the third basket on the question of contacts between religious faiths. Liechtenstein would have preferred another text which was duly registered in the journal.

Cyprus considered a clause in the section "Prior notification of major military manoeuvres" in the first basket "not merely unnecessary but also detrimental to confidence-building in a sensitive part of the world", i.e., the Mediterranean area between Cyprus and Turkey, but had come "to the conclusion that at this late hour we should not block consensus on the matter".

The actual texts of these statements are to be found in: Journal No. 246 of Committee I, C-Sub-committee 2, dated 19 July 1975; Journal No. 246 bis, idem, Journal No. 337, Committee I, A-Sub-committee 1, dated 19 July 1975, and Journal No. 46, Committee I, dated 20 July 1975.

9. See Luigi Vittorio Ferraris (ed.), *op. cit*., p. 69.

10. In French alphabetical order the participating states are listed as follows:

- (la République Fédéral d') Allemagne
- (la République Démocratique) Allemande
- (les Etats-Unis d') Amérique
- (la République d') Autriche
- (le Royaume de) Belgique
- (la République Populaire de) Bulgarie
- (le) Canada
- (la République de) Chypre
- (le) Danmark
- (l') Espagne
- (la République de) Finlande

- (la République) Française
- (le Royaume-Uni de) Grande-Bretagne et d'Irlande du Nord
- (la République) Hellenique
- (la République Populaire) Hongroise
- (l') Irlande
- (l') Islande
- (la République) Italienne
- (la Principauté de) Liechtenstein
- (le Grand-Duché de) Luxembourg
- (la République de) Malte
- (la Principauté de) Monaco
- (la) Norvège
- (le Royaume des) Pays-Bas
- (la République Populaire de) Pologne
- (le) Portugal
- (la République Socialiste de) Roumanie
- Saint-Marin
- (le) Saint-Siège
- (la) Suède
- (la Confédération) Suisse
- (la République Socialiste) Tchecoslovaque
- (la République de) Turquie
- (l') Union des Républiques Socialistes Soviétiques
- (la République Socialiste Fédérative de) Yougoslavie

11. In Luigi Vittorio Ferraris (ed.), op. cit., pp. 69-70 it is said that during the Helsinki Consultations "the rule of a President for each meeting was established".

12. Anatoli Kowaljow, ABC der Diplomatie [ABC of Diplomacy] (Berlin: Staatsverlag der DDR, 1980), p. 242. He says at the same time with astonishing frankness that the "USSR had delegated 30 to 35 collaborators in the Secretariat".

13. Luigi Vittorio Ferraris (ed.) op. cit., p. 73.

14. See Harold K. Jacobson, op. cit., pp. 89-90.

III. THE PARTICIPATING STATES AND THEIR OBJECTIVES

1. Introduction

What countries took part in the Madrid follow-up meeting and why these particular ones? Why were the USA and Canada included in a European conference? The rules of procedure provided for non-participating as well as participating states: what was the identity of the former and their role in the CSCE? These are the questions which the present Chapter must deal with before passing on to look at what objectives the participating states kept before them as they prepared for the Madrid Meeting. It was in the proposals, formally submitted in December 1980 to be incorporated in a concluding document, that these aims found expression, so the chapter closes with a summary of all 87 proposals, grouped according to country of origin, in order to show what each country hoped to achieve through the CSCE.

2. The Participating States

Thirty-three European states, plus the United States and Canada, were originally invited by the Finnish government to take part in the Consultations. Andorra and the Principality of Monaco were not on the original list. Andorra cannot be treated as a state in the fullest sense of the word according to international law because its foreign policy is the joint responsibility of France and Spain. Monaco was later invited to take part in the first and subsequent stages of the Conference and is a signatory to the Final Act.

The Albanian government was unique in being the only invited state to refuse the invitation. The reason given by Albania was that the direst threat to European security was the expansionist and aggressive policies of the United States and of the Soviet Union, and West German revanchism, and the Albanian government considered that as long as these conditions persisted there could be no fruitful conference on European security. Since that time Albania has never attempted to become one of the states participating in the CSCE and has remained the only European land not taking part. This brought the final number of participating states in the Conference and its follow-up meetings to 35.

With Albania and the European "mini-states" in mind, the Blue Book, in clause (54), set out how a state could attend the Conference as "observer":

> All European States, the United States and Canada shall be entitled to take part in the Conference on Security and Co-operation in Europe. If any of these states wishes to attend as an observer it may do so. In that case, its representatives may attend all stages of the Conference and of its working bodies, but shall not participate in the taking of decisions. Such a State may decide later to accept these decisions or some of them under the conditions defined by the Conference.

There have been no requests for observer status. The European "mini-states" such as the Holy See, Liechtenstein, San Marino, Monaco, all preferred to be full participants rather than observers. The provisions of the Final Act are so interwoven and the Act as a whole so carefully balanced, that it would have been difficult to allow a state to approve only some of the decisions. The rider "under the conditions defined by the Conference" was therefore certainly not superfluous (1).

In addition to the European states, the USA and Canada are full participants: both have troops stationed in Europe. At the very outset, when the Warsaw Pact countries, individually or collectively, first put forward the idea of an "all-European Conference" and/or a European "collective security system", Western European states made it clear that North American participation (the United States and Canada) would be an indispensable condition to their own involvement in the Conference. It was feared that the Soviet and Polish appeals for a "collective security system" in Europe was designed to weaken the ties between Western Europe and North America and that such a system would be dominated by the Soviet Union.

However, when the WP countries made their official proposals for a European Conference, it was not indisputably clear whether the US and Canada could take part. The Bucharest Declaration of July 1966 expressed no opinion on the question of whether the US and Canada were welcome to participate in the "collective security system" and the "all-European Conference". The Warsaw Pact countries' appeal for the promotion of good-neighbour relations, closer economic and commercial ties, more contacts and various forms of co-operation, was directed to "all European countries". The same Bucharest Declaration proposed further that the Conference should issue "a General European Declaration on co-operation in maintaining and consolidating European security" and that this Declaration "would be open to all interested countries". Were the US and Canada to be presumed "interested countries" in this context? The passage concerned with participation in the Conference was just as unclear: "Our [Warsaw Pact] countries are prepared to share in such a Conference at any time acceptable to the other interested parties, whether members of the North Atlantic alliance or neutral. The neutral European countries could play a positive part in convening the Conference". It was hard for Western countries to believe that the Warsaw Pact countries saw the countries of North America as potential participants in the proposed conference, since a large part of the Declaration was devoted to the "aggressive" post-war politics of America in Europe which "in collusion with the aims of West German revanchists" according to the Declaration "had nothing in common with the vital interests of Europe's peoples and security". This Declaration helped to contribute to West European fears that the proposal for the conference was meant to weaken the ties between Western Europe and North America.

The "Declaration on European Peace and Security" issued by 24 European Communist and Workers' Parties in April 1967 in Karlovy Vary, did nothing to allay these fears. "We fully support the proposal for holding a Conference of all European countries on questions of security and peaceful co-operation in Europe". The final sentence of this Declaration could not have been clearer: "The nations of Europe can themselves decide on matters of peace and security on their continent. May they take the destiny of Europe into their hands!".

The Budapest Appeal of 17 March 1969 took a much less aggressive tone over the US (and at the same time towards West Germany), but this appeal was still directed to "all European Governments" which were called upon to pool their efforts so that Europe would become "a continent of fruitful co-operation between equal nations, a factor of stability, peace and mutual understanding throughout the world". The Appeal stated further that: "An early meeting of representatives of all European states concerned to establish, by mutual agreement, procedures for convening such a conference and the agenda of subjects for discussions would be a practical step toward strengthening European security".

The question of participation in the Conference was resolved by the Finnish government which, by request of the Soviet Union, took the initiative at the beginning of May 1969 by handing over a Memorandum to the governments of all European states, together with those of the USA and Canada, in which it signified its readiness to assist in the preparation and holding of a European Security Conference in Helsinki. From then on it was established that the US and Canada would participate in such a conference, although this was not publicly acknowledged by the Warsaw Pact countries until much later.

The Warsaw Pact foreign ministers' Declaration in Prague, in October 1969, reiterated once more the Budapest Appeal of 17 March 1969 "to all European countries", and again said nothing further about which countries should participate. Six months later, in June 1970, the same ministers reassembled in Budapest and published a short, more or less uncontroversial communiqué. In this communiqué it was indicated that a document about the CSCE had been agreed upon and would be "conveyed to the governments of all the states concerned". This document clearly stated: "The question of participation at the conference has been clarified: participation is open to all European states, including the German Democratic Republic and the Federal Republic of Germany on an equal footing with each other and with rights equal to those of other European states, and also to the United States of America and Canada".

In connection with the CSCE the mode of participation of the GDR and the FRG did not turn out to be controversial but at that time, June 1970, the question was bound up with the state of affairs surrounding Chancellor Brandt's *Ostpolitik* and the Four Power talks about Berlin. In the CSCE the representatives of the GDR and the FRG have indeed taken part on an equal footing with each other and with rights equal to those of other European states, which can be interpreted as the first multilateral recognition of the GDR as a "European state". As far as the participation of the US and Canada was concerned, this was the first time that the Warsaw Pact countries as a group had recognized their right of participation, even if so far only in a confidential diplomatic memorandum adressed to other interested states. Public recognition was to follow in a year's time.

The NATO ministers had in the mean time declared publicly in their

Rome communiqué of May 1970, and were afterwards to repeat word for word in their subsequent communiqués, that in any conference that might be held "of course, the North American members of the Alliance would participate".

On looking back it is clear that an all-European conference on security and co-operation without North American participation would have been pointless for all kinds of reasons. It is difficult to imagine what purpose would have been served by the agreements concerning CBMs, if these had not applied to forces in Europe belonging to the United States and Canada. All the Madrid discussions about the mandate for the "Conference on Confidence and Security-Building Measures and Disarmament in Europe" would most probably have had little significance for the Soviet Union if the United States had not taken part. Moreover, the ten principles and the provisions in the field of economic and human co-operation of the Final Act would have meant a great deal less to East-European countries if they had not borne the signature of the President of the United States and the Prime Minister of Canada.

3. The Non-participating Mediterranean States

In practice the distinction between participating and non-participating states proved more important than that between participating states and observers. Rule (56) of the Blue Book introduces the new idea that *non*-participating states can take part in an international conference by contributing their own points of view: "The Conference and its working bodies will acquaint themselves, in such manner as they may determine, with the points of view held by non-participating states on the subject of the various agenda items". This leaves the Conference and its working bodies completely free to decide for themselves, where when and how - in writing or orally - they will hear these contributions.

Rule (57) makes clear which countries it has most in mind: "States situated in regions adjacent to Europe and to whom reference is made in the provisions of Chapter II, and in particular those of the Mediterranean States which have already expressed their interest in stating their views to the Conference are especially envisaged by this Chapter". The reference to Chapter II is to clause (15): "In considering questions relating to security in Europe, the Committee will bear in mind the broader context of world security and in particular the relationship which exists between security in Europe and in the Mediterranean area". In the same Chapter, moreover, clause (28) says: "In considering questions relating to co-operation in Europe covered by this mandate, the Committee will bear in mind the relationship which exists between such co-operation in Europe and in the Mediterranean".

This group of provisions came into being at the insistence of Malta who refused to approve the closure of the Helsinki Consultations unless all Arab Mediterranean states were invited to take part in the Conference, a proposal which, although it caused a sensation, aroused little sympathy among other participants. Malta was finally placated with the four clauses already quoted (2). They resulted in two pages of text in the Final Act under the title: "Questions relating to Security and Co-operation in the Mediterranean".

Other than some Mediterranean countries no state has ever made use of the possibility offered in clause (56). The countries referred to in clause (57) were Tunisia and Algeria. In the course of the first and the last stages in Helsinki, at the level of ministers and heads of state, Mediterranean and other non-participating states were given no opportunity to contribute to the discussions. In Geneva (1974/75) verbal contributions were heard from Algeria, Egypt, Israel, Morocco, Syria and Tunisia; in Belgrade (1977) from the same countries plus Lebanon; in Madrid (1980) from the same group minus Syria. In Madrid, after their hearing, the representatives of these countries were clearly put out by the way in which they had been treated. They had been conducted into the Auditorium precisely at the moment when they were permitted to make their contributions and shown out again by a representative of the Executive Secretary immediately they had finished, without being able to get any impression of how their interventions had been received.

In fact their contributions gave rise to no discussion and, later on, Western delegations let it be known that they were not interested in any further contributions from the countries concerned. What the content of the contributions was, can be gleaned from the following summary.

The *Israeli* representative indicated six specific areas in which it would be possible for European and Mediterranean countries to co-operate. These were: water conservation, desertification, the environment, agriculture, science and technology and solar energy. He pointed out that Israel had a special interest in the implementation of the provisions of the Final Act in the field of human rights and reunification of families, because of the emigration of Soviet jews to that country. He then warned the assembly of an increase in anti-semitism in Europe and called upon the states to prevent any recurrence of this phenomenon.

The *Egyptian* ambassador to Spain referred to the possibility of greater co-operation on security matters between the CSCE and the Mediterranean states and to recent European peace initiatives in the Middle East conflict. He appealed further for the right of self--determination for the Palestinians and the setting-up of a nuclear-free zone in the Middle East.

The *Tunisian* representative urged that the Mediterranean should become an "international zone of peace and security", and appealed for a "true dialogue" between the non-participating Mediterranean states and the CSCE states and noted with disappointment the absence of the PLO at the Madrid Meeting.

The ambassador of *Morocco* in Spain, noted Morocco's historic, economic and geopolitical relationship with Europe's countries and requested that Morocco should be allowed to take her part in decisions on all questions pertaining to the security of the region. He also lamented the absence of the PLO in Madrid. He went into the conflict in North West Africa in some detail and said that it could not be ignored by the CSCE.

The *Algerian* representative introduced a document spelling out a more definite series of principles regulating the relationship between the CSCE and the Arab states of the Mediterranean, and a document dealing with military security and co-operation in the area, as well as propositions in the field of economic relations and migrant workers. Algeria found it hard to understand why she was not allowed to participate in the actual work of the Meeting. Questions concerning disarmament and confidence-building measures which would affect her own region could not be dealt with in Algeria's absence. The Algerian ambassador finally enlarged on the importance of European countries having a good relationship with the Third World.

4. Objectives of the Participating States

Before they sent their representatives to Madrid the 35 governments had had to decide on their objectives for the meeting. In theory the CSCE consists of 35 independent sovereign states and what should follow here is a description of 35 sets of objectives. But in fact, on both Eastern and Western sides, points of view were coordinated so that it is possible to speak of two sets of objectives belonging to the two power blocs. The third group of participants, the NNA countries, could not be termed a bloc for they did not - at least not at this stage - act collectively. We shall begin with the official, governmental aims of the Western bloc and its most important member, the USA whose preparations were apparently the most intensive of those of all the Western lands. The objectives of the WP countries are examined next, with particular attention to those of the USSR and, finally, those of the NNA members.

4.1. Western Objectives

Within a year of the signing of the Final Act, American Congress had passed an Act establishing a governmental Commission on Security and Co-operation in Europe. It was "authorized and directed to monitor the acts of the signatories which reflect compliance with or violation of the articles of the Final Act of the CSCE, with particular regard to the provisions relating to Co-operation in Humanitarian fields". This also gave the Commission authority to monitor the US government's policy itself. The President supplies the Commission with semiannual reports, entitled *Implementation of Helsinki Final Act* which deal with the situation in East European countries with regard to the implementation of the Final Act (3). The Commission itself publishes a *CSCE Digest* with press reports on the same subject and also prepares, for instance, compilations of documents originating from Helsinki monitors in the Soviet Union (4). The Commission is bipartisan and consists of six senators and six members of the House of Representatives, further three Executive Branch commissioners (from the Department of State, Department of Defense and Department of Commerce), and finally a staff of more then a dozen members. The official US delegation in Madrid included on the list of participants five representatives from the Commission who were active in preparing speeches and other material for the delegation's use.

As far as the Commission was concerned, the most important purpose of the Madrid Meeting was naturally the review of implementation, as appears from its report which was submitted to the US Congress in the summer of 1980. According to this document the implementation review was to be frank and thorough and to cover all sections of the Final Act, giving a central place to human rights and the Soviet invasion of Afghanistan. There was no mention of fresh proposals for provisions of a concluding document. The only reference to new proposals said that "any new measures agreed upon must be balanced" (5). In conformity with this the USA in fact initiated only very few proposals although those they did were of great importance, for example, the proposal submitted jointly with Canada and later co-sponsored by Spain, on holding a meeting of experts on human rights, and also the proposal later co-sponsored by Denmark and Norway, to hold bilateral round table meetings between officials from the different states to discuss their respective approaches to all aspects of human rights and fundamental freedoms, and finally, the proposal jointly with Canada and later co-sponsored by Denmark, Greece and the UK, on convening a meeting of experts on family reunification.

There was more to the preparations in the USA than simply the monitoring activities of the Commission on Security and Co-operation; a subcommittee of the House of Representatives was devoted to CSCE matters and held regular hearings of experts from the USA and of witnesses originating from the East European countries on the subject of how the Final Act was being carried out in those countries (6). On the question of how the USA herself was implementing the Helsinki agreement the House published a detailed study under the title *Fulfilling Our Promises* which took a critical look at American policy (7). In all these activities the primary place was given to the question of the fulfilment of the Helsinki agreement rather than whether in Madrid new measures should be agreed. At the Madrid Meeting the US delegation was consistently less interested in reaching agreement on a substantial concluding document than other delegations.

In Western Europe, in preparation for the Madrid conference, deliberations between government officials from the EC countries took place in the framework of the "European Political Co-operation", the context in which the ten EC countries consult on matters of foreign policy. During these deliberations EC members introduced their new proposals and decided on common policy. In the end the EC group collectively submitted 13 proposals in Madrid, which made up half the Western total. All the EC countries except Ireland are also members of NATO and naturally this organization also held deliberations in 1980 to decide what political line to follow in Madrid. NATO did not, however, prepare collective proposals. During these deliberations at which the EC countries put forward their common policy for discussion, the NATO group as a whole evolved its own position with regard to the CSCE, which was eventually expressed in paragraph 8 of the Ankara Communiqué of 26 June 1980.

This communiqué already states the theme on which the meeting in Madrid was to play: the importance of maintaining the integrity of the Final Act. The NATO ministers agreed that emphasis had to be placed on full implementation of its principles and provisions: "Therefore, Allied representatives at Madrid will engage in a thorough, frank and measured review of implementation with a view to stimulating improvement". The Afghanistan question and violation of human rights were to occupy a central position. Besides this however, NATO countries would be prepared to discuss new "concrete proposals" but the consideration of new proposals would be influenced by the course of the review of implementation and would depend on the international situation at that time. The last condition found its expression in reality for it was the international situation that in December 1982 prevented the adoption of a concluding document which would contain new proposals. Among new proposals the Ankara NATO communiqué mentioned in particular the French one for a mandate for "negotiations on military significant and verifiable CBM's", also known as the European disarmament conference.

The NATO countries had two aims in view: a review of implementation and the introduction of new proposals to improve implementation where this was unsatisfactory. They put the highest price of all on fulfilment of already existing agreements and to them this was more important for the continuation of the CSCE process with its concomitant détente, than reaching new agreements. In their struggle to realise an in-depth implementation discussion Western countries appealed to the provision in the Chapter of the Final Act entitled "Follow-up to the Conference" which stated that the task of the Follow-up meetings was, among other things, a "thorough exchange of view on the implementation of the provisions of the Final Act and the tasks defined by the Conference". The West asserted that it had the right to discuss both the human rights record and the foreign policy of other states who had signed the Final Act. In the light of discussions in Belgrade two years earlier the West was well aware that the East European countries would point to Principle VI of the ten principles: "Non-intervention in internal affairs" which says in its first lines:

> The participating States will refrain from any intervention, direct of indirect, individual or collective, in the internal or external affairs falling within the domestic jurisdiction of another participating State, regardless of their mutual relations. They will accordingly refrain from any form of armed intervention or threat of such intervention against another participating State.

On the basis of this text (in its Russian version*) the East European countries claimed that other states had no right to "interfere" in their internal affairs and would not countenance their domestic policies being made the subject of an implementation discussion. They asserted furthermore that the provision quoted from the Follow-up Chapter of the Final Act is designed only to cover multilateral and bilateral implementation. Thus it was permissible in their view to raise for discussion the implementation of bilateral agreements, but not each other's domestic policy. Yet, according to the West the text of Principle VI is clear: it speaks not of non-interference but of non-intervention and this last concept is defined as "any form of armed intervention or threat of such intervention". This cannot mean that the participating states are forbidden to make a judgement of the way the provisions of the Final Act are carried out by other signatories.

NATO's Ankara communiqué said that the West was ready to submit new proposals and to discuss those of other countries. The Western proposals are given later in this Chapter. Their general aim was to point out the weakest areas of execution of the Helsinki agreements, largely in the field of human rights, economic co-operation, human contacts and free spread of information. Because these proposals high-

---

* the word *vmeshatel'stvo* covers both "intervention" and "interference"

lighted precisely those parts of other countries' policies which were most sensitive, it was inevitable that in the original wording the other countries found the proposals difficult or impossible to accept. In consequence such proposals reached the concluding document either in a much watered down condition or not at all. At their inception, before the Madrid conference began, the criterion had been what was desirable rather than what might be politically feasible. The consequences of this approach are dealt with in the context of the results of the Madrid Meeting, in Chapter X.

4.2. East European Objectives

NATO's Ankara communiqué had its counterpart in the "Declaration of the Warsaw Treaty States" which appeared in Warsaw on 15 May 1980 on the occasion of the twenty-fifth anniversary of the Warsaw Pact. It represented the results of the East European consultations in preparation for Madrid and described the CSCE as a victory for Socialism over the "cold warriors". The declaration also made known that, in Madrid, the WP countries would submit a proposal "to convene a conference on military détente and disarmament in Europe", and went on to state that, regarding the Madrid conference, "achievement ... of positive concrete results would also have a salutary effect on the general international atmosphere" (8). This became the WP countries' slogan in Madrid: what was required was positive concrete results, meaning a mandate for the wished-for disarmament conference, and no fruitless discussions on implementation of the Helsinki agreements.

The Soviet Union and her allies well knew what lay before them in Madrid as appears from an article by the Soviet writer, Valentin Kravtsov, published in *New Times* in September 1980, the month when the Madrid preparatory talks were to begin. The intentions of "the United States, Britain and some other close allies of the US", would be, according to Kravtsov, "to exert pressure on the Soviet Union under cover of every possible pretext, be it the Afghan events, the hypocritical manipulations with 'human rights' in the bourgeois interpretation, or the alleged failure of the socialist countries to observe the provisions of the Final Act" (9). In other words, the WP countries knew what the Western objectives were. They were prepared for a critical implementation discussion and showed a corresponding capacity for absorption of criticism during the first months in Madrid: they allowed Western criticism to sweep over them in anticipation of the second phase of the conference when new proposals would be introduced which they hoped would lead to the "concrete results" they wanted.

What NATO's Ankara communiqué had seen as the dichotomy of the implementation discussion and the introduction of new proposals designed to improve implementation, was interpreted by Kravtsov as follows:

> The Western participants in the [Madrid] meeting have two things to choose -- either businesslike deliberations and, consequently, tangible results of benefit to all Europeans, or polemics and recriminations, which, far from altering the Soviet Union's policy, would only poison the political atmosphere at the meeting and make it unproductive of results. The Soviet Union is all for the first alternative, but if the second is forced upon it, it is prepared to deal with it (10).

The stress laid on "results" is not surprising. The CSCE Follow-up Meeting in Madrid had to have "a positive outcome" because the CSCE was part of Leonid Brezhnev's comprehensive, world-wide "Peace Programme" and was therefore bound to succeed. The Peace Programme, the importance of which was stressed by the 24th (1971) and 25th (1976) CPSU Congresses, provided a number of initiatives in the field of arms control and disarmament affecting conventional and nuclear arms and missiles and also committed to "the promotion of détente and peaceful co-operation in Europe". The CSCE was an essential element here and because the Peace Programme was closely linked to the name and prestige of president Leonid Brezhnev it had already been decided that the CSCE follow-up meeting in Madrid would be a success.

In February 1981 the 26th CPSU Congress adopted the "Peace Programme for the 1980's" in which the CSCE again occupied a significant place, particularly in view of the results anticipated from it which were to include the mandate for a "conference on military détente and disarmament". This last had become such an important part of Brezhnev's Peace Programme that he was prepared, under certain conditions, to comply with Western wishes regarding the zone where the military confidence--building measures would be applied: "And now we want to propose that the zone for these measures should be substantially extended. We are prepared to apply them to the entire European part of the USSR, providing the Western states, too extend the confidence zone accordingly" (11).

In short, the most vital East European objective for Madrid was to achieve concrete results in the context of Brezhnev's Peace Programme.

4.3. NNA Objectives

Although the NNA countries do not form a political bloc with a single set of political objectives, they had one objective in common: this was to secure the continuation of the CSCE follow-up process in spite of political tension between East and West. For the NNA countries this goal took precedence over any other of the various national objectives which they cherished. Finland went even further by advocating, in an official proposal, the organization of meetings among diplomatic representatives of the 35 participating states, to be held in the periods between follow-up meetings, and to be referred to as: "the CSCE Committee".

For Yugoslavia "one of the main objectives of the Madrid Meeting would be to ensure the continuity of the CSCE, for this we consider to be a guaranty of positive and stable development of relations in Europe, this being of interest also for stability on a broader international plane" (12). In Madrid it was made clear, time and again, that all the NNA countries shared this aim although not exclusively for the reason quoted. For them CSCE meetings are a unique platform for discussion of European political affairs; a forum in which they enjoy full status and meet both Eastern and Western bloc countries on an equal footing. The aligned NATO and WP countries meet in other contexts and in bilateral US-USSR talks which exclude NNA states. Consequently the collapse of the CSCE would leave them once more in an isolated position, non-aligned and therefore outside the East-West dialogue. In the first year of the Madrid conference it was the NNA representatives who reacted most violently to the repeated Soviet refusals to accept definitively the principle that Madrid would be followed by a further meeting.

The second objective which NNA states held in common was the extension of the CBM regime: military aspects of security were of greater interest to most of them than the human dimension of the Final Act: various NNA countries can be said to have shown less interest in the implementation discussion than Western countries although later on the level of interest rose because of developments in Poland. Their original interest in military aspects is clearly betrayed by the fact that they submitted an extensive proposal with a number of detailed measures for improving and expanding the CBMs which had already been agreed in the Final Act. This was the only proposal prepared jointly by all the NNA countries (except Malta) to be submitted in Madrid (13).

5. The Proposals

Altogether there were 87 substantive proposals submitted at the beginning of the conference to be included in a final substantive Madrid Concluding Document. They took up more than 170 pages of English text as produced by the Secretariat. The proposals were submitted either in the Plenary or in the Subsidiary Working Bodies, a division which later proved to have no importance, either when the proposals were under consideration or when the Concluding Document was drafted. This division was also only a minor factor during the period of submission itself although it was commonly held that proposals of general interest should be submitted in the Plenary and more specific ones in the relevant Subsidiary Working Bodies. The division has been omitted from the accompanying Table 3-1, which shows instead the total number of proposals relevant to each of the Chapters of the Final Act, whether submitted in the Plenary or in one of the groups. Two proposals related to the Preamble of a Madrid Concluding Document, eleven to the first part of the first basket which contains the ten principles, eight to the second part of the first basket or the military aspects of security (five of these called for the convening of a disarmament conference) and twenty-six to the second basket, economic co-operation. The Chapter of the Final Act about the Mediterranean received six proposals, thirty were submitted in the third basket concerning human contacts and four fell to the Chapter on Follow-up.

The proposals varied not only in nature but also in length, scope and content. Some were relatively concrete while others might be simply declaratory and contain little that was actually operative. A long proposal could well be full of concrete ideas, but sometimes a proposal expressed in a few paragraphs was more important than one running to several pages. For this reason Table 3-1 is misleading in some ways because the units (i.e., one formally-submitted proposal) are not necessarily comparable, but it does at least give an impression of the

TABLE 3-1:
The Proposals for a Concluding Document

	Preamble	Principles	Military aspects	Basket II	Mediterranean	Basket III	Follow-up	TOTAL
European Communities and others		1		5		7		13
Combinations of Western countries		3		1		3		7
Belgium							1	1
France			1			1		2
Italy					1			1
Spain	1				1			2
SUBTOTAL	1	4	1	6	2	11	1	26
Combinations of East European countries		3		6		4		13
Bulgaria				1		3		4
German Democratic Republic						1		1
Hungary				2		1		3
Poland			1			2		3
Romania		1	3	3		2	2	11
USSR						1		1
SUBTOTAL		4	4	12		14	2	36
Combinations of NNA-countries		1	1	1		1		4
Austria				1				1
Finland							1	1
Holy See		1				1		2
Malta		1			3			4
Sweden			1	1				2
Yugoslavia	1		1	2	1	1		6
SUBTOTAL	1	3	3	5	4	3	1	20
Nordic countries				3		1		4
Finland-Hungary-Iceland						1		1
TOTAL	2	11	8	26	6	30	4	87

importance attached to different aspects of the CSCE by each of the 35 participating states.

Proposals could be submitted either by one country alone or by one country with the support of other co-sponsor countries. Just over half (45) of the total number of proposals were submitted by a single country and the rest (42) by a group of countries. A country that wanted to emphasize its own identity sometimes preferred to do without co-sponsors: this was the case with France and her two proposals, one on the Disarmament Conference and the other on the Cultural Forum. The first of these enjoyed the support of all NATO countries but France insisted on being its only sponsor, so that this proposal and the one on the Cultural Forum would become known as the French proposals. It is a striking fact in this connection that the greatest number of individual proposals came from Romania with 11 and Yugoslavia with 6, who thus underlined their special position in Europe. It was, however, open to any country wishing to do so to invite other countries to become co-sponsors of a proposal and these would normally be from the same camp. In theory, this was not necessarily the case, for the CSCE comprises simply 35 sovereign states and does not formally admit the existence of blocs or groups within its ranks. There was, however, only one proposal which was submitted by a combination of countries crossing East-West barriers: RM/H.6, which was an appeal for promotion of teaching of less widely-spread languages, was co-sponsored by Finland, Hungary and Iceland. All other collective proposals were submitted by one country with the co-sponsorship of other countries from the same camp.

Thirteen proposals were submitted by the Luxemburg delegation with the co-sponsorship of a number of other Western countries including all the members of the European Communities: Belgium, Denmark, France, the FRG, Greece (after 1.1.1981), Ireland, Italy, Luxemburg, the Netherlands and the United Kingdom. These were proposals which their experts had prepared long before in the context of European Political Co-operation (EPC) consultations or within the framework of the European Communities (EC) as far as the second basket is concerned and which had been agreed sentence by sentence by all ten member States. They were submitted by the Luxemburg delegation because Luxemburg was at that time the country presiding over the EC.

A short account of the content of all 87 proposals follows below.

In Madrid the proposals were dealt with subject by subject, but here, in order to give an idea of what each country or group of countries was primarily concerned with in the year 1980, the order of countries shown on the Table will be adopted. The proposals were aimed at improving the realisation of the objectives of the Final Act and they therefore indicate for each country at which points it considered the situation in Europe ought to be changed for the better.

5.1. Western Proposals

The delegations of the ten *EC countries* together with their co-sponsors submitted 13 proposals only one of which belonged in basket I and referred to the ten principles. This one (RM.19) was one of the most important proposals submitted by the West. It stated that irrespective of the political and social system of the country concerned, progress in the effective exercise of human rights and fundamental freedoms as set out in Principle VII should be constant and visible and it demanded furthermore the progressive removal of any existing legal, administrative or other measures which have the effect of jeopardizing the right of citizens of a country, individually or in groups, to (among other things) monitor the implementation of the provisions of the Final Act or make public their views on the question of implementation whether or not these are critical of the authorities in their own country or in other participating states. In other words it demanded freedom for dissidents and monitor groups in East European countries.

In basket II the EC countries submitted five proposals which had been prepared by national experts in Brussels and representatives of the European Commission. These representatives were also present in Madrid, temporarily attached to the delegation of the country occupying the EC presidency. This meant that they had to change delegation every six months but they took a consistently active part in fighting for the proposals, especially for those falling within the competence of the EC. The second basket proposals concerned the difficulties experienced over compensation transactions, with the request that the United Nations Economic Commission for Europe (ECE) should study these further (RM/E.2), the improvement of economic information and harmonization of economic and commercial statistics (RM/E.3), the improvement of business contacts, facilities and working conditions for representatives of foreign firms and in general the access by qualified sales or production representatives of the sellers to end-user firms (RM/E.4), the adoption of arbitration as an appropriate means of settling disputes in the field of trade and industrial co-operation (RM/E.18) and co-operation in the field of basic and advanced training for management staff (RM/E.19).

The seven EC countries' proposals in basket III were spread over all four sections of this basket, that is to say, human contacts, information, culture and education. Proposal RM/H.1 asked for free access for everyone to foreign embassies. Under human contacts came the important RM.11 proposal which threw out various ideas for improving the legal position of citizens who wished to leave their own country either temporarily or for good. These included reducing the processing-time for applications for exit visas, making the granting of exit visas the rule rather than the exception, allowing the applicants to renew their applications at once and taking no discriminatory measures against such applicants, making known the regulations relevant to obtaining an exit visa, reducing the cost of the exit visa and waiving any requirement for advance hotel reservation or currency exchange.

Yet another proposal in this area (RM/H.3) exhorted all states to take part in the European Inter-rail System of the UIC (International Railway Union) in order to promote individual youth tourism. Under "information" RM.12 proposed an increase in the dissemination of printed material from other participating states by, for example, developing the possibility of taking out individual subscriptions to foreign periodicals and by setting-up long-term agreements between firms for export and import of printed matter. The proposal also asked that foreign journalists should be allowed freedom of movement except in areas closed for security reasons. The journalists should also have freedom of consultation with their sources, including private individuals. As its final request the proposal asked for an end to jamming foreign radio broadcasts. Under "culture", RM.15 asked for free access for citizens of any country to reading rooms and cultural centres of foreign embassies. In "education", RM/H.2 wished to improve the facilities for visiting scientists and RM/H.4 to see the recommendations of the Hamburg Scientific Forum brought into effect.

Different combinations of *Western* countries submitted proposals in differing areas. The FRG, Italy, Portugal, Spain, Turkey, the United

Kingdom and the USA jointly submitted a proposal against terrorism (RM.14), in which Spain was the protagonist. Among other things it advocated bringing to justice, either by prosecution or extradition, those persons who are accused of having committed terrorist acts and said that countries should display the greatest diligence in preventing their respective territories from being used as bases for the preparation of terrorist activities or as sanctuaries after such acts have been committed.

Another proposal (RM.16) from Canada, Spain and the USA, called for a meeting of experts on human rights. On the same subject a proposal from the USA, Denmark and Norway (RM.26) recommended going over to bilateral, round-table meetings between officials from the different states to discuss their respective approaches to all aspects of human rights and fundamental freedoms.

In the field of economics a proposal was contributed by Spain and Portugal (RM/E.1) for better co-operation between host countries and countries of origin of migrant workers.

Basket III contained three proposals from Western countries. France, with Italy, Luxemburg, the Netherlands and Greece as co-sponsors (RM.9), called for more co-operation to preserve the historical heritage of European countries and for a UNESCO Conference on this subject. Proposal RM/H.21 from the USA, Canada, Denmark, Greece and the UK suggested convening a meeting of experts on family reunification at which experts from East and West would have to discuss the administrative problems which formed an obstacle to "family reunification" (emigration) from East Europe to the West. RM/H.11 came from the USA, Belgium Denmark, the FRG, Greece, Italy, Luxemburg, the Netherlands, Norway, Portugal and the UK and asked the states to agree to encourage libraries, research institutes and similar bodies in their territories to make catalogues and lists of open archival material available to scholars, teachers and students from other states.

Western countries submitted few individual proposals. At the end of February 1981 *Belgium* proposed that the next Follow-up Meeting should be held in about 2½ years' time in Brussels (RM/F.1).

France submitted two proposals. RM.8 was about the organization of a Cultural Forum to be attended by outstanding personalities from the world of the arts and of letters. On the same day, 9 December 1980,

France also submitted the most discussed proposal of the conference, RM.7, which called for the convening of a Conference on Disarmament in Europe, a proposal which had already been discussed extensively in NATO and to which the 15 NATO ministers of foreign affairs at Ankara (June 1980) had given their support for the second time, the first time having been their meeting in Brussels six months earlier. Its title was misleading insofar as the proposed conference, in its initial phase, was intended merely to adopt a coherent system of CBMs, and only after that, in a second phase, would the participating states examine how they could fulfil their expressed intention of continuing their efforts towards security and disarmament. The difference between the French proposal and the other four proposals for a disarmament conference lay in the four criteria which it imposed as qualifying characteristics on the confidence-building measures: unlike the CBMs which had already been agreed in Helsinki these were to be obligatory, verifiable, of military significance and to encompass all Europe from the Atlantic to the Urals.

On 2 February 1981 *Italy* submitted a proposal (RM/M.5) to convene by the end of 1982 in Venice a seminar of experts on economic, scientific and cultural co-operation in the Mediterranean; this was Italy's reply to an earlier proposal from Malta on the same subject (see below).

Spain was not only a co-sponsor of some of the Western proposals among which was one on terrorism and another proposed with Portugal on the subject of migrant workers, and of a proposal on information, acting in concert with the Neutral countries Austria and Switzerland, but submitted two more proposals entirely on her own: RM.37, which was a declaration about co-operation and détente designed to contribute to the Preamble of a Madrid Concluding Document, and RM/M.3 which was about co-operation on transport in the Mediterranean.

5.2. East European Proposals

As regards *Eastern Europe*, combinations of these countries submitted thirteen proposals, precisely the same number as the EC countries. The East European countries, however, worked on the principle that any proposal had to be submitted by one single country even if other countries were co-sponsors and they did not submit proposals as a group as was done by the EC countries. Three of their proposals touched on the ten principles in basket I. All three were briefly expressed in one or two paragraphs and reflected the formalistic East European approach to the principles. Bulgaria and the GDR devoted a single paragraph in RM.23 to a request to embody the ten principles in an appropriate form in bilateral and multilateral agreements. Likewise, RM./S.2, submitted by Poland and the USSR proposed that states should give expression in their national legislation to the same ten principles. Bulgaria, Czechoslovakia and the GDR called on all the states which had not yet done so to accede to the International Covenants on Human Rights, at the earliest possible date (RM.35).

In basket II combinations of East European countries submitted six proposals. The proposal from Czechoslovakia and the GDR (RM.25) was just as formalistic as the other East European proposals in the sense that it did little more than propose to strengthen the role of the ECE in its activities in the development of international economic co-operation thus contributing to the strengthening of peace and security. The proposal submitted by the GDR, Czechoslovakia and the USSR, RM.24, was short but unmistakeable, calling upon all participating states to refrain from any action which would impede trade and economic co-operation among them; in other words to cease to apply an economic boycott: this was to Eastern eyes one of the most important proposals in the second basket. Finally Poland and the USSR, in RM.5, proposed convening a high-level meeting on energy by 1982 at the latest, and asked for closer co-operation in the field of energy, especially within the framework of the ECE. Bulgaria, Hungary and Czechoslovakia in their proposal RM/E.10 expressed a wish for the participating states to create conditions favourable to industrial co-operation. Bulgaria and the USSR in their proposal RM/E.6 drew attention to the usefulness of the widest possible extension of the practice of concluding agreements for long-term programmes of economic, industrial and scientific and technological co-operation among states belonging to different social and economic systems. The proposal submitted by Bulgaria and Hungary RM/E.15 contained a single sentence: "The participating States, aware of the problems specific to the activities of small and medium-sized firms, will endeavour to create favourable financial, credit, administrative and other conditions to stimulate their participation in trade and industrial co-operation with enterprises and firms of other participating States". The main aim of this proposal was to counterbalance a Nordic proposal, supported by Western countries, on the same subject (E.5, see below).

Differing combinations of East European countries submitted four proposals in basket III. The most important was RM/H.13 which although it was expressed in simple terms might have had far-reaching consequences. It was submitted by Hungary and Poland and asked the states to ensure personal security for citizens of other participating states who were on their territory as members of official missions, such as diplomats, or for personal or professional reasons, such as tourists or members of sporting or cultural groups. The proposal went on to ask for improvement in procedures for the provision of legal and medical assistance for these strangers in a foreign land. The proposal continued by asking the participating states to help those seeking missing relatives in their countries.

Hungary and the USSR submitted a less controversial proposal, RM/H.12, encouraging youth tourism and visits to other countries for young people who were working, training or undergoing education. Proposal RM/H.17, submitted by the USSR and Czechoslovakia was unacceptable to the West for it suggested putting an end to the activities of Radio Liberty and Radio Free Europe broadcasting stations.

Finally, an important proposal co-sponsored by the GDR and the USSR, RM.28 ran to four pages of text dealing with the great and steadily growing responsibility of the mass media and journalists for disarmament, détente and mutual co-operation, the misuse of the mass media to propagate racialism, apartheid and war, the democratic transformation of the international information and communication system, the development of co-operation among radio and television organizations, the improvement of working conditions of foreign correspondents, the responsibilities of journalists not to (among other things) disseminate disinformation, tendentious information, lies or imputations, the right of the State to expel journalists in serious cases of slander. The document contained a series of obligations which journalists should meet and concluded: the participating States will ensure that their mass media and journalists, including foreign correspondents, observe the norms set forth in the present document in dealing with the life and politics of other participating States. Western delegates called this proposal an attempt to justify censorship.

Out of the 36 East European proposals 23 were submitted individually, without co-sponsorship by other countries. *Bulgaria* introduced one proposal in basket II and three in basket III: RM/E.9 exhorted the states to be more active in the dissemination of information made available within the framework of joint commissions on economic and scientific and technological co-operation. Bulgaria's basket III proposal, RM/H.8, made the same point with respect to information concerning the possibilities offered by bilateral cultural agreements, plans and programmes. In RM.22 greater attention was demanded for the problems of the "rising generation" (aged 6-16), which UNESCO was asked to study, while the organization of international meetings, festivals, assemblies and sporting events was also called for in favour of this age-group. Bulgaria's final proposal, RM/H.9 was for the states to stress the great importance of events linked to memorable dates in the history of their peoples in cultural as in other spheres.

There was a single proposal submitted by the *German Democratic Republic* (GDR), i.e., RM/H.10 expressing the wish to promote the intensified exchange of textbooks and schoolbooks and other educational information. *Hungary*, in its proposal RM/E.7, stressed that the states should promote a more active exchange of knowledge in the field of marketing and asked the ECE to examine the matter. Another Hungarian proposal in basket II, RM/E.8, encouraged international standardization and the conclusion of international arrangements on certification as recommended by the ECE. In basket III Hungary submitted RM/H.7 which proposed, among other things, to increase the transmission of high-level artistic and dramatic radio programmes, literary programmes, concerts and television films of other countries, both on a commercial and a non--commercial basis and to produce parallel or co-production programmes.

Poland submitted RM.6 without co-sponsors although it was well--known that this proposal had the firm support of all the WP countries and had been chiefly inspired by the USSR because it was in fact the long-expected proposal to convene a Conference on Military Détente and Disarmament in Europe scheduled to open on 20 October 1981 in Warsaw, the Warsaw Pact capital. This was a less specific proposal than the French one in respect of the criteria which had to be fulfilled by the CBMs which were to be discussed in the initial phase; there were no references to the area of application or to the need for verification of any CBMs which might be agreed. As in the French proposal the first stage of the Conference was to deal with CBMs. The second stage would be devoted to reaching agreement on measures aimed at lowering the level and the itensity of military confrontation in Europe, including the limitation of military activities and reduction of armed forces and armaments. The proposal touched upon the possibility that the disarmament conference might also consider and agree political and legal steps to reduce the danger of the outbreak of war in Europe, which certainly meant something of the nature of declaratory agreements on, for example, non--first-use of nuclear weapons.

Poland submitted two more proposals in basket III, the first concerning co-operation and exchanges in the field of education, in particular the implementation of universally recognized principles for the preparation of societies for life in peace (RM/H.14), and the second dealing with possibilities of improvement of co-operation and exchanges in cultural fields (RM/H.15).

Romania submitted eleven proposals on its own. In basket I, RM/S.3 dealt with unemployment and the right to work. Bearing in mind, as the text ran, that the participating states should be deeply concerned at the fact that millions of persons, and in particular young people, are victims of unemployment, the effects of which are particularly serious for human life and dignity, they were invited to adopt appropriate measures at the national level, including material guarantees, with a view to ensuring the full and entire exercise of the right to work.

Romania also submitted three proposals about the military aspects of security, beginning with RM.30 which proposed that a meeting of experts should be convened to draw up a treaty on refraining from force or the threat of force. RM.31 was the third proposal for convening a Conference on Confidence-Building and Disarmament in Europe and like the proposals from France and Poland envisaged two stages of which the first would be devoted to the examination and adoption of CBMs and the second, more radical than in the other two proposals, given over to military disengagement and general and complete disarmament. In RM.33 Romania offered a new set of CBMs which were to be agreed in Madrid itself: not to carry out multinational manoeuvres near the frontiers of other participating states; to freeze military budgets pending the conclusion of an agreement on their reduction; not to install new military bases, including sites of nuclear weapons and not to deploy new troops on the territory of other states in Europe; to give notification to all other participating states of major military movements and of air and naval manoeuvres taking place on their territory in Europe, as well as in its adjacent sea area or airspace.

In basket II Romania also submitted three proposals: RM/E.14 proposed expansion of industrial co-operation through joint ventures and expressed interest in the ECE as a framework for the creation of a permanent office to facilitate industrial co-operation (a remainder of a long-standing Romanian proposal to establish a Centre for Industrial Co-operation); RM/E.17 proposed facilitating the transfer of scientific and technical information and the convening of a group of experts to identify concrete ways and means of co-operation in the fields of contemporary science and technology and RM/E.16 proposed to encourage the development of scientific co-operation in the field of agriculture.

In basket III Romania introduced two proposals: RM/H.16 called for meetings devoted to problems related to youth and the support of forms and structures of multilateral youth co-operation; RM/H.19 invited all states to take firm measures aimed at prohibiting all forms of war propaganda, and to take legislative and other measures to suppress any manifestation tending towards the revival of fascism, neo-fascism, racism and chauvinism.

Two Romanian proposals in the Follow-up basket concerned the next CSCE Follow-up Meeting which it suggested holding in Bucharest. These proposals were RM.32 and RM.1; the latter had the distinction of being the very first proposal of the 87 submitted during the Meeting and was submitted on 12 November, the day after the official opening of the conference.

The *Soviet Union* on its own submitted only one proposal, RM/H.20 which called for greater co-operation with regard to the content of school history and geography textbooks and the inclusion in them of the most important facts of universal and pan-European significance, such as the struggle of the peoples against fascist aggression during the second World War and the crushing defeat of fascism.

5.3. NNA Proposals

Combinations of delegations from *Neutral and Non-aligned* countries submitted a total of four proposals, one in each important section. For the Principles section of basket I there was a proposal from Finland, Sweden, Switzerland and Yugoslavia (RM.20) urging the need for a second meeting of experts (the first had been held in 1978 in Montreux, Switzerland) to pursue the examination and elaboration of a generally acceptable method for the peaceful settlement of bilateral disputes. RM.21, submitted by Austria, Cyprus, Finland, Liechtenstein, San Marino, Sweden, Switzerland and Yugoslavia, that is the whole of the group of "Neutral and Non-aligned countries" with the exception of Malta, dealt with the military aspects of security, basket I, and put forward a number of concrete proposals for improving and expanding existing CBMs in respect of: prior notification of other military manoeuvres, exchange of observers, prior notification of major military movements, prior notification of naval exercises involving amphibious forces, prior notification of major naval exercises, openness of information concerning military expenditure, while recognizing the existence of additional measures which could usefully serve the common objectives of the Final Act. The proposal ran to five pages and yet received no consideration because discussion was centred on the proposals for a disarmament conference which itself would be the proper forum for dealing with these kinds of new CBMs.

Into the second basket fell Finland and Sweden's proposal RM/E.20 which sketched some guidelines for the treatment of migrant workers. The third basket received from Austria, Spain (not yet having entered NATO) and Switzerland a proposal on "information": RM.3 devoted four pages to concrete recommendations regarding possibilities of increasing the availability of foreign newspapers and journals, their sale price, the opening of CSCE reading rooms, co-operation between press-agencies and contact among foreign journalists and journalists' associations, their right to use their own sound and film equipment, their access to organizations and private individuals, their right to carry freely with them documents, reference material and technical equipment, their right to set up professional associations and their right not to be expelled.

Austria submitted one proposal on her own in the second basket; this was RM.4 dealing with co-operation to strengthen common efforts in order to solve longer-term energy problems and calling for a high-level meeting on energy within the framework of the ECE.

Finland put forward a proposal (RM.36) that suggested organizing meetings among diplomatic representatives of the participating states in the interim period between the follow-up Meetings, which meetings would be referred to as "the CSCE Committee". Adoption of this proposal would have been a step towards institutionalization of the CSCE by establishing a sort of permanent organ.

The *Holy See* submitted two proposals, one in the first and one in the third basket, dealing respectively with the importance of the effective exercise of freedom of thought, conscience, religion or belief (RM/S.1) and the access of religious faiths to the public media and the improvement of the exchange of information between them (RM/H.5).

Malta submitted four proposals, three of which were to do with the Chapter of the Final Act concerning the Mediterranean: the first noted the results of the Valetta Meeting of experts on co-operation in the Mediterranean (RM/M.1). The second and more controversial proposal urged the sponsorship of meetings of the participating states together with the eight non-participating Mediterranean states (Algeria, Egypt, Israel, Lebanon, Libya, Morocco, Syria and Tunisia) on security in the Mediterranean region (RM/M.2). The third proposal asked that these eight non-participating Mediterranean states should be invited to take part in the work of the Subsidiary Working Body on the Mediterranean in the course of the rest of the Madrid Meeting in 1981; this proposal (RM/M.4), the only one of the 87 which, as a procedural matter, was not designed to be included in a Madrid Concluding Document, did not get a consensus. Malta's fourth proposal (RM.10) called for the recognition of Malta's neutrality by the other 34 participating states, as a provision in the section on "Principles" of the first basket.

Sweden on her own submitted two proposals. RM.34 was the fourth proposal concerning the convening of a Conference on Disarmament in Europe. Just as in the other proposals on the subject, Sweden's scheme envisaged the first phase of the Conference as dealing with negotiation of enlarged confidence-building measures. These were to be designed so as to promote openness, restraint and disengagement and would have to conform to criteria such as political commitment to implementing the measures agreed upon, military significance (implying that ultimately the entire European region would be involved) and adequate verifiability. The Swedish proposal is distinguished from the earlier three proposals by its explicit definition of the objective of the negotiations, in the second phase, as arms limitation and reduction agreements covering conventional and also ultimately, nuclear weapons. The second Swedish proposal was RM/E.22 and recommended that appropriate action should be taken in order to facilitate and improve the possibilities of using arbitration as an instrument for settling disputes concerning international commercial matters.

Yugoslavia submitted six proposals without co-sponsors. RM.18 consisted of four pages of declaratory language about the Overcoming of the Aggravation of International Relations and Promotion of the Process of Détente, designed for the preamble of a concluding document of the Madrid Meeting. RM.27 was the fifth proposal for a Conference on Disarmament in Europe. This conference was also to take place in two phases, so as to deal with (a) transitional measures, which would comprise: limitation of military activities, the halting of the arms race, and military disengagement; and (b) measures of actual disarmament, which would apply both to conventional and tactical nuclear weapons; the last point here recalls Sweden's proposal on the same subject. With respect to nuclear weapons other than tactical ones, the proposal said further that in its second phase the Conference would also consider other nuclear weapons, with a view to formulating bodies to deal with the reduction of such weapons and their withdrawal from Europe. An important innovation in this proposal was the idea of preceding the Conference by a preparatory meeting charged with the task of defining the mandate more precisely and determining the time, venue and other modalities of the Conference.

The Yugoslavian proposals in basket II were about migrant labour, asking the ECE for more study of this subject (RM/E.12) and about North-South co-operation, calling upon the states to contribute to the common efforts towards the establishment of the New International Economic Order (RM/E.21). On the promotion of peace and security in the Mediterranean the Yugoslavian proposal (RM.17) was again declaratory in nature and called for the transformation of the Mediterranean into a sea of peace. The Yugoslavian proposal in basket III (RM.13), dealt with the organization of a Cultural Forum similar to the one described by France in greater detail in her own proposal.

5.4. Other Proposals

The five *Nordic* countries, Denmark, Finland, Iceland, Norway and Sweden jointly sponsored a total of four proposals, three of which were in basket II. The first of these, RM/E.5, proposed encouraging a greater participation by small and medium-sized enterprises in trade and industrial co-operation projects between the participating states and gave a summary of some possible means to this end. The proposal caught the attention of the ten EC countries, Canada and Switzerland all of whom asked to be added to the list of its sponsors. RM/E.11 recommended that the existing machinery of the ECE should be utilized to the fullest possible extent in order to continue and consolidate the implementation of the relevant provisions of the Final Act. RM/E.13 welcomed with satisfaction the results of the ECE High-Level Meeting on the Protection of the Environment.

The five Nordic countries submitted one proposal in the third basket, RM/H.18, in which they described a number of measures towards promotion of co-operation in the field of training of young scientists.

Of the 87 proposals only one was submitted by a combination of countries which cut across the different blocs. This was RM/H.6, submitted by the Neutral country Finland, the WP member Hungary and the NATO country Iceland. It originated with the Hungarians and acquired its other two co-sponsors later on. It contained a number of measures for the promotion of the teaching of less widely-spread or -studied languages and of the translation, publication and dissemination of works in such languages.

NOTES:

1. Compare Luigi Vittorio Ferraris (ed.), *op. cit.*, p. 85.

2. *Ibid*, pp. 85 ff and pp. 353 ff. See also Anatoli Kowaljow, *op. cit.*, p. 235.

3. These semiannual reports cover the periods June 1 - November 30 and December 1 - May 31, starting June '76, so that by the end of 1982 the Bureau of Public Affairs of the Department of State published its thirteenth report.

4. These compilations include *Reports of Helsinki-Accord Monitors in the Soviet Union* (February 24, 1977), *The Right to Know, the Right to Act; Documents of Helsinki Dissent from the Soviet Union and Eastern Europe* (May, 1978), *Reports of Helsinki Monitors in the Soviet Union* (November 7, 1978), *On the Right to Emigrate for Religious Reasons: The Case of 10.000 Soviet Evangelical Christians* (May, 1979), *Profiles: The Helsinki Monitors* (revised December 10, 1979), *A Thematic Survey of the Documents of the Moscow Helsinki Group* (May 12, 1981).

5. *Implementation of the Final Act of the Conference on Security and Co--operation in Europe: Findings and Recommendations Five Years after Helsinki*, Report submitted to the Congress of the United States by the Commission on Security and Co-operation in Europe on August 1, 1980 (Washington, D.C.: US Government Printing Office, 1980), pp. 6-7. In preparation of the Belgrade meeting the Commission published a similar report, then *two years after Helsinki* (September 23, 1977). After the Belgrade meeting the Commission published *The Belgrade Follow-up Meeting to the CSCE: A Report and Appraisal* (May 17, 1978). During the Madrid Meeting the Commission published besides a *seven years after Helsinki* report (November, 1982) several interim reports on the various phases of the meeting.

6. Reports of these hearings (all published by the US Government Printing Office in Washington, D.C.) include 15 volumes on *Basket III: Implementation of the Helsinki Accords* (February 24, 1977 - August 5, 1981); in the period just before and during the Madrid Meeting the hearings covered items like *The Helsinki Forum and East-West Scientific Exchange* (January 31, 1980), *Soviet Violation of Helsinki Final Act: Invasion of Afghanistan* (July 22, 1981), *Fifth Anniversary of the Formation of the Ukrainian Helsinki Group* (November 16, 1981), *The Crisis in Poland and its Effects on the Helsinki Process* (December 28, 1981), *Phase IV of the Madrid CSCE Review Meeting* (March 23, 1982), *Soviet Involvement in the Polish Economy* (April 1, 1982).

7. *Fulfilling Our Promises: The United States and the Helsinki Final Act, A Status Report Compiled and Edited by the Staff of the Commission on Security and Co-operation in Europe* (Washington, D.C., November 1979). With regard to other countries which produced reports on their own performance concerning the Helsinki Act, mention may be made of the Canadian Governments' *Commentary on Canada's Implementation of the Final Act of the CSCE*, published in October 1980 and distributed in Madrid. The Finnish Ministry of Foreign Affairs compiled a report on Finland, entitled *Follow-up to the Conference on Security and Co-*

-operation in Europe (Helsinki, 1980). The Polish Institute of International Affairs published as special issue no. 15 of Studies on International Relations Poland and the Implementation of the CSCE Final Act (Warsaw, 1980).

8. "Declaration of the Warsaw Treaty States", New Times, no. 21, May 1980, pp. 26 ff.

9. Valentin Kravtsov, "Towards the Madrid Meeting", New Times, no. 36, September 1980, pp. 5 ff.

10. Idem. The fact that Western and in particular United States aims were known to the Soviet Union is abundantly clear from, for example, I. Blishchenko and V. Shavrov, "US Hypocritical Human Rights Policies", International Affairs (Moscow) no. 4, 1981, in particular pp. 62-64.

11. Brezhnev's Report of February 23 to the 26th Congress of the CPSU in New Times, no. 9, February 1981, p. 28.

12. Mihajlo Javorski, "Yugoslavia and the CSCE", Review of International Affairs, no. 732, October 5, 1980, pp. 1-4.

13. This is made clear from, among others, Milorad Pesic, "European Co--operation and Security Pending the Madrid Meeting", Review of International Affairs, no. 728-9, August 5-20, 1980, pp. 1-7.

IV. THE REPRESENTATIVES AT MADRID

1. Introduction

It is interesting to note that neither in the last Chapter of the Final Act nor in the Blue Book or anywhere else is there mention of presentation of credentials by the representatives nor is there any commission charged with the examination and approval of such documents. It would seem that, in 1975, European states were so stable that it was unlikely that rival groups would claim to be representing one and the same state. Neither before, during nor after the Helsinki Consultations did it occur to a country to suggest that a system of credentials ought to be brought into force.

In practice it was found sufficient for the local embassy of a participating state (which is to say a state which had signed the Final Act) to supply the meeting's Executive Secretary with a memorandum containing the names of its country's representatives. Such a list was accepted by the Executive Secretary and the other delegations without reserve (1).

This Chapter's main objective is to discover who and what these representatives were and, to this end, will begin with some statistics. These will be followed by an account of the representatives' professional background, their relation to their home base (covering instructions and rapportage), their relations with the press and with pressure-groups and the role played by personality in the political arena where they belong. Because all representatives were members of national delegations the Chapter closes with a description of how the delegations set to work.

2. The Delegates

Some conclusions can be drawn from the analysis of the lists of participants regularly issued by the Executive Secretariat. These lists were no more than faithful reproductions of data supplied by the participating states themselves which makes comparisons between the various delegations a difficult process. The lists appeared in Spanish each name being followed by a description of functions such as "*miembro de la delegación"* [delegation member], *"agregado"* [assistant], *"consejero"* [counsellor], but it was not certain that these qualifications had one and the same meaning for every delegation; each descriptive term might well cover a range of functions. Moreover, some states listed only actual delegates whereas others would include their foreign minister or other government officials who scarcely ever set foot in the congress building. Nearly all delegations included among delegates their administrative secretaries, security officers or technicians in order to ensure their access to the building.

The first list of participants issued by the Executive Secretariat in November 1980 comprised 547 names. The US delegation had 92 members, the Soviet Union 30, Canada 28 and Spain 24. Those were the four largest delegations. The three smallest delegations came from Cyprus, Iceland and Monaco each with three members. Of the participants, 99, or 18%, were women. The names on the list can be divided into three categories which do not appear in the original lists but are given below in view of the conclusions to which they give rise.

1. Foreign ministers or other members of national governments, civil servants from national ministeries, members of parliament (from the USA and Canada), all more or less occasional visitors to Madrid, together with, for almost every state, staff who belonged to the national embassy in Madrid but were not themselves actively involved in the work in the congress building.
2. Members of the supporting administrative staff: secretaries, telex operators, technicians, security officers.
3. The actual negotiators involved in the daily work within the congress building. From the first list it can be estimated that approximately 270 of the 547 people named fell into this category, which is to say 50%. Of the actual negotiators 7% were women. But the percentage of 50 has to be reduced because not all the people on the list were present at any one time: some took it in turns to attend and there were always a few who for one reason or another were temporarily not in Madrid but at home. At an important Plenary gathering when in principle all active delegates were present there was a constant attendance of 180 to 200 people.

By 1982 these numbers had dropped. After the 1981 summer recess the October list gave a total of only 354 names with almost the same percentage of women as before, exactly 20% this time. The number of actual negotiators as defined in category three once more made up 50% of the total and 7% were women. Attendance at the Plenary sessions varied from 160 to 180.

By February 1982, after the Christmas recess, the number of names on the list had hardly changed at a total of 355; once more 20% were women. But this time only 40% were actual negotiators as defined in category three, the women nevertheless making up a constant 7%. Attendance at the Plenaries varied between 120 and 130.

The list of participants issued in the autumn of 1982 and the lists that appeared in the spring of 1983, gave the same picture as in February 1982 although with smaller numbers. The number of diplomats actually present went on decreasing because there was less work to be done and the Western and Neutral delegations in particular took the opportunity to give their diplomats a few weeks back at base until their presence in Madrid would be required once more.

Most of the negotiators were career diplomats and/or civil servants from foreign ministries (2), not necessarily specialists in the fields covered by their discussions and subsequent negotiations. That is to say they were not people who, because of special training or experience, might be called experts in such areas as human rights, international law, visa problems, cultural co-operation or on other problems with which they might have to deal. Of course the committees which dealt with matters in specialist fields like economic co-operation (second basket) and military affairs, would include experts drawn from the relevant ministry, economists from Economic Affairs or disarmament experts from Defence.

Members of parliament who paid fleeting visits to Madrid at various times throughout the Meeting (and were only included in lists of delegates by the US and Canada) normally remained in a passive role only very rarely intervening at a Plenary session and taking no active part in committees or actual negotiations. They were observers rather than participants or delegates.

Some delegates had previous CSCE experience following on involvement in the Geneva or Belgrade negotiations; the proportion seemed to be somewhat higher on the East European side than in the West and there is an impression that in general, among East Europeans, there was more effort to maintain continuity in CSCE staffing. That is not to say that Western and NNA countries ever ran short of CSCE specialists to counter-balance this advantage. Those with CSCE experience came into their own particularly in discussions on questions of procedure when they were able to cite precedents out of their own personal experience and produce authoritative interpretations of what were sometimes ill--defined CSCE procedures, on the lines best suited to themselves. In particular during the actual drafting of texts for the concluding document, it was important to be able to tell from experience which problem would call forth from the opposing side a certain form of words and in which directions it might be profitable to look for a solution. In discussions within his own circle the experienced CSCE delegate was able to play a major role in evaluating the opposing party's tactics and working out the necessary response.

3. Instructions and Reports

In recent years, theorists have laid considerable emphasis on the management aspect of international negotiations; the negotiator is seen as a manager who has to respond to a host of government groups, departments, pressure-groups and, in addition, non-government organizations. Gilbert R. Winham for instance describes SALT as principally an internal negotiation and quotes with approval an experienced US negotiator who said: "I would say about nine-tenths of my time of negotiation was done with my own side" (3).

What is valid for one type of international negotiation is not necessarily true of another. Conclusions drawn with justification from the SALT talks will not automatically apply to the CSCE. The issue at stake is significant (4). The SALT negotiations were concerned with safety interests. Now, more than one organized body at home, particularly in the US, had this subject at heart and considered itself competent to deal with it; for security matters are crucial to every country. Winham's theory seems to gain validity in proportion to the importance of the points at issue and therefore also to the number of home groups that would like to have a finger in the pie. In Madrid his theory, insofar as it applied at all, was borne out more with reference to the mandate for the disarmament conference than by other matters. Many of the subjects treated in Madrid were not controversial in Western democracies: for example, the Western proposal to guarantee all citizens free access to foreign embassies in their capital cities. The home front did not have to be "managed" in such cases and Western negotiators spent nine-tenths of their time round the negotiating tables.

The theory also tends to shift the centre of gravity of the decision-making process away from the competent authorities in the home capital to the negotiator himself, but if this really is its meaning then it must be said to conflict with reality as it was in Madrid. The seat of decision is and remains with the responsible authorities, the decision-makers in the capital, who issue instructions to the negotiator. It is true that the man in the field may himself contribute to these instructions by putting over his opinions to the decision-makers in the capital but this does not make him a policy-maker. He is bound to conform to the instructions he receives.

The negotiator receives his instructions before, during and after the negotiating process. This is because agreement on a text such as an important paragraph in the Madrid Concluding Document is normally reached, at the request of one or more of the parties involved, expressly: *"ad referendum"* or "subject to confirmation", a procedure well-known to all concerned. *"Ad referendum"* means that the negotiator gives his agreement in principle but reserves the right to come back on it if compelled to by his authorities at home. None of his colleagues will hold it against him if this is in fact what happens and he gives a reasonable account of why he has had to change his mind. "Subject to confirmation" implies greater reserves: in principle the negotiator will not be able to accept the agreement unless his government decides in consultation that he can. For this reason no agreement is deemed to have been reached until confirmed in this way. In practice the two cases *"ad referendum"* and "subject to confirmation", tend to merge into each other; common to both is the fact that one of the parties has made it clear that before he can give full agreement to what has been hammered out on a personal basis, he must be able to take instruction from his own side.

A delegate receives his instructions in various ways, either in personal interviews with specialists and policy-makers in his own capital, or in writing or by telephone. His *personal* contacts at home give the negotiator a general picture of the policy he is supposed to pursue. His briefings cover matters of a general nature but also points of procedure and tactics and sometimes questions of detail which may turn out to be important. They provide the background which enables him to interpret subsequent written instructions in the correct spirit and give him a feeling for the way his authorities are thinking, which should enable him to react to any unexpected contingency by taking up a position which he can be fairly sure will meet with his government's approval. The Madrid delegates kept the *telephone* under constant pressure during the conference; they used it to consult their home authorities when questions had to be settled quickly but also to seek further information on *written* instructions already received by telex or still anxiously awaited. The disadvantage of written instructions is that the written text, however carefully drafted, may somehow convey the wrong impression. On the other hand such a text, whether of only a few paragraphs or several pages long, confers the advantage of setting down the national position in black and white so that there can be no misunderstanding between the different groups at home and the negotiators in the field whereas a telephone conversation involves no more than a dialogue between two people. Written instructions may consist merely of general indications but can become extremely detailed when required. Negotiators sometimes need no more than broad guidelines and yet on other occasions they may ask for instructions on the use of a single word or the substitution of a comma for a semi-colon.

It is of interest to know when it is that general instructions are thought to suffice and when these become more specific. To draw a line between substantive matters and tactics, allotting the latter largely to the responsibility of the delegation while leaving the former in the hands of authorities at home, is hardly useful (5). Tactics themselves may be of great importance. The night when the Western caucus agreed to stop the clock and the next night when they decided to bring that fiction to an end, (events which will be discussed in Chapter VIII) more than one Western delegation was on the phone to its capital to get the blessing of its government before giving its agreement: too much was at stake for the delegation to take full responsibility. At various other times when the West decided on a certain strategy, the same consultations took place. To set up tactics, or indeed procedure, against substantive policy as a distinct field of activity seems irrelevant to the question of the nature and purpose of instructions.

Richard Pedersen, basing his opinions on his experiences in the US delegation to the United Nations, has put forward the following hypothesis: "In general it may be stated that the larger the country, the greater the resources, or the more thoroughly organized it is, the greater the degree of control the foreign office will exercise" (6). Here two different criteria for the degree of control by the foreign office are given: on one side the size of the country and the amount of resources it has, and on the other the degree of organization of its administration, two criteria which do not necessarily go hand in hand. All the 35 countries at Madrid were developed countries and could be taken to have reached more or less the same degree of administrative organization, so the question that remains is whether the hypothesis is right in postulating that the larger the country the more specific the instructions its delegation receive. Although of course it made a good deal of difference that some delegations had the support of a large body of interested experts at home, it would be too much to say that delegations from such large countries by definition received more detailed instructions than those from small countries. Yet it is hardly surprising to learn that the US or FRG delegations did receive more copious instructions than, say, the Monaco delegation. In order to explain why this should be so it is perhaps more illuminating to work from the assumption that the larger countries had more *interests* in the conference than their smaller counterparts.

The limits to freedom of action imposed on the negotiators and the degree of detail gone into in the instructions were to a large extent governed by how much interest national authorities felt they had in the issue under discussion and the importance they therefore attached to it. Reciprocally, the negotiators would seek detailed instruction much sooner in cases which they knew were considered at home to be vital than in those which they knew were of little significance there. A few examples will serve as illustration.

Both the Bulgarian and Romanian delegations had strict instructions to see that the Madrid Concluding Document included texts dealing with exchanges among young people and there instructions did not appear easy to reconcile. Bulgaria wanted the emphasis to lie principally on the problems of the "rising generation", children from the age of 6 to 16, whereas Romania preferred to concentrate on contacts between young people aged from 16 to 24. Agreement was eventually reached largely by virtue of the fact that most of the other delegations from large or small countries had been given enough latitude in their instructions to allow them to accept any reasonable text. Bulgaria and Romania, however, found it necessary to apply to their superiors for instructions because they knew that the subject was of interest at home.

A second example is the case of Malta, itself a small country whose representative nevertheless found himself acting under strict telephoned and written instructions during discussions on the paragraphs in the Madrid Concluding Document concerning security in the Mediterranean. The same was true of his Greek, Turkish and Yugoslavian collegues but not, for example, of the Nordic delegations who had only general directives on this subject. The US delegation was also under stringent instructions not so much because the USA is large as because she has security interests in the Mediterranean where the sixth fleet is stationed.

The FRG provides a further example for when it came to proposals on reunification of families and international exchange of visits between family members, its delegation had to conform to precise instructions and was left little freedom of manoeuvre. This is a subject which touches the Federal Government more than other Western countries.

If it is accepted that the density and degree of detail of instructions are determined not by the size of the country or its administration but rather by the interests that it feels it has in any particular issue, then it will come as no surprise to learn that almost every delegation received precise instructions when it came to drafting the mandate for the European disarmament conference for here the issue involved touched everyone's security interests. Yet the rule still held true that for some countries (e.g., USA) there was more at stake in the military field than for others (e.g., Monaco) and therefore one delegation might have less play than another in its instructions on the subject. Most countries also attached great importance to areas where the material was of an ideological character: for example human rights, and freedoms such as freedom of expression. Instructions to delegations from socialist East European countries allowed a certain latitude for the third basket when it was a question of bilateral co-operation and exchange in the field of culture and education, but when it came to anything under the heading "Information" (circulation of foreign periodicals, liberty to take out subscriptions to foreign periodicals or access of religious faiths to mass media) then these delegations were once more bound hand and foot. These were matters which impinged on state ideology and were therefore of importance to their home capitals.

All that has just been set down with reference to the scope and complexity of instructions may also be said to apply to the rapportage sent home by a delegate: the coverage he gives to developments at his end will largely be determined by the amount of concern he knows there is for them at home. The difference in this case is that the size of the delegation as well as that of the home administration affect the extent of the coverage. Members of small delegations have less time to spend on comprehensive rapportage than members of large delegations in which there are more man-hours available. Similarly, administrations of considerable size, with specialist departments for each area, can devote more time to reading than those with a smaller personnel and are therefore more interested in receiving copious reports. Hence the total quantity of rapportage emanating from delegations from large countries exceeds what is produced by those from small countries, and yet, in both cases the proportion of this total allotted to each subject depends on the interest it is thought to arouse in the home capital.

4. Relations with the Press

A delegate is not only in constant contact with the authorities in his own capital city but is also required to deal with the press and pressure groups. For the press the delegate is a source of information, whereas he is on the receiving end of whatever information the pressure groups may use in order to influence him. First of all some remarks about the relationship with the press.

There were always journalists about in the congress building, at times in their hundreds but usually just a few, depending on whether an important session was taking place or not. However, the longer the conference went on the fewer were the journalists who followed its proceedings in the congress building; its newsworthiness declined steadily. The journalists who continued to be in regular attendance had every opportunity of keeping abreast of how discussions were proceeding whether in the Plenary or at informal gatherings. Such information Western journalists acquired principally in the course of personal conversations with delegates from their own country who seldom refused to answer any pertinent question they cared to put (7). The value of the Madrid Meeting as a propaganda forum escaped none of the Western and Neutral delegations and publicity was something sought after rather than shunned. Western delegates sometimes found this extra duty burdensome and time-consuming especially as in the nature of things the journalists were most numerous and insistent precisely when something important was happening and the delegate himself was most under pressure. On the other hand there were Western delegates who regarded a dialogue with the press as an opportunity for expressing their experiences and observing an outsider's reaction which at the same time forced them to distinguish the relative importance of the various events in which they themselves had been immersed.

There were not many secrets in the congress building. Rules (80) and (85) in the Blue Book distinguish between open sessions (the inaugural and closing sessions) and the remaining sessions which are not open, and between those documents which may be made public and those which may not. In fact, however, none of the sessions or documents at the Madrid Meeting were secret in the sense that journalists were unable to come by whatever information they wanted about them. Yet this does not mean that all such information actually found its way into Western and Neutral news media. Neither T.V., radio or newspapers were invariably interested in all the information their reporters had or might have had, and they were also selective in the way they used it, laying greater stress on the aspects which they considered of public interest. Only the reporters for Radio Liberty and Radio Free Europe were able to count on their broadcasting stations having an unfailing appetite for daily reports from Madrid.

As a rule journalists were given little or no information on the positions taken up by national delegations during internal negotiation, that is to say about the progress of talks within delegations or within Western caucuses. No Western delegation wanted to give the opposite side a chance to play off one Western partner against another. In any case there was little demand for such information; journalists were more interested in positions which had been made clear in the conference discussions themselves and here they were given every facility.

In addition to personal contacts with members of the delegations there were also official press conferences for interested journalists given by heads of delegations who explained and defended their national point of view. These official occasions were open to all members of the press and not exclusive to the journalists of one particular country so they were rather less "confidential" than the briefings fed only to journalists of the same nationality.

Western journalists often found the Soviet delegation's press conferences disappointing: their questions were met only with a repetition of well-known answers without any further explanation or substantiation. One Western journalist remarked: "East European representatives appear to have no idea of press relations. In Madrid they have the opportunity of influencing journalists from all parts of the West by presenting good sound arguments for their case but this opportunity they simply fail to grasp".

Western negotiators did not normally attempt to influence Western journalists in the sense of using or misusing them in the course of the game of negotiation in order to convey a message to the other side. It is, however, not to be denied that Western spokesmen were well aware of the effect on public opinion at home of the nature of Western publicity about this conference so that considerable care and attention was devoted by most Western delegations to press-relations.

All the same, Western journalists must sometimes have had the feeling that they were being used in the propaganda battle against the communist world. They were fed with speeches made in the Plenary on the subject of how human rights were being violated by various communist regimes and on their treatment of dissidents; but the mission confided to these journalists by their editors was not to report on the situation in Eastern Europe but on the progress of the Madrid conference.

5. Relations with Pressure Groups

During the first year of the conference in Madrid the Netherlands delegation received one or more letters from a grand total of 101 different interest groups pleading in general terms for the furthering of their aims during the conference. After summer 1981 the stream was reduced and the letters received were from organizations which had already written earlier. The 101 different interest groups were based in 22 countries: USA and Canada, eight other NATO countries, four Warsaw Pact countries, five Neutral lands, while Jamaica, Israel and Australia each provided a single letter. The most prolific countries were the USA (18 organizations), France (16), and the FRG (10). The following classification is designed to give some impression of the sort of organization which showed interest in the Madrid Meeting. Each organization has been assigned to a single category according to the salient features of its letters but it must be said that a certain random element does persist because various organizations could have been put equally well into more than one category.

1. The largest group of letters came from 37 different associations of emigrants from East European countries, but 3 from associations of Turkish exiles and 1 from Indonesian exiles: e.g., the "World Federation of Free Latvians" based in Munster (FRG) or the "World Congress of Free Ukrainians" writing from Toronto, or the "Community of Romanians in France";
2. Letters came from 14 Helsinki Watch or Monitor committees like the "US Helsinki Watch Committee" and the "Belgian Helsinki Committee";
3. Letters came from 13 human rights organizations, such as the Finnish "League for human rights and freedoms";
4. Letters came from 12 peace movements: the Sofia-based "World Parliament of the Peoples for Peace" and the "Youth Committee for Peace" from Paris are two examples.
5. 8 organizations of war veterans and war victims sent letters: from Paris the "World Veterans Federation" and also from France the "Co--ordination Committee of Associations of War Veterans and Victims of Seyne-sur-Mer" are again two examples;
6. 6 religious organizations including the "Islamic Council of Europe" in London and the "Estonian Evangelical Lutheran Church" from Stockholm, sent letters;
7. Finally, letters were received from three political parties, one trade union and three scientific institutes.

The great majority of the letters comprised circular letters sent to every delegation at the conference; they were expressed in general terms and on the whole required no answer.

There were other manifestations of public opinion in Madrid, for at the start of the conference in November 1980, the city was transformed into what was termed by *Le Monde* (22.11.80) "a city of dissidence". H. Gordon Skilling, Professor of Political Science at the University of Toronto, gives the following description:

> During the critical 10 days at the opening of the conference a veritable "counterconference" was taking place in Madrid as groups and individuals gathered to lobby the CSCE delegates, transforming the city, in the words of *Le Monde*, into "a city of dissidence". There converged on Madrid a large number of celebrated Soviet dissidents in exile (Gen. P. Grigorenko, L. Alekseyeva, V. Bukovskiy, N. Gorbanevskaya, L. Plyushch, and others), exiles from Czechoslovakia, Romania, and Poland, and representatives of various ethnic groups and human rights organizations, such as the Helsinki Watch, the Interreligious Task Force on Soviet Jewry, the World Congress of Free Ukrainians, the Gesellschaft für Menschenrechte, and the Anti-Bolshevik Bloc of Nations. Although this gathering was not so dramatic or as well-publicized as similar parallel meetings at earlier international conferences in Stockholm and Vancouver, it nonetheless exerted considerable influence on world public opinion.
>
> These groups and individuals conducted press conferences, gave interviews to the press, and held public meetings to discuss human rights and détente. There was an exhibit of *samizdat* literature, a concert in honor of human rights activists, and a few hunger strikes and demonstration marches in various parts of the city. A Latvian cut his wrists outside the congress center; others put up a huge banner of protest against Soviet occupation of the Baltic states on the stadium opposite the congress hall. Six Canadian Latvian girls attended a public session in national costume and attracted the attention of the cameramen of the mass media. The death of Andrey Amalrik, who was killed in an automobile accident en route to the conference, was the occasion of a service in Russian in a small Russian Orthodox church in Madrid. This memorial tribute was attended by the American delegate Max Kampelman and other delegates (8).

Most delegates were not directly or personally involved in these events but got to know about them by reading the newspapers. The question of whether this sort of happening "exerted considerable influence on world public opinion" is one we shall not attempt to answer here, if indeed there is any possible answer. A question which may be more fruitful to discuss is whether as R. Winham has suggested, "interest-group activity may be having a more profound impact on foreign policy than many observers realize" (9).

In discussing this question it may be useful to employ the classic distinction between policy formulation and policy execution which is found again in Winham (10). Then it may well be said that interest-group activity may be having an influence on foreign policy *makers* who may feel obliged for some reason to take into account the interests of certain groups when they formulate their policies. But the question posed in the context of this Chapter is rather whether the *delegates* in Madrid, whose role was an executive one, allowed themselves to be influenced by the flood of letters they received from interest-groups and private citizens, the personal interviews some of them had with representatives of these organizations, by the "counterconference" or other demonstrations outside the congress building or by the massive peace marches which took place in their home countries. In other words, were they influenced by public opinion in whatever form? It must be said from the outset that in theory and in practice the answer to this question must take account of the fact that the negotiator is bound to follow the instructions he is given and has no right to depart from them in response to the claims of any interest-group. To do this would be for him to falsify the relationship he enjoys with his responsible authorities.

Every delegate is nonetheless to some extent a prey to the influence of public opinion even when he is acting in a purely executive capacity, for the negotiator is after all only human. He may himself sympathize with the expressions of such public opinion or be entirely in disagreement, yet they may affect the spirit in which he carries out his instructions, his own sense of conviction and hence his power to convince.

During the discussions on implementation of the Final Act some delegations, while expressing their national point of view, did at times refer in general terms to the letters received in Madrid although no direct quotations were used. These letters were also a stimulus when speeches were drafted, and had a hand in creating the ambiance of both plenary and committee discussions. It was not unusual to hear a general appeal to public opinion (on the side of the speaker) in support of the national position. There were however, in addition, appeals to public opinion on the opposite side: the Soviet and other East European delegations repeatedly drew attention to the peace marches in Western Europe in the autumn of 1981, using them as justification for their contention that all the peoples of Europe were in favour of disarmament, which was only prevented by artificial obstacles created especially by the Reagan government but also by some West European governments.

6. Personality versus Political Power

In the literature there is a preoccupation with precisely what qualities make a good negotiator (11). William Zartman and Maureen R. Berman in their contribution to the subject, start from the axiom that "negotiators are made, not born and that there is something about the process that can be taught and learned" (12). According to these authors a negotiator must learn to try to understand the other side; in addition he must acquire patience, self-confidence and physical and mental stamina and tenacity; he must learn to build up relationships of trust and exercise various other learning skills (13). However, these seem to be skills which are useful to every human being whose aim is to live in harmony with his neighbours, business acquaintances, friends and family.

Can the negotiator's personality and qualities have no influence then on the results of his negotiations? Opinions differ on this question. In the context of their theory Zartman and Berman are inclined to think that there may well be an effect: "Negotiators themselves often point to the positive impact that a good personal working relationship can have on a negotiation and a negotiator's credibility" (14). Arthur Lall takes much the same view in his theory although he imposes the condition that the negotiator must be "in direct touch with or able to approach the sources of authority in his government". He lays great stress on this condition (which is hardly surprising from a diplomat from a country like India where personal relations play a more important role than organization): "Assuming that a good working relationship exists between a negotiator and the sources of authority in his government, the personal qualities of the negotiator - his tact, energy, understanding and sensitivity, as well as his capacity to engage in informal discussion - are of direct relevance to the success or failure of a negotiation" (15). Gilbert Winham sums up the literature on the subject: "The literature on negotiation especially emphasizes the proposition that *who* the negotiator is will affect the outcome of the bargaining" (16). He himself, however, reaches a different conclusion calling in case (like Zartman & Berman) what the practitioners themselves say: "Even though personality factors can create 'problems', practitioners rarely admit in interviews that personality was ever decisive in negotiation; occasionally they will describe particular negotiators they have known who have been successful because of technical competence, even though their personalities were not what one would expect would bring success in negotiation" (17). Mastering the substantive material on which negotiations are being carried out Winham finds, in the end, just as important a factor as personality or cultural background.

There is no doubt that negotiators who at crucial moments can be seen to have the relevant material at their fingertips are effective in determining the results. They clearly have much influence in international negotiations as they probably also have at a national level in negotiations between business men or employers and employees. The problem remains: is personality of direct relevance to the success or failure of an international negotiation or not? The answer must take account of the fact that the role of personality is ultimately limited by the nature of the instructions received and by the instructions under which the opposite side is working. On these conditions and conscious of the fact that in bilateral negotiations the personality of the negotiator may play a different role than in multilateral ones, the following remarks can be made on the basis of experience of multilateral negotiations.

At a great multilateral gathering like the Madrid Meeting, a delegate's impact on the course of the conference depends not on his personality and his personal qualities alone but also on the political power behind him: both these elements are important. In connection with the second element it may be said that Western delegations in Madrid were unanimous in accepting that important informal meetings within small groups should normally include a member of the US delegation in addition to the "President of the Ten" representing the EC countries. These two represented the two most considerable Western political powers. Such informal groups also included a Soviet delegate on the East European side supported by one or more members of the East European delegations.

Indeed, as far as the Soviet delegation was concerned, the US delegation continued to be the most important delegation with sufficient political weight to make it an acceptable business partner where really important matters were at stake and this in spite of the fact that the US delegation was one of the delegations most deeply involved in the arraignment of the Soviet Union for violations of the provisions of the

Final Act during the discussions on its implementation. Eastern and Western delegations more often than not got the impression that for the Soviet delegation, the US delegation was the sole natural partner in negotiations.

This is not to say that American representatives alway dominated discussions in the conference chambers while the rest of the Western and Neutral delegations sat meekly by. On the whole the importance and influence of a delegate depends not only on the importance of the country he represents but also on his strength of personality and the force of his arguments. He is listened to with attention if and when he has something to say. Of course, a delegate from a large and important country is more likely to have something of interest to say to the conference than his colleague from a smaller country. But during unprepared discussions on problems which arise suddenly, delegates from small countries have a chance of affecting the course of the debate by forceful argument, particularly, but not exclusively, when it is a question of procedure. There were many times during the Madrid discussions when representatives from smaller countries proved the importance of their presence. They also came into their rights in the *"chef-de-file"* system of the EC and Western caucuses, where particular delegates were appointed as spokesmen for the whole group on particular subjects (18).

The total effect of the personality factor on the final result of the conference, the Madrid Concluding Document, is difficult to evaluate; an assessment would require an experimental parallel: the same conference held under identical political circumstances and thus with the same political instructions but with different actors. It is not unlikely that such a conference would have resulted in a different text for many of the phrases of the present document represent political compromises thought out by the negotiators themselves. Of course those phrases found their inspiration in the instructions emanating from the capital cities, and might be amended in accordance with further instructions before being given their final sanction, but still the original drafting lay, in a great number of cases, with the negotiators. This means that the drafting abilities of delegates was a significant factor in arriving at the final text.

Personality and political power are both elements of such importance that it is difficult to assess the influence of one as distinct from the other. It is true that the most graceless stammer proceeding from the mouth of a delegate from a powerful land, if such a thing ever occurred, would render the opposing party far more attentive and figure much more in reports sent home, than the most brilliant rhetoric coming from the representative of an obscure country. Yet even this does not nullify the personality factor altogether. With this in mind the following conclusions are given:

1. A particular representative of a certain country may have markedly more influence in multilateral discussions than either his predecessor or his successor in the same role. One member of a delegation can be more influential than another of the same delegation.
2. Two delegations from countries of equal political weight may affect the course of events to different degrees according to their personnel.

Both these conclusions eliminate the variable of political power and stress the importance of personality.

Finally there is the question of the qualities which determine the influence wielded by a delegate. The answer, which has an instinctive rather than scientific feel to it, is that the relevant factors are his power to convince, his ability to find the right arguments at the right time, his analytic grasp of the negotiating scene at any one moment, his skill in penetrating the intentions of his opposite number thus enabling him to set up a strategy for the immediate future and, last of all, his ability to react to unexpected situations in a way which later analysis will deem to have been adequate.

7. National Delegations

All delegates were members of their national delegations. Although these were important organs in the complex structure of the conference they must not be seen as the smallest and therefore primary decision--making organs. It was outside rather than within their national delegation that individual experts in particular areas were confronted with the problems on which they were expected to pronounce an opinion, and they did not necessarily have time to consult their colleagues on every occasion. Delegation meetings provided a unique opportunity to discuss their experiences either as a prelude to the decisions they would have to make as experts in their caucus or in plenary committees, or as an analysis after the event. Indeed the meetings formed a valuable and therefore indispensable part of the work of every delegate.

National delegations of only a few members did not hold formal meetings like those held by larger delegations. In general, delegation meetings had three functions: (1) exchange of information and consequent reflection on what had already happened and was about to happen; (2) discussion of specific problems encountered by individual delegates in their own areas and (3) discussion of the instructions received from the home capital and of what from among the various developments which filled every day, should be included in reports back to base. The importance of instructions and rapportage has already been dealt with earlier in this Chapter. The degree of co-operation and mutual consultation between members of a delegation was largely determined by the personality of the delegation chief and his personal interest in the work and problems of his fellow-workers. This was something that differed from delegation to delegation but most delegations of any size and political weight met at least daily, early in the morning before the caucus meetings or plenary committees began or in the late evening when they were all over.

With regard to exchange of information it is important to note that most of the delegates devoted their time to only one or two problem areas of the many subjects discussed during the conference; they had their specialized area and always discussed the same subjects with their fellow experts in the caucus or in conference committees. The delegation meetings were useful because the delegate and the head of delegation himself, was able to glean from the general exchange of information what was happening in the other committees in which he took no part. It was possible, for example, to tell whether a particular delegation's attitude in a caucus or plenary committee was an expression of the national political line followed by that delegation in every caucus or committee meeting, or whether it might be merely the result of the personal attitude of the delegate concerned. Discussion also revealed which committee was making progress and which was, for the moment, marking time. The exchange of information enabled delegates to get an overall picture of the running of the whole machine in which they themselves were only tiny cogwheels.

With regard to discussion of specific problems it is important to note that when a delegate had been confronted with special problems and needed advice then the delegation meeting was the time and place for him to consult his head of delegation and his colleagues. Problems arose not only in the conference committees but also in the caucuses of friendly experts, and could not always be resolved *in situ*.

They covered both tactical and substantive matters but might be important enough to be passed from the level of experts to that of heads of delegation. The delegate would then receive his instructions from his head of delegation during the meeting of the delegation.

NOTES:

1. It should be noted, however, that the Turkish delegation has made it clear on several occasions that the Turkish government does not recognize the actual "Government of the Republic of Cyprus" or her representatives at the CSCE meetings.

2. In exception to this, besides a number of staff from the Congressional Commission on Security and Co-operation in Europe as permanent US delegates, for the first six months of the conference up to the summer of 1981, the US delegation included as full members not only professional diplomats but also eight members of Congress as well as 30 "public" representatives. On the Soviet side, Yuri N. Rakhmaninov, member of the Soviet Committee on Security and Co-operation in Europe, was also member of the delegation of the USSR, while the USSR embassador to Spain, Mr. Dubinin, as an old time CSCE expert from Geneva and Belgrade, occupied the post of deputy chairman of the Soviet delegation.

3. See articles by Gilbert R. Winham, "Practitioners' Views of International Negotiation" World Politics, vol. XXXII, no. 1, October 1979, pp. 116 ff; and "International Negotiation in an Age of Transition", International Journal, vol. XXV, 1979-80, p. 9, where he quotes, with agreement, Winthrop Brown: "Negotiation, like charity, begins at home".

4. Winham himself would have to assent to this for he stresses "the weight that practitioners give to cognitive variables (e.g., issues) at the expense of affective variables (e.g., personality or culture)" and also observes "Negotiation theory tends to emphasise the elements of the bargaining situation that are similar, regardless of what is being bargained over; practitioners assume that *what* is being bargained essentially shapes the nature of the interaction". Given the truth of this remark, which can hardly be overstressed, it can be said to follow, that whether or not his theory that negotiation is primarily a management process is true depends on the "issue", "what is being bargained over". Gilbert R. Winham "Practitioners' Views of International Negotiation", pp. 116 and 122-123.

5. This distinction is for instance made by Richard F. Pedersen, "Diplomacy in the United Nations", mimeographed paper, (Cambridge, Mass.: Center for International Studies, 1960), p. 93.

6. Ibid, p. 100.

7. The official records of the closed sessions of the official organs of the conference were of no use to journalists. Not only did they appear some days after the sessions had taken place, but also failed to supply any information of importance either. For example the journal for the 99th Plenary Meeting read as follows:

   1. Date: Friday, 18 December 1981 (afternoon meeting)
      Opened: 3.40 p.m. Closed: 6.25 p.m.
   2. Chairman: Mr. F. van Dongen (Netherlands)
   3. Subjects discussed: Agenda item 8
   4. Statements: Malta, Italy, Netherlands, Hungary, San Marino, German Democratic Republic, Switzerland, Austria, USSR, Portugal, Sweden,

Ireland, Czechoslovakia, Luxemburg, Liechtenstein.
5. Next meeting: Tuesday, 9 February 1982, at 11.00 a.m.
Chairman: Poland.

Nobody could possibly have guessed from this that it was in this week that the military take-over in Poland had taken place and that on the very last morning and afternoon before the Christmas recess there had been emotional interventions from Western and Neutral countries on the subject and strongly-worded retorts from the East Europeans.

8. H. Gordon Skilling, "CSCE in Madrid", Problems of Communism, vol. XXX, July-August 1981, pp. 6-7.

9. Gilbert R. Winham, "Practioners' Views of International Negotiation", p. 127.

10. Ibid., p. 129.

11. See, for instance, Daniel Druckman, Human Factors in International Negotiations: Social-Psychological Aspects of International Conflict (Beverly Hills: Sage Publications, 1973), p. 72 and his contribution to Daniel Druckman (ed.), Negotiations: Social-Psychological Perspectives (Beverly Hills: Sage Publications, 1977), pp. 29 ff. and pp. 247 ff.

12. William Zartman & Maureen R. Berman, The Practical Negotiator (New Haven: Yale University Press, 1982), p. 16.

13. Ibid., pp. 16-41.

14. Ibid., p. 29.

15. Arthur Lall, Modern International Negotiation: Principles and Practice (New York: Columbia University Press, 1966), p. 333.

16. Gilbert R. Winham, "Practitioners' Views of International Negotiation", p. 123.

17. Gilbert R. Winham, "International Negotiation in An Age of Transition", p. 17.

18. For the role of small countries in multilateral negotiations see Johan Kaufmann, op. cit., pp. 186-187.

V. THE FORMAL SETTING OF THE DECISION-MAKING PROCESS

1. Introduction

Previous Chapters have considered general procedural rules in the CSCE and the question of which countries were involved and who their representatives were in Madrid. This covered the static elements which were of influence on the Madrid negotiations. Before we turn to the actual course of events in the conference this Chapter will deal with the formal modalities which were intended to control this course of events. They comprise what is known as the Purple Book*. The Purple Book is the result of negotiations during the meeting set up to prepare for the Madrid conference and contains rules on the agenda and time-schedule to be followed, subjects which raised considerable feeling during the Preparatory Meeting. The question is now how these modalities worked out in practice.

One of the things the Purple Book did was to set up a number of working groups and to grant to the Plenary the right to institute other such groups. A chart (Figure 5-2) is given of the formal organizational structure in 1981 (the 1982 situation when all Drafting Groups were abolished and replaced by a single group, is described in the next Chapter) and a description of how the groups functioned and their relation to the Plenary. In anticipation of what will be described about the formal and actual settings of the decision-making process in the present and next Chapter, Figure 5-1 shows all the various groups with the periods of their functioning.

2. The Purple Book

The task of the Madrid Preparatory Meeting, which ran from 9 September to 10 November 1980, was to "decide on the appropriate modalities for the main Madrid Meeting" as had been agreed two years earlier in Belgrade. The political result of this preparatory meeting was "the Purple Book", a compromise which came into being only at the end of a long tug-of-war. At the beginning of the Preparatory Meeting the West

---

*see Annex no. 3

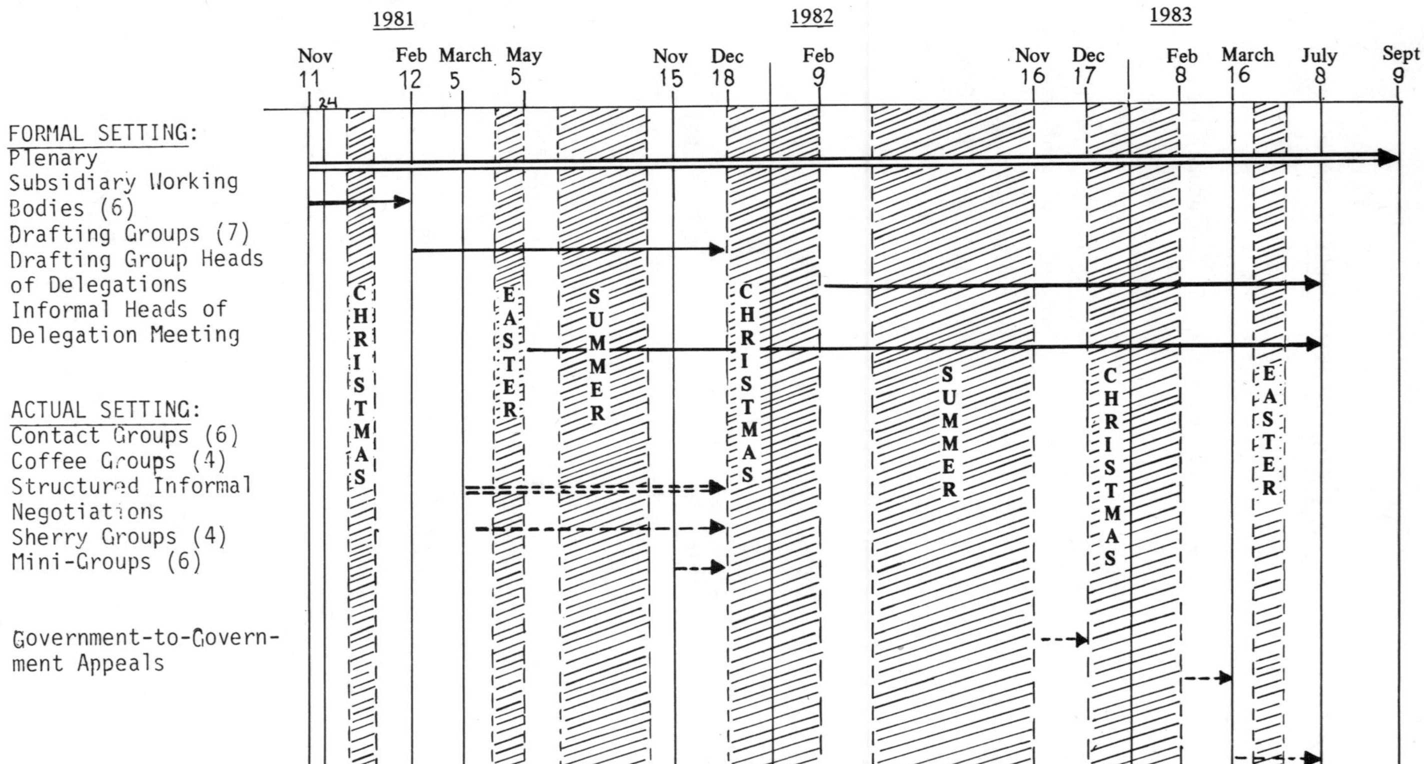

Figure 5-1:
The Formal and Actual Setting of the Decision Making Process in Phases.

was willing to adopt, for Madrid, the Yellow Book which had served the Belgrade Meeting, but a proposal to this effect, put forward by Spain, was rejected by the East European countries. The most important bone of contention was the question of how long the discussion of the implementation of the Final Act should go on and whether, as had been the case in Belgrade, this should be seen as a self-contained section of the main meeting distinguished both in time and nature from the phase when new proposals would be made.

The task of a follow-up CSCE meeting like the one in Madrid was considered to be twofold: a review of the implementation of the Final Act's principles and provisions, on one hand, and the introduction of new proposals designed to further this implementation, on the other. It was the review of implementation which was of paramount importance to the West. During the Preparatory Meeting therefore, Western representatives fought hard for an extensive review of implementation which would form the basis for discerning more clearly the necessity for new proposals designed to improve it. East European countries, however, claimed to be looking to the future and therefore wanted to focus attention especially on new proposals and more specifically on those concerning a European disarmament conference on an East European model.

As will be seen there were other problems but they were related ones. In the end a compromise was adopted a few days after the official opening of the main meeting. The compromise formula was later given the document number CSCE/RM.2 but is better known as the Purple Book from the colour of its cover when the book was later published by the Spanish government.

2.1. Agenda

The Purple Book consists of:

- Agenda
- Organizational Framework, timetable and other modalities of the Meeting
- Working Programme including the grid for the period 11 November - 19 December 1980
- two Statements by the Chairman

The Agenda lists eleven subjects which had to be dealt with:

1. Formal opening of the Meeting;
   Address by a representative of the host country;
   Address by the Secretary General of the United Nations or his representative.
2. Opening statements by the representatives of the participating States.
3. Contributions by:
   (a) the United Nations Economic Commission for Europe (ECE) and UNESCO;
   (b) the non-participating Mediterranean States.
4. Reports of the Meetings of Experts and of the "Scientific Forum", held in accordance with the relevant provisions of the Final Act and of the Concluding Document of Belgrade.
5. A thorough exchange of views both on the implementation of the provisions of the Final Act and of the tasks defined by the Conference, as well as, in the context of the questions dealt with by the latter, on the deepening of their mutual relations, the improvement of security and the development of co-operation in Europe, and the development of the process of detente in the future.
   Examination of proposals concerning the above questions.
6. Questions relating to security in the Mediterranean will be discussed, in accordance with the relevant provision contained in the Concluding Document of the Belgrade Meeting, in the Plenary and in the subsidiary working body M, in the context of item 5 of the Agenda.
7. Definition of the appropriate modalities for the holding of other meetings in conformity with all the provisions of the Chapter of the Final Act concerning the Follow-up to the Conference.
8. Drafting of a concluding document which will include decisions relating to the above-mentioned items of the Agenda.
9. Adoption of the concluding document.
10. Closing statements by the representatives of the participating States.
11. Formal closure of the Meeting.

These subjects were not to be taken chronologically in the given order although, of course, the item which was taken first was indeed the formal opening of the Meeting and the last one its formal closure. For the rest there were guidelines which, after long negotiations, had been provided in the Purple Book's "organizational framework, time-table and other modalities" with its annex: "working programme". What these guidelines for the most important agenda items were will now be examined.

Items 1, 2 and 3(a) were to be discussed in open plenary meetings during the first week, from 11-14 November. The address by the Secretary General of the United Nations or his representative, which formed the third part of the *first* item, was in fact given on the very last day of that week when items *two* and *three (a)* had already been dealt with. The speaker, the Deputy Secretary General of the United Nations' Office at Geneva, was unable to attend any sooner because there had been so much doubt as to whether the Meeting would begin at all. After that, in the second week, a start was to be made straight away in closed plenary sessions with the first sentence of item *five* which read: "a thorough exchange of views both on the implementation of the provisions of the Final Act and of the tasks defined by the Conference". This was known as the review of implementation or the implementation debate.

Preferably during the third week, suggested the Purple Book, the programme was to revert to items *three (b)* and *four* which comprised hearing the contributions from the non-participating Mediterranean States and the reports of the three Meetings of Experts which had taken place since Belgrade. These contributions were indeed delivered at the end of the third week. During this week and after, however, the implementation debate (item *five*, first sentence) was again to be pushed forward, and was supposed to be completed by the end of the sixth week. The examination of the proposals, or second part of item *five*, could then start after the Christmas recess, in the seventh week, which began on 27 January, and was to be finished by 11 February. Item *six:* questions relating to security in the Mediterranean, was to be treated "in the context of item five of the agenda", which meant that everyone had the right to refer to these problems in the course of their interventions, while at the same time they were to be dealt with in a separate Subsidiary Working Body.

Item *seven:* "Definition of the appropriate modalities for the holding of other meetings in conformity with all the provisions of the Chapter of the Final Act concerning the Follow-up to the Conference", is not allocated any particular time at all in the Purple Book. Just as in Belgrade, the Western countries had wanted this item included in order to underline its importance. It was impossible to confine its discussion to a limited period; it came up at regular intervals, in interventions in the Plenary, during negotiations in the Follow-up Subsidiary Working Body and Drafting Group and in the lobbies, at dinners, lunches and parties. It never functioned as a separate agenda item to be treated on its own at a particular moment, and it had never been meant to do so.

The *eighth* item on the agenda: "Drafting of a concluding document which will include decisions relating to the above mentioned items of the agenda" was supposed to come up on 12 February 1981 and round about this date it did in fact do so. This period of drafting was supposed to last not longer than three weeks for: "every effort should be made to agree on the concluding document not later than 5 March 1981" runs the Purple Book. One year later, on 12 February 1982, during a plenary session the Soviet delegate asked the chairman to say which item, according to the agenda, was supposed to be under discussion at that moment. The answer was that it was item eight. This brief incident was significant because on 12 February 1982 nobody was working on item eight, "drafting of a concluding document", because the debate was concerned exclusively with developments in Poland on account of which twenty Neutral and Western foreign ministers had travelled to Madrid. In progress was a continuation of the implementation discussions which really belonged under the first sentence of item five. However, at the Purple Book's adoption, the Western countries had expressed a unilateral reservation or "tacit assumption" to the effect that if new violations of the Final Act should occur after 1 January 1981 they would comment on them (see below under "cut-off").

These new violations did indeed occur, in their opinion, and for this reason the debate on implementation, far from confining itself to the period prescribed in the Purple Book, continued up to the end of the conference. Political reality proved stronger than the procedures which had been agreed. This divergence from agreed procedure was possible by virtue of an unwritten law of the CSCE: no representative of a sovereign state may be prevented from speaking in a Plenary session on whatever subject he chooses provided it has some connection with the Final Act. That means that a country's political decision to bring up a certain subject in Plenary is of more weight than the question of whether the subject itself is in order according to the Purple Book.

The period of drafting, which was supposed to last no longer than three weeks, lasted 69 working weeks over a period of 2½ years, followed by eight "Malta weeks".

2.2. "Optical Division"

In paragraph 2(a) of the final chapter, "Follow-up to the Conference", the Final Act calls for: "a thorough exchange of views both on the implementation of the provisions of the Final Act and of the tasks defined by the Conference, as well as, in the context of the questions dealt with by the latter, on the deepening of their mutual relations, the improvement of security and the development of co-operation in Europe, and the development of the process of détente in the future".

At the insistence of the West, the Yellow Book which contained the agenda and other modalities of the Belgrade Meeting, had introduced a perceptible space before the second part of the sentence beginning with "as well as", to indicate that two separate agenda items were involved, namely the review of implementation 'as well as' the introduction of new proposals:

> A thorough exchange of views
>
> > both on the implementation of the provisions of the Final Act and of the tasks defined by the Conference,
> >
> > as well as, in the context of the questions dealt with by the latter, on the deepening of their mutual relations, the improvement of security and the development of co-operation in Europe, and the development of the process of détente in the future.
>
> Examination of proposals concerning the above questions.

In Madrid, at the start of the Preparatory Meeting, Spain proposed the adoption of the complete Yellow Book as guideline for the Madrid Meeting. As explained above, this was rejected by East European countries not least because they objected to this visual separation which had given the Western countries in Belgrade the right to hold a detailed discussion about implementation. In the end, item five of the Agenda in the Purple Book did not display the lay-out which the Western countries had wanted but one of the "Statements by the Chairman" reads: "On the occasion of item 5 of the Agenda the Chairman noted the general understanding of the Meeting that this item of the Agenda contains two distinct elements".

In fact the loss of the "optical division", as it was called, had no influence on the course of the discussions in Madrid: five to six weeks were devoted exclusively to deliberations on the implementation of the Final Act. The Purple Book had left open the possibility of submitting substantive proposals early on during that period because it stated that such proposals "should be submitted *not later* than during the fifth week after the beginning of the Meeting". However, the East European delegations in no way attempted to change the course of the discussions during those weeks by an anticipatory introduction of important new proposals as had been feared by the West.

2.3. "Cut-Off"

It was important to East European countries that at the end of the review of implementation phase, after six weeks, these discussions should be closed and that the following stages, which were the introduction of new proposals and the drafting of the concluding document, should not be interrupted by a return to questions which belonged to the first phase. This the Western countries refused to accept, referring to it as "cut-off" and claiming that representatives of sovereign states had the right to speak at any time on any subject which they cared to raise. The "cut-off" nevertheless found its way into the Purple Book because paragraph 4 of its chapter "Organizational Framework" reads in part: "The thorough exchange of views on the implementation of the provisions of the Final Act and of the tasks defined by the Conference will be completed by the end of the sixth week".

The Western delegations assumed, however, that in conjunction with this a tacit agreement existed allowing all representatives the right to expose any fresh violations of the Final Act which might occur after the end of the sixth week. The existence of this tacit agreement has never been acknowledged by the East European delegations. Yet, during 1981 and 1982, long after the end of the first six weeks, Western and Neutral representatives repeatedly raised the subject of new violations of the Final Act on the part of East European countries which could not but respond to these accusations. They almost always concerned new measures taken against dissidents and, from December 1981 onwards, developments in Poland.

2.4. Time Schedule

The lengthy negotiations about the amount of time which should be allocated to each phase (review of implementation, introduction of new proposals, drafting of the concluding document) led to more specific detail on this point in the Purple Book than had been the case for

Belgrade's Yellow Book. In the end it was agreed to devote five weeks exclusively to the review of implementation, after which would come a "mixed week". This would be the last week before the Christmas recess and might be occupied both by the review of implementation and by the introduction of new proposals. This only becomes clear from taking in conjunction two extracts from different paragraphs in the chapter "Organizational Framework" in the Purple Book: one, which has been quoted already, states that the review of implementation would have to be completed by the end of the sixth week and the other stipulates that "Examination of the proposals submitted will be preceded by explanatory statements starting during the sixth week".

In the event the mixed sixth week lived up to its name: the review of implementation was rounded-off by general statements from representatives giving a broad survey of their earlier interventions, while the introduction of their most important new proposals occupied the rest of the time. As a result, during the Christmas recess, delegations were able to consult their experts at home about the various proposals which had been put forward, which was what the East European countries had said they had wanted. On the other hand the Western countries had also seen their wishes complied with for they had retained the right to discuss the implementation of the provisions of the Final Act during the six weeks right up to the Christmas recess.

2.5. Final Closing Date

During the preparatory discussions most of the Western countries wanted to see a closing date included in the working programme while East European countries were not keen on the idea. The Purple Book eventually says on this subject: "Every effort should be made to agree on the concluding document not later than 5 March 1981; the date for the closure of the Meeting will be decided by the Meeting itself". The latter part of the sentence, after the semi-colon, rather detracts from the value of the former because consensus for the closure of the Meeting would now be needed, a consensus which could be frustrated by any one delegation. On the other hand, some sort of target date had been agreed. However, on 5 March, in the various Drafting Groups, the bargaining process on the many proposals which had been introduced had only just begun and nobody seriously thought of stopping right in the middle.

Later, another English expression was used more often than not when a target date was indicated: the participating states would express "their resolve" to bring the Meeting to a close within a certain period. The Madrid Meeting finally ended on September 9, 1983.

2.6. Follow-up

From the outset of the Preparatory Meeting Western representatives were surprised by the refusal of the East Europeans to accept as an established fact that the Madrid conference should in any case pronounce an opinion about the date and place of a third Follow-up meeting after Madrid. The official East European reasoning was that whether such a follow-up meeting should take place at all would be dictated by how the main Madrid Meeting went and, first and foremost, by the results of this Meeting. Without this knowledge it would be premature and illogical to take for granted that a follow-up meeting to Madrid would take place.

The message this contained for the West was clear. If the conference in Madrid was to be used in the same way as in Belgrade, as an opportunity for endless attacks on the Soviet Union and some of her allies and if this Meeting failed to result in an European disarmament conference, then further CSCE follow-up meetings would cease to be of any interest to the Soviet Union. This official Soviet stand aroused in the Western camp a correlative mistrust of the Soviet Union's motivation in the CSCE Madrid Meeting and this led to increased obstinacy in the matter of laying down there and then that the Madrid Meeting should fix the time and place for the next similar meeting, as had been done in Belgrade.

At length the Soviet Union agreed to the following solution to the conflict. The Agenda for the main Madrid Meeting was to contain as item seven: "Definition of the appropriate modalities for the holding of other meetings in conformity with all the provisions of the Chapter of the Final Act concerning the Follow-up to the Conference". A statement by the Chairman would further read: "On the occasion of the registration of item 7 of the Agenda the Chairman noted the general understanding of the Meeting that the definition in the concluding document of the appropriate modalities for the holding of other Meetings includes setting the date and place of the next Meeting similar to the present one". To Western eyes the Soviet Union's having accepted the inclusion of this statement by the Chairman in the Purple Book implied its commitment to setting the date and the place of a follow-up meeting after Madrid although the language was less forceful than the wording used in the Yellow Book for the Belgrade Meeting which stated twice that the Belgrade Meeting would "in any case" fix the date and place of the next similar meeting.

During the main Madrid Meeting the Soviet Union seemed ready to accept the principle of holding a further follow-up meeting but only on condition that simultaneously the time and place of a European disarmament conference should be fixed. This became clear at last in a Bulgarian proposal for a paragraph in the concluding document in which the same sentence mentioned both the time and place of the disarmament conference and that of the third follow-up meeting. This complied with the provision of the Purple Book quoted above but included the WP condition that agreement should first be reached on the mandate for the disarmament conference which the WP countries wanted. But it was on this mandate that West and East disagreed. The Soviet Union persisted with her strategy up till December 1981: if the NATO countries wanted a third follow-up meeting then they must pay the price of amenability on the question of the mandate for the European disarmament conference.

2.7. Consensus

During the Preparatory Meeting there were two provisions which gave rise to no difference of opinion; they became paragraph 9 and paragraph 15 of the "Organizational Framework" of the Purple Book. The first, which also formed part of the Yellow Book, reads: "The rules of procedure, the working methods and the scale of distribution for the expenses of the Conference will, *mutatis mutandis*, be applied to the Meeting". This refers to the so-called Blue Book which contained the rules of procedure for the conference's organization from 1973-75, in Helsinki, Geneva and Helsinki again, in particular to Chapter VI of this Book which is called "Rules of Procedure" and has been dealt with in the second Chapter of the present book. That Chapter has already indicated that the most important stipulation in the Blue Book was the one making a consensus indispensable for all and every decision. The provision from the Purple Book, quoted above, meant to say that all rules of procedure, including the one on consensus were to be taken over from the Blue Book.

FIGURE 5-2: The Formal Setting of the Decision-Making Process (1981)

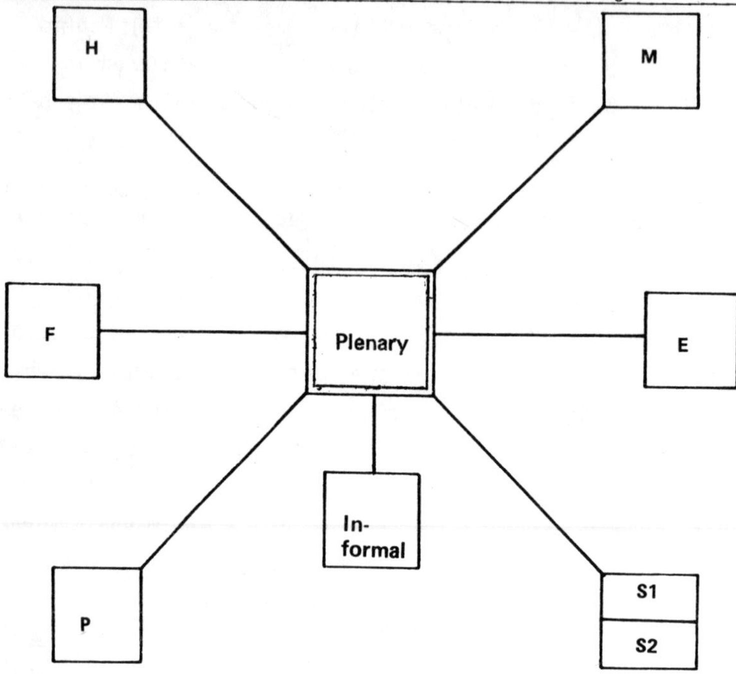

Explanation

= Subsidiary Working Body until 12/2/1981, thereafter a Drafting Group, consisting of experts from 35 delegations. Characteristics:

- chairmanship rotates at each new session
- delegations sit behind the nameboards of their countries in alphabetical order
- held in the presence of a representative of the Executive Secretary and members of his staff such as administrative secretaries and interpreters.

S (= Security), E (= Economics), M (= Mediterranean), H (= Humanitarian Co-operation) and F (= Follow-up) were set up by the Purple Book; P (= Preamble of the Draft Concluding Document) and INFORMAL (= Informal heads of delegation meeting) were set up after Easter 1981 by the Plenary. S met alternately as S1 on the Ten Principles and S2 on military affairs, with different complements of experts.

The Purple Book finally closes with paragraph 15 which could not be clearer: "Nothing in these decisions can prejudice the principle of consensus".

3. Working Methods

Just as had happened in Belgrade the Purple Book instituted some "Subsidiary Working Bodies" which were to become Drafting Groups from 12 February 1981 and were then to prepare the Madrid Concluding Document. The Purple Book also gave the Plenary the right to establish other Subsidiary Working Bodies which, after Easter 1981, it did. For the whole of 1981 the formal structure of the Madrid Meeting was as shown in Figure 5-2.

4. The Plenary

The plenaries were held in Madrid in an auditorium with rising tiers of seats in front of which was a podium on which a table was placed. The chairman sat at this table flanked by other members of his delegation on his left and the Executive Secretary on his right. The delegations occupied the auditorium seats in alphabetical order according to the French version of their countries' names. There was room for 14 or 15 people in the space allotted to each delegation, which was ample for most delegations. In the first months there were three closed plenary sessions every week, from 16 February 1981 only two, and each session normally lasted for two hours but could be longer or shorter depending on the number of speakers who had put their names down to take part. In tranquil periods this number could be quite small but at certain moments it might rise to twenty or more.

The sittings sometimes lasted longer than two hours because a delegation was using its right of reply to the full. This right could be granted at a delegation's request when all the listed speakers had finished. Its object was to allow the delegation to reply to questions, remarks or accusations which had been addressed to it. This right had been established in the Blue Book, rule (87), "During the meeting the Chairman shall keep a list of speakers and may declare it closed with the consent of the meeting. He shall, however, accord the right of reply to any Representative if a speech after he has declared the list closed makes this desirable". It was, in practice, left to the delegation itself to decide when it was "desirable" for it to exercise its right of reply and upon what grounds. In Madrid the right was not abused. It was quite often common knowledge before the session which delegation was to be addressed; this delegation would then insert its name on the speakers' list at some point after the expected speech so that it would have a good chance of making, prior to delivering its "prepared statement", at least some sort of not entirely improvised response to the critical remarks which had been made.

If it came to the point of taking up positions on an important subject or if in the course of the implementation debate the politics of another country were to be attacked or defended, the order of speakers from allied delegations often fell into one or other of two patterns corresponding to West and East. In the case of the EC countries the President of the Ten would put his name down as the first Western speaker and speak on behalf of the Ten. The US representative would take the floor after him, followed by the remaining EC delegations which associated themselves explicitly with what the President of the Ten had said and then added to it in conformity with their own national outlook. On the Eastern side it all happened in reverse order. First to take up positions or respond to Western points were non-Soviet W.P. delegations who put their names down to speak early on. After the ground had been prepared in this way came the Soviet delegation, as one of the last on the list, welcoming and agreeing with the interventions of its "comrades" and finally delivering the principle defence of their case. On many occasions it was clear that the Soviet delegation was determined to have the last word.

Statements made in the plenary sessions were prepared in advance and read out from a text. At the few open sessions the representatives spoke from a tribune on the podium; at closed sessions from their seats in the chamber. In the Plenary there was seldom question of a true debate in the sense of a direct exchange of ideas, views and opinions. First of all the list of speakers had to be got through. What at times did happen during the implementation debate was that one delegation, having been criticized by another for violations of the Final Act and having therefore put itself down to speak a little later, would then allow itself some unfriendly observations about the first speaker who would inevitably use his right of reply at the end of the sitting to return to the arena. These were interesting moments for those present, especially because in such situations the representative concerned had to show both a considerable capacity for improvisation and adequate knowledge of the subject under discussion. Sometimes the heads of delegations were able to predict such contingencies, and would see to it that their team of experts was sitting next to them. Yet the responsibility still lay with the head of delegation who had to exercise all his powers of judgement to decide how and in what tone to react.

There was always a good attendance at the plenary sessions. Speakers never had to address an empty or half-empty chamber as happens at other international conferences or in national parliaments. It is difficult to say, in a word, why this was so. In general the members of the delegations found themselves emotionally involved even when the conference had been going on for a long time and it had become possible to predict the content of speeches in the Plenary because they had been heard so often before. Everyone knew approximately what was going to be said and who would say it, but wanted to be there to hear it all the same. It was assumed that the heads of missions were always present, which was true. Formal sub-committee meetings were held at different times from the Plenaries so that all delegates would be able to attend.

5. The Subsidiary Working Bodies

As explained in Chapter II above, during the Helsinki Consultations the participants had come to the conclusion that the areas covered by the various proposals were so diverse that concrete results could only be hoped for if working groups were set up in each field. The West agreed to the setting up of the working groups because these would facilitate the inductive or "bottom-up" approach to drafting texts. In this connection the Blue Book therefore recorded the possibility of Committees and Sub-committees being formed at a later stage.

The Purple Book stipulated that for the Madrid Meeting there should be a number of "Subsidiary Working Bodies" (SWBs) which would then become known as "Drafting Groups" after 12 February 1981. Just as had been done for Belgrade in the Yellow Book, the Purple Book described five SWBs for the Madrid Meeting, each designated by a single letter:

S Subsidiary working body on: Questions relating to Security in Europe

E Subsidiary working body on: Co-operation in the Field of Economics, of Science and Technology and of the Environment

M Subsidiary working body on: Questions relating to Security and Co-operation in the Mediterranean

H Subsidiary working body on: Co-operation in Humanitarian and other Fields

F Subsidiary working body on: Follow-up to the Conference.

The task of the SWBs , which consisted of experts of the 35 delegations, was to deal with a number of agenda items at the same time as the Plenary. Among these the only one of importance was item 5, the review of implementation of the Final Act and the examination of new proposals. The period allotted for this work was the 6½ working weeks between 24 November 1980, and 12 February 1981. During this time, according to the Purple Book, the groups would be "guided in their work by the Plenary". This did not mean that in practice the Plenary passed resolutions about the work to be accomplished by the SWBs, nor that these groups reported to the Plenary on their progress.

Subsidiary Working Bodies - later on Drafting Groups - led an independent life. Their relationship with the Plenary, which was the main body of the Meeting (said the Purple Book) was carried on indirectly through the national delegations. Nearly every day the members of these delegations would report the most important events in their working groups to their heads of mission who might then advise or instruct these members on the line they ought to follow in their groups. If the head of delegation considered that crucial issues were at stake then he would make an intervention in the Plenary, in order to communicate his approval or disapproval of what was happening in the relevant working body or drafting group. But such interventions never resulted in the Plenary actually issuing directives which would be binding on the working bodies.

Although the Subsidiary Working Bodies and Drafting Groups did thus lead an independent life, yet there was a clause in the Purple Book which attached a real meaning to the Plenary's authority over them. Paragraph 8 of the "Organizational Framework" ran: "Meetings of the Plenary and the subsidiary working bodies will be held during the first six weeks according to the working programme attached to this document as an annex.

Subsequent working programmes will be adopted by the Plenary", which meant that the Plenary was to decide how many times a week any working group could meet. The group itself as such could exercise no influence here.

The importance of the organization of the working programme, or grid, as it was commonly called, was that there were tactical issues involved. If nothing particular was happening then the grid of the previous two weeks would be adopted unchanged for the following two weeks, but if for some reason the grid had to be changed then the caucuses of allied delegations (see next Chapter) would hold discussions to consider the advantages and disadvantages of the new grid. The personal viewpoints of the representatives played a part here, for example in discussions on the expected duration of the conference and whether speeding up the work of the groups would lead to an early conclusion, and also whether such an acceleration was about to be used by the opposing side as a means of applying pressure.

In addition, the time available had to be apportioned between the various subsidiary groups, account being taken of the facilities available, which implied establishing an order of priority. From the grid which was laid down in the Purple Book for the four weeks before the Christmas recess,* it can be seen that the group dealing with the first basket was allowed to meet six times a week, the two groups concerned with the second and third baskets each five times a week, and that the two working groups on the Mediterranean and the Follow-up were to share five meetings over three weeks.

In Geneva and Belgrade the Austrian, Finnish, Swedish and Swiss delegations had held the prerogative for drafting a scheme for the grid. In Madrid it was the Swiss delegation alone which provided the draft for a new grid which was then discussed in the various caucuses of allied delegations. After that, the authors of the draft would have a meeting with two Western and two East European representatives in order to try to come to an agreement. These negotiations involved constant reference back to the caucuses. An agreement reached by this procedure would then be announced in the Plenary by the Swiss representative after which the chairman would formally invite the delegations to voice any objections against the proposed working programme.

---

* see Annex no. 3

SWB meetings normally lasted for 2 hours, sometimes running to 2½, but seldom longer. The delegations sat with their country's name displayed before them round a large oval table which had room for two members from each delegation, thus seating seventy people, with an extra two for the chairman and a representative of the Executive Secretary. Extra members of a delegation could be accommodated in a second and third row of chairs behind the front row. The size of the national delegations differed according to the delegation and the basket under consideration. For the third basket, for example, the Soviet delegation officially consisted of seven members and the United States of four, while from countries such as Iceland, Liechtenstein, Malta, Monaco and San Marino there were sometimes no delegates present at all.

Representatives spoke from their places and what they said was interpreted simultaneously into the five other official languages which could then be heard through earphones. Whoever wanted to speak put his name down on the chairman's list of speakers (as was the case in the Plenary), choosing his position on the list himself according to whatever reason weighed most with him: delegates who had an important point to make usually wanted to speak early on, thus leaving time for friendly delegations to lend them support later, but it was sometimes thought better to let the opposing party begin so as to be able to react to its arguments. In any case the important factor for choosing a place on the list was how the meeting was expected to run. If there was any time left when the speakers' list had been exhausted, those who wished to speak could raise their hands. It was during this final period of the meeting that real discussions sometimes occurred, with direct exchanges of opinion and immediate reactions to remarks from the other side. During the review of implementation and examination of new proposals, the first part of the "discussion" consisted only of long monologues which were nonetheless not invariably tedious.

The SWBs were instructed by the Purple Book to deal with all aspects of item 5 of the Agenda and, more precisely, to spend the first four weeks on the review of implementation, and later 2½ weeks on examining new proposals. They were also the object of two more directives: (1) The Purple Book stipulated that work on item 5 of the Agenda would be "carried out on the basis of a balanced and adequate allocation of time". This implied that more or less the same amount of time was to be spent on each of the different parts of each basket and yet this period was always to be adequate for a careful treatment of the subject in hand. This meant, for example, that East European delegations were not allowed to use up all the time allocated to the third basket in talking exclusively about educational and scientific co-operation, nor could Western delegations limit their discussion to "human contact" and "information" alone.

(2) The Purple Book said in addition that the SWBs would "conduct the examination of this point (5) of the Agenda in a sequential and structured way according to the Final Act". This meant that the subjects were to be treated one after the other in the order laid down in the Final Act and following a structured programme which was to be agreed on by the group itself.

As a consequence of these two directives the first meetings of the SWB dealing with security, or the first basket, were taken up by a procedural wrangle over how to share out the time between a review of the principles on one hand and a review of the military aspects of security on the other. This was not the case for the other baskets where programmes were soon agreed in informal consultation between representatives of a few delegations, and adopted under a gentleman's agreement.

6. Drafting Groups

In January and the first part of February the 87 proposals submitted provided plenty of material for discussions in the Plenary and in the Subsidiary Working Bodies. Officially, this was the period allowed for examination of the proposals. Each delegation gave a comprehensive explanation of its own proposals and commented only in general terms, if at all, on proposals from other countries. From 12 February onwards the Subsidiary Working Bodies were turned into Drafting Groups, "in order to assist the Plenary in drafting the concluding document of the Meeting", (Purple Book). As an approximation to what was actually done this phrase must certainly be taken in its most formal sense. Neither the Plenary nor these Drafting Groups ever drafted a single sentence, with the exception of DG-M.

During the drafting period allocated by the Purple Book, which was from 12 February to 5 March 1981, all that took place in the different

Drafting Groups was a second reading of the proposals, following their first reading in the SWBs. This was now organized systematically according to a specific subject, all proposals relevant to the subject in question being brought under consideration at the same time. In this way each proposal was exposed to a more concrete critique from the opposing side. It was in the Drafting Groups rather than in the SWBs that it became apparent which particular phrases out of the proposals were unacceptable to the opposite party, and which phrases could be made acceptable by changing the wording.

In brief, this was the time when the most salient problems concomitant to the proposals were brought to light. References to earlier interventions during the review of implementation could not be avoided and here again fundamental positions had to be defended. These matters of principle now appeared as it were in the guise of certain phraseologies in the proposals, and were fought for or criticized by the different parties. Considering the number of proposals and the fact that these covered so wide a field and came from so many different countries, it now seems perfectly reasonable that the time available should have been taken up by this type of intervention.

By about 5 March 1981 the Drafting Groups had fulfilled their task of giving a second reading to the proposals and the question paramount in corridors and coffee bars was how the actual drafting could best be tackled. Opinion favoured following the example of the Belgrade Meeting and setting up "contact groups" because there were practical reasons why it would have been difficult to carry out the actual drafting in the Drafting Groups themselves. In these groups, just as in the SWBs, the delegates sat round a large, oval table, seating seventy people, in alphabetical order according to their countries' names. This was an arbitrary arrangement for the alphabet can have no political significance.

7. Working Bodies Created by the Plenary

The Purple Book gave the Plenary the right to create further Subsidiary Working Bodies in addition to those mentioned above: "Other subsidiary working bodies may be set up by the Plenary to deal with specific questions". The Plenary did this in two cases and later on also took the step of abolishing all Drafting Groups and replacing them by one single group. These decisions were actuated not so much by the rule out of the Purple Book quoted above but by the feeling that exists in the CSCE that the Plenary is entitled to take whatever decision it likes provided a consensus is achieved. This was the reality which was reflected in the Purple Book when it described the Plenary as "the main body of the Meeting". At Eastertime in 1981 the Plenary lived up to its description by creating two new organs.

The first of these, the "informal Heads of Delegation Meeting" had one morning a week reserved for it. The idea originated with the West, with support from NNA countries, but was quickly accepted by the East. In the great auditorium where the heads of delegation gathered officially in the Plenary, the ambiance favoured monologues rather than business-like discussion, whereas informal meetings round an oval table, as in official sub-committees, were more conducive to direct debate on points of difficulty which had arisen in sub-committees. These meetings were to be chaired by the current Plenary chairman. Members were to be addressed informally by their names and not as "the distinguished representative of...". The object was to avoid polemic and pass from confrontation to conciliation. The result was, however, that this organ became a prolongation of the official Plenary, giving representatives the chance to discuss even more directly and more concretely substantive and procedural problems as well as new violations of the Final Act. Political reality outside the congress building frustrated conciliation and the East-West confrontation penetrated even as far as these informal gatherings.

The Plenary's creation of a new Drafting Group, DG-P, was nearer to following the letter of the Purple Book: "other subsidiary working bodies may be set up by the Plenary to deal with specific questions". The specific question was the consideration of the Preamble of the draft concluding document submitted by the NNA countries on 31 March 1981. Like the other Drafting Groups the DG-P converted itself into a "contact group", a species which will be dealt with under that heading in the following Chapter.

NOTES:

1. For the scheme of organization of the Geneva negotiations see Anatoli Kowaljow, op. cit., p. 237.

VI. THE ACTUAL SETTING OF THE DECISION-MAKING PROCESS

1. Introduction

The last Chapter described the Madrid conference in its formal setting characterized by its Subsidiary Working Bodies and Drafting Groups. Experts from 35 delegations sat round the table in alphabetical order, under a chairman taken from each delegation in turn, session by session; it was the concrete expression of the principle of equality between the participating states. But from March 1981, when negotiations on the text for a concluding document had to begin, the official Drafting Groups, although they continued to meet at the times indicated on the grid, did so with a difference. Following its opening, each meeting almost immediately closed, the members present re-arranged themselves round the table and the name-boards of the countries disappeared. Warsaw Pact and Western countries sat down opposite one another and the NNA countries took up an intermediate position round the end of the table. The latter also supplied a permanent chairman for each group, known as the "co-ordinator". These gatherings were the "contact groups" which did the work of drafting even though only the Drafting Groups themselves were officially recognized. The principle of equality had given way to political reality.

The present Chapter describes the actual setting of the decision--making process as it developed in the course of almost three years: contact groups, coffee groups, structured informal negotiations, sherry groups, mini-groups and the government-to-government approaches during the end-game. The Chapter ends with an account of the functions and operation of the most important decision-making organs throughout the conference: the caucuses of friendly delegations which sent their representatives as spokesmen to the informal gatherings. Figure 6-1 is a chart of the informal structure of the decision-making process in 1981.

2. Contact Groups

In Geneva during the second stage of the Helsinki Conference (1973-1975), there had been Committees for each basket, subdivided into sub-

Figure 6-1: The Informal Setting of the Decision-Making Process (1981)

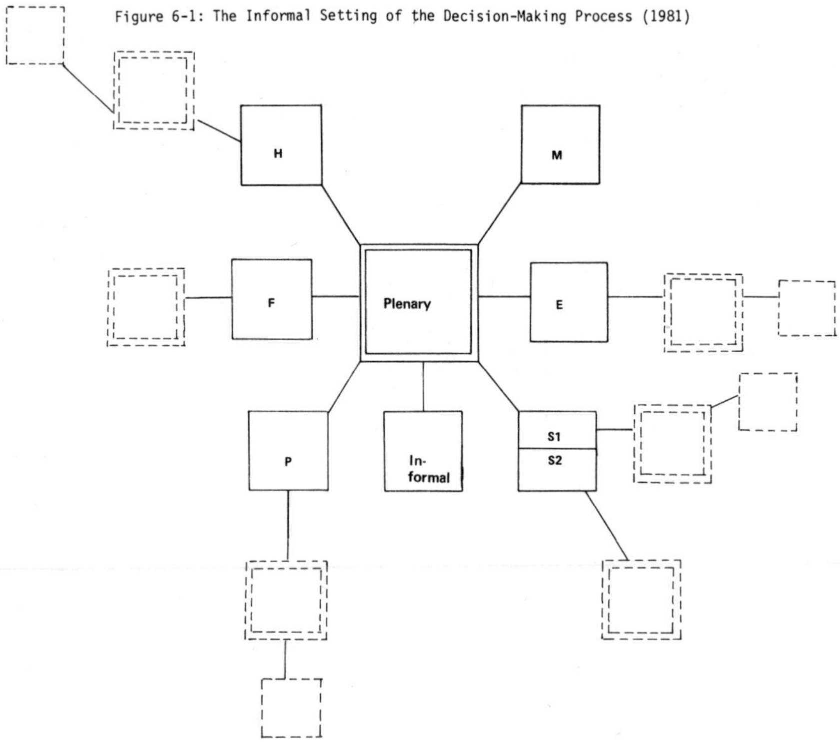

Explanation

= Official Drafting Group consisting of experts from the 35 delegations (see also Figure 5-2, page 142):
- the chairman changes with each session
- delegations sit in alphabetical order behind their country's name-boards
- representative of the Executive Secretary is present with staff such as administrative secretaries and interpreters

= Contact Group consisting of experts from the 35 delegations:
- permanently chaired by a "co-ordinator"
- seating arrangement without name-boards in political blocs opposite each other with NNA countries at the side
- no representative of the Executive Secretary present but staff such as secretaries and interpreters

= Coffee Group set up by the contact group to deal with one specific problem, consisting of experts from the most interested delegations (a few delegations from either side)
- temporary, deals with one problem
- no chairman but sometimes under the same permanent "co--ordinator" as the contact group but with more direct discussion between the relevant experts
- no representative of the Executive Secretary present and usually no staff such as secretaries and interpreters.

-committees which were in practice more important than the Committees themselves. It was in the sub-committees and especially in the mini-groups to which they gave rise, that the real work of drafting was done. Gathering together in mini-groups and other selective groups outside the formal programme of meetings was looked at askance from the beginning by the very smallest delegations who were afraid their points of view would go unheard. Although they could not prevent the proliferation of informal mini-groups, these delegations did manage to make sure that all informal gatherings should be open in character and thus accessible to everyone, just as were the formal meetings. It had been in Belgrade that "contact groups" had first come into being, but they had accomplished very little at that time because the SU was not then interested in any substantial work of drafting.

The term contact group is also current in UN jargon. Within the UN however, contact groups are groups drawn from countries which are all of one mind and negotiations take place between, for example, the contact group of the Group of 77 developing countries and the contact group of West European and other countries. In the CSCE on the other hand, contact groups have a different purpose for they create an informal bargaining place where negotiations can take place between opposed parties.

In Madrid a contact group would come into being after representatives of the various political groupings had met in the corridors and agreed that the time was ripe to find a more effective method of getting results and so to change over to informal debates in committees newly formed for the purpose. In each of the formal Drafting Groups it was the East European delegations, in particular the Soviet delegation, who first suggested changing over to negotiations in an informal context. When the representatives of the different political groups had reached agreement in the corridors, the Drafting Group's official chairman-of-the-day would announce at the end of the formal meeting that directly afterwards an informal group would reassemble, at which meeting anyone wishing to attend would be welcome.

There were some technical points of importance in which the sessions of the contact groups differed from those of the Drafting Groups. The most important of these concerned the seating arrangements. No sooner had the official Drafting Group formally risen for lack of speakers, some few minutes after it had begun, than the nameboards of the countries which had been displayed in front of each delegation were removed and the delegates proceeded to arrange themselves in a completely different way at one end of the oval table round which they had previously been sitting in official alphabetical order. The WP countries clustered round the Soviet delegate on one side of the table while the Western countries sat down on the other side next to the American delegate, the President of the Ten and other principal Western spokesmen. East and West were now face to face and there was free reference to "the other side of the table" and "delegations on this side of the table" when different political groupings were referred to. In between East and West round the end of the table, sat delegates from the NNA countries, one of whom acted as chairman of the meeting. There were some delegates who picked their seats with great care in order to express the political position of their countries: one Romanian delegate took care to sit as far as possible from his Soviet colleague while still remaining on the East European side of the table and, before Spain entered NATO there was a Spanish delegate who stuck to the Western side but inserted himself carefully between the remotest Western delegate and the NNA delegates.

The chairmanship of contact groups did not pass from one country to another as it did in the official Drafting Groups and this made the proceedings of the contact groups more effective. Each contact group, throughout its existence, worked under the same chairman or, more accurately, under the same delegation from one of the NNA countries. The contact group in Madrid dealing with the ten principles of the first basket was chaired by a member of the Finnish delegation, the group dealing with the military aspects of security by a Swedish delegate; for the second basket a member of the Yugoslavian delegation presided, for the third basket an Austrian and for the Follow-up and the contact group set up later to deal with the Preamble, a Swiss. The group on security in the Mediterranean was intended to have a member of the Holy See in the chair, but to all intents and purposes this contact group never came into being.

These chairmen were called "co-ordinators" which was supposed to indicate that they were not official chairmen as described in the rules of procedure. At the very outset, in Helsinki, the NNA countries had set themselves up as co-ordinators of informal discussion groups and they retained this role in Geneva and later in Belgrade. In Madrid the NNA countries took it on themselves to choose which of them would become co-ordinator of which group. Neither Western nor East European countries were able to exert any influence on this selection, although some of them did seriously attempt to do so. When the NNA delegations had taken a unanimous decision on sharing out the groups between themselves, a decision which had sent some of them scurrying to the telephone to get instructions from their home base, then Western and East European delegations simply had to accommodate themselves to a *fait accompli:* the member of the selected delegation sat down in the chairman's seat of the contact group without further ado and politely enquired of the remaining delegations whether they had any objections to his henceforth carrying out the role of co-ordinator.

In Madrid the role of co-ordinator did not primarily involve drafting compromise texts although some co-ordinators did attempt this. At crucial moments they might well contribute to the formulation of a text which would be generally acceptable, but so might any ordinary delegation. Their importance lay rather in the part they played when discussion turned to matters of procedure such as the question of which subjects should be dealt with at a particular session of the group. For the co-ordinator, one important question was whether to begin with important proposals, or the most important parts of a proposal, which would also be the most controversial and on which it would be hardest to reach a consensus, or to start with less controversial proposals or paragraphs of a proposal which were of much less political importance. East Europeans were always determined to take the easier proposals first so as to establish a large volume of agreed language on different subjects which could then be held up as proof of the success of the Madrid Meeting. The West fought against this because its priority was to reach agreement on a small number of proposals important to it in the area of human rights, human contacts and information: it stressed quality rather than quantity. It fell to the co-ordinator to fulfil the important task of steering a path somewhere between these two approaches so that the contact group could get on with its work. Which text should be considered? Was the best course to break off discussions for a time when a certain text seemed to offer no basis for agreement, or should the co-ordinator stimulate the discussion at all costs and propose no matter what compromise text in order to arrive at a solution? The way he tackled these situations determined his influence on the group. Sometimes, however, the best of co-ordinators must have felt considerable frustration in the face of the Western and East European delegations' inflexible attitudes and uncompromising solidity which rendered all his efforts useless.

The co-ordinator had informal contacts with the most important spokesmen on both sides of the table and was aware of the currents of opinion in each camp and in general how the land lay. Before each session he was usually informed of any important decision which had been taken recently in either camp so that he could trim his sails to the wind. A co-ordinator's influence on the course of events depended first of all on the strength of his personality. The way he went about his work in and out of session determined his acceptability to the other delegations. But ultimately whatever his ability the limiting factor was the instructions which the delegations brought with them into the deliberating chamber; these were the framework inside which he was obliged to work.

Discussion in the contact group, unlike that in the Subsidiary Working Bodies or Drafting Groups, was carried on between only a handful of representatives from East and West even though nearly all the delegations were present; each political group appointed its spokesmen and other delegations were usually disciplined enough to sit and listen without joining in, so there was a real dialogue between East and West with direct communication between one side of the table and the other. If in the face of an unforeseen situation any spokesman felt the need for new instructions from allied delegations, he would ask the co--ordinator for a coffee-break which would then be used for mutual consultations in the corners of the room. This was also sometimes the moment for a man-to-man exchange between the principal opponents from East and West: if this concerned a particular text a quick interchange of proposals could take place or it might be concluded without further delay that an impasse had been reached and there was no more to be said.

3. Coffee Groups

As the work of the contact groups progressed the conflicts involved gradually came into view more and more clearly via the sequence of written text proposals from each side. If the general understanding of a contact group was that a certain problem had been sufficiently discussed and that a solution lay, or ought to lie within the bounds of possibility, any delegate, or the co-ordinator himself could propose to call together a coffee group on this problem. The difference between a contact group and a coffee group was slight but not without importance. The contact group met directly following the end of the official Drafting Group scheduled in the grid, although this Drafting Group had itself lasted no more than a few minutes. That meant that the number of sessions of a contact group, together with their time and place, were fixed, through this link with the official Drafting Groups, according to the grid set up by the Plenary. A coffee group, in contrast, could meet whenever it liked, at the convenience of its members and without interpreters. Of even greater importance was the fact that whereas in the contact group all the delegations were present even though only a few spokesmen took part, the coffee group limited itself to the spokesmen themselves. So in the coffee groups the conversation was even more direct and when proposals for new versions of a text were bandied to and fro every attempt was made to dispense with the usual exhaustive defensive pleas because these could be taken for granted.

Once again at coffee group sessions a delegate might ask the co-ordinator for a "coffee break" and not with the intention of drinking coffee, but, as in the contact groups, in order to consult with his friends or make direct contact with his opponents in order to discover whether a solution on a controversial point might be obtained by altering a word here, or a comma or semi-colon there, in the phrase under discussion.

Coffee groups got their name from the idea that they were supposed to assemble round a table in the coffee bar. They soon grew, however, into the unofficial gatherings just described which took place in small meeting rooms for the practical reason that a noisy coffee bar is far from the ideal place for negotiations or actual drafting. What did take place in the coffee bar were *rendezvous* arranged in advance between representatives of Western, East European and Neutral delegations in order to discuss substantive or procedural matters. Most of these meetings were mainly concerned with procedural problems. In addition the coffee bar was the natural place for Eastern and Western delegates to meet each other and try out any new ideas in order to test their probable reception. There were also business lunches and dinners which afforded similar unstructured and informal opportunities for interchange of ideas and discussion of solutions to current impasses. The economists of the second basket even held regular lunch parties to discuss their problems.

4. Structured Informal Negotiations

After the 1981 summer recess the Formal Drafting Groups and thus also the informal contact groups met less frequently than in the spring of that year. During the first half of 1981 everything that the contact groups had found it possible to agree was put down on paper, comprising approximately 30 pages. Problems still remaining at that stage, however, seemed to be unsolvable. As the month of November 1981 went by, the meetings of contact groups suffered the same fate as those of the Drafting Groups: no sooner did they begin than they were brought to an end for lack of speakers. Now both the meetings together took no more than ten minutes. Discussions did sometimes take place but offered no new perspectives. It was stalemate on all sides.

In this situation some of the NNA delegations (first Finland and later Switzerland and Yugoslavia) in informal bilateral talks separately tried to find solutions for the main points of difficulty, in particular those that concerned the mandate for a disarmament conference. All attempts failed. The NNA delegations then decided to take a combined initiative to break the deadlock. They invited in turn to their private offices for consultations, a group of three from the NATO caucus and three from WP countries. Informal but structured talks like these had also taken place at critical moments in Geneva and Belgrade, with the same object which was to sketch in the furthest limits of each side's willingness to compromise in order to define what was politically feasible. On the basis of these consultations the Austrian delegation, in the first instance, produced a new draft concluding document, After talks within the NNA group this document was presented in the Plenary by all NNA delegations (with the exception of Malta) on 16 December 1981 and became document RM.39.

5. Sherry Groups

The same week in December 1981 the Plenary decided to wind up all expert Drafting Groups, including also expert contact and coffee groups, and to replace them with one single Drafting Group at the level of heads of delegation. This group was given the task of dealing with the NNA draft for the concluding document, RM.39, mentioned above. In the spring of 1982, however, the Western delegations refused to go on with negotiations on a substantive and balanced concluding document because it seemed to them that in view of the situation in Poland it would be unjustifiable to do so. They therefore kept silent in the Drafting Group, enacting what was called by East European delegations a "conspiracy of silence".

In the autumn of 1982 Western delegations were once more prepared to continue negotiations in this Group, principally so as to be able to introduce their own new proposals which they would then expound and defend. The actual negotiations on the NNA draft RM.39 of 16 December 1981 and the new Western proposals of November 1982, took place in coffee groups which now acquired the name of "sherry groups". There was no difference between these sherry groups and the coffee groups of an earlier period except that the sherry groups assembled on the initiative of one of the NNA delegations rather than by decision of a contact group, and were held at the level of heads of delegation rather than at expert level. The old contact groups themselves had become redundant, for in these groups the possibilities of discussion had been exhausted.

A chart of the informal structure as it looked in the autumn of 1982 is given in Figure 6-2.

FIGURE 6-2: The Informal Setting of the Decision-Making Process (1982)

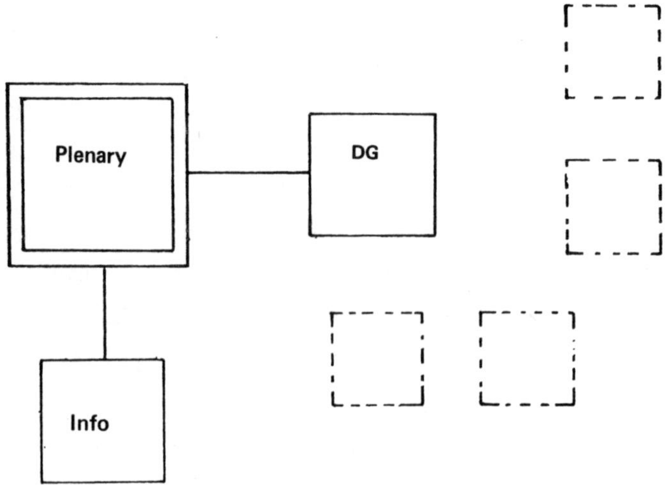

6. Mini-Groups

The sherry groups were scenes of much debate and yet only a single sentence was agreed. After the Christmas recess two political developments occurred which improved the outlook for progress in drafting. The Western countries declared that they were ready to begin serious negotiations and that they would adopt a flexible attitude where the language of their proposals was concerned although they were not willing to depart from the substantive content. This was a political decision which gave Western negotiators room for manoeuvre in an attempt to find language with which East European countries could agree. The NNA countries said they were ready once again "to act as go-between for East and West", although not for more than four or five weeks. To this end they proposed to set up mini-groups for which they would provide chairmen and which would meet at regular times. Before Christmas they had called the sherry groups together for *ad-hoc* discussions on sentences or groups of sentences. Now each chapter of the draft concluding document had its own permanent mini-group organized for it for systematic discussion of all the problems still unsettled in that chapter according to a fixed timetable. It was the same idea as that of the contact groups two years before, with the difference that now not all 35 delegations were welcome but only three from the East, three from the West and three from NNA countries.

The mini-groups reported to the Drafting Group on the progress they made. The mini-groups' grid was fixed by the Drafting Group and distributed by the Executive Secretariat which meant in fact that the official rules of procedure had been officially breached in favour of an informal setting of the decision-making process. There was a swift reaction to these events from Romania (who for reasons of principle sent a delegate to every meeting of each mini-group) and from Malta and Yugoslavia. They claimed that this formal recognition of the informal setting was too great a violation of the basic rules of the CSCE. These basic rules start indeed from the principle of sovereign equality of all the participating states and therefore imply the necessity for all meetings to be open-ended and chaired by each delegation in turn in daily rotation. These protests led to dissolution of the mini-groups, but not before the NNA delegations had seen their way to the projection of a revised RM.39 document which they wrote on the basis of the intensive discussions that had taken place in these groups. This document appeared on March 15.

The informal chart of the conference during the three weeks of operation of the mini-groups in February and March 1983 is given in Figure 6-3.

FIGURE 6-3: The Informal Setting of the Decision-Making Process (1983)

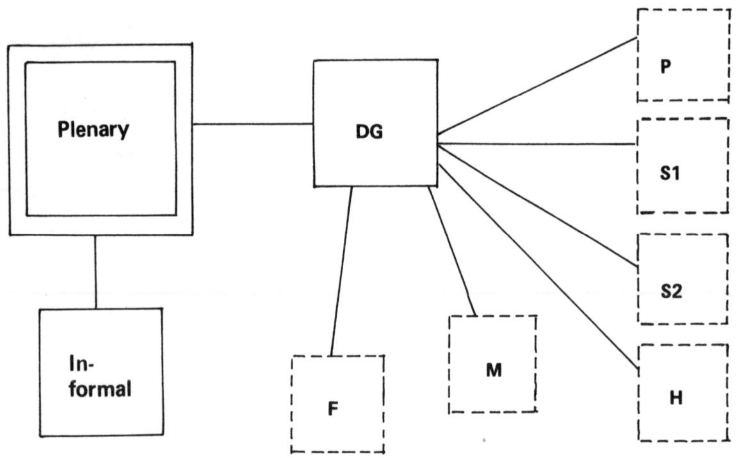

Explanation

P = mini-group dealing with the Preamble
S1 = " " " " Principles
S2 = " " " " Military aspects
H = " " " " Third Basket
M = " " " " Mediterranean
F = " " " " Follow-up

7. Government-to-Government Appeals

During the final phase of negotiations, "the end-game", which lasted three months (April-July 1983), the Madrid negotiators had little or nothing to do for weeks at a time, but in the capital cities, certain steps were taken at regular intervals. On 18 April the heads of government of six NNA countries (Austria, Cyprus, Finland, San Marino, Sweden and Yugoslavia), sent via their embassies, a personal collective letter addressed to their colleagues of the other participating states, appealing to them to take a political decision to conclude the Madrid Meeting without delay on the basis of the NNA draft of March 15, RM.39 revised. But on 3 May the Western countries proposed four more amendments to this document, involving deletion of various words and the addition of a few phrases one of which provided for the calling of an expert meeting on human contacts in Switzerland.

On 6 May the Soviet leader Yuri V. Andropov informed his 34 colleagues in a personal message that he was prepared to accept RM.39 revised, but without any changes. The implication of the Soviet message was that they rejected the amendments proposed by the West which were at the same time declared unnegotiable. Because the West continued to insist on negotiations on these amendments an impasse ensued which lasted for eight weeks. Every week five official meetings took place but for lack of speakers almost every meeting was brought to a close immediately after its opening, thus allowing the eighty or so diplomats present to return whence they came. There were no more informal meetings at all, except in the case of the linguistic experts who employed the time in comparing the various language versions of RM.39 revised (1).

On 1 June the Romanian Foreign Minister unexpectedly summoned together all the CSCE countries' ambassadors in Bucharest in order to announce that Romania, in spite of the fact that she was a Warsaw Pact member, was prepared to start negotiations on the Western amendments, a number of which she considered acceptable. In addition, the Romanian minister withdrew the Romanian amendments which had been proposed a few weeks before in Madrid but which had evoked no response whatsoever.

Far from breaking the impasse the Romanian move had the opposite effect of hardening Moscow's resolve to refuse every alteration in RM.39 revised and not even to declare any of them negotiable.

On 10 June, in Paris, the NATO Foreign Ministers at their half-yearly meeting urged the Soviet Union to change its attitude and negotiate a solution of the few remaining issues, but Moscow was not impressed.

In the end the Madrid impasse was resolved through the action of the President of the Spanish Government, Felipe Gonzales who, on 17 June, invited the 35 heads of delegation to his residence in Madrid in order to put before them a compromise which came down to acceptance of about 50 per cent of the four Western amendments. The President then left for an official visit to Washington where the "Spanish initiative" was one of the subjects of his discussions with President Reagan who was finally convinced that this was a move of great importance.

Two days later the same Spanish initiative was "noted with interest" and to all intents and purposes accepted by the European Council of the ten EC foreign ministers who happened to be meeting in Stuttgart.

A week later the Ten, followed by all the other Western countries, officially accepted the Spanish initiative in Madrid. The following day the West German Foreign Minister, Hans-Dietrich Genscher, sent a personal letter to his counterparts in Moscow and the other Warsaw Pact capitals, urging them to do the same.

The same day, 28 June, that this letter was delivered through the West German embassies in the WP capitals, an unscheduled urgent meeting of WP state leaders took place in Moscow, which lasted only a few hours and in which the chief subjects under discussion were the Geneva negotiations on INF which accounted for the major part of the discussion, and also the Madrid negotiations, in respect of which it was decided to accept the Spanish initiative. On 1 July in Madrid the Soviet delegation, with reference to these WP discussions in Moscow, informed the Plenary that the Soviet Union and her allies were, after eight weeks, at last prepared to resume negotiations "within the framework of the Spanish initiative".

The actual text that Felipe Gonzales had read to the 35 delegation leaders in his residence on 17 June, was purposely unclear on a few crucial points. The task of the negotiators in Madrid was now merely to get acceptance for the interpretation of the text most favourable to their party. This was done as informally as possible by a number of representatives of the Western, East European and NNA caucuses. The caucuses themselves met during the whole of this period in order to programme their representatives. The final moment came when both the WP caucus and the NATO caucus gave their representatives leave to approve the deletion of a certain comma in the Russian translation of the English text of the mandate for the European disarmament conference and consensus was reached on the Madrid Concluding Document (leaving aside Malta, but that is another story).

8. Caucuses

This Chapter has already referred to representatives of a caucus who carry out negotiations on behalf of the caucus. A caucus is a group of friendly delegations who work in mutual consultation. In the case of the WP, NATO and EC caucuses these consultations led to the establishment of caucus positions taken up jointly by all members of the caucus. The group formed by the NNA countries presented itself as such in the Plenary and working groups on the occasions when these countries jointly proposed a draft concluding document, but did not otherwise claim to be a caucus, insisting rather on being simply a group of individual countries. In fact the 35 individual countries of the CSCE did make up three political blocs: NATO (with the addition of Ireland known as the Western countries), WP and NNA countries. Each block had its own caucuses both at the level of heads of delegation and at the level of experts. Inside and outside these three groups other caucuses formed.

Within these political groupings the nuances of national character remained. When East European countries were charged in the Plenary with violation of the Final Act, the style of presentation differed accorded to which Western delegation was presenting the charge; similarly one East European country would put problems in a different way from another and one Neutral or Non-aligned country would be ready to compromise sooner than delegates from another NNA country. Yet although all the interventions made and the positions adopted thus bore the stamp of a national identity, it was affiliation to the particular group in question which played the decisive part.

The geo-political unity of the five *Nordic countries* found expression in the Nordic caucus of which the composition was unique in that it consisted of three NATO countries: Denmark, Iceland and Norway and two Neutrals: Finland and Sweden. The heads of mission of these countries met once a week, the chair being taken by each country in turn in alphabetical order of their names in their own languages. During their weekly discussions members of these five delegations found that their points of view on current problems showed remarkable affinity. Similarity of language (except in the case of Finland) and cultural background brought with them considerable homogeneity of outlook when it came to determining national positions although this was never expressed in Plenary or working groups as a joint Nordic view. The composition of this caucus might lead one to suppose that it would be the perfect channel of information from the EC and NATO caucuses through Norway to the NNA group and vice versa. Certainly, exchange of information about the positions of these groups did take place in this caucus, but this was not exclusive to the Nordic group. Personal contacts between Western and NNA delegates at all levels were intensive enough not to need such a specific channel, even though at some critical times the Norwegian and Danish delegates did prove to be better-informed about events in the NNA group than other Western delegates.

The *WP caucuses* comprised all seven countries of the Warsaw Pact: Bulgaria, Czechoslovakia, the German Democratic Republic, Hungary, Poland, Romania and the USSR. Their heads of mission met once a week in one of their embassies, the chair passing from one to another in alphabetic order according to their countries' names in Russian. They held further *ad hoc* meetings at this level and also at experts' level whenever problems came up on which they had to take a joint stand. These would usually take place in some corner of the congress building just before the meetings. Exactly what was discussed and decided at consultations and how decisions were reached, it is difficult for an outsider to say. The world was always shown a united front although its presentation was marked by national variations: some East European delegations had a much less conciliatory attitude to Western or Neutral proposals than others. During meetings of the contact groups it always became clear which East European delegation it was which was the chief objector. Yet their solidarity was such as to prevent any divergence in policy.

Can the solidarity shown by WP countries be compared or equated with that of Western countries? Do both reflect the same inner processes? The aim of the EC and NATO caucuses at all levels was to reach a common position by means of exchange of information, consultation and deliberation. Within the WP caucus exchange of information can scarcely have been optimal; Western delegations found that they were sometimes better informed about Soviet positions than their East European colleagues. Furthermore, Western delegates received the impression that "consultations" within WP caucuses on important matters consisted mainly of listening to the Soviet delegation's opinions, and any deliberations confined themselves to the question of how best to defend these positions.

As has already been said, the *Neutral and Non-aligned* (NNA) countries considered themselves as a grouping rather than a caucus. Their heads of delegation normally met once a week, chaired in rotation according to their countries' names. Further meetings, both at the level of heads of delegation and at the level of experts, were held *ad hoc* as the situation demanded which sometimes led to frequent meetings and sometimes not. Such *ad hoc* meetings were chaired by the delegation most involved in the subject under discussion, which usually meant the delegation which was acting as co-ordinator in the contact or mini-group on this subject. The group was extremely diverse, consisting of the four traditionally Neutral countries: Austria, Finland, Sweden and Switzerland, joined by the three European Non-aligned countries Cyprus, Yugoslavia and Malta as members of the worldwide Non-aligned movement, as well as two countries which are traditionally neither neutral nor member of the Non-aligned movement, Liechtenstein and San Marino. Monaco and the Holy See did not join this group, thereby remaining the only ones among the 35 not to participate in any caucus. The difference between the two was that Monaco was seldom represented in Madrid whereas the Holy See's delegate was always in attendance.

At crucial moments the NNA group, or at least some countries within it, took the initiative in an attempt to break a deadlock between East and West by presenting a draft document or a draft decision of the Plenary. This would serve as a compromise, or, more precisely a formulation of what was politically possible, given the positions taken up by Western and WP countries. These efforts involved repeated rounds of discussion at NNA meetings because of the great variety of their own national positions which none of the NNA delegations were entitled to disregard in view of the instructions they had received from their own capital cities. NNA countries have little in common apart from the fact that they belong to no alliance; the political positions and cultural backgrounds of, say, Sweden and Cyprus, or Switzerland and Yugoslavia, are poles apart. Yet joint documents appeared nonetheless although they were not always sponsored by all the NNA countries.

The *EC countries* formed the most closely-knit bloc which consisted of Belgium, Denmark, France, the Federal Republic of Germany, Greece (after 1 January 1981), Ireland, Italy, Luxemburg, the Netherlands and the United Kingdom. When the President of the Ten spoke in the Plenary and specifically pointed out that he was speaking as such and represented the ten member states of the EC, this was clearly a direct expression of the political determination of the Ten to strive after a common foreign policy. None of the other caucuses stressed their solidarity to the same extent. Yet each of the ten countries retained its national identity and character in its individual contributions. The ten heads of mission met regularly in their caucus three times a week for at least an hour in the offices of the delegation which was supplying the President at the time. The ten EC experts at working group level met when necessary in their caucuses to prepare either for their NATO caucus on the same level or for the actual 35-country contact group or for both. These EC expert caucuses normally met with the same frequency as their contact group, which meant in some cases every day and in others once in two weeks. At all these meetings information was exchanged, instructions compared and positions decided with respect to matters of substance and to the tactics which were to be employed during the coming day or week. When the defence of common proposals was discussed (and more for the third basket than for the others) then tasks were shared and the spokesmen would often be supplied in advance with arguments both to strengthen their position and to counteract criticism expected from the opposition. In the drafting phase in most of the EC caucuses, concrete text proposals were produced, discussed, criticized or adopted so that the spokesmen in question had plenty of material at their disposal when they started negotiations with East European delegations.

Instructions received by the EC delegations from their home capitals were first of all given a hearing in the EC caucus. At the end of this stage a common viewpoint was normally achieved, from a synthesis of the various national attitudes, and could be presented either in the NATO group or in the 35-country group itself. A delegation which, because of its instructions, found itself at loggerheads with the rest of the EC countries, was at liberty to carry on with its own point of view into negotiations with the 35 but this happened very seldom because the delegation concerned usually preferred to maintain the solidarity of the group and submit to the majority. No formal votes were taken. In some cases a delegate would give way to arguments of principle advanced by one or more colleagues but in other cases the latter in turn would be ready to adapt themselves to his opinion when it concerned a matter of special importance to him; in this way a single national delegation could find its own special position adopted as the joint EC stance.

There were various reasons why the EC caucuses at each level held intensive consultations. The chief point was that the political goal of the ten countries of the EC is to achieve a common foreign policy. Where in the second basket economic affairs within the competence of the European Commission were concerned, an obligation to co-operate followed as a direct consequence from the Treaty of Rome. The Ten together form not only a juridical but also, and primarily, a political reality, embodied in the European Political Co-operation (EPC) in the framework of which the foreign ministers as well as their director generals for political affairs meet regularly and discuss, among many other things, CSCE affairs. For these meetings the ten heads of mission in Madrid had to make a regular joint report on progress in the CSCE and received in exchange their collective instructions. This intensified the feeling of solidarity.

Another more practical reason for the intensity of consultations among EC countries was that each EC caucus had a permanent chairman for six months. The presidency of the EC at Brussels is passed on every six months and in consequence this was also what happened in every caucus of EC delegations in Madrid. The other caucuses had a rotating chairmanship so that there was a different chairman for each successive meeting. During a period of six months the EC President's national delegation felt a special duty to provide leadership and develop new ideas with regard to all important matters dealt with by the conference. It is beyond question that a permanent chairmanship favourably affects the dynamism and cohesion of a group. This is not to say that the President was the only person to speak on behalf of the Ten. Within the Ten the system of *"chef de file"* had already been instituted in the CSCE long before the Madrid Meeting began. According to this system it was arranged that for each specific subject in the Final Act a particular delegation was responsible, which therefore initiated the study of the subject in its own country, had proposals prepared and itself acted as spokesman during negotiations. The responsibilities were shared out according to the importance of the subject to any particular country: the FRG, for example, was particularly interested in Human Contacts, from the third basket (reunification of families), France in the subject of Culture from the same basket and in the Military Aspects of Security from the first basket; Human Rights, which were also in this basket were the object of special attention from the UK. In Madrid the *chef de file* system was carried through in great detail because the treatment and care of each subject or sub-subject and ultimately of each paragraph in the draft concluding document was handed over as a special responsibility to a separate EC delegation (or to one of the non-EC NATO delegations).

The *NATO caucuses* consisted of the fifteen and later sixteen member states of NATO: Belgium, Canada, Denmark, France, the Federal Republic of Germany, Greece, Iceland, Italy, Luxemburg, the Netherlands, Norway, Portugal, Spain (since 1982), Turkey, the United Kingdom and the United States. At the beginning of the preparatory talks in September 1980 Spain had already expressed her desire to be present at NATO consultations. At the level of heads of missions the NATO caucus met in normal times twice a week for discussions which usually lasted for two hours in the offices of one of the delegations. Both at the level of heads of mission and at that of experts, regular NATO caucus meetings covered essentially the same ground as the EC delegations had done in their caucuses earlier on, but normally in less detail. In the NATO caucuses it was more often a question of the overall lines of strategy or tactics to be followed and the discussion was more general. The seven non-EC members of NATO (Canada, Iceland, Norway, Portugal, Spain, Turkey and the United States) often brought in a fresh point-of-view on problems which had already been gone over extensively in the EC caucus and this new element, based on instructions from home or on personal conviction, could give the discussions a new impetus. Between the EC members and the non-EC members there was seldom any direct conflict which could not be resolved; the feeling that Western solidarity had to be maintained was too great. This solidarity resulted equally in the abandonment of some national positions so as not to spoil the show for other NATO delegations who were pushing proposals of particular interest to themselves. Not all Western proposals sponsored by some combination of Western countries enjoyed the whole-hearted support of every other Western country; a few of these proposals were even objected to on matters of principle by one or two countries; but Western solidarity restrained these countries from expressing their views openly at the negotiating table during negotiations with the other side.

More than one EC delegate found it a time-consuming effort first to take part in an EC caucus and then in a NATO caucus to discuss the same subject. Political considerations apart, an obvious practical solution would have been to combine the two caucuses into one. This was impossible, however, because there is one member of the EC who is not a member of NATO, Ireland. For internal political reasons this country refused to be present at any gathering of the NATO caucus whatsoever, although this would have been accepted by the other Western countries. This situation raised both formal and practical problems but resulted nevertheless in the EC and NATO caucuses each acquiring a distinct identity.

The *chef de file* system used by the EC countries was accepted by the NATO caucuses and extended to the effect that in the various contact groups the NATO caucuses appointed one or more spokesmen, in addition to the EC spokesmen, from the ranks of the non-EC members of NATO.

The chairmanship of NATO caucuses passed normally from country to country in successive meetings in alphabetical order according to English names. Only two NATO expert caucuses, which did not meet regularly, had permanent chairmen, namely the expert group for the Mediterranean and the one for the second basket. The rotation of the chairmanship of the other NATO caucuses did little to promote the efficiency of NATO deliberations; there was no permanent leadership, able, like the presidency of the Ten, to assume responsibility for the efficacious operation of the group. Yet, at crucial moments the NATO caucuses played a greater role than the EC caucuses. When it was necessary to hold deliberations in between times such as during coffee--breaks in the official meetings, it was the NATO caucus that met (and not the EC caucus) and important decisions were often taken at just such emergency meetings. During the last phases of the conference the final decisions were definitely taken by the NATO and not the EC caucus.

Finally, so as to complete the picture, mention must be made of a caucus which functioned only in the second basket, dealing with economic co-operation, where experts from all countries with a capitalist economic system met regularly to evolve a common policy towards socialist countries. This group of *non-state trading countries* had 21 members made up of the sixteen NATO countries plus Ireland and the four Neutral countries.

The CSCE, which consists of thirty-five individual countries, in fact consisted of the following groups:

- the five Nordic countries,
- the seven WP countries,
- the four Neutral countries,
- the seven NNA countries: the four Neutrals and the three Non-aligned countries,
- the nine: the seven NNA countries plus Liechtenstein and San Marino,
- the eight: the nine minus Malta,
- the ten members of the European Communities,
- the sixteen NATO countries,
- the seventeen Western countries: the sixteen plus Ireland,
- the twenty-one non-state trading countries: the seventeen plus the four Neutrals,
- the thirty-four: the thirty-five minus Malta.

NOTES:

1. During these eight long weeks there was time enough for a "toilettage" of the various language versions of the draft concluding document RM. 39 revised. Finishing touches were applied with greater thoroughness than had been the case in Geneva and Belgrade. Delegations who were interested gathered in informal groups to compare the Executive Secretariat's official translations of the document with the original English text on which agreement had actually been reached. The NNA delegations were able to find sufficient multilingual diplomats to supply political leaders for each group: one to deal with the translation of the English text into Russian, another for the one into French, and so on. Western delegations had the support of experts in Russian, flown in from Washington, London and Bonn. The discussions proved to be most animated on the very points which had already provoked lively exchanges during the negotiations on the English text; the English compromise texts that had been worked out contained nuances which had then proved difficult to translate satisfactorily into the other languages.

VII. THE RESULTS OF THE DECISION-MAKING PROCESS AND THEIR LIMITS

1. Introduction

Previous Chapters have considered the factors which determined the course of the decision-making process. The following ones will be devoted to a description of the results of this process looked at from the angle of precisely what influence was exerted by the rules of procedure, in particular that of consensus, on these results. It was the rule of consensus which circumscribed the outcome of the process. The present Chapter describes the manner in which this rule imposed limits on the review of implementation in Madrid. Before embarking on this we must, however, look back to the Final Act which formed the common basis for all the discussions and the point of departure for all 35 participating states in their attempts to produce a new, substantive document which would be the outcome of the Madrid conference. The Final Act itself was the result of negotiations which had continued over several years, during which period the consensus rule played a decisive role which gave the final document all the characteristics of a compromise. The analysis which is applied here to the Final Act, then serves in an analogous way, to dissect the Madrid Concluding Document.

2. Limits of the Final Act

Chapter II has already shown that the moral force of the Final Act is all the greater because this Act was approved by consensus rather than by variable majorities. On all points where the 35 countries found that their interests conflicted there is, of course, a strong flavour of political compromise. Considering that every word had to be agreed by each of 35 countries, it is remarkable that the final text contains as great a proportion of clear language as it does, particularly in the formulation of the Ten Principles.

What now follows is not meant as an authoritative exposé or analysis of the Final Act but simply attempts to discover the actual effect of the consensus rule on the substantive result of a decision-making process dominated by this rule.

When all participants have identical interests, the common cause can be readily expressed by careful drafting. A simple example of such a provision is the one in the Final Act dealing with the exchange of observers at military exercises. All parties in Geneva wanted the invitation of observers to their military exercises to be arranged as occasion arose, on a voluntary basis, so it was not hard to find a formula expressing what was an identical interest. Another example is the section in the Act dealing with improvement of the environment for here there was no opposition from any country.

However, where different interests were in conflict or partly in conflict, rather than identical, then compromise solutions had to be adopted. This meant that the text would not be ideal for any of the parties concerned but merely the best that could be achieved under the circumstances (1). In the CSCE consensus means that a text is accepted as soon as it provokes no further opposition. There are in consequence three possible results.

1) *Maximum results*. There may be a situation in which some countries attach great importance to an issue and other countries much less or none at all, but these last consider that the issue contains no threat to their own interests so that they have no objection to seeing the issue form part of the concluding document. In this case the countries heavily involved get what they want and there is a maximum result. Interests which are harmless as far as the majority is concerned but to which even a tiny minority attaches importance, are protected. Such a result can be the outcome of one party's giving way simply because it wants to accommodate the other, without demanding any favours in return, or through a package deal by which one party accedes to the wishes of another on condition that the latter is ready to make reciprocal concessions. The result is maximum in that in the final expression all the parties see their own wishes reflected, none of which is too damaging to any one party.

This was one of the factors contributing to the great length of the Final Act. In every one of its sections the maximum consequence of the consensus rule is to be found: the desires of each party, even of the smallest possible minority, had to be represented. An example of this is the entire section dealing with "Questions relating to Security and Co-operation in the Mediterranean" which was of importance to only a few and tolerated by the rest. This tendency to express a compromise solution by simply including every demand can sometimes also be found in small sections of the texts such as the one under "Meetings among Young People", which stipulates that the participating states intend to further the development of contacts and exchanges among young people by encouraging increased exchanges and contacts among "young people working, training or undergoing education ...". East European countries originally wanted this text to apply principally to young working people, to which the West had no objection but wished to extend it to other categories of young people as well. The result was a maximum compromise which leads one to wonder whether any sort of young people (except those out of work) fall outside the definition.

No harm is done here but in other cases the consequences can be more important and Valery Chalidze dubs this form of compromise "a false symmetry". The example he takes is from the section "Contacts and Regular Meetings on the Basis of Family Ties". Here the governments "confirm that the presentation of an application concerning contacts on the basis of family ties will not modify the rights and obligations of the applicant or of members of his family". This refers to the situation of citizens in some East European countries who apply for an exit visa and find that in consequence their civil rights become attenuated. In this case the compromise was between Western countries who wanted the text to speak of "rights" and East European countries who wanted to put in "obligations". Chalidze, who was an active member of the Moscow Human Rights Group prior to the disavowal of his citizenship by the Soviet Government in 1972, accuses the Western negotiators of having made too great a concession in allowing "obligations" to be added to "rights" in this context. He claims that

> "This formulation is wrong in principle and in its consequences. In any discussion of rights, it is natural to assume that the inhabitant of a country is bound to fulfil his civil obligations if nothing is stated to the contrary in an international agreement. In Helsinki, only the protection of rights was the topic of conversation. The participating states had no intention of trying to broaden the duties of citizens. ...
> The point is that "obligations" can be defined by the state and therefore used to oppress individuals" (2).

But it may be claimed that the sentence quoted means that the applicant's status may not be changed in any way, which is to say that by making his application an applicant should not incur any more obligations than rested on him in the past, and that all his rights must continue to be recognized so that consequently no vexatious measures can be taken against him.

2) *Minimum results*. At the opposite pole the combination of the negotiation process with the rule of consensus, may lead to a minimum compromise. The degree of conflict between the various interests involved is then so great and the interests themselves so mutually exclusive, that the result is minimal and varies from no text at all to one which says little or nothing. Here again one side may attach great importance to its own objectives but in this case they are so unacceptable to the other side that the result is minimal. Examples from the Final Act are more difficult to find precisely because the issues concerned are either completely absent from it or represented to a minimal degree. The two possible variations of the situation are that conflicting interests lead either (a) to no text at all, or (b) to a minimum text.

a) The most striking example of no text at all is the Concluding Document of Belgrade, 1978. All that this document says is that the parties could not agree: "Consensus was not reached on a number of proposals submitted to the Meeting". The proposals referred to numbered about ninety. As has already been said, in order to demonstrate this form of compromise in the context of the Final Act, it is necessary to look for proposals which did not ultimately appear in the Final Act, like the Western proposal for guaranteeing free access for the citizens of any country to foreign embassies in their country; or the Western proposal on "family reunification" (and thus emigration), which would have outlawed discrimination against applicants on the grounds of the country to which they wish to emigrate; or the proposal to guarantee privacy of letters.

b) Proposals which are of great importance to one party but damaging to another, can result in a minimal text which is rendered harmless by its very reticence. It is possible for an extensive draft proposal to be reduced to a single phrase in the common concluding document. An extreme example of this is the expression "free and full development" in the second paragraph of principle VII in connection with the inherent dignity of the human person. This expression is all that remains of a proposal on protection of individual freedom and prohibition of arbitrary arrest, put forward by Switzerland and rejected by the SU.

3) *Ambiguity*. Finally, a type of compromise much in evidence is the use of ambiguity, calculated vagueness or restrictions, escape clauses and loopholes. All the parties, for whatever reason, accept the inclusion of the issue in the concluding document but, in order to find a common denominator for all the different interests involved, recourse is had to constructive ambiguity, calculated vagueness or loopholes. The ambiguity and vagueness which are all too evident in the Final Act are far from exclusively the result of the incapacity of diplomats to express an issue clearly, but often spring from politic attempts to resolve opposing viewpoints. Calculated ambiguity is often helpful (3).

An example of calculated vagueness and ambiguity is the following sentence:

> The participating states note the expansion in the dissemination of information broadcast by radio, and express the hope for the continuation of this process, so as to meet the interests of mutual understanding among peoples and the aims set forth by this Conference.

In Geneva, during negotiations on the third basket, this was one of the most difficult paragraphs. Jamming of Western radio transmissions (Radio Free Europe, the Voice of America, *die Deutsche Welle* and the BBC) occurred to a lesser degree in the months of negotiation than before that time, and the intention was to express recognition of this fact in the first part of the sentence: the phrase "the expansion in the dissemination of information broadcast by radio" was finally produced by the West as a euphemism for the decrease in jamming and was accepted as such without comment by the East European countries. The words "so as to meet" cut both ways, for East European countries take them to mean "in such a way as to meet" implying that if, in their eyes, such transmissions fail to pursue what they construe as "mutual understanding", they must either be discontinued by one side or jammed by the other. The official "Polish View" on this paragraph is that: "The implementation of this provision should lead to the elimination of information slanderous to the socialist states and harmful to the idea of security and co--operation in Europe" (4). In Madrid this interpretation of the words "so as to meet" was expressly spelled out by East European representatives whereas the West insisted that, on the contrary, the provision stated that the expansion of radio transmissions was necessary "so as to meet", i.e.: in order to promote mutual understanding.

A second example of calculated vagueness is to be found at the end of the text in the Final Act on military confidence-building measures which speaks of "the importance that the participants in negotiating fora see to it that information about relevant developments, progress and results is provided on a appropriate basis to other States participating in the CSCE and, in return, the justified interest of any of those States in having their views considered". The origin of this vague provision was the conflict, dating from long before the CSCE began, between those countries which wished to establish a connection between the CSCE and the MBFR talks and those which did not. The result of the Geneva discussions on this problem was the paragraph quoted which leaves wholly unanswered the questions of precisely in what way or on what "appropriate basis" the information vaguely referred to should be made available and to which other states. In practice this has happened and happens still on a bilateral basis entirely outside the CSCE framework. But no reader would ever surmise that what is meant here are the MBFR talks. It may nevertheless be asked whether this vague passage has not acquired, or may not in the future acquire, precisely in virtue of its vagueness, an added significance which, if it had consisted solely of a specific reference to the MBFR talks, it would not have had.

Another recognized example of calculated vagueness is the word "adjoining" in the following quotation from the same section on confidence-building measures: "Notification will be given of major military manoeuvres which take place on the territory, in Europe, of any participating State as well as, if applicable, in the adjoining sea area and air space". The adjective "adjoining" was consciously chosen as a term which has no precise definition in international law and thus leaves ample room for interpretation. Nobody knew and nobody wished to know exactly what degree of proximity "adjoining" might cover. And another compromise appear in the same sentence with the expression "if applicable" the interpretation of which is left to the reader, which means of course the sovereign state concerned.

Loopholes, escape clauses and restrictions appear in the Final Act most frequently when it comes to concrete recommendations for specific measures. Then expressions such as "where necessary" or "as appropriate" appear, leaving to the reader - or sovereign state - the task of deciding when the measure in question is necessary or appropriate. Such loopholes are the work of a party which feels little inclination to meet the wishes of the opposite party and yet is ready to do so on condition that a means of escape from the recommended measure is provided. The consensus rule sees to it that the party demanding the strongest escape clause wins because it can refuse its assent under any other circumstances.

Even if the final level of commitment is quite low either because of the weakness of the verb or the vagueness of the formulation or the size of the loophole, it can still be preferable to one party to let the issue in question appear, rather than resign itself to the alternative of having no text at all. The urge to bring a certain problem to light may well be stronger than the reluctance to accept any necessary concessions in the form of vagueness or escape clauses.

For example, the West was keen to point out the fact that in some East European countries visas and other documents required for leaving the country were so expensive as to prevent many people from going abroad on either a temporary or permanent basis. In the Final Act the section in "Human Contacts" which deals with Contacts and Regular Meeting on the Basis of Family Ties reads: "They will take such steps as may be necessary to ensure that the fees for official travel documents and visas are acceptable"; the section on Reunification of Families: "They will lower where necessary the fees charged in connexion with these applications to ensure that they are at a moderate level"; and the section on Travel for Personal or Professional Reasons: "They will endeavour gradually to lower, where necessary, the fees for visas and official travel documents". Exactly when the fees may be acceptable or moderate, and in relation to whom, is left undefined and thus also when it may be necessary to lower them, while the level of commitment of the verb "to endeavour" is low. Nevertheless the problem of the prohibitive price of travel documents has been aired and is seen to exist.

Escape phrases such as the ones that have been mentioned together with "where possible", "where desirable" or "within their competence", were used by all parties whenever they felt the need. In Geneva and later in Madrid, the East European countries used, in addition, other methods to set limits on their commitment. They wanted to rob the recommendations on "Co-operation in Humanitarian and Other Fields" of their force by prefacing this whole chapter with a preamble and including mini-preambles for the sub-headings. These would make clear that co-operation depended on, national "laws and regulations" and bilateral "mutually acceptable conditions".

To have accepted the first of these conditions would have meant an explicit sanctioning by the CSCE of the national East European "laws and regulations" and created a barrier to the exercise of measures which were designed to open the way to freer movement of people, ideas and information. The second expression "under mutually acceptable conditions" was meant to establish that the provisions of the third basket did not have to be carried out automatically but were to be preceded by a bilateral mutual decision on the conditions of their enforcement. In spite of Western objections both these expressions do appear in the Final Act (the first in Principles I and X and the second in the mini-preamble to the "Human Contacts" section of the third basket), but in such a way that, to Western eyes, they cannot be interpreted in East European fashion (5).

In the Madrid Concluding Document there are no references to "mutually acceptable conditions" in spite of efforts from the East Europeans to introduce these references. References to national "laws and regulations", however, appear several times; twice as unequivocal restrictions of the actual commitment entered into. On the first occasion, paragraph (13) of the section on Principles from the first basket, in consequence of a NNA compromise text, the right "freely to establish and join trade unions" is now to "be exercised in compliance with the law of the State and in conformity with the State's obligations under international law" (see Annex 4, page 300). The West strove in vain for consensus on deletion of the extra word "and".

Laws and regulations come for the second time to the West's disadvantage in the footnote to paragraph (10) of the section on Information from the third basket. This states that "import of printed matter may be subject to local regulations which will be applied with due regard to the journalists' need for adequate working material" (see Annex 4 page 312). As in the first case, the West was prepared to concede the change resulting in the reference to "local regulations" as the price demanded by the East Europeans for acceptance of the main text. The alternative would have been total silence on these problems. It was the usual choice: a less than ideal text or no text at all.

3. Limits of the Review of Implementation

One of the results of the follow-up meeting in Madrid was the extensive review of implementation of the Final Act, an account of which is given in Chapter X. It is an unwritten rule of the CSCE that each participant has the sovereign right to bring up in the Plenary any subject which has any connection with the Final Act. Up to the very last day of the conference Western and Neutral countries continued to make frequent use of this right to draw attention to new violations of the Final Act, but there was nothing approaching dialogue between the opposite parties. East European countries maintained that Western criticism of their domestic human rights policies was illegal interference in their internal affairs. This opinion set a limit on the significance of the review of implementation. A further limit was provided by the fact that on various questions the Final Act could be interpreted in more than one way, which meant that each of the parties could choose the interpretation which suited it best.

Principle VI, "Non-intervention in internal affairs", was invoked by the West to accuse the Soviet Union of unlawful threat of intervention in Polish affairs, yet East European delegations made use of the same Principle in order to reject Western criticism of the military takeover in Poland on the grounds that this criticism itself was interference in Polish affairs. Moreover they accused the US of indulging in economic coercion, which this Principle forbids, because of the US economic boycott which was designed to influence Poland's domestic policy. Principle I: "Sovereign equality, respect for the rights inherent in sovereignty", and Principle VIII: "Equal rights and self-determination of peoples" were used by the West to demonstrate violation of the Final Act by the Soviet and Polish governments on the ground that the Polish people had been denied the right of self-determination. On the other hand, the Polish delegation cited the same Principles in order to reject Western criticism as unlawful: the Polish people had itself, in a legal and constitutional manner, determined its own fate on 13 December 1981 in perfect freedom, and decided on its domestic political status entirely in accordance with these two Principles.

These were not the only sections of the Helsinki document which lent themselves to use by each of the parties involved in order to defend its own policy or condemn that of an opponent. And yet it would be wrong to join with K.J. Holsti in regarding the Final Act as a "source of conflict" which, because of its ambiguity and differing interpretations "has, if anything, increased east-west conflict". Holsti is confusing cause with consequence (6). The ambiguity of various parts of the Final Act and the fact that those parts can be interpreted in different ways, is not the source of increased East-West tension but a reflection of it. The document is a child of its time, reflecting the existing fundamental incompatibilities between opposed political systems. It was these incompatibilities which stood in the way of simple language and unambiguous interpretation.

Once it had been signed by the 35 heads of government it did become an instrument with which to flog the opposing side. The susceptibility of important parts of the Final Act to interpretation in more than one way presented every party with the opportunity of claiming that the infringement lay not with him but with the other party. It could not be expected anyhow, that any of the 35 sovereign governments would admit that its policy was not in line with the Final Act. It is true that the Poles and the Turks did admit that the need for law and order in their lands meant that for the moment not all the Helsinki obligations could be fulfilled, but they added immediately that this was an exceptional situation which would be brought to an end as swiftly as possible. The constant ultimate aim of their policy was complete fulfilment of the Helsinki objectives (7).

None of the 35 sovereign states was inclined to indulge in self-criticism and that meant that the review of implementation could not lead to a common communiqué containing any sort of judgement on any particular land, and even less to a decision to bring sanctions to bear against such a land. The country itself would never have given agreement on such an issue and under the rule of consensus agreement from every country is a *sine qua non*.

4. Limits of the Madrid Concluding Document

It has been explained how the consensus rule set limits to the political aspirations of the 35 participating states. The Final Act reflects not what these states thought of as ideal but what was politically feasible. The same is true of the Madrid Concluding Document. This too bears every trace of the consensus rule. Each phrase is the result of political negotiation between many countries and can be no more than a compromise. The Madrid Document is clear where common interests could be identified, maximum where it deals with uncontroversial matters - even if these were of importance to only a few countries - and minimum, vague or ambiguous on controversial subjects.

The analysis which follows, based on these terms, is not intended as an authoritative analysis of the Madrid Concluding Document. As was the case in our analysis of the Final Act, a few illustrations serve to point to the three types of result consequent on the rule of consensus. The analysis is in no way a political appreciation of the document.

Identical interests, whether appearing in Western, NNA or East European proposals, were quickly identified and agreed. The proposals in question were mostly those on combatting terrorism and on co-operation between states in economic and trading affairs and in culture and education. In June 1981, only six months after negotiations began, all texts on these subjects had been provisionally agreed. The various proposals for a European disarmament conference also brought to light identical interests but for two years differences of opinion persisted on the extent of territory to which the confidence-building measures that this conference was to agree, should apply. As is generally true of the Madrid Concluding Document, the mandate ultimately agreed for the conference on "Confidence-and-Security-Building Measures and Disarmament in Europe", as this conference is now entitled, is clear-cut where interests coincided and less clear on controversial issues.

1) *Maximum results*. The very extent of the Concluding Document is one example of maximum result. All participants did their best to get their own national interests represented in the final document and the result was a maximum, 35 pages of text or, as the joke went in Madrid, "one page for each country".

From a Western point of view some of the East European proposals for the chapters on co-operation in economic, cultural and educational areas were virtually superfluous but they were also harmless enough to be included in the final document. They were therefore approved and went forward to add their contribution to the maximum Madrid result. The chapter on co-operation in the Mediterranean was another maximum solution, desired by only a few countries and tolerated by the rest.

On a smaller scale a further example of maximum outcome is to be found in the last paragraph of the section "Human Contacts" in the third basket. The paragraph is relatively long and encourages "exchange among young people". Although no-one had any major objections to intensification of contacts between young people, not all countries found this paragraph necessary. But the whole paragraph is itself a maximum compromise because it incorporates all the important elements of the four proposals on the subject. Romania, in her proposal, had wanted to "encourage and promote pan-European activities for young people" and it later transpired that "young people" meant those aged from 16 to 19. Bulgaria had wished special attention to be paid to the problems of "the rising generation" afterwards defined as those between 6 and 16. Because the two delegations found it impossible to agree on a single text to cover both age-groups the paragraph now takes a maximum form, "young people", according to the Romanian proposal, on one line, being followed by the problems of "the younger generation", reflecting the Bulgarian one, on a succeeding line (see Annex 4, page 310).

2) *Minimum results*. The most minimum result a proposal can have is not to be mentioned at all in the concluding document because the opposition was too strong. East European proposals that, on the whole, got no mention in the Madrid Concluding Document include the GDR/USSR four-page proposal on the responsibility of the mass media and journalists for disarmament, détente, mutual co-operation between states etc. (RM.28) and the Romanian two-page proposal on the responsibility of the states to prohibit war propaganda, fascism, neo-fascism, racism and chauvinism (RM/H.19). Texts of this sort were unacceptable to Western and Neutral countries because of the implied derogation of the freedom of the press.

One proposal to which some of the East European delegations persistently returned was designed to incorporate in the Madrid Concluding Document the principle of "the right to work" but this was constantly met from the West with its counter-proposal "the right to strike", which led to stalemate so that neither "principle" ultimately reached the final document.

Western proposals which were left out in the Madrid Concluding Document were those on the prohibition of interference with foreign radio broadcasts (RM.12), non-expulsion of journalists because of articles published in their newspaper (RM.12), free access of all citizens to reading rooms and cultural centres belonging to foreign embassies (RM.15) and, most important of all, freedom of expression for dissidents and Helsinki monitors. The chief Western proposal on this subject (RM.19) was entirely omitted except for the provision that the participating states "recall the right of the individual to know and act upon his rights and duties in the field of human rights and fundamental freedoms, as embodied in the Final Act, and will take the necessary action in their respective countries to effectively ensure this right" (page 299). Only careful comparison reveals the single but significant departure from the text of the Final Act, this being the addition of the words "will take the necessary action in their respective countries to effectively ensure this right". On freedom of expression for the Helsinki monitors the West had to be satisfied with the vague phrase in the Introduction to the chapter on the Principles where the participating states express their determination (page 298): "... to encourage genuine efforts to implement the Final Act".

3) *Ambiguity*. The Madrid Concluding Document is consciously ambiguous or vague where it deals with anything both important and controversial. This was the only possible way to express political compromise. Those who put forward their important but controversial proposals were willing to put up with the derogatory conditions which were the price of consent because they found it important simply to indicate the existence of the problem they were dealing with. A few examples will serve to illustrate the point.

Using calculated vagueness, for example, the NNA countries managed to construct a compromise between the Western proposal to make the Preamble roundly express the fact that around twenty Western and Neutral ministers had come to Madrid in February and March 1982 in order to discuss the situation in Poland, and the East European refusal to allow any mention of it at all. The consensus rule pre-empted the least censure of any one of the states which would have to contribute to consensus. The NNA solution was to add to the third paragraph of the Preamble which had already been agreed, where it read "Opening statements were made by all Heads of Delegations among whom were Ministers and Deputy Ministers of Foreign Affairs of a number of participating States", the sentence: "Some Ministers of Foreign Affairs addressed the Meeting also at later stages" (page 296). This has then to be read in combination with the additional words proposed by the NNA countries "at times represented at a higher level" in the third sentence of paragraph (9) of the same Preamble which finally reads: "Therefore, the participating States, at times represented at a higher level, considered it necessary to state, at various stages of the Meeting, that strict application of and respect for these principles, in all their aspects, are essential for improvement of mutual relations between the participating States" (page 297).

Few readers of the Madrid Concluding Document will immediately guess that these two sentences, read together, refer to the discussions on the situation in Poland in February and March 1982. Readers of the last sentence of the same paragraph which runs: "The necessity was also stressed that the relations of the participating States with all other States should be conducted in the spirit of these principles", will be even less likely to put two and two together and conclude that this sentence read together with the first two phrases of this paragraph represents the Western and Neutral countries' condemnation of the Soviet Union's conduct in Afghanistan.

Another less important example of conscious vagueness is the phrase defining who is to take part in the Cultural Forum to be held in Budapest in 1985. The original French proposal envisaged participation of representatives only from the world of the arts and that of letters, and not government officials. But the text now states that the Forum "will be attended by leading personalities in the field of culture" (page 313), words which leave each government free to decide who the "leading personalities" are and to identify them with government officials if it so wishes.

Constructive ambiguity can be found in the mandate for the expert meeting on human rights where it reads: "They decide to convene a meeting of experts of the participating States on questions concerning respect, in their States, for human rights and fundamental freedoms, in all their aspects, as embodied in the Final Act" (page 300). Leaving aside the fact that the last six words in themselves constitute a restriction, the ambiguity is concealed in the words "in their States". It was only by inserting these words into one of their compromise proposals that the NNA countries made it possible for the SU to approve the mandate, for the East European countries in contrast to the Western countries took the words to mean that each country would only be allowed to talk about the human rights situation in its own territory. Up to the very last minute the West did its best to get "in their states" altered to "in those states" to make it say clearly that anyone would be allowed to discuss any case of violation of human rights in whichever of "those" states it occurred.

It must not be supposed that the inclusion of these illustrative examples is meant to prove that every vagueness in the Madrid Concluding Document is calculated or every ambiguity a constructive one. The drafters sometimes missed possible interpretations of certain phrases. Moreover, in some cases, over a two-year period, many different drafters in turn may have tinkered with the same text so that an unambiguous historical interpretation is no longer possible.

Loopholes, escape clauses and restrictions were always introduced at the positive wish of one or more delegations impelled by the urge to procure for themselves a possible means of withdrawal from their commitments in the future. The following text gives an extreme example:

> They also reaffirm their willingness to take, within their competence, reasonable steps, including necessary security measures, when appropriate, to ensure satisfactory conditions for activities within the framework of mutual co-operation on their territory, such as sporting and cultural events, in which citizens of other participating States take part (page 310).

This resulted from the proposal from Hungary and Poland (RM/H.13), to ensure personal security for citizens from their countries who were in other countries as members of sporting or cultural groups. Western countries could not have accepted this proposal without the qualifications "within their competence", "reasonable", "necessary", "when appropriate" and "within the framework of mutual co-operation", but Hungary and Poland considered it so important simply to draw attention to the problem that they were prepared to accept the necessary loopholes.

Clear examples of loopholes only occur on a few occasions in the section on the "Principles". Two of these, procured by the West, concern the word "appropriate" which occurs twice in the first two paragraphs (page 298). In paragraph (10) on religious freedom, the word "necessary" comes twice and there are two references to the constitutional framework within which religious faiths must work, which mean that this paragraph does not apply to religious faiths not recognized by the government of the country in question (page 299/300). In all these cases the restriction has been applied wherever action is demanded.

Various kinds of escape clauses come in the chapters on Economic and Human Co-operation much more frequently than in the section of Principles. These chapters contain continual demands for actions, and expressions like "where necessary", "in case of need", "as appropriate", "as a rule" and "where possible" are the opposition's response. It is a matter for some amazement that there should be any passages at all in the Madrid Concluding Document that are without loopholes.

NOTES:

1. Edward McWhinney calls the Final Act an example of "the all too frequent sloppiness and repetitiveness and looseness and imprecision of language" of a general détente agreement. He attributes this not only to the fact that the parties to the Act were numerous but also and largely to the fact that "too many" of the negotiators were not professionals but "skilful amateurs doubling in too many highly specialized technical fields at the one time or even passengers along for the ride". He thereby fails to see that the shortcomings of the Helsinki Act to which he refers proceed more from necessary political compromise than from amateurism. The negotiations by "amateurs" in Geneva were closely monitored by experts in capital cities. Edward McWhinney, *The International Law of Détente, Arms Control, European Security, and East-West Co-operation*, (Alphen a/d Rijn: Sythoff & Noordhoff International Publishers BV, 1978), pp. 183-184.

2. Valery Chalidze, "The Humanitarian Provisions of the Helsinki Accord: A Critique of Their Significance", *Vanderbilt Journal of Transnational Law*, vol. 13, nos. 2-3, Spring-Summer 1980, pp. 438-439.

3. Cf. I. William Zartman and Maureen R. Berman, *op. cit.*, pp. 123 and 182-183. See also Barry Buzan, *op. cit.*, p. 345.

4. Marian Dobrosielski, "The Conference on Security and Co-operation in Europe; Its Origins-Development-Meaning", Polish Institute of International Affairs, *Conference on Security and Co-operation in Europe: A Polish View* (Warsaw: PWN-Polish Scientific Publishers, 1976), p. 55.

5. For the East European interpretation, see *Ibid.*, p. 54 and Jerzy M. Nowak, "All-European Co-operation in the Field of Culture, Education and Human Contacts", *Ibid.*, p. 208.

6. K.J. Holsti, "Bargaining Theory and Diplomatic Reality: the CSCE Negotiations", *Review of International Studies*, 1982, no. 8. pp. 167 ff.

7. Hungary alone among the WP countries admits to being not yet able to fulfil all provisions of the Final Act. For her the Final Act is an objective towards which she is working but which she adknowledges to be, for the moment, unattainable without risk to the internal stability and integrity of the state.

VIII. THE DECISION-MAKING PROCESS: PROCEDURE AS ISSUE

1. Introduction

In previous Chapters the factors influencing the decision-making process have been set out, namely the rules of procedure, agenda and other modalities, the participants and their objectives, the formal and informal decision-making organs as well as the limits imposed on the process by the most important rules of procedure. The Chapters that follow will be devoted to the process itself. The present Chapter discusses the consequences of the application of the most important rules of procedure to decisions of a procedural nature. For this purpose three debates on procedural points will be described in detail, debates at which tension reached a high level, thereby reflecting East-West relations outside the congress building: first of all the night of the stopped clock, then the day when the Polish chairman refused to let a number of Western and NNA foreign ministers speak and, thirdly, the night of silences.

Rules of procedure are normally susceptible of more than one interpretation and it is therefore generally not difficult to make use of them for political ends. The consensus rule particularly lends itself to political use because it confers the power of veto on every participant. There is no doubt that at critical moments the consensus rule actively influenced the development of events, as will be demonstrated later on in this Chapter, but whether the actual result of the process would have been different if a different rule had been in force remains an open question. The same question is raised by the other rule out of the Blue Book which was of great importance during the three debates, the rule which laid down that the chairmanship should be rotated daily according to alphabetical order. The conduct of the chairmen during the Plenary sessions in question, all three of whom happened to belong to WP countries, was strongly criticized by Western and NNA delegations. The chairmen certainly did attempt to bend the course of events in their own direction but whether the actual result of the discussions would have been other if there had been different chairmen, is another question.

In the last part of the Chapter, these questions will be discussed further.

2. 11 November 1980: The Stopped Clock

The date for the opening of the main Madrid Meeting had already been decided in 1978, in Belgrade, as 11 November 1980 and to this the Soviet Union had agreed, even if reluctantly. Yet during the preparatory Meeting in Madrid the Soviet delegation claimed to have no interest at all in the main Meeting's taking place or at least to set little store by it. This was a ploy by which the Soviet delegation tried to get the Western countries to give in to its demands on the agenda and timetable. What happened was that throughout October the East European delegations refused to begin serious negotiations on the outstanding problems concerning the agenda and timetable. The message seemed to be that if the West wanted the main Meeting to take place then that would make the West the *demandeur* and therefore the West would have to pay a price because otherwise the East Europeans would see to it that no main Madrid Meeting took place at all. The price they asked was the adoption of their East European proposals for the agenda. Whether this was a bluff or if those countries were truly interested or not in the Meeting were questions which could not be answered at that time. On the assumption that it was indeed a bluff the West called it by a simple procedural move. This move was designed to force the Soviet Union and her allies to show their colours: did they want to fulfil the Belgrade agreement to open the Madrid Meeting 1980 on 11 November, or not? In order to get an answer to this question the NATO countries decide to abandon the fiction of the stopped clock during the evening of 11 November so as to allow the Spanish government the opportunity of opening the main Meeting that same day.

The clock had been stopped at the end of the previous day, Monday 10 November, by joint decision of the 35 participants of the Preparatory Committee, to enable them to continue the work which was supposed to be completed before the 11th. The Hungarian representative was in the chair. All the clocks in the congress building were stopped at 11.56 p.m. The sitting rose four hours after midnight to be resumed later that day as if it were still a few minutes to midnight on the previous day. During the night some delegations from Neutral countries had circulated a new compromise text of the agenda and timetable and the Spanish Foreign Minister had had conversations with the US, Luxemburg, Netherlands and Soviet delegations exploring every possibility of agreement. Still the Soviet delegation showed no inclination to budge and the head of the American delegation told the press that prospects were bleak. Western delegates rang their wives to say they would soon be home. After the NATO countries had decided on 11 November to give up the make-believe of the stopped clock (at the same time pushing forward consultations with the other delegations in the corridors) the Netherlands representative declared in the Preparatory Committee that he no longer wished to associate himself with the temporary consensus which had created the stopped clock, so that according to his watch it was now 7.15 p.m. on Tuesday 11 November 1980.

There was at once a violent reaction from the Soviet side. The Soviet representative claimed that because a consensus had been necessary for stopping the clock there would also have to be one if the clock was to be started again but this time the Soviet representative would refuse to agree. He also took the Netherlands' intervention as a vote of no--confidence in the Hungarian chairman who, if the clock were re-started, would have to make way for his successor, the Irish representative, whose turn came on 11 November. This, the Soviet delegate felt, was an insult to the Hungarian, who had chaired the meeting with admirable objectivity.

An obvious consequence of abandoning the stopped clock was indeed that the Irisch representative would take over the chairmanship from his predecessor, but at that time NATO countries had not the least notion of bringing discredit on the Hungarian chairmanship. However, the chairman adopted the thesis of his Soviet colleague and found that there was no consensus for bringing the stopped clock fiction to an end. Western delegates retorted that a consensus for this was not necessary because the stopped clock consensus had been for only a temporary stoppage and it was expressly on this condition that they had joined it. A confused debate followed on the question of when a consensus was definitive and when not. The confusion was increased when the Maltese representative asked the chairman for a "coffee-break" which would provide an interval and give the delegations the opportunity to get together for mutual consultations and perhaps arrive at a solution. The chairman replied that a consensus would also be needed for the coffee-break and asked if everyone felt he could agree to a coffee-break.

Although it is true that, as for any other decision, a consensus is required for a coffee-break, the chairman and delegations normally allow a coffee-break whenever it is demanded. In this case Western delegates said they had no objections provided that after the break the Irish representative took over the chair. The East Europeans also had no objection but only on condition the Hungarian representative resumed the chair. To the irritation of the Western delegates the chairman now continued the debate and showed no inclination to adjourn for a coffee--break in spite of repeated requests to this effect from Malta, supported by Spain. The situation was saved in the end by the Spanish Foreign Minister who had arrived meanwhile. He informed the Committee that he held the mandate of the CSCE's Belgrade Meeting to open the Madrid Meeting on 11 November 1980 and would therefore be delighted if all the representatives present would come to the auditorium of the congress building in an hour's time in order to be present at the inauguration. The Hungarian chairman then finally adjourned the session.

The Spanish Foreign Minister officially opened the Madrid Meeting at twenty minutes to midnight on 11 November. He announced that at 12 p.m. a working group of experts under Spanish chairmanship would start to push forward discussions on the agenda for the Meeting and that the next plenary session would begin at 11 a.m. on the following morning. After that he brought the inaugural meeting to a close, amid derisive laughter from the press gallery (*"por el ridículo del acto"*, [because the scene was so ridiculous], as one serious Spanish newspaper commented the next morning). Journalists in their hundreds from the press, radio and television had waited throughout the length of the day to witness this grand gathering of 35 countries and the whole meeting eventually lasted no more than three full minutes.

Over the two preceding days, of course, many informal negotiations had taken place in between the official sessions of the Preparatory Committee. The NATO and WP caucuses were almost continuously in session discussing the most recent compromise proposals. Each had settled down in a separate part of the congress building and had sent out "messengers", making use of the Swiss delegate as go-between. He was himself in contact with his own group of Neutral and Non-aligned countries. Throughout the day itself the Spanish delegation had devoted its energy to trying to discover how to get the inaugural plenary session under way on that same day in spite of all the obstacles. Western countries naturally had no objection to a brief official opening ceremony; the East European countries finally agreed to it on condition that the Preparatory Committee would operate again, later, as a conference working body on the conference's agenda. Only a few days after the formal inauguration a consensus on the agenda was achieved. The compromise proposal, later known as the Purple Book, was worked out jointly by the NNA countries and presented by Sweden. In order to underline the importance of this final attempt at compromise, the Foreign Ministers of Austria, Cyprus, San Marino, Sweden and Yugoslavia and the Prince of Liechtenstein came to Madrid and took an active part in its defence. To the surprise of Western delegations, the Soviet delegation, which usually claimed to have to refer back to Moscow at length for instructions in such important matters, was now able to give its consent to the proposal with very little delay.

3. 9 February 1982: The Polish Chairman

In accordance with the rule of alphabetical order, that is, by pure chance, the chairman of the first plenary session after the Christmas recess 1981 on 9 February 1982 was the Polish delegation. This had long been foreseen; the Netherlands had chaired the last session before the recess and, in French, *Pologne* follows *Pays-Bas*. During the recess the Foreign Ministers of the NATO and EC countries had published communiqués declaring their intention of coming to Madrid during the week of 9 February in order to express their concern about developments in Poland following the military takeover. Ministers from Neutral countries were ready to follow their example. Yet in the afternoon of 9 February the Polish chairman was able to prevent thirteen representatives from speaking in spite of the fact that their names were on the speakers' list and these included the Foreign Ministers of seven countries. Their journeys to Madrid were thus rendered fruitless.

During the preceding nights and days there had already been procedural squabbles on another point, the order of speakers on the speakers' list. Negotiations on this question were carried on between the outgoing chairman, a member of the Dutch delegation, and the current chairman, member of the Polish delegation. At the same time each of them was also representing his own caucus. In these negotiations two clauses from the Blue Book were invoked: rule (87), which for various reasons will be quoted again several times, says, in part: "During the meeting the Chairman shall keep a list of speakers...". On the basis of this rule the Polish delegate insisted that he, as current chairman, was bound to keep the list of speakers up to date. According to him this meant that only speakers who had given their names to him during the Christmas recess (these happened to be from exclusively WP delegations with Poland itself first on the list) or did so now, would be given the floor during the session under his chairmanship. This implied that on 9 February all the East European delegations would be able to speak first, before a single Western minister got the chance.

Western delegations invoked a different rule from the Blue Book: rule (70) which reads under (c): "In the interval between meetings of the Conference, the functions of the Chair shall be exercised by that Minister of Foreign Affairs who presided over the immediate preceding meeting of the Conference". So in Western eyes it was the Netherlands representative who by virtue of having been the last chairman before the recess in December should still continue to exercise his chairmanship until the Polish representative took over from him on 9 February. This meant that the speakers' list kept by the Netherlands ought to take precedence over the Polish one. First on the Dutch list was the name of Canada who in the first few days of January had applied to the Netherlands Embassy in Madrid, and it was followed by various other Western delegations who had added their names during the past weeks.

Both WP and NATO caucuses at length decided not to make this conflict a matter of principle. The negotiators were empowered to combine the two lists into one. The West agreed to the WP demand that the first speaker should be from an East European country (which turned out to be Hungary) which would be followed by Canada and then Belgium representing the ten EC countries. Another East European delegation would come next and then the US and so on according to a pattern which could be described as normal (see Chapter V). In normal political circumstances the problem of who would be first speaker at a session and who would occupy the next few places would not have given rise to any difficulty. But the WP countries, irritated by the NATO and EC communiqués announcing the Western ministers' intention of coming to

Madrid in order to speak on Poland, now set great store on an East European's being at the head of the list of speakers. His speech would not, of course, make any mention of events in Poland but refer only to the necessity for promoting détente and international peace. It was to attain this end that rule (87) was invoked.

The West took this as a sign that the Polish chairman intended, just as they had thought, to misuse procedures in order to hinder the course of the debate on 9 February. During the Christmas recess Western experts had given much thought to the question of which procedural rules the chairman might be going to use on 9 February to stop the Western ministers speaking on Poland and had discovered many ways in which this might be done although they did not in fact tumble to the method the Polish chairman eventually chose to adopt. It was thus with considerable distrust that the Dutch negotiators met the Polish delegation, especially as the Polish Deputy Foreign Minister had declared in loose terms to the press, first in Warsaw and then when he arrived in Madrid, that, as chairman he would not tolerate any imputations against Poland. This deepened Western suspicions so that during negotiations on the Polish speakers' list the NATO caucus wanted to have some guarantee that all the speakers on the list would get the chance to speak; provided there was this guarantee the order of speakers became less important. But on the eve of the ninth the Polish delegation leader would guarantee nothing. He told the Dutch delegate that at the end of the morning he would ask the meeting whether the session should be continued or not. This question would be put to the meeting even if the list of speakers should not be exhausted. As an "objective chairman and instrument of the Conference" he would follow the wishes of the Plenary but could guarantee nothing about the attitudes that might be taken up by his political friends in the WP. Western delegates and the ministers present had thus been warned, but they saw no means of altering the line of action which the Polish delegation leader had in all fairness explained to them.

So it fell out. Eight speakers took their turn in the morning and there were thirteen still to come when, at the beginning of the afternoon, the chairman made the following proposal. As chairman of the Plenary he was, he claimed - and this was a claim he was to repeat many times later on - no more than an institution of the Conference, bound as such to implement earlier decisions by the participants. On 14 November 1980, the working group of the Plenary which had been set up to produce the agenda and time-table for the Madrid Meeting, had decided, as could be seen from Journal 4 of that day, that the Meeting's working hours would be from 10.30 hours to 13.00 hours and from 16.00 hours to 18.30 hours. Furthermore, the Plenary of 18 December 1981 had approved a grid which envisaged a morning session of the Plenary on 9 February 1982 but no afternoon sitting on the same day. As it was already past 13.00 hours, continued the chairman, the morning session could be taken as having ended unless there was a consensus to reverse both the earlier decisions. Was there such a consensus to enable the session to continue? This was the chairman's question.

It was clear that there would be no consensus to continue the session because the WP countries would refuse to join in. First to react was the Austrian representative, a veteran of CSCE procedure. He said that he was aware of the Journal 4 decision but that normal practice had always been to disregard the time limits when the list of speakers was still not exhausted, a practice based on rule (87) of the Blue Book which said: "During the meeting the Chairman shall keep a list of speakers and may declare it closed with the consent of the meeting". It followed from this that a consensus was necessary to close the list of speakers and *end* the meeting whereas to *continue* the meeting, which was to say to maintain it in progress, required no consensus. Thereupon began a debate which lasted for five hours and which was described to the press by the Spanish Foreign Minister, who left in disillusion after a few hours, as Kafka-esque. It was in fact more confused than Kafka-esque and is summarized here schematically because a chronological account might well give the impression of being lifted from a Kafka novel.

The WP delegations insisted that the chairman was right: there had to be a consensus if the morning session was to continue and as far as they were concerned there was no consensus. The grid of 18 December 1981 provided only for a morning session of the Plenary. Journal 4 of 14 November 1980 laid down that a morning session had to end at 13.00 hours. A clear distinction was to be made between morning and evening sessions because rule (70 b) of the Blue Book says: "If the Conference should meet both in the morning and in the afternoon, the two meetings shall be regarded as constituting two distinct meetings". In order to call a new meeting for the afternoon there would have to be another consensus. All the rules of procedure quoted above were "standing orders" and, the Polish chairman said, "it is well-known that in British law, on which the CSCE's rules of procedure are based, standing orders can only be suspended by consensus".

Western and NNA delegations continued to assert that the morning session was still in progress because there had been as yet no consensus to close it. The grid of 18 December 1982 had fixed a time for the session to begin but not the moment of its ending. Journal 4 of 14 November 1980 contained a decision of a working group which had never been confirmed by the Plenary and which was not part of the Purple Book which the Plenary had approved. This decision on the part of a working group of a Follow-up Meeting was in any case subordinate to the June 1973 Helsinki decisions which approved the Blue Book. The latter required that a meeting should be closed only by consensus, for rule (87), already quoted earlier by the Austrian representative, stipulated that the list of speakers could only be declared closed by the chairman with the consent of the meeting. Normal practice, based on this rule, had always been therefore that anyone who had put himself down on the speakers' list or still wished to do so would be granted the right to speak by the chairman. Never before in the history of the CSCE had a representative whose name appeared on the speakers' list had his right to speak refused by the meeting's chairman. Was this an attempt on the part of the Polish chairman to impose Polish martial law on the CSCE? The Norwegian Foreign Minister concluded, with emotion: "If you believe that you can stop people from the free West using their right to speak, you are mistaken, sir!". This brought a spontaneous round of applause from Western and NNA delegates, the first time such a thing had happened in the CSCE's history.

The reaction of the Soviet side and the Polish chairman was to declare that the "normal practice" referred to by the NNA and Western countries had been a deviation from the rules, based on a silent consensus, a consensus which did not exist in this case. Consensus was necessary for departing from fixed procedures, not for their application. Rule (87) from the Blue Book did not say that consensus was necessary for the closure of a meeting. This rule said: "During the meeting the Chairman shall keep a list of speakers..." but said nothing about the duration of the meeting and this duration was established only by Journal 4 which said the meeting had to end at 13.00 hours.

Gradually the discussion worked round to another point. Western and Neutral delegates pressed the chairman to put certain questions to the meeting. The most important of these was: "is there consensus to close the session?" Before complying with this request the chairman granted the right to speak to other delegations who had requested it. To do this was, from a procedural point of view, contestable, for "points of order" (the discussion consisted entirely of points of order) are supposed to be taken one by one, no new point being started before the previous one has been completed. And yet the chairman allowed other delegations to speak first if they so wished. This gave East European delegations the chance to remark that the question which the chairman had been asked to put was out of order because the meeting had to be closed in the very absence of a consensus for it to continue. The chairman was then able to declare that a lack of consensus was manifested that he put the question ("is there a consensus to close the session?") before the meeting. Here the chairman drew criticism from Western and Neutral countries because his conduct made the fulfilment of his duty contingent on whether there was opposition to it.

Another question which Western and Neutral countries repeatedly urged the chairman to put to the meeting was of a purely political nature and asked whether there was any objection to the French Foreign Minister's (he was next on the list to speak) and the other Foreign Ministers' speaking to the substance on that day. In the end the chairman found that he was obliged to follow the advice of the Executive Secretary to comply with this request. As soon as he had finally put this question to the meeting, several East European delegates raised their hands to show their opposition to the French Foreign Minister and the other listed speakers' speaking to the substance that day. This was a political point for the West. However, two East European representatives immediately asked for the floor in order to contend that the question should never have been put to the meeting because it was not a legitimate one and could therefore never have obtained the consent of the meeting. The Maltese representative pointed out, furthermore, that the question had been improper because it did not lie within the power of the Plenary to decide whether a country's representative could speak or not: it was already his given right.

In a coffee-break, later on, the NATO caucus decide to finish with the debate, which appeared to be leading nowhere. There was no point in going on. But it was emphasized that the end should come according to the Western interpretation of the rules of procedure: the Western countries announced that they were ready to give their consent to closing the meeting, whereupon the consensus to do so was complete.

The epilogue to the discussions should not be forgotten. A day later, the Polish delegate gave a political defence of his conduct as chairman. He asked who had been responsible for his being obliged to apply the rules of procedure in such a severe fashion. His answer was that it had been the NATO countries. His delegation had not come to Madrid to listen to prepared speeches and ready-made accusations which were damaging not only to Poland but also to the Madrid Meeting and the whole CSCE process because they made dialogue impossible. He spoke of the "NATO scenario" which he described as having been detected long before, but which had failed. The intention had been to turn the Madrid Meeting unilaterally into a branch of NATO, but NATO had disregarded the fact that Poland herself was a full participant in the CSCE. The Polish delegation had therefore been driven to pay strict attention to the rules of procedure. This statement from the Polish delegation astonished Western and NNA delegations. The Polish delegation's application of the rules of procedure had been not strict but unjust. Moreover, in his declaration the Polish delegate had admitted to having used the procedures solely as means to a political end, the overtoppling of what he liked to call the "NATO scenario".

4. 5 March 1982: The Night of Silences

In the weeks that followed this procedural debate of the 9th of February, efforts were made to make it clear to the Soviet Union and Poland that the West was not ready to carry on "business as usual" as long as repression continued in Poland. After 9 February Western delegations refused to go on with work on the Concluding Document on the grounds that it would be a mockery to sign a document which contained commitments on the promotion of détente, the refraining from threats of violence, the furthering of international human contacts, the free exchange of information and, for example, greater freedom of movement for foreign journalists, when at the identical moment these very principles were being violated in Poland. Therefore, in the Drafting

Group which was supposed to finalize the Concluding Document the Western delegations remained silent, to the irritation of the WP countries who accused them of "a conspiracy of silence". WP countries wanted to get on with the Concluding Document in order to show the world, or at least their own home public, that, in spite of events in Poland, the West was prepared to carry on with negotiations.

This the West was not prepared to do and the NATO caucus decided to use every possible means to force the WP countries to agree to a long summer recess, in the hope that autumn would bring a better political climate. In place of the "conspiracy of silence" in the Drafting Group, the more logical course was chosen of refusing to approve any work programme which included a meeting of this group. The Soviet delegation would certainly press for a work programme with two or more Drafting Group meetings and was not in favour of a long recess: "We did not come to Madrid to listen to indictments of Poland and then be sent home again for months on end", was the Soviet reasoning, "we came here to do business in the Drafting Group". The NATO caucus knew therefore that its refusal to approve a grid including any meetings of the Drafting Group would lead at the very least to an extended procedural debate.

The NATO caucus had considered what the consequences would be if by the end of the last day of the week, 5 March, no agreement had been reached on the programme of work for the following week. Would it mean the end of the Madrid Meeting? The answer was: no. The Madrid Meeting had been set up by consensus in Belgrade and could only be terminated by another consensus. Without this the conference would go on for ever, with or without grid. In Belgrade the practice had been that if a Plenary failed to reach agreement on the work programme for the following days it would meet again on the next working day in order to continue discussing the programme.

The Plenary session which began on 5 March was chaired by the Czechoslovakian representative, in response to whose enquiry the Swiss delegate had to reply that no agreement on a work programme had yet been reached in the corridors of the building. After the representatives who had put their names on the speakers' list had spoken (the main theme was once more developments in Poland), at the beginning of the afternoon, again the Swiss delegate had to report that still nothing had been agreed in the corridors on the programme of the next week, and as far as he could see there was no prospect of agreement. This led to the first silence: despite appeals from the chairman none of the delegations was prepared to come forward with concrete proposals for a work programme. The Maltese representative finally drew the conclusion that the Plenary ought to be closed, and reassemble on the next working day to continue discussing the work programme. To this the Soviet delegate immediately replied that there was no reason why the discussion on a grid should not begin at once, for as long as there was no work programme there was also no fixed time and date for the next Plenary. The coffee-break which followed brought no improvement: no-one would budge. After the coffee--break there was a further long silence which led the chairman to propose yet another coffee-break. The GDR then proposed going on with the work programme of the past week which would mean that there would be two Drafting Group meetings, wereupon the Belgian representative (Belgium was President of the Ten) proposed a work programme consisting exclusively of two meetings of the Plenary.

A verbal battle now followed between some East European representatives and the West over whether the Purple Book required the work programme to include a Drafting Group meeting or not. There was at this time only one Drafting Group, set up in December 1981 to replace all the Drafting Groups which had been instituted according to the Purple Book a year earlier. The Soviet delegate claimed that the present Drafting Group was legal successor to the Drafting Groups referred to in the final paragraph of article 4 of the Purple Book and these had been given the explicit task of assisting the Plenary in drafting the concluding document of the Meeting. Now the Plenary was still officially occupied with item 8 on the agenda: "drafting of a concluding document", and the Plenary had no right to dispense with the Drafting Group until all its item 8 work was completed. A work programme with no Drafting Group was subversive of the Purple Book and the CSCE in general, for to liquidate this group would be a blow to any prospects of adopting a substantive concluding document. Western delegations replied by observing that the Drafting Groups referred to in the Purple Book had long ceased to exist and the Plenary, as the main body of the Meeting, was entitled to organize its own work and to decide for itself whether or not it needed the assistance of a Drafting Group.

After a silence and yet another coffee-break (during which the NATO caucus decided to go on keeping silent) East European delegations repeated their arguments but, in the absence of any reactions from the West, were forced to come to a halt. The silence which followed was broken by the representative of Malta: "Procedures have already been seen to have political implications but now keeping silent has also acquired political meaning. We just sit, and look, and stare! Another coffee-break? Even coffee-breaks are no more use". Nevertheless a coffee-break followed and directly after it the Maltese once more put his view that the meeting ought to be closed and reconvened on the next working day, which was Monday, following Belgrade practice in cases when agreement on a work programme had not been reached. To this, however, the Soviet delegation now explicitly refused its consent; it was determined to hold out against closure of the session as long as no consensus was forthcoming for the GDR delegation's proposal for a programme including two meetings of the Drafting Group. In doing this the Soviet delegation took up a position opposite to the one it had occupied on 9 February for it now recognized a consensus as necessary for the closure rather than the continuation of the meeting.

When midnight had passed another problem arose. Was the Czechoslovakian representative, who was the current chairman, to make way for the next day's chairman who was from the Turkish delegation? He did not do so. In Belgrade, if meetings went on for long, beyond midnight, it had been the custom for the chairman sometimes to remain in office and sometimes to change, according to the meeting's consensus. On this occasion the Czechoslovakian did not find it necessary to follow the "daily rotation" rule from the Purple Book. The Soviet delegation devised the following argument to support him: rule (70) of the Blue Book asserted that the chairmanship changed with each meeting but here there was no question of a new scheduled meeting because it was the same meeting which was in progress; so it was also unnecessary to have a new chairman. The insertion of a coffee-break did not mean that the ensuing period constituted a new meeting. It followed that after a fresh coffee-break the chairman in office had to continue to fulfil his duties. It was the same problem as has already been described as contributing to the events of 11 November 1980 after the clock had been restarted and the Hungarian chairman refused to make way for his successor. But this time the chairman's refusal to stand down brought a sharp reaction from

NNA countries who argued that daily rotation meant that the chairmanship had to change with the day: when the day changed so must the chair. The CSCE principle of equality demanded daily rotation of the chairmanship because otherwise the unallied countries would be to an important degree dependent on the whims of the two military pacts which together constituted a large majority.

A fresh coffee-break produced no further results; informal discussions in the corridors only led to a hardening of positions. Once more the chairman asked who wished to speak and met with no reply; it was now 2.40 a.m. This time the silence lasted for fifty minutes. The interpreters must have thought that the hundred or so diplomats in the chamber had taken leave of their senses. Fifty minutes of silence in a full chamber is a long time. Some diplomats read the paper, some nodded off and some gossiped with their neighbours. Silence may speak louder than words. The British representative called it: "an eloquent silence". Its effect may be to raise the tension more than any discussion. Finally the chairman announced that the Executive Secretary had managed to get the coffee bar re-opened. It had been shut for several hours but the attendants had been fetched from their beds. Did anyone object to a coffee-break? The answer being a silence, so it was decided and it was during this interval that the negotiators from the various caucuses agreed on a formula for putting an end to the night's performance. The meeting would not be closed, for this the WP countries refused, but a coffee-break would be called extending until 11 a.m. on the following Monday. It was then 5.30 a.m. on Saturday morning so the coffee-break would last 54½ hours. On the Monday morning the meeting would continue. Whether the Czechoslovakian or the Turkish representative as next in alphabetical order, would then preside over the meeting, was left undecided.

During the weekend Western delegates realized what a strange situation they were in, thanks to the inexorable consensus rule. The Soviet delegation was not willing to consent to the Plenary session's being closed unless the GDR proposal for the work programme was accepted. But the West was not willing to accept this proposal. So the session would go on for ever and ever, perpetually under the chairmanship of the Czechoslovakian representative since he refused to stand down until the session ended. And this situation could continue for as long as the

Soviet delegation wanted.

The same weekend saw negotiations taking place in the hotel rooms of Madrid on the initiative of NNA countries; representatives from the caucuses took part and agreement was reached on a package deal. The most important elements of this agreement were that it was agreed to have a working programme for one week which would include some meetings of the Drafting Group as proposed by the GDR, but at the end of the week the Madrid Meeting would go into recess until the beginning of November, which fulfilled the wishes of Western countries. In November, drafting of a concluding document would be continued and therefore the first work programme in November would also include meetings of the Drafting Group. Western and NNA countries had achieved their most important aim, an agreed recess until the autumn. East European countries had succeeded in having the appearance kept up that the Madrid Meeting's Drafting Group was still negotiating a substantive concluding document, in spite of the situation in Poland, and would continue negotiations in November. Throughout the three meetings of the Drafting Group held in the last week before the recess the West maintained its silence. Some NNA countries did speak but there was no question of serious negotiations on the concluding document.

On Monday the Czechoslovakian representative again took the chair in the Plenary but as, according to the package deal, the meeting was to last no more than a few minutes, Western and NNA countries made no objection. Later in the week they signed a protest on principle against his having remained in the chair.

5. Consensus on Procedures

From the three sequences of events which have been described here emerges the crucial importance of certain rules of procedure: consensus, daily rotation of the chairmanship and the fixing of the grid by the Plenary. They were of great influence on the *course* of the decision--making process. It may still be asked, however, whether they were of crucial significance in determining the political *result* of that process. Would not other procedures have led to the same result? In the absence of relevant conclusions drawn from simulated scenarios there can be no definitive answer, but some remarks can be made.

On the day when the clock was re-started the aim of the Western countries was to get the Soviet Union and her allies to show their colours and to reveal whether they were prepared to stand by the Belgrade agreement to begin the Madrid Meeting precisely on 11 November 1980; the West also had a second objective which was to induce the Soviet Union to take a more flexible attitude to the still unresolved differences of opinion on the Meeting's agenda. Both these objectives were achieved. Whether the Soviet delegation also succeeded in getting what she wanted by the tactics she employed in the same period must remain a mystery as long as it remains unclear what she did want. Would the result of the political process have been different if other procedures had been followed?

Under other rules of procedure the West would still have struggled to attain the same goals and would probably also have reached them. Moreover, on looking back it can be presumed that the Soviet Union would have been unlikely to have continued her refusal to let the Madrid Meeting begin (perhaps not on the 11 November but a few days later) because she was too interested in what she considered the primary interest of this meeting; the creation of a mandate for a European disarmament conference which would fit in with Brezhnev's Peace Programme. At the time the political climate was bad, but not bad enough to cause any of the 35 participants to want to break off the CSCE follow-up process. On the contrary, all 35 countries, though for a variety of reasons, saw the holding of the Madrid Meeting as offering political advantages. That is why it was held.

On the day that the Polish chairman to all intents and purposes muzzled Western and Neutral Foreign Ministers and prevented them from speaking on Poland, his declared objective was to frustrate the "NATO scenario". This, in his own opinion, he achieved: "Your scenario failed. The Madrid Meeting has not become a branch of NATO. In your NATO communiqué you had lost sight of political reality. You had disregarded the existence of Poland herself as a full participant in CSCE". This is taken from the later statement by the Polish chairman. The Polish delegation also admitted afterwards in personal conversations that in all conceivable circumstances, whatever the procedural rules had been, it would have striven to reach the same political goal. An expert in Warsaw had had to spend several days researching in order to discover procedural means of frustrating the course of the 9 February meeting. What he unearthed in the end was Journal 4. Would the day have gone differently if the procedures in force had been different?

It is hard to say, but given the political situation at that time in Europe the "NATO scenario" was unlikely to have had a smooth run. The same expert in Warsaw would have seen to that, for his terms of reference were to find a means at all costs. Poland achieved her political aim on that occasion although whether it was a politically reasonable aim in itself, is another question. Both the Soviet and the Polish delegations quickly perceived that their attitude on 9 February had been counter--productive for this "debate on the Polish crisis" attracted far more attention throughout the world than if the normal course of affairs had not been upset by their interventions. Their decision not to repeat the performance at the following Plenary on Friday was therefore a politically conscious decision. The *International Herald Tribune* of the day after the 12th ran a front-page story under the headline: "Moscow drops attempt to block foes in Madrid" and analysed correctly:

> The Soviet Union abandoned efforts Friday to block discussion on the Poland crisis at the Madrid Conference on Security and Co--operation in Europe, and Western foreign ministers resumed their attacks on the Warsaw military government for suppressing the Solidarity union movement. The switch in Soviet tactics appeared to spring from an awareness that the Warsaw Pact had suffered severe damage to its image Tuesday when Poland, which chaired that day's session, touched off an angry, seven-hour procedural dispute and prevented eight foreign ministers from speaking.

In corroboration of this, on Friday 12 February it appeared that the procedural problems which had dominated the debate on 9 February could be resolved quite simply if all parties were, for political reasons, prepared to do so. At the beginning of the morning session on 12 February, without any discussion and within thirty seconds, an Austrian proposal to hold not only a morning session but also an afternoon session so as to have time for all the speakers whose names already made up a very long list, was adopted. After this the meeting went forward without any further procedural discussion.

The Western aim in the night of silences was to show the East European countries that it really was not prepared to carry on with business as usual and that it would be politically realistic to react positively to the initiative from some of the Neutral countries proposing a long summer recess. This aim was fulfilled: a few days later the Soviet delegation accepted an agreed recess of several months whereas at the beginning it had been against it.

As a consequence of the developments in and round Poland, international relations had become so bad that none of the Western or Neutral countries could think of seriously and realistically negotiating a substantive concluding document. Other procedures would simply have driven the West to approach its goal by another path. It would again be speculation to assert that the goal would have been reached in any case but any other result in the given political situation would seem unlikely.

In the three cases political aims were paramount and were attained by making use, justly or unjustly, of the rules of procedure in force, as would have been the case if other rules had been in force. Ultimately the Madrid Meeting was a reflection of political reality and this reality can never be confined in a procedural straitjacket, least of all at times of political tension. Reality is stronger than paper.

IX. THE DECISION-MAKING PROCESS: SUBSTANCE AS ISSUE

1. Introduction

Whereas in previous Chapters attention was focused on the application of the Rules of Procedure to the decision-making process, the present Chapter is primarily devoted to the substantive content of that process. One of the objectives common to all participants was agreement on a substantial and balanced concluding document which would contain new provisions relating to every area of the Final Act. Proposals for such provisions were prepared in the capital cities. This Chapter begins by describing the course of such a proposal up to the moment when it was accepted by the 35 states for inclusion in the substantial concluding document, and gives an account of the drafting techniques which were used in reaching the necessary agreement.

Throughout its evolution into a final provision any proposal is the object of negotiation; in Madrid, because of the rule of consensus which required co-operation from every party before a provision could be finally accepted there was a special dominating feature in such negotiations and this is the subject of the next section of this Chapter. It is the question of the identity, among all the participants, of the *demandeur* or in other words, the party which has the greatest interest in reaching the agreement. In the light of this an analysis is made of the roles played by each of the parties (initiators, vetoers, brokers and controllers), and finally the whole process is regarded from a historical point of view and expressed in terms of "turning points".

2. From Proposal to Provision

Before its official presentation as described in the last part of Chapter III, a proposal would already have been the object of deliberations, first of all in the capital city between the various competent government bodies and then, as far as Western or WP countries were concerned, between the different members of the alliance. How these consultations ran differed according to the degree of cohesion present among the members of the group and to the nature of the subject itself.

The accompanying chart illustrates the course followed by a proposal in the area of co-operation in humanitarian and other fields. For the Western side, the path of an EC proposal is given because it followed the widest possible course. The explanation in the present section gives the deviations to be expected in the case of proposals of a different nature and from other sources.

The chart refers exclusively to eighty per cent (i.e., 30 of the 35 pages) of the NNA comprehensive draft for a substantive and balanced Madrid concluding document, RM.39, dated 16 December 1981, on which, in the expert contact groups, provisional agreement had been reached earlier in the year.

After its inception and development in the capital city of one of the EC countries, the idea leading to a proposal would then be presented by an official of the relevant foreign ministry to the EPC work group which, under the official title of *"Sous-Comité CSCE"*, met regularly under the chairmanship of whichever country currently held the Presidency of the European Communities. This work group was a subsidiary committee of the "Political Committee" of the Directors General for Political Affairs which meets regularly in the framework of "European Political Co--operation" (EPC) for consultations towards evolving a common foreign policy on important questions. EC proposals on economic co-operation were not discussed in this work group but in Brussels in a committee known as the *"Groupe ad hoc CSCE"* in the presence of a representative from the European Commission, since such proposals often concerned subjects which, according to the Treaty of Rome, were within the competence of the European Communities. Consultations on proposals connected with military aspects of security were held entirely outside the EPC and were discussed in one of the subsidiary committees of the permanent Nato Council in Brussels.

The deliberations of the EPC work group would result in collective instructions addressed to the expert EC caucuses in Madrid and including the actual text of the proposals which were to be put forward. These would then be presented by the Presidential delegation - at the time covered by the chart the Luxembourg delegation - after the NATO caucuses had been asked which Western countries would be willing to act as co-sponsors. In the NATO caucuses the non-EC countries also sought co-sponsors from among the other delegations for their national proposals.

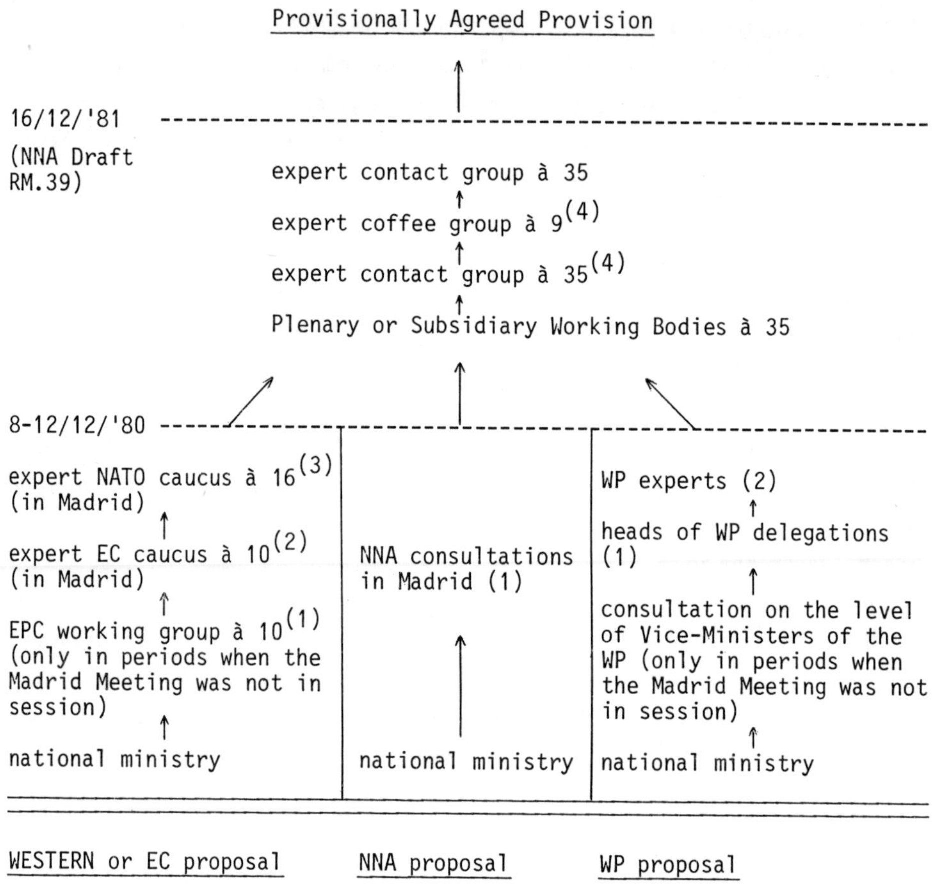

Figure 9-1: The Course of a Proposal for the Third Basket

(1) in case of disagreement the matter was referred back to the national ministries for new instructions.

(2) ditto to heads of delegations and/or national ministries.

(3) ditto to expert EC caucus, heads of delegation and/or national ministries.

(4) ditto to allied expert caucuses.

The texts of the proposals would then be passed to the staff of the Executive Secretary and translated into the other conference languages before being circulated to all 35 delegations. In the Plenary or the pertinent Subsidiary Working Body (SWB) Western proposals were introduced and defended from 27 January 1981 onwards by the original sponsors acting as the first *"chefs de file"*. When on 12 February 1981 the SWBs were replaced by "Drafting Groups", all proposals received a second reading during which the opposing party had the opportunity of commenting on them. This filled the period up to 5 March 1981 as described in Chapter V under "Drafting Groups".

The real work of drafting took place in the expert contact groups. The work of these contact groups began with the submission of "non-papers" or proposals put forward anonymously be one delegation or group of delegations. The sponsors' names did not normally appear on the papers which meant that the sponsors could maintain their flexibility because their proposal, submitted as a non-paper, had no officially identifiable source. Naturally the identity of every non-paper's authors did become clear from the text but because it was officially anonymous, negotiations were easier.

The first non-papers were no more than re-drafts of the original proposals officially submitted to the Executive Secretary a month or so earlier. The texts had been somewhat streamlined, shorn of superfluous preambulatory language and contained some cosmetic concessions, which meant that account had been taken of the criticism which the proposals had received, even though none of the changes affected the substance of the proposal itself. These initial non-papers were known as "consolidated non-papers". In most contact groups Western delegations switched over almost at once to introducing "comprehensive" non-papers which included their own "consolidated" non-papers and, in addition, a revision of any of the official East European proposals which might be acceptable once Western revisions had been incorporated. All totally unacceptable East European proposals were disregarded in these Western non-papers. Then East European delegations also began to circulate non-papers.

It was on the basis of all these non-papers that the contact groups struggled to find common ground on each subject, a process which involved discussion of every sentence and phrase.

3. Drafting Techniques

At that time there were various methods available for getting down to the real work of drafting. One well-known technique which had been used in Helsinki, Geneva and Belgrade was the use of square brackets. The "square brackets" technique consists of setting out conflicting opinions on the same subject next to each other in the same sentence using square brackets for the sensitive area. An oversimplified example might be the sentence by which one party claims that "John is a good boy": this leads to two possibilities. The opposition may refuse to utter any opinion about John, in which case the first party can require the chairman to circulate the text to all participants with the sentence about John in square brackets: "The participating states agree that [John is a good boy]". If, on the other hand, the opposition does want to say something about John in the concluding document, then they can propose their own opinion for inclusion, namely: "John is a bad boy" and the text circulated by the chairman would read: "The participating states agree that John is a [good] [bad] boy". The minimum compromise would be: "The participating states agree that John is a boy" which would simply acknowledge John's (or the problem's) existence.

An alternative solution might be to say: "John is sometimes good and sometimes bad" which would give the original sponsors of the proposal the satisfaction of having the fact that John could sometimes be good, recognized by the opposition. A solution such as "According to some participating States John is a good boy and according to others a bad one" would certainly reflect the difference of opinion between the two parties but would be in conflict with the consensus rule for this would raise the question of how many states thought John was good and how many bad. How many is "some"? Should not "some" be replaced by "several" or "most"? Then it would come to counting heads.

Finally there is one other solution; the sentence might read: "Different views were expressed as to John's qualities", and it was this type of expression which was the best that could be managed in the concluding document of the Belgrade meeting. It ran: "different views were expressed as to the degree of implementation of the Final Act reached so far", to which may be compared the Madrid Concluding Document: "... different and at times contradictory opinions were expressed as to the degree of implementation of the Final Act reached so far by participating States".

The example involving John is dealing with a non-operative evaluation of an existing situation, the question being whether John is a good boy or not. In the same framework a paragraph which was operative, demanding action, would raise greater difficulties. The original proposal might have read: "The participating States decide to give John every encouragement to persist in the good courses he is following", and the counter-proposal might have been: "The participating States decide to give John every encouragement to desist from the bad courses he is following". Then, as basis for further discussions, the chairman would have circulated the following text: "The participating States decide to give John every encouragement to [persist in] [desist from] the [good] [bad] courses he is following". Details of the possible compromise variations can be left to the reader's imagination.

In Madrid, when it came to the real drafting, the Soviet delegation appeared to have received stringent instructions from Moscow not to accept the square brackets system although it had done so in both Geneva and Belgrade. The Soviet delegation justified its refusal by the claim that this method had been seen to have a slowing-down effect in Geneva and also made it difficult to reach results which satisfied all parties. But the Soviet delegation was prepared to change over to the use of dots. To return to the example used above, in this system the sentence which was to be used as a basis for further negotiations would read: "John is a ... boy", after which discussions would have to continue until all parties came to agreement on a qualification for John (1).

The dots method was used in Madrid only a few times at the beginning of the drafting exercise. It gave rise to the following sentence for example: "The Conference ... will consider ... questions in Europe". This was the first sentence approved in the contact group dealing with the mandate for a European disarmament conference. It was this conference to which the words "the Conference" referred. The intention was to wait until further discussions made it possible to find appropriate words to fill in the name and thereby indicate the function of the conference (first group of dots) and subsequently also the subjects which would be dealt with at that conference (second group of dots). Western military experts' connivance in this sentence was not unanimously welcomed by their political authorities; agreement here might be interpreted to mean that agreement to hold the conference had been reached before its mandate, or terms of reference, had been decided, whereas the intention of the West had actually been to agree formally to the calling of the conference only after its mandate had been settled. East European propaganda was now able to trumpet forth that in Madrid all 35 countries "had reached agreement on holding a disarmament conference".

In Madrid the method of approving sentences containing rows of dots as a basis for further negotiation was not much used. It was preferred to regard as "provisionally agreed" only those lines or parts of lines of which every word and comma had been unanimously accepted. Such unanimity was reached by exchange of many non-papers containing drafts and re--drafts of the same paragraph, variations on previous non-papers submitted by the same side or the opposing party, or sometimes, as a result of clarificatory discussion, a new formulation of the same problem from a totally different viewpoint.

Approximately twenty non-papers, most of which were submitted over a period of only two weeks in the coffee group created for this purpose, contributed to the draft which was finally approved for the three--sentence preamble to the third basket of the Concluding Document. In most cases, however, negotiations on a particular line occupied a much longer period, which could include long intervals between proposals. One sentence, dealing with freedom of movement for journalists in the country where they are accredited, was finalized only after exchange of about fifteen non-papers which were submitted from the beginning of February to the second half of July in 1981.

On 31 March 1981 eight NNA countries presented their first complete draft for the whole concluding document. This draft took over the various texts upon which agreement had already been reached in different contact groups and also put forward new formulations, based on the non-papers in circulation, for the many questions which were still open. After that negotiations continued on the basis of this document. One advantage was that it was no longer necessary to base the negotiations on the whole unwieldy mass of non-papers produced by East European and Western countries. But the method of drafting remained the same: when a certain paragraph from the NNA document was to be dealt with, alternative versions would be proposed in the appropriate contact group, either orally or in non-papers, until the co-ordinator of the group was able to conclude that the text had obtained a consensus.

About eighty percent of the Madrid Concluding Document was achieved in this way. In view of the fact that there seemed to be no possibility of agreement between East and West on the remaining twenty percent, the NNA countries, on the basis of the discussions which had already taken place on these problems, once more produced a compromise document which appeared on 16 December 1981 and became known as RM.39. Nearly a year later in November 1982, the Western countries proposed around twenty extensive amendments to this document, all of which concerned passages on which no provisional agreement had yet been reached in the contact groups. In principle these amendments then took the same path as shown in the Chart on page 214, with the difference that all formal and informal groups of experts were omitted, and all negotiations took place only at the level of heads of delegation.

This time the actual negotiations were done in so-called sherry groups, and later, mini-groups (see VI, 5 and 6). The technique for drafting was once more the exchange of non-papers, each of which gave rise to new discussions, on the basis of which the NNA countries put together their last compromise, RM.39 revised. The West now filed four amendments which involved deleting two words, alteration of two other words and addition of two important new paragraphs. Once the Spanish government had put forward its compromise, and this compromise had been accepted in the Plenary by everyone, as a basis for further negotiation, all that was at stake was two words and the problem of the manner in which the expert meeting on human contacts should be called into existence. Negotiations on the last phrases finally took place between a few representatives of East and West and the NNA countries, round a table in the coffee-bar. As soon as the last comma had been agreed and the three caucuses - always on call in expectation of their representatives' reports - had approved the compromise which had been reached, the Plenary was summoned, at 22 hrs. 15 July 1983, and the Austrian representative presented a total package of amendments to RM.39 revised. In this meeting of the Plenary, the representatives of the various caucuses, now formally stating by name the countries they represented, explicitly gave their provisional approval.

Two procedural problems were solved by this way of doing things. Some time before, the 35 delegations had already decided in principle to meet daily, but only as the Plenary. Between the coffee-bar and the Plenary there was no longer any kind of Drafting Group which would have had to accept the final compromise texts before they could have been presented to the Plenary.

The second problem was that of Malta whose attitude threatened to prevent a consensus. Because all delegations except Malta actually voiced their agreement in the consensus through their spokesmen rather than merely giving passive assent by keeping silent (which is all that is required by the CSCE consensus rule), the chairman was able to say that a consensus had been reached "except for Malta" who had not been named in the lists of countries recited, whereupon he appealed to Malta to add her own consent. There was thus "a consensus of 34" which put the choice squarely before Malta whether or not to join in.

4. Aspects of Negotiation

There is an extensive literature on the subject of international negotiations and it is not our intention to go into it to any great degree. Only a few aspects of negotiation come under scrutiny and these have been selected because they proved to be important in Madrid in consequence of the most significant procedural rule, that of consensus.

4.1. The Demandeur

In order to have a clear insight into one's own negotiating position and also into that of the opposing party, it proved to be important in Madrid to have a constantly renewed awareness of which of the two parties was the *demandeur*. It is remarkable how little use is made of this concept in the literature on negotiation even though the question of the identity of the *demandeur* dictates a considerable part of the negotiator's strategy. The *demandeur* is the party which is asking for something and of whom it is well-known that he sets more store by a certain decision than the other party concerned although the decision can only be taken with this party's consent. This means that the second party can set a price on its consent and the *demandeur's* position is weak (2). Under the consensus rule every decision requires the co--operation of all parties, each of whom is therefore entitled to set its own price for consent, and the demandeur must concede all along the line, at least if the proposal is a controversial one. If all parties have an interest in a proposal, as for example in the proposal to combat terrorism or the ones on cultural co-operation, negotiation is confined to formulation of the common interest. But the importance of who is playing the role of *demandeur* in other cases can be shown in the following examples.

During negotiations on the Final Act (Geneva 1973-75) East European countries got themselves into the position of *demandeur* by pointedly striving for agreement on a principle declaring the existent boundaries in Europe to be inviolable now and in the future; in their eyes this meant international recognition of the post-war *status quo* in central Europe. In order to achieve this object they were obliged to pay the price asked by the West which was commitments in the field of human rights and human contacts. Some of the Western delegations let it be known at crucial moments that the success or failure of the CSCE was in general not of vital interest to them and an agreement on the inviolability of frontiers even less, unless they themselves should thereby obtain satisfaction on the subject of human rights and human contacts.

A second example: in Chapter VIII a description has already been given of how during the Preparatory Meeting in October 1980, the Soviet delegation boasted of its entire indifference to the question of whether the main Meeting would start on 11 November 1980, while Western and NNA countries showed that it mattered very much to them, so that they were, in Soviet eyes, in the position of *demandeur*. Western and NNA countries were keen to see the CSCE follow-up process begun for reasons connected with international and internal politics. Yet they did not allow themselves to have the role of *demandeur* thrust upon them nor did they let themselves be misled into making concessions, because they were convinced that the Soviet Union and her allies were no less susceptible to being cast in the *demandeur* role. Western delegations were convinced that the Eastern delegations had, in fact, just as much interest in continuing the follow-up process and that their manoeuvres were mere bluff. It was to call this bluff that the West decided to put an end to the fiction of the stopped clock and find out whether the Soviet Union was willing to begin the Madrid Meeting on 11 November 1980 or not. The operation was a success; the role of *demandeur* proved to be shared by both sides.

Such an analysis of the situation enjoys the advantage of hindsight; at the time the negotiators felt instinctively that this was the situation but did not necessarily reason it out in such terms.

A third example shows that it can at times be even less clear who the *demandeur* at a conference is. At the conference in Madrid Western (and NNA) negotiators found themselves in a difficult position because on several questions which were to them very important, such as human rights, human contacts and information, they were the petitioners. They had submitted far-reaching proposals for improvement of the situation in relation to these questions in (East) Europe. They attached great importance to these proposals which were of indifferent interest to the East European delegations. The latter finally announced, in November 1981, that as far as they were concerned no further progress could be made on these crucial items as long as the West made no move on the mandate for the disarmament conference. But the Western delegations did not allow themselves to be bullied in this way into making concessions on the subject of this mandate. They realized that the Soviet Union was squarely in the position of *demandeur* as far as the disarmament conference went and ready to pay a price to ensure that it would be held. The West was, or said it was, less interested than the SU in this conference. Some Western countries totally denied being to any degree at all *demandeur* in this case while others were slightly less confident, depending on their domestic political situations. All Western negotiators were, however, in agreement that the mandate for a disarmament conference would only be obtained if the Western conditions relating to it were fulfilled. That was the price to be paid by East European delegation for seeing their wishes granted.

Why is the *demandeur's* position a weak one? He must take the initiative time and again in order to reach his object. This is because the other party has little or no interest in the decision so dear to the heart of the *demandeur* and can therefore wait on events and will do so as long as he thinks that such is the best way to avoid a decision which does nothing to advance his interests. He can also achieve his "interdiction goal" by initiating a counter-proposal and playing for stalemate, a strategy which he might prefer to simply blocking the decision with a veto. Stalemate is sometimes easier to explain and more acceptable to public opinion outside the conference than a stubborn attachment to the right to veto (3). The counter-proposal will also be used if the other party is convinced that it will ultimately be impossible to avoid consenting to the decision. From his point of view the most reasonable course may then seem to be to make a counter-proposal and so give evidence of goodwill towards the *demandeur* and at the same time be in a position to limit the damage to his own interests by careful phrasing of the decision itself.

But, in general, the initiative remains with the *demandeur* and each new initiative involving the formulation of the decision, which must follow rejection of the previous text by the opposite party, is bound to be an attempt by the *demandeur* to move a little nearer to the position of the other party and will thus be of a concessionary nature. In theory the opposing party can go on saying no until the asking price is paid. The only alternative allowed by the rule of consensus when the parties cannot agree is to end up with no text at all which leaves the party which is in no way playing the role of *demandeur* in a comfortable position.

4.2. Roles to be Played

In the light of the remarks which have been made above on the identity of the *demandeur*, some further exploration will now be made of the roles which were played by different delegations in Madrid. The pattern for this analysis is the role distribution described by Robert W. Cox and Harold K. Jacobson in order to give an account of the influence of actors in international organizations, a pattern which seems relevant to the way negotiations went in Madrid. The authors speak of initiators, vetoers, controllers and brokers as four roles in which an actor may be influential (4). The pattern is thus concerned with functions which might be performed by an actor. For our purposes the actor is always a national delegation and not an individual (5).

"In each decision some actor or group of actors must take the initiative and hence become the *initiator*", say Cox and Jacobson. All delegations in Madrid were initiators for they all submitted proposals. Unless their proposals were such as could lead to formulation of a common interest, the proposers found themselves cast in the role of *demandeur*. Where very controversial subjects were concerned, East European delegations tended however to stick to their guns for shorter periods than their Western counterparts and thus occupied the position of *demandeur* for a shorter time. Controversial proposals which they initiated included the scheduling of a new principle on the right to work, summoning a high-level meeting on energy, and particularly their various proposals on the establishment of the responsibility of the mass media to strive for objective information, mutual understanding between peoples, détente, peace and security, and to struggle against fascism, racism and chauvinism.

The proposals on the subject of the responsibility of journalists were particularly unacceptable to Western and Neutral countries because what was implied was an invitation to censorship. The East European delegations did not insist on these proposals for long but re-introduced them later on as counter-proposals when they thought the Western countries were being too obstinate over their own controversial proposals. To the Western proposal "not to interfere with the reception of broadcast information from the other participating states" which meant in fact to stop jamming foreign radio broadcasts, the Soviet delegation proposed to qualify the word "information" by adding "which is objective and serves the purpose of peace, security, understanding between peoples and halting the arms race". In this way the East Europeans emphasized their own position and set the price which the West was expected to pay in order to have its proposal accepted: a prohibitively high one. This tactic of countering unacceptable proposals with equally unacceptable counter--demands was used by both the East Europeans and the West.

"The real initiators are not always the formal initiators", say Cox and Jacobson: "For example, international officials sometimes prepare draft resolutions that are then submitted by members of national delegations". Another possibility is that one delegation may lay a compromise proposal before a second delegation for it to submit either because the policy of the first delegation's government prevents it from doing so itself or in order to increase its acceptability to third parties. At times in Madrid the Soviet delegation used the not unknown tactic of not actually offering a concessionary text but alluding to possible compromises which might be acceptable, after which the onus was on the opposing side to work these allusions into a viable compromise text. For whatever reason this tactic may be employed it has the consequence that the compromise submitted by the formal initiator remains open to attack from the other party which has thus placed itself in the role of vetoer.

In the words of Cox and Jacobson, *vetoers* are actors who have the power "to block initiatives" and "to prevent a decision by whatever means they may require". Wherever the consensus rule holds sway every participant has in fact the power to prevent any decision. Who were the most frequent vetoers in Madrid? As appears from the table of proposals in Chapter III, East European countries put forward more proposals than either Western or NNA countries (the numbers were 36, 26 and 20 respectively). They would therefore have more right to the denomination "initiator" than the others and in consequence less claim to the title of "vetoer". Where important controversial East European proposals were concerned (see above), the West did indeed act as vetoer. But the majority of the East European proposals were on subjects not in themselves among the most controversial, such as economic, cultural and educational co-operation between states, where agreement could usually be reached. In the much more delicate area of the human dimension the Western countries played the role of *demandeur* as well as initiator (certainly after the beginning of November 1982 when, for political reasons, they had put forward new or renewed proposals) and East European countries had to take the role of vetoer. Thus, because these Western proposals took much longer to discuss than most of the East European ones, the East European delegations, particularly the Soviet delegation, spent longer periods as vetoer than the West.

Little mention has so far been made of the role played by the NNA countries who nevertheless initiated twenty proposals. But, with a few exceptions (Yugoslavia, Malta) they did not act as *demandeurs*, either because their proposals were not too controversial or because they did not lay too much emphasis for too long a period on getting them accepted. In one area they were recognized by all the remaining parties as initiators and this was the field of procedure; they took the initiative for drafting the weekly work programme and in decisions to take a long or short recess. Especially when a long recess was mooted, Western and East European countries left the initiative to the NNA countries so as to avoid the odium of not being prepared to carry on with the normal negotiations.

NNA countries seldom took the role of vetoer in the sense of blocking a proposal which was acceptable both to Western and Eastern countries. They knew very well that their potential role was that of broker. According to Cox and Jacobson, *brokers* are those who "serve as go-betweens among the participants and as consensus builders". At critical moments the NNA countries did all they could to bridge the gap between Western and East European opinions while simultaneously doing their best not to betray their own positions.

"There are some actors whose known or surmised views may have to be taken into account because of their control of sources of their formal authority, or for some other reason. They can be called *controllers*". Cox and Jacobson seem to be speaking here of the influence brought to bear by these actors on potential initiators even before the latter have submitted their proposals. When the initiators formulate their proposals they take account of what they assume to be the controllers attitudes. By this reasoning the role of controllers in Madrid can be allotted to the SU and US in relation to their allied partners. The members of each alliance took into account the expressed or unexpressed views of their major ally. Of course this is not to say that they therefore took no account of the views of the remaining partners in the alliance: no-one would want to submit a proposal which clashed with the interests of one of his allies. A member of an alliance would tend always to recognize the interests of another member and because the interests of a superpower are wider than those of a small country the controller's role would fall to the superpower rather than to the latter.

5. The Process in Phases

The actual negotiating process occupied 63 working weeks spread over 30 months (27 January 1981 - 15 July 1983). The eight so-called "Malta weeks" which followed, are not dealt with in this context. At the outset no-one either intended or expected the negotiating process to run for so long; its course, and therefore the length of time it lasted was influenced by both external and internal factors, but the former were the most important. In this Chapter internal factors are regarded as those inherent in the development of the negotiating process itself, and external factors as political developments outside the congress building, which affected the course of the negotiations.

The following analysis makes use of certain concepts developed by

I. William Zartman. In an article published at the beginning of 1975, Zartman analysed the process of negotiation in terms of "turning points", important moments punctuating the process. The first of these he calls the "threshold of seriousness", the second is the moment when agreement is reached on the "formula", if not the "framework", for solving the problem and the last is called "the crest" (6). Five years later, together with Maureen R. Berman, he published *The Practical Negotiator* in which he describes phases: preceding the first turning point comes the "Diagnostic" phase, also called "Bringing about Negotiations", followed by the "Formula" phase "Defining Solutions", after which comes the "Detail" phase, "Working out Agreements", upon which the negotiators get the feeling of being on the home stretch (7). The phases are marked off by points which are identical with the "turning points" of his 1975 article but which he no longer refers to as such. Zartman and Berman emphasize that "the notion of stages or phases of a negotiation is an analytical one that, while corresponding to reality, is far sharper in concept than is ever the case in human events" (8).

As long as this reservation is kept in mind Zartman's conceptual framework forms a useful tool for analysing the course taken by the negotiating process in Madrid. Yet at the same time two further reservations have to be made. Like other theorists, Zartman describes the process of negotiation as if it stood in isolation and followed its own laws so that his analysis takes no account of external outside factors affecting it. The Madrid negotiations on the other hand were extremely sensitive to external factors, i.e., political events outside the conference building.

The second reservation rests on the fact that the Madrid conference had at least two separate functions, a "normative function" involving the negotiation of a substantive concluding document which was to include new commitments in all areas of the Final Act, and a "rule supervisory function" involving an exchange of views on compliance with the Final Act by the participating states; it is only to the first of these functions that Zartman's concepts can be applied.

What follows applies therefore only to the second column in the appended historical survey of the process (Table 9-1). The first column lists a number of external factors which influenced the negotiating process and the third column divides the whole course of the conference

External factors	
27/12/'79 : Soviet invasion of Afghanistan 1979/1980 : Treatment of dissidents in some Eastern European countries	
23 Febr. : Brezhnev on CBMs - 26th CPSU congress	
10 May : EPC meeting Venlo (Netherlands) on Poland	
Oct./Nov. : Peace Marches in Western Europe 11 Nov. : Reagan on arms control 13 Dec. : Martial Law in Poland	
Developments in Poland	
8 Oct. : Dissolution of Solidarity 10 Nov. : Brezhnev-Andropov 13 Dec. : Suspension of martial law in Poland	
1979 : NATO two-track decision (INF-deployment)	
Idem	

TABLE 9-1: The Negotiating Process in Phases

Highlights of the negotiating process (turning points underlined)	Phases (focus of attention)
11 Nov. : the Stopped Clock	Preparatory Meeting 9 Sept. - 10 Nov. '80 negotiating the Purple Book
8-12 Dec.: submission of proposals	Phase I 11 Nov. - 19 Dec. '80 review of implementation
5 March (1981): beginning of the drafting 31 March (1981): first NNA draft for concluding document	Phase II 27 Jan. - 10 April '81 examination of proposals
Intensive negotiations in informal groups	Phase III 5 May - 27 July '81 drafting the document
16 Dec. (1981): second NNA draft for concluding document (RM.39)	Phase IV 27 Oct. - 18 Dec. '81 search for solutions
9 Febr.: the Polish Chairman 5 March: the Night of Silences	Phase V 9 Febr. - 12 March '82 review of implementation
9 Nov. : new Western amendments	Phase VI 9 Nov. - 17 Dec. '82 new Western proposals
15 March (1983): revised NNA draft for the concluding document (RM. 39 revised)	Phase VII 8 Febr. - 25 March '83 preparing the end-game
3 May : four Western amendments 6 May : Soviet rejection Western amendments 17 June : Spanish compromise 15 July (1983): provisional agreement à 34 6 Sept.: adoption of the concluding document	Phase VIII 19 April - 9 Sept. '83 the end-game

into eight phases according to natural breaks such as Christmas and Easter recesses. These divisions are purely historical and bear no relation to the analytical phases proposed by Zartman.

During each of the eight phases both functions of the conference mentioned above operated but the third column also indicates which of the two aspects predominated in each phase.

5.1. Phase II (27 January - 10 April 1981): Examination of Proposals

The process of negotiation began with the examination of new proposals at the beginning of the second phase. The first phase (11 November - 19 December 1980) was devoted to the initial review of implementation of the Final Act. The preceding preparatory phase (9 September - 10 November 1980) had served to establish the agenda and other procedural matters for the main meeting.

One of the internal factors contributing to the length of the conference was the multiplicity of proposals at the start of the second phase, to be dealt with and incorporated into a substantive concluding document, and also the variety of their content; there was enough material for months of discussion. However, if the situation in Madrid differed from that of the first follow-up Meeting in Belgrade, which had lasted only five months, it was not in the number of proposals - for this was identical - but in that in Belgrade in January 1978 the SU had indicated that she was not interested in negotiations on these proposals because she set no store by a substantive concluding document. Three years later in Madrid, in contrast, the SU was ready to start negotiating on all proposals, apparently because she was now keen to reach agreement on a "Conference on Military Détente and Disarmament in Europe" (the East European title), a mandate for which could only be included in a concluding document which was balanced as well as substantive or, in other words, one which also contained commitments on other aspects of the Final Act. The importance that the SU attached to such a disarmament conference was underlined by President Brezhnev's speech on 23 February 1981 which caught everyone in the conference building by surprise: he said that under certain conditions he was willing to include "the entire European part of the USSR" in the new régime of confidence building measures that might be agreed at this disarmament conference. Here Brezhnev unexpectedly fulfilled one of the four conditions of the Western proposal for the conference.

The fifth of March 1981 can be taken as what Zartman would call "the first turning point" in the long process which ensued. Round about this date real negotiation began in the contact groups. The moment conformed to Zartman's theory for he says: "At some stage, an important Turning Point of Seriousness has been reached: the perception by each side that the other is serious about finding a negotiated solution - that is, that the other is willing to 'lose' a little to 'win' a little rather than to win or lose all in a non-negotiated approach" (9). At this time the West made the assumption that the SU was prepared to lose just sufficient to win the mandate for the disarmament conference. To say the least of it, the West did not wish to exclude this possibility and for domestic political reasons affecting various West European countries could no longer afford to do so without being branded as the nigger in the woodpile.

Even though far from all Western and Neutral negotiators were personally convinced that there was any real chance of achieving a substantive concluding document, there was now no alternative to crossing the Threshold of Seriousness. The fact that all parties now did so meant that all had given silent assent to what Zartman terms a "referent principle" (10), in this case the attempt to achieve "a substantial and balanced concluding document" (11) in the context of which "substantial" indicates the wish to arrive at a series of meaningful commitments, and "balanced" to the wish to cover all areas of the Final Act. In the attempt to achieve this object, the contact groups spent March 1981 in trying to reach agreement on all 87 of the proposals that had been put forward. In these negotiations a second referent principle also obtained, and this was that every provision in the Madrid concluding document had to be "an improvement" or "step forward" in relation to the Final Act, meaning a clarification or further specification of the Final Act's provisions. This principle was used by all parties as an argument for or against proposed texts; ultimately the referent principle of the whole CSCE process is the Final Act.

In the contact groups drafting followed the inductive method, focusing from the very beginning on the details of the proposals. Thus Zartman's Formula and Detail Phases went on simultaneously. While it gradually became clear during this phase that agreement might be reached, but only on proposals that Western and Neutral countries held to be of less importance and not on those to which they attached greater importance, two parallel developments came into existence. The Neutral delegations, on the one hand, were working towards drafting an integral, substantive concluding document in order to see whether differences of opinion could be accommodated in that way, while on the other hand plans were growing among both NNA and EC delegations to try for an early adjournment of the conference for a considerable period without agreement on a substantive concluding document. The first of these developments resulted in the first complete NNA draft for a concluding document which was put forward on 31 March 1981. This date would qualify as "a second turning point", in Zartman's terminology, and the NNA document itself as "a substantive framework for agreement and a set of criteria for resolving details" (12) because in the months to come it played a primordial role as comprehensive guideline. It was based on a number of texts that had already been agreed in contact groups and on the many non--papers containing draft texts, which were in circulation. One of the postulates which had governed its drafting had been that proposals that stood no chance of success because one of the parties opposed them on matters of principle, should not be included. Therefore, in spite of the acclaim which greeted the document it also became the target of criticism from both sides, singling out unacceptable paragraphs or lamenting the omission of others. The document was nevertheless adopted as a basis for further negotiations.

While this document was being prepared, one of the Neutral delegations was at the same time fostering a plan to obtain early closure of the meeting with the issue of a short document of the Belgrade type, with no content whatsoever, in view of the fact that there was no real chance of a substantive document. However, few of the other delegations gave their support to this plan. Among EC delegations there was another plan which would have come into effect immediately after the coming Easter recess, when a deadline would have been set for closure (mid-June) on the understanding that if by then there should still be no prospect of agreement on matters of substance, the EC countries would wish to adjourn the conference for one or two years. There was increasing apprehension among these delegations that the Madrid CSCE meeting would cease to be essentially a follow-up meeting, and become instead of a permanent nature, finally perhaps turning into a permanent forum dealing largely with questions of disarmament (as the SU seemed to want, according to these EC delegations), and that the human rights dimension would be mislaid in the process. Should the CSCE find itself institutionalized in this way, it would mean a complete betrayal of the follow-up process.

During the last weeks before Easter the Soviet delegation, in contrast, took pains to appear totally unflurried: better late than never seemed to be its attitude to the mandate for a disarmament conference and its patience was unshakeable.

5.2. Phase III (5 May - 27 July 1981): Drafting the Document

After Easter there was an unexpected reversal of these positions due to external factors. The Soviet delegation had patience no longer and pressed for an early closure of the conference with a substantive document. The SU's objective, the European conference on military détente and disarmament, had suddenly gained urgency as part of Brezhnev's Peace Programme. The Soviet delegation was even willing to make some concessions on passages dealing with other areas of the concluding document in order to achieve its ends. On the other hand the Foreign Ministers of the ten EC countries had decided in Venlo (The Netherlands) on 10 May 1981 that, in view of tensions in and around Poland, they would not be leaving Madrid for the present. Speaking as President of the Ten, the Dutch Foreign Minister told the Press, after the Venlo meeting had concluded, that the Madrid conference must not break up at least for the time being.

Whatever the original objectives of the EC countries - and they had been twofold, discussion of implementation of the Final Act and consideration of new proposals - their priorities were now changed as far as Madrid was concerned. For the Ten, the Conference's most important function was now "informational"; for them, it had become the sole forum for daily dialogue with Moscow at a time of political crisis. The ten West European governments could not now allow the Madrid discussions, which continued unexpectedly to offer such a forum, to be unseasonably interrupted.

So those Western representatives in Madrid who had been in favour of early adjournment for a long period were obliged to lay their plans aside.

This phase therefore saw the continuation of intensive negotiations on the first NNA draft for a final document. The pace was slow. But these twelve weeks ultimately produced 30 pages of agreed text which two years later came to make up eighty per cent of the Madrid Concluding Document.

5.3. Phase IV (27 October - 18 December 1981): Search for Solutions

After the summer of 1981 no-one could any longer be justified in excluding the possibility of the materialization of agreement on a substantive concluding document before Christmas. For Western countries in that autumn of mass peace marches in Western Europe, the Madrid conference had again become important but for reasons different from before. It became part of their comprehensive effort to negotiate with the Soviet Union on arms control. In his speech of 11 November 1981, President Reagan referred to the Western proposal in Madrid (from France) for a European disarmament conference as one of his four initiatives on arms control alongside the negotiations that he was proposing in Geneva on INF and START, and the on-going negotiations in Vienna on MBFR. This unexpected role taken by the Madrid Meeting in Western foreign policy was also expressed in the West German-Soviet communiqué of 25 November 1981 after party leader Brezhnev's visit to Bonn, in which both sides expressed their determination to bring the Madrid negotiations for a "Conference on Confidence and Security Building Measures and Disarmament in Europe" - as the European disarmament conference had meanwhile officially become known - to a satisfactory conclusion before the end of the year. It was now the "normative function" of Madrid which had priority in Western foreign policy.

In the conference building in Madrid it was striking to hear the degree of emphasis used by the Soviet and other East European delegations in pointing to the mass marches for peace in Western Europe as a sign that "the peoples of Europe" wanted disarmament, a desire that the Soviet Union claimed was frustrated by the Reagan administration and its closest allies. In this way the SU made use of the Madrid conference to appeal to a secondary audience, in this case the peace marchers, the "peoples" who were protesting against their governments in the struggle for peace (13).

In spite of the reasonable climate of international political East--West relations in the autumn of 1981, negotiations in Madrid hung fire.

In the various contact groups not a single sentence could be agreed. The problems before them were small in number but provoked lengthy discussion and seemed unable to generate common language. All parties were waiting for agreement to be reached on the mandate for the European disarmament conference which everyone now wanted, but agreement proved elusive. The differences in opinion on the mandate resisted all attempts at a semantic solution because they affected the security interests of the states most nearly involved. But until the mandate had been settled none of the parties was inclined to take an amenable attitude to the remaining issues. The West even went so far as to retract one or two of the summer's concessions, retreating into more hardline positions on these issues. The Soviet delegation made it perfectly clear that it would refuse any compromise on these subjects until agreement was reached on the mandate for the disarmament conference.

First to produce an initiative to force a breakthrough was the Finnish delegation which, on express instructions, put forward some compromise suggestions for the mandate. Although this particular effort failed, its consequence was that all four Neutral delegations, as a group went into direct, intensive consultation with both Eastern and Western delegations on either side, to find a solution for all the questions that still remained undecided. These consultations resulted in a package deal put together by the Austrian delegation and officially presented jointly by all the NNA delegations, with the exception of Malta, on 16 December 1981 under the connotation RM.39. Its NNA sponsors repeated what they had said about their first draft, that this comprehensive draft for a concluding document was "not the ideal text but the only one that seemed likely to be achieved".

This document was intended to be what William Zartman would call "a third turning point", or "the crest". For this he provides various definitions not all of which apply to the situation in Madrid at that time. For instance it was not true that in Madrid at that moment "enough was agreed upon to constitute an acceptable accord" (14); the situation was rather that it was anticipated that the NNA draft would provide the basis for an accord after a short final round of negotiations. But wholly in accordance with Zartman's theory, the moment could be distinguished from the second turning point in that for internal political reasons, the agreement itself (including the mandate for a European disarmament conference) had now become of great importance to the majority of participants even though its content might not be entirely satisfactory for them. In the first weeks of December the situation could be described in Zartman's words as follows: "it would not be inaccurate to say that, at that point, the agreement itself becomes a positive good in the eyes of the parties, to be defended against loss just like the other demands of the parties" (15). All this was changed however as soon as the consequences of the military takeover of 13 December in Poland became known; the desirability of reaching agreement on a concluding document evaporated in face of the fact that one of the participating states was at the very same moment acting in conscious violation of its provisions.

5.4. Phase V (9 February - 12 March 1982): Review of Implementation Once Again

During the Christmas recess the Madrid forum regained its importance for Western politics in its "rule supervisory" role. The ten EC foreign ministers, and subsequently the NATO ministers, sent out communiqué's in which they declared their intention of travelling to Madrid that February in order to express their concern about the way in which, under Soviet pressure, human rights in Poland were being violated. The NNA ministers followed suit. The first week after the conference resumed on 9 February was entirely dominated by discussions on the fulfilment of the Final Act and its violation by Poland and the Soviet Union, interrupted by the procedural debates described in Chapter VIII, 3 and 4. These debates reflected the international situation while political will to see agreement on a concluding document "as a positive good in itself" had completely vanished. The problems about the mandate for the European disarmament conference were not discussed at all and neither were the remaining questions which were still to be decided on the NNA draft of 16 December. In the Drafting Group which had been set up in December to deal with these questions the Western delegations refused to speak, a "conspiracy of silence" against which the East European delegations were powerless. The Soviet delegation emphatically rejected any "linkage" made by the West between events in Poland and the subject of negotiations in Madrid: "By artificially linking different questions it is impossible to solve a single international problem", they said. For Moscow the most important object of the Madrid conference remained what it had always been: the calling of a European conference on military détente and disarmament. The US delegation was singled out as arch villain in the "crude attempt to undermine the very idea of convening the conference, to make it dependent on factors totally unrelated to the Madrid meeting" (16).

5.5. Phase VI (9 November - 17 December 1982): New Western Proposals

During the summer recess NATO heads of state and governments met in Bonn on 10 June and issued a "Document on arms control and disarmament" in which, just as in the autumn of 1981, the CSCE was set beside START, INF and MBFR as a platform for negotiations with Moscow on arms control measures. "In CSCE, the proposal for a Conference on Confidence - and Security - Building Measures and Disarmament in Europe as part of a balanced outcome of the Madrid CSCE Follow-up meeting would open the way to increased transparency and enhanced stability in the whole of Europe from the Atlantic to the Urals".

In the political "Declaration" to which this Document was annexed, on the other hand, the CSCE was not mentioned by name, and although the Declaration did contain a single paragraph referring indirectly to the conference, this gave no indication that government leaders in the West still retained any hopeful expectations of an early conclusion to the conference (17).

During the preparations within NATO for resumption of the conference it became apparent that the NATO countries were not all in agreement on the policy to be followed that autumn in Madrid. One body of opinion was in favour of maintaining the refusal to negotiate on the NNA draft RM.39 of 16 December 1981 for a concluding document. An agreement still failed to regain its character as a positive good in itself because the international political situation still did not justify it: on 8 October, in Poland, the trade union SOLIDARITY had been banned. The Soviet Union's recent record on human rights (greatly reduced Jewish emigration, disconnection of international automatic telephone links, dissolution of the Helsinki monitor group in Moscow) gave even less reason for the West to take an amenable attitude in Madrid.

The other body of opinion held that a significant concluding document as a new code of conduct for relations in Europe was worth fighting for in order to keep the East-West dialogue going both in spite of the international tensions and because of them. The result of these disparate opinions was a compromise within NATO by which amendments to the NNA draft of far-reaching significance in the light of the recent events in Poland and the SU would be put forward in order to start negotiations off. The CSCE work group of the ten EC countries then formulated these amendments which were put forward by the West on 9 November 1982. One of them gave an account of the implementation discussions on Poland held in February and was therefore totally unacceptable to East European countries.

A further Western amendment renewed in the clearest terms the earlier Western proposal regarding the prohibition of interference with foreign radio broadcasts: the participating states were to "undertake not to interfere with the reception of broadcast information from each other". Western countries also demanded protection of the rights of monitor groups. The nucleus of this proposal was that each state should "take the actions necessary to ensure the freedom of the individual to express his views concerning the respect shown by governments, including his own, in law and practice, for the Final Act". Another proposal with the same end in view asked the states: "not only to refrain from impeding but also to encourage all efforts to implement the Final Act". Yet another Western proposal was one to "ensure the right of everyone freely to form and join trade unions of his choice" which was part of a wider proposal concerning the right to free trade unions. Finally there were about ten drafting amendments which were designed to improve the NNA text in a Western sense. In conclusion, on the basis of earlier Western proposals, detailed agendas were put forward for two expert meetings, the first to be held in Ottawa "concerning respect for human rights and fundamental freedoms, in all their aspects, as embodied in the Final Act", and the second in Washington "on Human Contacts as set forth in Section 1 of the humanitarian chapter of the Final Act".

For the West this sixth phase of the conference became therefore a time for introduction and defence of new amendments. The recent unsatisfactory record of practice in East European countries was brought in as justification for these new measures. For the West the function of Madrid had once more become "normative".

East European delegations fought the amendments because they saw them as unrealistic. They claimed that they had been put forward simply because they would be unacceptable to East European countries. Their delegations repeatedly threatened to introduce counter-proposals equally unacceptable to the West, but they never seriously carried out their threat, contenting themselves with outlining the counter-proposals which they might put forward if they so wished. They labelled the Western proposals as a provocative attempt to prevent achievement of a substantive concluding document and its corollary, the mandate for a European disarmament conference. The calling of this conference was, as ever, still the Soviet Union's prime objective (18). The Soviet delegation itself declared flatly that its aim for this phase of the Madrid Meeting was to reach agreement on the mandate for a disarmament conference before Christmas of that year. To this end the SU was prepared to take a step in the direction desired by the West on the subject of the mandate's content but the West found that this did not go far enough to make agreement possible.

5.6. Phase VII (8 February - 25 March 1983): Preparing the End-Game?

At the beginning of this phase the NNA countries issued a collective declaration which had been prepared during intensive mutual consultation in the Christmas recess. Two years earlier such political cohesion among NNA countries regarding the Madrid Meeting would have been unthinkable. The common urge to save the CSCE now drove them more than ever towards a communal policy. In somewhat authoritarian tone they offered "for the last time" their services as "honest brokers" between East and West, for a further three or four weeks, and proposed to set up for this purpose "mini-groups", each of which would take one chapter of the draft concluding document, RM.39, and resolve whatever questions still remained to be decided within it. In addition, the NNA countries declared that if after these three or four weeks there was still no prospect of a substantive concluding document, this would be the end of the Madrid Meeting's credibility and they would seek an early conclusion to the conference without such a document.

Both East and West greeted the NNA countries' initiative with enthusiasm. Both sides felt the need to terminate the conference, with a commitment to begin a European disarmament conference before the end of the year. The start of that conference would then coincide with the possible beginning of implementation of the NATO decision of December

1979 to deploy intermediate range ballistic missiles in Western Europe, if INF talks in Geneva failed. Discussion in the corridors began to give weight to this question; in the next phase (see below) this was even more clearly the case.

In the mini-groups set up by the NNA countries intensive negotiation continued on the phrases out of RM.39 remaining to be settled and on the far-reaching Western amendments of November 1982 in relation to these passages. It was a question of a mere twenty sentences in a document of 35 pages. Half of these were actually agreed in the mini-groups.

At the end of the four weeks that the NNA countries had allowed East and West to come to agreement, the NNA countries decided that sufficient perspective had been filled in to arrive at a substantive concluding document and they announced that they would now produce a revised version of their RM.39 draft with compromise solutions for the few points that were still open questions. The new document was issued on 15 March 1983 and classified as "RM.39 revised". As far as the formulation of the mandate for the European disarmament conference was concerned this new document was favourable to the West, but there were glaring omissions when it came to what the West had hoped for with regard to reinforcing the human dimension of the concluding document.

It now remained for the political authorities at home to decide during the Easter recess whether "RM.39 revised" was acceptable or not, and therefore whether it would form the last turning point - "the crest" - in the words of Zartman. The original RM.39 draft for a concluding document presented on 16 December 1981, and intended as "the crest", had missed its target due to external factors because of which the West had consciously relapsed into what Zartman would have called "the Detail Phase" as described above.

5.7. Phase VIII (19 April - 15 July 1983): The End-Game

The "end-game" as it was called in Madrid, lasted for about three months and was then followed by the so-called "Malta weeks". In fact, for most of this three month period there were no negotiations. The final NNA draft for the concluding document (RM.39 revised) was accepted by Moscow on condition that no changes at all would be made. But the West, supported by NNA countries, insisted on four amendments concerning four words in the draft and the addition of two passages, one on the prohibition of radio jamming and one on calling a meeting of experts on human contacts (to discuss the emigration policies of some of the participating states, which left more and more to be desired). Besides this there was a phrase in the mandate for the European Disarmament Conference which was susceptible of two interpretations on which the West asked for further clarification. The Soviet delegation had no inclination to begin negotiations on any of these amendments. Finally, Romania and Malta had both filed additional amendments which were acceptable to no--one. Stalemate lasted for two months.

The end-game now played itself out as psychological warfare. In veiled terms in their formal speeches, and openly in personal conversations, East European delegates asked their colleagues from the West and from NNA countries whether they were really ready to risk everything that had been achieved in the draft concluding document (RM.39 revised) which covered 35 pages of text and could be called for eighty per cent a Western document, for the sake of those four Western amendments. The East European delegates claimed that it would mean no concluding document at all and thus no European Disarmament Conference in autumn 1983, and yet had not the West German Foreign Minister more than once told the press that he wanted this conference to begin in the autumn? The West was in the position of *demandeur* for an early end to the Madrid Meeting and was therefore bound to accept the draft for a concluding document unchanged. Moscow, on the other hand - so their argument ran - was not interested in the conference's early closure. Because the continuation of Madrid into the autumn would provide an ideal forum for Moscow's complaints against deployment of INF missiles, just as the West, a year earlier, had used the Madrid forum to criticize developments in Poland, the continuation of the Madrid conference into the autumn would be more to Moscow's taste than the start of the European Disarmament Conference in Stockholm. Moscow might then threaten to withdraw her assent to RM.39 revised in view of the deterioration of détente to be expected over the summer. "The CSCE process wil not survive the autumn" was the foreboding cry of these East European delegates.

Some of the NNA and Western delegates were impressed by this line of argument but most of them were not, arguing that in the end the Soviet Union was *demandeur* for the European Disarmament Conference and would therefore ultimately be willing to start negotiating on the four Western amendments. In any case no-one in the Western camp was ready to give in without more ado to East European threats. It was vital to strengthen the human dimension in the concluding document by means of these four Western amendments.

In the end it was a compromise initiated by the host country Spain and including about fifty per cent of the four Western amendments that, on 17 June, broke the impasse. When the West and Moscow declared it possible to negotiate on this compromise, and Moscow, in addition, wanted to finish negotiations within no more than a few days, delegates felt that at long last the home-stretch, in Zartman's terminology, had been reached. On 15 July 1983, 34 of the 35 delegations reached "provisional agreement" on the Madrid Concluding Document. The fact that the home--stretch subsequently extended itself far beyond the wishes of any delegate was due to Malta's insistence on certain amendments unacceptable to the rest. Even a theory like Zartman and Berman's cannot be expected to foresee a "Malta phase", lasting eight weeks.

5.8. The Malta Phase (15 July - 6 September 1983)

In Madrid, delegates had expected some "Malta weeks" but not the extension of this period over two months. This phase lasted longer than in either Helsinki 1973, Geneva 1975 or Belgrade 1978 (see Chapter II under 4.1.) largely because in Madrid none of the remaining 34 countries was prepared for the fourth time to be bullied by Malta's tactics. Malta's plan once again was to block consensus for the close of negotiations for as long as her wishes were not complied with.

Malta's representative had already declared his intention, long before negotiations reached their close, to employ the usual Maltese strategy unless all her proposals were accepted. Her proposal for recognition of a special sort for her own neutrality had already been approved in spite of the fact that other countries were against it. Malta's remaining proposals concerned, first of all, a reconfirmation of the passage in the Final Act - only included in 1975 by virtue of the Maltese strategy - declaring that the states would strive towards "reducing armed forces" in the region of the Mediterranean, secondly the inclusion of the Mediterranean in the area of application of the measures to be decided by the Stockholm disarmament conference, and, finally, the calling of a CSCE meeting on security in the area of the Mediterranean Sea to be attended not only by experts from all 35 CSCE countries but also by experts from the non-participating Mediterranean states: Algeria, Egypt, Israel, Lebanon, Libya, Morocco, Syria and Tunisia. These proposals were politically so unrealistic that East and West, together with the NNA countries, were driven to create a "consensus of 34" and use as a threat the possibility of approving and implementing the Madrid Concluding Document without Malta's assistance, even if this would mean in fact the beginning of a "CSCE-Mark 2".

At the end of July the ministerial sessions designed to close the Madrid Meeting were fixed for 7, 8 and 9 September. The conference did not, however, then go into recess for the summer. Each delegation left a single member behind in Madrid with the task of attending weekly plenary meetings during August and carrying on negotiations with Malta. The 34 delegations made up a "caucus" with the object of consultation on tactics to be used against Malta. Only Romania hesitated before joining this "caucus". On 25 August, when Malta still refused to conform to the consensus of 34 and even became more adamant in her demands, the threat to approve the concluding document without her agreement began to be put into action. The Spanish Minister of Foreign Affairs invited his CSCE colleagues by means of bilateral diplomatic Notes "to attend a meeting of Ministers of Foreign Affairs, in Madrid on 7, 8 and 9 September". This meeting would take place at Spain's initiative and thus outside the framework of the CSCE.

On 5 September the 34 delegations agreed that during this meeting the 34 ministers would "affirm their determination to put into effect the draft concluding document", including its annexes and chairman's statements, "and to implement them from now on in letter and in spirit, comprising all the texts in their entirety". This meant that both the disarmament conference in Stockholm and the other meetings of experts would take place, with or without Malta. Furthermore, the 34 ministers would "welcome a decision by the 35th state to join them at any time, in order that the concluding document can be adopted and the Madrid Meeting can be concluded by consensus". This was formulated in a statement to be made by the chairman on behalf of the 34 countries. When it became clear to Malta that all 34 countries were party to this declaration, including Romania, thus making it inevitable, she gave way and, on 6 September she joined in the consensus in exchange for a chairman's statement on her proposals. This had been prepared by Sweden meanwhile, but had no binding force whatsoever.

At the ministerial sessions on 7, 8 and 9 September which were now able to take up their role as closing sessions of the CSCE Follow-up Meeting in Madrid, in conformity with the agenda of the Purple Book, the Malta problem was forgotten: East European ministers concentrated their interventions on the necessity of military *détente* in Europe, and Western and Neutral ministers drew attention in general to the violation of human rights in Eastern Europe and in particular to the shooting down of a South Korean Boeing-747 airliner over the Russian island Sachalin, on 1 September; review of implementation once again.

NOTES:

1. During the Preparatory Meeting Sweden once circulated a compromise draft for the disputed agenda for the main Madrid conference, in which the most important paragraph looked like this:

   "A thorough exchange of views

   [............................
   ....
   ,]

   Examination of proposals concerning the above questions".

   When the Soviet representative read this proposal he asked: "Since when has Sweden been a member of NATO?". An explanation is to be found in Chapter V under "optical division"; the visual separation which the NATO countries had wanted was taken over in principle in the Swedish proposal which furthermore indicated, by the use of square brackets, that the paragraph's lay-out might be the subject of argument and that, as shown by the lines of dots, Sweden did not wish to make any pronouncement on the text itself.

2. Compare Newhouse: "It is hard for the other side to react to a self-appointed demandeur other than to exploit him". John Newhouse, Cold Dawn; The Story of SALT (New York: Holt, Rinehart and Winston, 1973), p. 270.

3. Compare Zartman and Berman: "Stalemate is better as a tactic than veto; it is less vulnerable, less likely to become an issue or subject of attack itself, and it is friendlier". William Zartman and Maureen R. Berman, op. cit., p. 77.

4. See Robert W. Cox and Harold K. Jacobson et al., The Anatomy of Influence; Decision Making in International Organization (New Haven and London: Yale University Press, 1974) pp. 12 ff.

5. It is relevant here to take account of the conclusion reached in Chapter IV: "A particular representative of a certain country may have markedly more influence in multilateral discussions than either his predecessor or his successor in the same role. One member of a delegation can be more influential than another of the same delegation". The role of broker, for example, may be played better by a certain representative than by his colleague from the same NNA delegation. One representative may be less acceptable as "controller" than his predecessor in the same office.

6. See William Zartman, "Negotiations: Theory and Reality", Journal of International Affairs, vol. 29, no. 1, 1975, pp. 69-75, in particular pp. 74 and 75.

7. See Zartman and Berman, op. cit., in particular pp. 87, 143 and 188-189.

8. Ibid., p. 9.

9. Ibid., p. 87.

10. "Referents are principles of justice on which both parties can agree. They can be such philosophical principles as equality, split-the--difference, compensation, or special rights". Zartman, op. cit., p. 71.

11. After the Easter recess of 1981 all delegations claimed to be pursuing "a substantial and balanced concluding document". As in the case of many CSCE notions it is impossible to tell who first used this expression, but it seems likely to have been one of the NNA delegations at the presentation of the first NNA draft for such a document.

12. See Zartman and Berman, op. cit. , p. 143 and Zartman, op. cit., p. 75.

13. Kowaljow underlines that an unbreakable rule of Soviet diplomacy is to apply the Leninist principle to address oneself not only to the primary audience, the governments, but at the same time to the secondary audience, the peoples who, according to Lenin, must be helped in opposition to their governments "to take action in problems of war and peace". Anatoli Kowaljow, op. cit., p. 47.

14. Zartman and Berman, op. cit., p. 188. See also Zartman, op. cit., pp. 75-76.

15. Zartman and Berman, op. cit., p. 188.

16. The argument on "linkage" was a central theme in the Soviet delegation's interventions in the Plenary during this phase in Madrid. See L. Baturin, "Détente in Europe and Its Opponents", International Affairs, no. 7, 1982, p. 12.

17. The text of the Declaration's paragraph read as follows: "Our purpose is to develop substantial and balanced East-West relations aimed at genuine detente. For this to be achieved, the sovereignty of all states, wherever situated, must be respected, human rights must not be sacrificed to state interests, the free movement of ideas must take the place of one-sided propaganda, the free movement of persons must be made possible, efforts must be made to achieve a military relationship characterised by stability and openness, and in general all principles and provisions of the Helsinki Final Act in their entirety must be applied. We, for our part, will always be ready to negotiate in this spirit and we look for tangible evidence that this attitude is reciprocated".

18. Compare Rakhmaninov: "It is obvious that an agreement in Madrid on holding a conference on military detente measures would help build up confidence between states. And this, naturally, would facilitate the solution of other questions discussed at the meeting". Y. Rakhmaninov, "The Key Problem of European Security", International Affairs, no. 12, 1982, p. 20.

X. THE MADRID RESULTS

1. Introduction

The limitations imposed on the Madrid results in consequence of the rule of consensus have already been discussed in Chapter VII. It comes as no surprise, therefore, to find that the Madrid Concluding Document is no marvel of juridical art. The results themselves are given below in further detail with the object of relating them to the main objectives held by the participants on their arrival at Madrid three years earlier (see Chapter III under 4 and 5). To what extent were these objectives realized? Our aim here is thus not to ascertain Madrid's significance for European history or whether the Madrid results are liable to change the world at large, but to give a description of the Meeting as a decision-making process and of the way in which its conditions influenced that process and thereby its results.

2. The Review of Implementation

It has already been explained in Chapter III that one of the two important aims of the Western countries in Madrid was to hold a searching discussion on the records of the participating states in fulfilment of the Helsinki agreements. For this reason, during the Preparatory Meeting, the West fought a long battle for recognition of the principle, already accepted in Belgrade, that the implementation discussion should be a discrete and independent element of the main meeting. Although in the end this effort was, on paper, less successful than in Belgrade (see Chapter V) in practice this proved to be of little importance.

Discussions on fulfilment of the Final Act occupied not only the first six weeks of the conference in their entirety (as envisaged in the Purple Book), but also continued to form a major part of the deliberations right up to the last phase of the Meeting two-and-a-half years later. The West's vindication of this state of affairs had a two-fold basis. In the first place, the Purple Book, which envisaged the conference's finally ending on 5 March 1981, had laid down the proportion of time which was to be spent on the implementation discussion and the proportion which was to be taken up with new proposals. With the prolongation of the conference beyond that initial four months, it became incumbent for the same proportion of the total duration to be devoted to the implementation discussion as had originally been fixed. In the second place the West had unilaterally reserved the right to continue the implementation discussion beyond the first six weeks if new facts should arise to make this appropriate. The sort of thing that was envisaged and which it would be impossible to pass over without comment might be new arrests of dissidents in East European countries or military intervention by the Soviet Union in Poland. This right which the West had appropriated to itself, was much exercized by both Western and Neutral countries, for there was no lack of new facts to act as stimulants.

Discussions on fulfilment of the Final Act came to a head in the weeks following 9 February 1982 when the subject of discussion was mainly the situation in Poland. The leader of one of the Neutral countries' delegations was then finally driven to remark that the discussions were "exceptionally harsh, accusational and bitter" more than ever before in the history of the CSCE. The NNA countries then decided that it would be wiser to push for a long summer recess because the "dialogue" that was taking place between East and West was damaging to the CSCE process. With the help of the Western countries this aim was achieved, as has been described in Chapter VIII under the heading "The Night of Silences".

Autumn 1982 produced an international situation less provocative of heavy-fire implementation discussions. A few of the Neutral countries did address themselves to Turkey, with greater emphasis than ever before, on the subject of the large number of political prisoners in that country, and Romania was asked by Western countries to explain her recent emigration measures which required Romanian women wishing to join their husbands abroad to provide a prohibitively large amount of money in foreign currency as restoration of what their education had cost the Romanian state. In the Spring of 1983, when Western countries were seriously interested in negotiations on a substantial concluding document, there was little implemenatation discussion for fear this might jeopardize the chances of achieving agreement on such a document.

2.1. Themes Discussed

From the very beginning the implementation discussion was well-prepared, sharp and at certain times emotional. On occasion it could also be businesslike particularly when economic co-operation between states was concerned, and now and then in the third basket, when it was to do with cultural co-operation. Originally the discussions took place in the Subsidiary Working Bodies as well as in the Plenary, but later primarily in the Plenary because the SWBs had been turned into Drafting Groups, and, subsequently, into contact groups.

In the Plenary the most important Western theme at the beginning of the conference was the Soviet invasion of Afghanistan which was claimed to be in conflict with the United Nations Charter and with various Principles of the Final Act. Reference was made in particular to the final lines of the section of the Final Act containing the Declaration on the Ten Principles: "The participating States declare their intention to conduct their relations with all other States in the spirit of the principles contained in the present Declaration". However, the Soviet delegation was never willing to put up a defence on the Afghanistan question because, according to the SU, the Western accusations constituted interference in the internal affairs of Afghanistan.

Yet Western as well as Neutral countries repeatedly gave warning that détente would not be able to survive a "second Afghanistan" (for which read: Poland). In addition to Afghanistan there were also other themes pursued from the Neutral and Western side: the treatment of Helsinki monitor groups in various East European countries; misuse of psychiatric science; maltreatment, internal exile and discrimination in the case of dissidents, applicants for exit visas, religious minorities, Jews, the Tartars in the Krim, the Baltic peoples and the Ukrainians. In the course of such discussion concrete facts and actual names of victims were regularly cited.

The Soviet reaction to accusations from the West sharpened increasingly as the accusations themselves became more heated. If a Western delegate delivered its charge in a moderate tone, either there would be no response at all or the Soviet representative, or that of some other East European country, would simply say that the intervention in question did not indicate a businesslike approach to the conference, likely to enhance the possibility of the Madrid Meeting's achieving a constructive result, and that it was unnecessarily polemical in tone.

If a Western delegation cited the names of dissidents or referred to them explicitly, the Soviet delegation would react by saying that the Western countries were taking "criminals" under their wing, puppets of imperialistic circles, and ask why they should take such an interest in criminal elements. When, after a fierce attack, the Soviet representative chose to respond in kind, the subsequent tirade usually contained one or more of the following standard expressions: slander, hypocrisy, fairy--tales, poisoning the atmosphere in Madrid, cheap propaganda, defence of criminals transgressors and betrayers of their fatherland, an imperialistic outcry from the USA, sterile polemics.

In February and March 1982, during the debates on the situation in Poland, East European delegations expressly appealed to principle VI which, they claimed, forbade interference in the internal affairs of Poland. In the conference's first year they had seldom appealed directly to this principle even though in general they rejected interference in domestic policies: "We shall not stand for interference in the internal affairs of our countries, particularly by countries where human rights are violated daily and on a massive scale", as one of the East European heads of delegation put it.

This in turn led him to draw attention, in general terms, to wrongs existing in Western countries.

The more urgently the West went into the domestic situation in some East European countries the more the representatives of these countries pointed to the state of affairs in Western countries: "Is it not paradoxical that those who express concern about human rights in socialist countries, should be precisely those countries where human rights are violated, continuously, systematically and on a massive scale?" was the question of the leader of the Soviet delegation, who followed this up by mentioning, among other things, the high figures for unemployment in the West and the situation in Northern Ireland. In the debate on Poland the same spirit inspired him to launch a direct attack on American foreign policy: "Who are these people who dare to set themselves up in judgement on Poland? They turn out to be the very same circles in the United States that give support to the Israeli aggressors, the bloodstained junta in El Salvador and the Pinochet régime in Chile, racism in South Africa and other dictatorial régimes, and to the anti--humanitarian decision by Reagan to resume production of chemical weapons".

Interference in the domestic politics of other participating states was not admissible and yet because the West did it East European delegations also claimed to be justified in doing so. They pointed to what, in their eyes, were "massive", "structural" violations of human rights in the West: the enormous unemployment figures, organized criminality, racial discrimination and anti-semitism in certain Western countries in general, and more specifically the treatment of Northern Ireland's hunger strikers by the United Kingdom, the murders of negro children in Atlanta, president Reagan's handling of the airline leaders' strike and the maltreatment of IRA members imprisoned in the Maze Prison in Northern Ireland.

In the face of such accusations the West's defence usually followed certain lines: criticism from East European delegations was welcome in so far as nobody would wish to deny them the right to bring up any conjectured violations of the Final Act in the West. Thanks to freedom of the press and freedom of expression in the West, everyone was aware of the evils which had been brought in evidence and the Western governments concerned were already doing their utmost to provide a remedy wherever there was real injustice.

2.2. Basket Discussions

What follows is an account of the more detailed discussions in the various Subsidiary Working Bodies during the first weeks of the conference in the autumn of 1980. In general, the themes raised by the West in the SWB for the *first* basket, dealing with "Questions relating to Security in Europe" were the same as those mentioned above, with the addition of more detail: Afghanistan, violation of human rights in some East European countries, the discriminatory treatment of religious believers, unofficial trade unions, Helsinki monitor groups, Jews and other minorities. Facts and numbers were cited. Favourable developments in East European countries also received their share of Western attention. When criticized, East European countries based their defence not only on their assumption that the Final Act did not allow "interference" in their domestic policies, but also on articles of their own constitutions and laws which forbade just such discrimination.

When the section of the First Chapter of the Final Act concerning military aspects of security came up, both the US and the USSR traded accusations on who was responsible for the arms race. Western delegations reproached East European countries with poor compliance with the Final Act provisions about prior notification of military exercises and said that Western military observers were not given adequate opportunity to view WP exercises. Eastern delegations criticized Western countries for holding large-scale manoeuvres near their borders (which the Final Act does not forbid). Western delegations drew attention to the way in which they had carried out the provisions in the Final Act concerning advance notification of military manoeuvres, and East European countries in turn vaunted their merits in the field of disarmament initiatives.

One of the main themes dealt with in the SWB for the *second* basket concerned co-operation in the field of energy, which was stressed particularly by East European delegations; a subject broached in particular by Western and Neutral countries was the difficulty they experienced in having to use compensation transaction in trade with East European enterprises which insist on paying in finished products rather than in currency. They also raised the problem of their difficulties in obtaining the necessary economic data for putting their business relations with East European firms on a long-term basis. The Eastern side in turn described their own difficulties in trading with the West: the EC's alleged "discriminatory" quantitative restrictions and the high US tariffs. Other subjects which came up were the possibility of co-operation in the field of environment (pollution of the Danube, for example), trade practices of some East European countries (dumping) and the problems of migrant workers, which were stressed by the labour--exporting countries of Southern Europe.

The *third* basket comprises a variety of subjects. The West brought up problems such as: the difficulty of obtaining exit visas in some East European countries; censorship of the press and radio and the limited distribution of Western newspapers and periodicals in the same East European countries. Western and Neutral delegations condemned the treatment of scientists in the SU as an insufferable abuse of psychiatric science. This criticism was dismissed by the Soviet delegation as being based on doubtful sources of information. Western and Neutral delegations claimed furthermore that their journalists were not allowed complete freedom of movement in Eastern European countries and that radio programmes sent out by the BBC, the *Deutsche Welle*, the Voice of America and Radio Free Europe were jammed.

The East European delegations, after first drawing attention to their own performance in fulfilment of the provisions of the Final Act, then pointed out that Western countries showed no interest in East European newspapers and periodicals. They also complained of the lack of security measures experienced by their sporting teams and other groups when they were in the West, and in general of the way certain specified countries complied with their consular and cultural bilateral agreements. As to their jamming of foreign radio programmes, they stated that in general the Western press and radio broadcast gave false information about their countries, were the vehicles of fascist and revanchist propaganda and in no way promoted peace and mutual understanding between peoples. The Voice of America and Radio Free Europe were in conflict with the ideals of the Final Act because they had been created to foster hatred between European peoples.

2.3. Détente and Implementation

During the review of implementation a controversy arose over the relationship between détente and the commitments entered into in the Final Act. For socialist countries détente is virtually a mechanical, irreversible process and, since the Final Act was signed, a fact. If the continuity of this process is hindered in any way this automatically influences fulfilment of the provisions of the Final Act. Thus the degree of détente has a decisive influence on how far these provisions will be implemented. Progress in détente, or better mutual understanding between the states, would lead to better implementation of the Final Act.

To illustrate this point of view the Soviet delegation recalled the boycott of the 1980 Olympic Games in Moscow by certain Western countries. This had been the consequence of the shortcomings of the relationship then existing between East and West. The same deterioration in détente had also been responsible for the breaking off by the West in 1980 of arrangements with the SU for exchange visits by cultural groups and scientists. It was only if détente were allowed to improve that increase and development of cultural and other contacts might be expected. According to the Soviet delegation the repercussions of this philosophy were to be heard in the Final Act, particularly in the mini-

-preambles to the provisions on human contacts, information and culture, in the third basket. There it is stated indeed that the participating states desire to continue efforts towards progress in these field "with the continuance of détente", "with the development of mutual understanding" and "with the further improvement of their relations". Western and Neutral delegates cited other parts of these mini-preambles which implied that, on the contrary, it was fulfilment of the provisions of the Final Act that would contribute to détente and better understanding between peoples, and not *vice versa*.

In general the Western view was that the East European philosophy put everything the wrong way round. For the West détente is influenced by (among other things) how far the commitments entered into in the Final Act are realized. Better implementation of the provisions of the Final Act would lead to better mutual understanding and progress in détente. The East European delegations were using wrongly the quotation from the Final Act which read "with the continuance of détente": the word "with" which represented an ambiguous compromise reached after much discussion in Geneva, was not, according to the West, to be interpreted as imposing a condition, as would have been the case if the word had been "if". "With" denoted an interaction between détente and implementation of the Final Act. Continuance of détente for example and the mutual understanding between peoples depended, claimed the West, on what was done by governments in the fields of human rights and human contacts. The East European philosophy would seem to condemn all the dissidents in the Soviet Union and the Jews who wanted to emigrate, to play the role of hostages to détente. The Olympic boycott and the decrease in cultural exchange had followed from Soviet policies regarding Afghanistan and human rights and it was precisely those policies which were a stumbling block to détente.

In Madrid the Soviet delegation was not prepared to reach any agreement on the paragraphs of the section "Human Contacts" in the third basket, which were so important to the West, unless agreement was first reached on a preamble for the whole of the third basket which would reflect the East European philosophy on the relationship between the development of détente and progress in the implementation of the Final Act as set out above. Western negotiators were not prepared to formulate a preamble which complied with the Soviet requirements. The result was the present unclear and ambigious text of that preamble (see Annex 4, page 309).

However, in the last weeks of Madrid the Soviet Union unexpectedly proved to be willing to accept the calling of an expert meeting on human contacts, but only on two conditions. Consensus on this question was not to be recorded in the Concluding Document itself but only in a chairman's statement annexed to this document. Furthermore, this statement had to include a clear expression of this philosophy on the relation between détente and fulfilment of the Final Act. After a few days of negotiations during which the fate of the Madrid Meeting hung in the balance, a solution satisfactory to the Soviet delegation was found. This consisted in quoting word for word a part of the mini-preamble of the section on "Human Contacts" of the Final Act, including the words: "Desiring in this spirit to develop, with the continuance of détente, further efforts to achieve continuing progress in this field". The West was prepared to pay this price in order to achieve the summoning of the human contacts meeting in Bern for 1986.

3. The Madrid Concluding Document

3.1. First and Third Basket

The Western countries had two aims in view: a review of implementation of the provisions of the Final Act and the introduction of new proposals to improve implementation where this was unsatisfactory. Therefore, the criterion for the proposals they introduced had been what was desirable rather than what might have been politically feasible, as explained in Chapter III above, under 4.1.

The Western countries had thus directed their principal proposals at those aspects of East European implementation of the Final Act that they considered to be most unsatisfactory, and these proposals were for this very reason extremely difficult if not impossible for the East European countries concerned to accept. Western countries could not have expected the Madrid Concluding Document to set out these proposals just as they were, in black and white; the rule of consensus would have prevented that from happening. No East European country would be ready first to indulge in self-accusation and then meekly to promise amendment.

The fact that nevertheless partial success was gained on a few points, is to be attributed to a variety of reasons including the patience shown by the West and the fact that in the end the countries of Eastern Europe showed themselves more attached than the West to the summoning of a European disarmament conference; at critical moments in Madrid the West was prepared to outsit the Soviet Union at the negotiating table.

The important Western proposals in the first and third baskets concerned the mandate for such a disarmament conference; provisions on progress in the effective exercise of human rights; the right of every citizen to monitor the implementation of the provisions of the Final Act by his own government; the calling of an expert meeting on human rights (first basket) and another on human contacts (third basket); the free access of citizens to foreign embassies and reading rooms belonging to these embassies; improvement of regulations for the granting of exit visas to those wishing to leave their own country either temporarily or permanently; the waiving of any requirement for currency exchange by visitors to East European countries (GDR); wider dissemination of foreign publications; prohibition of interference with foreign radio broadcasts; a code for expulsion of foreign journalists; freedom of movement for foreign journalists; free access of these journalists to their sources including private persons; and, finally, in relation to events in Poland, the right to have free trade unions and a reference to the right of self--determination.

A number of these subjects are to be found in the Final Document of Madrid expressed in a manner not entirely unsatisfactory for the West. The mandate for the European disarmament conference corresponds largely if not very obviously, to Western objectives (pages 301-302, especially paragraph 4). An expert meeting on human rights is to take place in Canada in April 1985 (page 300) and one on human contacts a year later in Switzerland (pages 316, 317). On the regulations for granting exit visas to those who wish to leave their own countries temporarily or for good, the first six paragraphs of the section on "Human Contacts" in the third basket represent a further clarification and specification on the Final Act (pages 309, 310). Access to foreign embassies is enshrined in the sentence: "Access by visitors to these missions will be assured with due regard to the necessary requirements of security to these missions" (page 310). The first four paragraphs of the section on "Information" encourage a wider dissemination of foreign publications, although here the differences between the new text and the corresponding text of the Final Act are not always so obvious (page 311).

Remaining Western proposals are represented in the Madrid Concluding Document either minimally, inadequately or only in such a way as to add little to what has already been said in the Helsinki Final Act. Proposals not appearing at all in the Madrid Document are the most important provisions of RM.19 on human rights (although the commitments of the Final Act on this subject are confirmed, pages 299, 300); the proposal to waive any requirement for currency exchange by visitors from other states; proposals on the prohibition of jamming of foreign broadcasts and on the non-expulsion of foreign journalists and the proposal to open reading rooms or cultural centres attached to foreign embassies.

But there were also East European proposals which have failed to appear in the Madrid Concluding Document. These concern the responsibility of the mass media and of journalists to promote disarmament, détente and mutual understanding between states, to fight racialism, *apartheid* and war and not to disseminate disinformation, tendentious information, lies or imputations, proposals which the West saw as invitations to state censorship and an implied end to freedom of the press. The same was true of the Romanian proposal on the responsibility of the states to take measures aimed at prohibiting all forms of war propaganda, fascism, neo--fascism, racism and chauvinism. The Romanian proposal for a meeting of experts to draw up a treaty on refraining from force or threat of force had just as little success in getting into the concluding document, and both the proposal from a number of East European countries to bring the activities of Radio Liberty and Radio Free Europe to an end and another proposal to give the state the right to expel journalists, met with the same fate. The important East European proposal on commitments to ensure, among other things, personal security and medical assistance for visitors from other participating states, did give rise to provisions in the concluding document, although qualified by the necessary restrictions (page 310). The proposals to insert the Ten Principles of the Final Act in international treaties and national legal systems are reflected in the first two paragraphs of the section on "Principles" (page 298). The rest of the East European proposals mostly had in view the intensification of co-operation in cultural and educational fields and have found their niche, usually in shortened form but without much difficulty, in the sections on "Culture" and "Education" in the third basket (pages 312-314).

The most important NNA proposal projected a new series of confidence-building measures which were not discussed in Madrid because before that could happen the criteria to which they would have to conform - now laid down in the mandate for the Stockholm conference - had to be established and agreed. Discussion of these measures would now form part of the Stockholm negotiations. The proposal from some of the NNA countries for a second meeting of experts on peaceful settlement of bilateral disputes had its outcome in the meeting fixed for March 1984 in Athens (page 301). The extensive proposal from Spain, Austria and Switzerland in the field of "Information", took a course largely parallel to that of the Western proposals on the same subject. Some of the ideas contained in that proposal are completely missing from the Madrid Concluding Document (including the opening of CSCE reading rooms and the possibility of foreign journalists' forming professional associations) the remainder having found a place although not in such uncompromising terms as their proposers would have liked. The Finnish proposal for meetings among diplomatic representatives in the interim period between follow-up Meetings was not included in the concluding document. The Holy See's two proposals on the exercise of religious freedom do appear in the concluding document but in a qualitatively minimal manner (pages 299, 300 and 310). The proposals from Malta on security in the Mediterranean and on her own neutrality, are also present in the document but also not in the form originally envisaged by the Maltese authorities (pages 308 and 301). Ideas from the Yugoslavian proposal on détente gave rise to certain sentences in the introduction to the chapter on "Principles" (page 298), and the Yugoslavian concept of the Mediterranean as a "sea of peace" can be detected in the phrase in the chapter on security in the Mediterranean, which runs: "... and make peace prevail in the region" (page 308).

3.2. Second Basket

The chapter "Co-operation in the field of Economics, of Science and Technology and of the Environment", the so-called second basket, occupies about a quarter of the whole document (pages 302-308). This chapter was the first to be completely agreed and agreement took place as early as June 1981 which was two years before the rest of the document was ready. In this basket there were no proposals so controversial as to take up much time with search for compromise formulae. On many points the participants' interests were identical or aroused little controversy: this was certainly the case, generally speaking, in matters to do with encouragement of co-operation in trade and industry, expanded exchange of contacts and information on economics and the recognition of the interests of migrant workers and those of small enterprises.

In these matters the Madrid Concluding Document has little new to offer nor does it add much of importance to the Final Act and the resolutions of the ECE.

The European Communities initiated five proposals, three of which were regarded by the West as a whole as the key issues in this basket. These were the proposals on improvement of business contacts, on the improvement of economic information and harmonization of economic and commercial statistics and, finally, on the difficulties experienced over compensation transactions. Here, Western objectives were successfully achieved and paragraphs (3), (4) and (6) could be seen in Western eyes as a modest if not significant advance on the Final Act (pages 303-304).

The most important East European proposal sought to make the states agree "to refrain from any actions which would impede trade and economic co-operation", i.e., to refrain from economic sanctions. Its outcome is to be found in paragraph (2) of this chapter, in the phrase: "they reaffirm their intention to make further efforts aimed at reducing or progressively eliminating all kinds of obstacles to the development of trade" (page 303), which does not go beyond the wording of the Final Act. Another important East European proposal was the one calling for a High Level Meeting on Energy, but the East did not insist on this and the reference to it in paragraph (9) adds nothing to the Final Act (page 305).

The five NNA proposals in this basket were virtually uncontroversial and simply made their contribution to the Madrid Concluding Document's coverage.

3.3. Follow-up to Madrid

Finally, among the results of the Madrid conference may be reckoned the various follow-up meetings projected in the Madrid Concluding Document. Chief of these is the third follow-up Meeting in Vienna at the level of representatives appointed by Ministers of Foreign Affairs, which has the task of reviewing the way in which the participating states carry out not only the Final Act but now also the Madrid Concluding Document. The Madrid Document also provides for three meetings of experts, on peaceful settlement of disputes, on human rights and on human contacts; for a "Cultural Forum" to include among its participants government officials as well as representatives from the artistic world; for a "Seminar" on co-operation in the Mediterranean, to be held in Venice and attended by representatives of the participating states joined by representatives of the eight non-participating Mediterranean states; for a commemoration of the tenth anniversary of the signature of the Final Act, leaving the form it should take and at what level it should occur for the Finnish government to decide, and, finally, for a "Conference" on CSBMs and Disarmament in Europe. This conference is, according to the Madrid Concluding Document, "a substantial and integral part" of the CSCE follow-up process, not therefore a "conference" in the original CSCE sense of the word, but rather a "meeting", but scheduled to last longer than the normal six weeks for a meeting of experts and therefore not referred to as such.

The variety of these follow-up meetings is another example of maximum result; each one was proposed by a different country. Not all Western countries were originally in favour of expert meetings, fearing that discussions on specific subjects in these meetings might come to replace treatment of the same subjects in the main follow-up Meetings which would thus be diminished in value. East European countries objected particularly to the expert meetings on human rights and human contacts. The clearer it became that within the Concluding Document there was to be nothing in the human dimension sufficient to counterbalance the conference on relief of military tension, the more the two North American participants (Canada and the USA) in particular, insisted on the two expert meetings they had proposed, one on human rights and the other on human contacts, in order to redress the balance. In the end the US government declared that it would be unable to accept any Madrid Concluding Document that did not contain as balance to the disarmament conference not only the human rights meeting but also that on human contacts.

The Madrid Concluding Document eventually envisaged the following meetings:

1983		
25 October	Preparatory meeting for the European Disarmament Conference	Helsinki
1984		
17 January	Start of European Disarmament Conference	Stockholm
21 March	Expert meeting on the Peaceful Settlement of Disputes	Athens
16 October	Seminar on Co-operation in the Mediterranean	Venice
21 November	Preparatory meeting for the Cultural Forum	Budapest
1985		
23 April	Preparatory meeting for Human Rights	Ottawa
7 May	Expert meeting on Human Rights	Ottawa
1 August	Tenth anniversary of the CSCE	Helsinki
15 October	Cultural Forum	Budapest
1986		
2 April	Preparatory meeting for Human Contacts	Bern
15 April	Expert meeting on Human Contacts	Bern
23 September	Preparatory meeting for the Third Follow-up Meeting	Vienna
4 November	Third Follow-up Meeting	Vienna

3.4. Reservations and Interpretative Statements

The possibility of adding interpretative expositions to the text of the concluding document, offered by Rule (79) of the Blue Book, was less frequently used in Madrid than it had been in Geneva. The device of the "chairman's statement", on the other hand, came into play more often. Finally there was once again a single political reservation.

This last was the usual statement issued by the Turkish delegation "in connexion with the adoption of the Concluding Document of the Madrid Meeting". The delegation said in a brief letter addressed to the Executive Secretary and attached to the Journal of 20 July 1983, No. 318, that the Turkish government maintained its formal reservation against Cyprus (made in Helsinki in 1975), which it had repeated in Belgrade and during the Madrid Preparatory Meeting, on fulfilment of the Final Act (see Chapter II under 4.2.). The Government of the Republic of Cyprus made a four-page statement, attached to the Journal of 21 July, No. 319, in which it said that "such a 'reservation' arrogantly challenges both the constitution of the Conference and its Rules of Procedure as contained in the 'Final Recommendations of the Helsinki Consultations' and in fact is incompatible with participation therein". The sole interpretative statement on the text of the Madrid Concluding Document also came from Turkey. On 28 July 1983 (Journal No. 324) the Turkish delegation declared:

> In the course of negotiations in connection with Article 4 Paragraph 3 of the Conference on Confidence- and Security-building Measures and Disarmament in Europe of the document RM.39/Revised, we have noted with satisfaction the understanding, that the zone of application of the CDE (Conference on Disarmament in Europe), does include the area referred to under major Military manoeuvres Section of the Final Act. It was understood, without doubt, that all the CSBM's to be decided at the CDE Conference will also be applied in this area of the Zone. However, it has not been found possible to include this understanding with the same clarity in the written text of the Document that we are going to adopt. Therefore, my Government deems it necessary to unilaterally register this understanding in the Journal of the day.

The area in question is one stretching 250 km each side of the frontier between the USSR and Turkey, outside Europe.

Rule (79) of the Blue Book makes no mention of chairman's statements. These are statements made by the chairman that meet with no opposition or, in other words, on which there is consensus. Whereas an interpretative statement is a unilateral declaration, a chairman's statement is an expression of consensus. Such a statement was used in Geneva on one occasion in order to register an interpretation of the Final Act (see note 7 Chapter II). In Belgrade a chairman's statement was appended to the Yellow Book and dealt with the interpretation of various points of the agenda of the main Belgrade meeting. The Purple Book has a chairman's statement attached dealing with interpretation of two points of the agenda for the main Madrid Meeting.

For the text of the Madrid Concluding Document six chairman's statements were registered, two of which were appended to the document itself and were thus destined to be published at the same time as the document, and four others that appeared only in the Journals and will therefore swiftly be lost to view. The difference in status accorded to these two sorts of chairman's statement followed the conscious decision of the Plenary. In the case of the two appended statements the reasons for their attachment to the text were in one case technical and in the other political.

The first annexe is about the organization of the Venice Seminar on co-operation in the Mediterranean and consists of a text which was considered too long to be included in the Document itself. The second contains the Swiss invitation to hold a meeting of experts on Human Contacts, in Bern; Moscow did not wish this to be included in the Document itself, but preferred to underline its exceptional character by setting it apart; the actual decision to hold this meeting is prefaced in the annexe by a *considerandum*. Journal No. 324 of 28 July, contains three chairman's statements all with the object of providing solutions to linguistic and translation difficulties. Of these, the most important refers to paragraph (7) of the section entitled Human Contacts in the third basket (see page 310). The West feared lest the English word "visitors" (which occurs to denote people who should be allowed access to foreign embassies) should be interpreted as referring only to people in possession of a specific invitation to an embassy. The Russian word used in the corresponding position could also be interpreted in this way. The Soviet delegation confirming that this interpretation would be incorrect, a chairman's statement was agreed as follows:

> The Chairman notes that in registering the provision on access to diplomatic and other official missions and consular posts in the section *Co-operation in Humanitarian and other Fields* of the Concluding Document of the Madrid Meeting the understanding was reached that the phrase "access by visitors" refers to visitors who have an invitation as well as to visitors who have none.

The second case was that of the Russian translation of the English phrase "practising or prepared to practise" in paragraph (10) of the Principles Section of the first basket on religious freedom (see page 310). According to Western linguists the Russian translation favoured by the Soviet delegation was inadequate. The Chairman's statement says therefore that the Russian-language version of this expression has "the same meaning" as the English and the other language versions. The third case was about the French translation in the Preamble, paragraph (9) (see page 297), where it says *"violations graves"* with reference to violations of the Final Act, the expression agreed during the negotiations having been "serious violations". The Soviet delegation wanted to replace *"violations graves"* by *"violations sérieuses"* which, according to the French delegation, was not French. The chairman's statement now says that *"violations graves"* is an "adequate translation" of "serious violations" and the other language versions of this phrase.

The Maltese problems were solved by approval of the following Chairman's statement (6 September, Journal No. 333) in which the qualification "when appropriate" gives the whole declaration a contingent character as far as the other states are concerned:

> On the question of Security in the Mediterranean the Chairman stated that the participating States had duly taken note of the proposals concerning questions relating to security in the Mediterranean as embodied in the Helsinki Final Act. The Chairman further noted that the participating States were ready to give support, when appropriate, to initiatives which Malta and other participating States concerned may launch in the post-Madrid period to maintain and amplify the contacts and dialogue of the participating States in terms of the Helsinki Final Act, as initiated by the CSCE with the non-participating Mediterranean States to include all States of the Mediterranean, with the purpose of contributing to peace, reducing armed forces in the region, strengthening security, lessening tensions in the region, and widening the scope of co-operation, ends in which all share a common interest, as well as with the purpose of defining further common objectives.

During consultations on the drafting of this chairman's statement some Western delegations still felt uneasy: despite the loophole furnished by the words "when appropriate", they felt that they were taking on too strict an obligation to accept whatever initiative Malta might make. The Austrian delegation in its capacity of chairman of the day of the NNA countries obliged these Western countries by appending the following interpretative statement to the original chairman's statement:

> It is the understanding of our Delegation that no initiative taken on the basis of the Chairman's statement on the Security in the Mediterranean would be considered to be a CSCE meeting unless it had obtained the consensus of all 35 participating States.

Thus in the last few minutes before definitive acceptance of the Madrid Concluding Document, once more an element new to CSCE history was introduced. An interpretative statement on which agreement had been reached in informal discussion was appended to a chairman's statement that had been accepted informally at an earlier stage.

3.5. The Madrid Concluding Document: a Catalogue of Contemporary Problems

The Madrid Concluding Document is a document of its time. It draws attention to the problems that characterize the relationship between East and West in the Europe of the early eighties, and yet stops short of solving them. Post-Madrid Europe is no different from before. The Final Act of 1975 was a volume crammed with promises for a better future and increased détente between East and West, but Madrid's final document came into being during a period during which East-West relations reached a very low level, even lower than during the first CSCE review conference in Belgrade in 1978 when East and West were totally incapable of coming to substantial agreement. It is therefore no wonder that after nearly three years of negotiation the substantive document that emerged should have been a document which neither Eastern nor Western critical opinion will find completely satisfactory. Yet from a political point of view it was the best that could be achieved and on some points of importance it is even surprisingly clear.

It catalogues contemporary problems but fails to solve them. Comparison of the text of the Madrid Concluding Document with corresponding passages in the Helsinki Final Act shows marked improvement or closer definition only on a certain number of points. What also emerges is that a number of issues which appeared in the Final Act are missing from the Madrid Concluding Document. These were problems that the 35 states apparently no longer found worth highlighting in 1983. This throws the remaining problems that were retained in the Madrid Document into greater relief for it was those problems that were regarded as important enough to keep their place on the agenda after the Final Act, even if the commitment expressed was little more than a restatement of that Act. Still other problems were passed over in silence because they were so controversial that it was impossible to get consensus on how they should be stated. The rule of consensus made its own contribution to the fact that what the Madrid Concluding Document proved to be was a detailed account of the problems that all parties were able to agree should be solved.

XI. CONCLUSIONS AND RECOMMENDATIONS

1. Introduction

In the introductory Chapter the basic problem underlying the present study was stated as follows:

> What conditions concerning agenda, institutional framework and rules of procedure determined the organization, course and results of the Madrid Meeting and - in view of the aims of the CSCE as laid down in the Helsinki Act - what modifications of these conditions would be acceptable to the 35 participating states in order to increase the efficiency of decision-making at future meetings?

Three basic questions were derived from this statement of the problem: first of all what were the conditions of the Madrid Meeting; secondly, how did these conditions affect the organization, course and results of the Madrid Meeting, and finally how could these conditions be acceptably modified to increase the efficiency of decision-making in the future?

On the basis of findings from the preceding Chapters the answers to these questions will be summarized in the three following sections of this chapter.

2. The Madrid Conditions

a. agenda

> The CSCE agenda covers virtually every aspect of security and co-operation in Europe. The fact that there is no theoretical agreement as to whether internal events and circumstances can come under discussion does not limit the scope of the agenda in practice.

The communiqué dialogue conducted between NATO and the WP countries between 1966 and 1972 established that if a CSCE was to be organized it should be able to deal with almost all aspects of security and co-operation in Europe. This broad agenda was first reflected in the Final Recommendations of the Helsinki Consultations (the so-called Blue Book) and was confirmed in the Final Act. The follow-up meetings in Belgrade and Madrid were therefore entitled to include in their implementation discussions and proposals virtually all issues that they considered important to their mutual relations. Moreover, the fact that new items totally absent from the Final Act were added to the agenda in Madrid, the right to form free trade unions and the protection of visiting sporting and cultural groups are two examples, means that from now on gaps discovered in the Final Act can be filled at follow-up meetings.

In Belgrade interpretation of the Final Act's principle of non--intervention led to discussions that seemed to augur ill for discussions in Madrid: was the CSCE entitled to concern itself with, for example, the implementation of the principle on human rights in other CSCE states, or was this contrary to the Final Act? WP countries held that in the CSCE only bilateral implementation of the Final Act could be discussed and not the circumstances inside any one country. But in Madrid every country maintained its right as sovereign state (and there is no CSCE procedural rule that can deny this right) to bring up for discussion in the Plenary, at any time it wished, any problem that related to the letter or spirit of the Final Act. This meant in practice that the agenda of the follow-up meeting in fact covered all the most important problems troubling the relations between the participating states. This does not mean, however, that a meaningful dialogue on these problems followed or that consensus on their solution was found, for the same rule of consensus limits the possibilities of achieving such results.

b. institutional framework

> The CSCE follow-up system projected in the Final Act is envisaged as a framework at a low level of institutionalization. Follow-up meetings are only mandated to take decisions of an informational, rule-supervisory or normative nature.

In spite of suggestions from the academic world and initial attempts by both WP and NNA countries to achieve a permanent organization, preferably linked with the UNO, in the end the Final Act only envisaged a framework at a low level of institutionalization. It was first of all decided that a second follow-up meeting should only take place by a consensus decision of the first follow-up meeting. Then CSCE rules of procedure and working methods were declared valid for all meetings *mutatis mutandis* but the date, duration, agenda and other modalities of each follow-up meeting were left to be decided by a preparatory meeting in each case. Finally the Final Act decreed that there should be no permanent secretariat but that an *ad hoc* secretariat with limited competence should be set up for each follow-up meeting.

The Madrid Meeting attempted to raise the level of institutionalization of the CSCE by declaring the agenda, and other procedural modalities laid down in the Purple Book, valid for the Vienna follow-up Meeting as well, even if *mutatis mutandis*.

The Final Act lays only limited tasks on follow-up meetings and it is indeed difficult to widen the functions of such meetings. Consensus on sanctions against alleged non-fulfilment of the Final Act can never be reached because the State involved will always refuse to co-operate. Consensus on rule-creating standards will be equally difficult to reach because states would rather bow to a consensus of a supposedly politically binding nature than to a consensus of a legally binding nature.

c. rules of procedure

> CSCE rules of procedure are based on the principle of equality expressed in the consensus procedure for decision-making and in the rule of rotating the chairmanship which applies in every organ of the conference. Notwithstanding the formally prescribed procedure the working method is inductive. The Executive Secretary is charged with technical tasks alone, among which language services are the most labour intensive and hence the most expensive. Rules prescribed for publicity are strict but in practice there is a high degree of openness.

In the very first days of the Helsinki Consultations preceding the CSCE in November 1972 agreement was reached on the most important rules of procedure. The principle of sovereign equality of all 35 states was established then, with the condition furthermore, that the participating states would not take part as members of military alliances. The two most important rules of procedure sprang from the principle of equality: the rule of consensus and rotation of the chairmanship.

Some mitigation of the consensus rule is offered in the Blue Book by its negative formulation on this point: consensus can be achieved "in the absence of any objection" which means that positive approval of a decision is not required: silence means consensus. Objections to decisions have moreover to be submitted as "constituting an obstacle" to the taking of the decision in question. Finally there are the resources of formal reservations and interpretative statements which can be added to decisions, but little use has ever been made of these in the history of the CSCE.

Mitigation of the consequences of the rule of rotation of the chairmanship and at the same time of the rule that makes it incumbent to sit round the table in alphabetical order, principles that reflected an ideal of equality rather than political reality, was obtained by going over to informal organizational structures as soon as actual drafting of the concluding document had to start. Permanent "co-ordinators" provided by the NNA countries took the chair and the alphabetical arrangement gave way to one in which the main political groups found themselves face-to--face.

As far as working methods are concerned, the formal procedural framework places the Plenary at the centre of the decision-making process with the task of guiding the Subsidiary Working Bodies in their work; Drafting Groups are supposed to assist the Plenary in drafting the concluding document. In practice however, the actual drafting took place in a variety of autonomously operating informal organs which never in fact worked on the basis of guidelines previously received from the Plenary.

One of the points at which the low level of institutionalization appears is in the terms of reference for the Executive Secretary and his secretariat, who are empowered to deal only with technical matters. The major part of the work of the secretariat is the language services it provides since the CSCE recognizes six working languages (English, French, German, Italian, Russian and Spanish).

On paper, CSCE meetings are not entirely public yet in practice the CSCE might be called "an open book". The forum aspect of the CSCE means that all its participants are looking for publicity and therefore openness.

3. The Madrid Experience

a. organization of the meeting

Since 1973 the number of CSCE participants (35) has remained stable and will most probably continue to do so.

Use has never been made of the possibility offered by CSCE rules of procedure of attending the conference as "observer" without participating in the taking of decisions, and this is unlikely to happen in the future. Albania is the only country that might still attend as observer, or as participating state bring the total number of CSCE states to 36, but up to now it has preferred to remain in isolation. In the opposite sense a reduction of the number of participants is equally unlikely. In Madrid, during the Malta phase, the meeting threatened to create a "positive" consensus of 34 because of the lack of a "negative" consensus of 35 on acceptance of the Madrid Concluding Document, but Malta preferred not to be excluded from the CSCE in this way.

The influence of the special category of participating states known as the "non-participating Mediterranean States", on CSCE decision-making is nil.

Although the Final Act offers an opportunity to non-participating (Mediterranean) states to offer their views on questions relating to security and co-operation in the Mediterranean, almost all the fully participating states appeared to have no interest at all in these views.

In Madrid, as before in Belgrade and Geneva, the CSCE was a conference of diplomats and government officials. Visiting members of national parliaments and "public members" in delegations had no influence on the decision-making process.

Different delegations included among their numbers, for short periods, members of their parliaments, not as negotiators but as observers. The US delegation sometimes included "public members" who played a modest role in the implementation discussion. Notwithstanding the forum aspect of the CSCE, decision-making was done by diplomats, mostly career diplomats, and other government officials.

The absence in CSCE rules of procedure of any

> regulation on the presentation, examination or approval of official letters of credence by representatives of the participating states gave rise to no problems.

CSCE practice is that a diplomatic Note from the embassy in the host country, and later from the delegation to the meeting itself, to the Executive Secretary, giving a list of representatives of that country, is sufficient to give these the right to speak and take part in decisions. Such Notes are accepted as credentials by the Executive Secretary and the other participating delegations without any discussion. The only problem was over Turkey's refusal to recognize the representative of Cyprus and this was easily solved by unilateral declarations on the part of each of these countries.

b. course of the meeting

> Provided a consensus could be reached, the Plenary of the Madrid meeting arrogated to itself the right to take any decision it thought fit; in its own opinion the Plenary was all-powerful.

In exceptional cases in Madrid the Plenary reached consensus for a specific interpretation of established rules of procedure. The underlying thought was that as long as consensus was obtained, the Plenary was all-powerful and could take any decision, as it saw fit, as an opportune interpretation of the procedures laid down in the Purple or Blue Books. In December 1981 therefore, the Plenary decided to replace all the Drafting Groups set up according to the Purple Book at the level of experts, by a single Drafting Group at the level of Heads of Delegation. In July 1983 and as a departure from the rule of daily rotation of the chairmanship, the Plenary decided to change to twice-daily rotation during the final ministerial days in September.

Thus the Plenary is all-powerful except in so far as there must be consensus for its decisions so that it is still open to any country to refuse to depart from the established rules of procedure or to interpret these in an exceptional fashion.

> Drafting of the concluding document, one of the tasks of the Madrid Meeting, took place outside the formal setting of the meeting.

Just as had been the case in Belgrade and in Geneva, neither the Plenary nor the official Drafting Groups drafted a single sentence for the concluding document in Madrid, with the exception of the official Drafting Group for the Mediterranean where the East-West opposition did not have a dominating role. Drafting took place informally in a variety of circumstances: contact groups, coffee groups, structured informal negotiations, sherry groups and mini-groups, and there were also many informal contacts in coffee-breaks, in the coffee bar and at lunches or even dinners, on occasion, which cleared the way towards the solution of drafting problems. In the end it became necessary to go as far as government-to-government appeals in order to arrive at a final result.

In spite of the official rules of procedure the existence of political groupings of allied nations played a crucial part in the internal decision-making process of the Madrid Meeting.

Although the formal rule is that all states participating in the conference should do so as individual states independent of whatever "military alliance" they may belong to, the caucuses of these political groups formed part and parcel of the Madrid decision-making process and were in fact the most important decision-making organs. As the meeting pursued its lengthy course, spokesmen became less and less reluctant to speak on behalf of their own group and more and more inclined to call a spade a spade. The CSCE, which consists in theory of 35 independent countries, disclosed itself in Madrid as an assembly of political groups reflecting the reality of the political situation. The NNA countries, finding themselves more and more often in a buffer position between two antagonistic blocs, became increasingly prepared to consolidate themselves into a third bloc and to undertake the role of broker in the negotiations.

Application of the consensus rule to matters of procedure had on various occasions dramatic effects on the immediate course of decision--making in Madrid, but not on its results.

There were in Madrid at least three occasions on which the scene might have been described as Kafka-esque.

a) On 11 November 1980 a procedural discussion took place on how to apply the consensus rule in order to restart the stopped clock so that the Main Meeting, as desired by the West, would be able to begin on that day according to the schedule agreed in Belgrade. The Meeting did indeed begin on that day but it seems likely that it would have done so in any case even if other procedures had been employed.

b) On 9 February 1982 the Polish chairman attempted to use the consensus rule to prevent thirteen speakers from making speeches on the situation in his own country; even if other procedural rules had been in force he would still have made use of them for the same purpose. But political reality cannot be confined in a procedural straitjacket and Western concern about events in Poland did manage to draw worldwide attention through the forum offered by Madrid.

c) In the night of silences, on 5 March 1982, the West used the consensus rule to enforce the initiation of a long summer recess. The object was achieved but would probably also have been achieved if different rules of procedure - for example a voting system - had been in force.

> Application of the consensus rule to matters of substance in Madrid meant that in the decision-making process all drafting bodies were open-ended and all participants enjoyed equal rights in decision taking. However, equal rights should not be confused with equal political influence.

Negotiation on the Madrid Concluding Document took place between representatives of the caucuses, in large or small informal groups. However informal the Drafting Groups were, it remained a condition that consensus had to be reached on every word of the document. In theory therefore, and in practice, all these groups continued to be accessible to all delegations in order to allow them the opportunity of exercising their veto if necessary. In very limited sherry- or mini-groups the absence of other delegations was entirely on a voluntary basis and represented an exercise of self-discipline.

The conclusion that an equal right to withhold consensus does not mean an equal right to exert influence, is for example borne out by what happened in the Malta phase. A positive "consensus of 34" would not have been a possibility if the thirty-fifth country had been the US or the SU. Clearly the opinions of these two countries carry more weight than those of, say, Monaco.

c. results of the meeting

> The review of implementation of the Final Act occupied not only the first six weeks of the meeting in their entirety, as envisaged in the Purple Book, but also continued to form a major part of the deliberations right up to the last day of the Madrid Meeting, two-and-a-half years later. Whether or not certain topics were considered by some delegations as purely internal affairs, other delegations persisted in talking about them.

The consequence of the principle that each participant had, as sovereign state, the right to speak in the Plenary on any subject it liked, as long as it was connected with the Final Act, was that none of the Western and Neutral countries would give up their right to continue the implementation discussion to the bitter end and to make speeches on what other states considered to be their own internal affairs. The chairman, who is not a single individual but a delegation occupying the chair, cannot be expected to call his fellow delegations to order for he is not allowed to make a chairman's ruling: such a ruling could never be challenged because the chairman's voice itself would be needed to complete the consensus for a challenge.

> The Madrid Concluding Document, reflecting the limits of drafting under consensus conditions, catalogues contemporary problems but fails to solve them.

Although the Madrid Meeting finally adopted a so-called "substantial and balanced concluding document" this document betrays every characteristic of the result of a drafting process based on consensus. It exhibits a maximum drafting result on less controversial issues, a minimum result where politically sensitive matters are concerned and ambiguous texts where agreement to disagree was preferred to no text at all.

> External rather than internal factors explain the long duration of the Madrid Meeting. Notwithstanding heightened tensions between participating states and also their various political configurations, the CSCE follow-up process stayed alive.

The Madrid Meeting, taking place as it did in a period of heightened East-West conflict, was able to serve as an appropriate forum for discussion of the bones of contention that lay between the participants: the human rights condition, economic boycotts, or the situation in and around Afghanistan and Poland. The pressing need to discuss these problems contributed to the Meeting's long duration; a concluding document would have been agreed much sooner if it had not been for the Polish problem and other East-West tensions. The final outcome of all the conditions governing the Madrid Meeting which have been discussed in this book is that we still have at our disposal a forum in which critical implementation debates can be held. The reverse of the coin is that those same conditions, by producing compromise normative formulations and rule-supervisory promulgations unsupported by sanctions, limited the actual effect of the Madrid follow-up Meeting. Implementation of the Final Act and the Concluding Document of Madrid is a matter of concrete fact which perversely remains outside the conference chamber. However, although compromise formulations of the same kind as dominated Madrid are to be found in the mandates for future meetings announced in the Madrid Concluding Document, the very holding of these meetings will itself constitute a fact in the reality of post-Madrid Europe. With or without détente, the CSCE is here to stay.

4. Recommendations

The conclusions to be drawn from the material described in this book will now be summarized in the form of a series of recommendations each followed by a discussion. The recommendations have been so designed that each one is capable of execution independently of the rest but they should also be regarded as interrelated and together constitute a package.

a. agenda

RECOMMENDATION 1: Participating states should exercise the greatest restraint in putting forward proposals to be approved by the next follow-up meeting: a single political group of countries should contribute not more than one proposal per basket, focussed on the most important problem in the relations between the 35 states.

RECOMMENDATION 2: Neither a substantive concluding document nor any other comprehensive final document should be aimed at: the function of such a document can be performed by a small number of separate chairman's statements.

The Madrid Concluding Document is an extensive document representing nearly three years of negotiation on 87 proposals. The repetition of such an exercise is not to be recommended. Madrid, never again! The provisions contained in the Madrid document vary in importance. The most important Western and East European proposals occupy a disproportionate place. It would seem to be more efficient and less time--consuming if negotiations were concentrated only on proposals that are of essential interest in the relations between the 35 states. Whether such negotiations would be likely to achieve results would depend, as always, on the political climate of the moment, but it would at least become swiftly apparent what the prospects were for a useful outcome.

The Final Act does not require the follow-up meetings to produce a final document at all. Towards the end of the Madrid negotiations the mechanism of the chairman's statement proved to be an effective method of reaching consensus. The less text there is to be agreed the less time consensus takes to reach. On the other hand the consensus rule might still be used to veto one chairman's statement until agreement is reached on a different one; conditional linkages of this sort are unavoidable where the rule of consensus has absolute force. Therefore the pattern of negotiations would remain unchanged. As a result, the "balance" desired by the participating states would grow out of the negotiations themselves.

If follow-up meetings confine themselves in future to the approval of a limited number of chairman's statements, this is not to prevent any future Conference - say once every ten years - from attempting to achieve a balanced and substantive concluding document which might then include the chairman's statements from preceding years or use these statements as a starting point for negotiations.

b. the follow-up system

RECOMMENDATION 3: The Preparatory Meeting in Vienna should take a decision on the duration of the interval between the Vienna Meeting and the fourth Follow-up

> Meeting, one of say two years. The main Vienna Meeting should then decide on the periodicity and duration of follow-up meetings in the future (for example, biennial meetings of perhaps six weeks before and six weeks after a Christmas recess). The possibility of interim meetings between regularly scheduled follow-up meetings should be left open.

In Geneva, during negotiations on the Final Act, it was the East European countries that fought for an automatic succession of follow-up meetings; the West preferred to envisage the taking of a specific decision for holding each succeeding follow-up meeting. During the Preparatory Meeting in Madrid positions were reversed because the East European countries were not inclined to take a decision for holding a third follow-up meeting after Madrid, while the West, together with the NNA countries now laid great stress on it. The question of whether there would be a further follow-up meeting at all, a point sometimes hotly discussed in Madrid during the first two years, now appears to have been somewhat academic; which of the 35 participating states can afford, politically, to stop the CSCE follow-up process? The CSCE is here to stay.

There is nothing in the Final Act to prevent strengthening the institutionalization of the CSCE and regulating the follow-up process. Certainty on the question of whether there will be a fourth follow-up meeting after Vienna, would improve the climate of negotiation in Vienna.

The Executive Secretary (see Recommendation 13) should be given the right, during periods between follow-up meetings and at the request of one of the participating states, to call a meeting of CSCE ambassadors which could then decide to convoke an *ad hoc* CSCE meeting at the level of representatives of ministers of foreign affairs. This might be done in the event of sudden crises in relations between the 35 states in consequence of alleged flagrant violation of the letter or spirit of the Final Act. The rule-supervisory function of the CSCE (or, in CSCE shorthand, the implementation discussion) would be strengthened in this way. Even if the meeting of CSCE ambassadors should be unable to decide on calling an *ad hoc* meeting of the normal follow-up type, because of lack of consensus, a rule-supervisory gesture would nevertheless have been made.

RECOMMENDATION 4: Every encouragement should be given to the efforts already begun by the Madrid Meeting to declare the existing rules of procedure, agenda, working programme and other modalities of follow-up meetings valid, *mutatis mutandis*, for future meetings as well. The Blue Book and the Purple Book should be recognized as regulating the conditions of all succeeding follow-up meetings.

The Madrid Concluding Document provides that "the agenda, working programme and modalities of the main Madrid Meeting will be applied *mutatis mutandis* to the main Vienna Meeting, unless other decisions on these questions are taken by the preparatory meeting ...". This means that both the Purple Book and the Blue Book have been declared to apply to Vienna unless there is a consensus to depart from them. Thus no further consensus is required in order to formulate new rules of procedure. Recommendation 4 more or less comes down to changing the words in the quotation given above from "the main Vienna meeting" to "all other Follow-up meetings". This would palpably lighten the task of every preparatory meeting preceding a follow-up meeting and so increase the efficiency of preparation. The degree of institutionalization of the CSCE would be raised by this measure.

RECOMMENDATION 5: The Executive Secretary from the most recent host country should be held to be responsible for the CSCE secretariat up to the moment at the beginning of the succeeding follow-up meeting when the Executive Secretary from the new host country takes over the responsibility.

This recommendation follows the rule from the Blue Book that the retiring chairman remains responsible until the new session begins. The retiring Executive Secretary should be obliged to bear responsibility for his secretarial tasks up to the moment when he can hand over his responsibility to his successor by means of a symbolic handshake, a gesture that would then serve to underline the continuity of the CSCE.

In the interim period up to this moment the retiring Executive Secretary would carry out the tasks allotted to him in Recommendation 13.

RECOMMENDATION 6: The two jobs of a follow-up meeting, review of implementation of the Final Act and examination of new proposals, should not have to be done at separate times but could from the very beginning of the meeting go on simultaneously.

In Madrid the West wanted to follow the same programme as had been followed in Belgrade, devoting the first weeks of the meeting to discussion of implementation alone and only subsequently going on to examination of new proposals. In fact the implementation discussion continued in Madrid from first to last. Much time would be gained if new proposals were introduced immediately after the meeting's opening and their examination initiated in formal or informal working groups in parallel with the Plenary's discussion of implementation. The Purple Book's timetable would have to be adapted to this purpose, under the *mutatis mutandis* rule.

RECOMMENDATION 7: The trend begun in Madrid to make greater use of the possibility of organizing expert meetings, should be continued. Each succeeding follow-up meeting should pay more attention to the results of such interim meetings.

In Belgrade it was decided to hold one expert meeting on peaceful settlement of disputes, one on co-operation in the Mediterranean and also a Scientific Forum. Three expert meetings were decided on in Madrid together with one forum, one seminar, a commemoration of the tenth anniversary of the Final Act and a disarmament conference extending over a long period. This proliferation of expert meetings reinforces the multilateral CSCE follow-up process. Any tendency for such meetings to detract from the importance of the real follow-up meetings will be annulled if the follow-up meetings make fuller use of the results of the expert meetings, both in discussions and in the formulation of the concluding chairman's statements.

RECOMMENDATION 8: However unrealistic organizational links with UNO organs may appear to be, the practice of engaging certain of these organs in the CSCE process should be actively continued.

In the options for an institutional framework for the CSCE suggested by theorists in the early seventies, much attention was paid to the possibility of establishing organizational links with the UNO. Among the suggestions was one for a regional framework with links to the Security Council. The options as a whole are now of little more than academic interest because it is clear that consensus for their adoption will never be achieved in the CSCE, if only for the reason that various

CSCE members, such as Switzerland and the Holy See, are not UN members and have no wish to be connected with it. In the Madrid Concluding Document the CSCE states issued one invitation and six recommendations to the ECE and on one occasion expressed their interest in UNESCO activity. The ECE came in for special mention because it is itself concerned with the same subjects as fall into the second basket of the Final Act, over the same geographical area. On the other hand, non--European members of UNESCO and other UN organs cannot be expected to interest themselves in purely European affairs. Yet where CSCE countries succeed in reaching agreement during follow-up meetings, to delegate certain responsibilities to UN organs, this should be encouraged in the interest of avoiding duplication. It is not the role of the CSCE to duplicate the activities of functional or regional UN organizations.

c. the rules of procedure

RECOMMENDATION 9: In the context of the application of the rule of consensus to both procedural and substantive matters, it would be more effective to attempt to reach an early consensus firstly by abandoning the effort to achieve an extensive concluding document and aiming for a small number of chairman's statements instead; secondly by going over to drafting in informal work groups at an earlier stage, and thirdly by giving the NNA co--ordinators of such work groups the right to frame Informal Single Negotiating Texts.

The desirability of changing the consensus rule with regard to procedural matters may well be open to question but what is certain is that the rule of consensus can only be replaced by consensus and this consensus will never now be achieved. The same is true with regard to whether in the case of substantive matters the consensus rule should be altered to allow some sort of voting procedure: consensus on this is no longer possible.

If the rule of consensus is there to stay in the CSCE, then what must be looked for is how to achieve results more quickly than was the case in Madrid. It is more difficult to get consensus for an extensive concluding document like that of Madrid than for a restricted number of chairman's statements. The lesson of the Madrid experience is that agreement can be reached in a reasonable time on the text of a chairman's statement because it has a concrete content which can be grasped from the beginning. If, in parallel with official treatment of the agenda, informal negotiation is started at an much earlier stage, considerable time is saved. During the informal negotiations the NNA co-ordinators might make use of Informal Single Negotiating Texts, at an earlier stage, as was the practice in UNCLOS III, in order to put forward their perception of a possible basis for consensus.

RECOMMENDATION 10: More intensive use of formal reservations and interpretative statements should not be encouraged.

Formal reservations and interpretative statements are necessary escape mechanisms which accelerate the decision-making process if adequate use is made of them. The only way of making them more attractive would be to give them a status equivalent to that of the decision to which they refer; this could be done by appending them to the decision itself together with which they would then be published. However, if it were known that such unilateral declarations would receive the same publicity as the final documents, other delegations would feel obliged to state their views on the subject as well. As a maximum result the concluding documents would be accompanied by 35 unilateral declarations.

It would therefore be better to continue the practice followed in Madrid and to regard this escape mechanism as a last resort enabling a delegation to avoid blocking consensus without losing face. An intensive use of unilateral interpretative statements and formal reservations would open the way for each state to dine *à la carte* and, in the end, rob consensus of its meaning as the ideal of the CSCE.

RECOMMENDATION 11: If the change-over to informal negotiation happens at an earlier stage (see Recommendation 9) there will be no need to interfere with the rule of daily rotation of the chairmanship; the provision for departure from this rule in the Blue Book should be used if a formal drafting group itself goes over to actual drafting.

Daily rotation of the chairmanship is an expression of the principle of equality of all the CSCE states which gives it an interest which far outweighs its drawbacks. The drawbacks themselves can be avoided by leaving the actual drafting to informal working bodies. In Madrid the one formal drafting group in which actual drafting was done was the one on co-operation in the Mediterranean where the East-West conflict had no role to play. In such a situation it is possible to revert to rule 71 (b) of the Blue Book and establish "a basis of rotation in accordance with practical arrangements".

RECOMMENDATION 12: In the absence of an extensive concluding document as an objective, this having been replaced by the ideal of a small number of chairman's statements, the Plenary should fulfil its role as central organ in the formally-prescribed procedure by establishing guidelines at an early stage, which should lay down the number of chairman's statements to be agreed and the areas they should cover, so that the bottom-up approach can function more effectively.

The bottom-up approach would be more efficient if the negotiators in formal or informal work groups had a general principle of reference at their disposal from the beginning. If the Plenary, which, according to the Purple Book, is the main body of the meeting, indicated the number and subject matter of the chairman's statements (for example one per basket) then the structure of the final result would already be established which would prevent a succession of events similar to the Malta phase.

RECOMMENDATION 13: The Executive Secretary for technical matters should be given the following additional responsibilities:
a) before the Meeting: to formulate and distribute the Purple Book *mutatis mutandis;*
b) during the Meeting: to report on any complaints about fulfilment of the Final Act received during the interim period; to provide technical support for co-ordinators in arriving at single negotiating texts;
c) after the Meeting: to provide a clearing house for complaints about violation of the Final Act or the Madrid Concluding Document and to call a meeting of the CSCE ambassadors if requested to do so by a CSCE state.

The last line of the Final Act reads: "The services of a technical secretariat will be provided by the host country". According to the Blue Book the Executive Secretary is to be concerned only with technical matters. Within such limits it is impossible to create an institutionalized permanent, international CSCE secretariat. The recommendations given above are only intended to increase the permanence and degree of institutionalization of the CSCE to the extent possible within these limits. As, in future, the Purple Book is only to be "adjusted" in order to serve for the next follow-up meeting, and these "adjustments" are considered to be merely of a technical nature, the Executive Secretary and his secretariat may properly frame and circulate a draft for the adjusted Purple Book. During the Meeting the Executive Secretary and his secretariat should be more actively and intensively involved in the NNA co-ordinators' efforts to produce their negotiating texts and made fully responsible, for example, for registration and distribution of proposals, amendments, textual changes and decisions on which agreement has been reached, or in other words given the job of archivist and registrar.

In the interim period, that is, after any one Meeting, the secretariat should act as clearing house for complaints put in by participating states on fulfilment of the Final Act and the Madrid Concluding Document by other CSCE states. These complaints would be published and distributed by the secretariat. If any state so required, the secretariat would call a meeting of CSCE ambassadors, empowered to decide to convoke an *ad hoc* CSCE meeting following a consensus (see Recommendation 3). This new function for the secretariat would lay stress on the importance of the multilateral CSCE follow-up process.

RECOMMENDATION 14: It should not be automatically considered necessary for every document to be translated into all official languages with the least possible delay.

In Madrid the language staff accounted for the largest portion of all costs of the executive secretariat. Yet consensus will never be reached for dropping any one of the six official languages. Costs might rather be reduced by circulating all emphemeral documents in only one working language, the one in which they were originally drafted, leaving it in case of need to the delegations' language experts themselves to translate them. Such an arrangement would mean that secretariat translators would be required only in the last phase of the meeting in order to prepare the various language versions of the texts previously agreed by consensus.

<u>RECOMMENDATION 15</u>: Journals of closed sessions should be produced only if there are decisions, formal reservations or interpretative statements to be registered. The verbatim texts of the opening and closing statements during the open sessions should be published only in the language in which they are delivered.

In Madrid 336 Journals amounting to 803 pages issued in six languages were published and distributed on a wide scale. A small number contain records of consensus on particular decisions or reservations and interpretative statements included at the request of one or more delegations. The rest are of no interest because all they contain is lists of which delegations contributed to the session, without the text of what was said. To carry out empty routines of this sort is totally superfluous.

The verbatim record of statements at the Madrid opening sitting filled 350 pages and of this record 782 copies were distributed, 100 in German, 270 in English, 73 in Spanish, 166 in French, 60 in Italian and 113 in Russian. The closing statements had a similar circulation. Publishing only a single text containing each statement in its original language would mean a significant saving of costs. The states themselves could then make what translations they liked in their own home capitals.

<u>RECOMMENDATION 16</u>: All Plenaries should be open to the public but all meetings of both formal and informal working bodies should remain closed.

Opening all the Plenaries to the public would represent a recognition of the CSCE's character as a forum and would also strengthen its rule-supervisory function. As the fact of the matter is that each delegation at present supplies the press with texts of its own interventions in the Plenary it would seem more efficient simply to allow the press to be present at the sessions.

ANNEX 1

BLUE BOOK: CHAPTER 6: RULES OF PROCEDURE

(64) The States participating in the Conference on Security and Co-operation in Europe shall conduct their work as follows:

(65) 1. All States participating in the Conference shall do so as sovereign and independent States and in conditions of full equality. The Conference shall take place outside military alliances.

(66) 2. The representation of the participating States at each stage of the Conference shall be determined in accordance with the provisions laid down in Chapter 1 of these Final Recommendations.

(67) 3. The working bodies of the Conference shall be the Co-ordinating Committee, the Committees and the Sub-Committees. These working bodies will function during the second stage of the Conference. However, the Co-ordinating Committee will meet at the site of the second stage before the opening of the second stage in order to settle questions relating to the organization of that stage.

(68) The working bodies of the Conference may, if they so wish, set up such working groups as they may consider useful. The working bodies and working groups of the Conference shall be open to all participating States.

(69) 4. Decisions of the Conference shall be taken by consensus. Consensus shall be understood to mean the absence of any objection expressed by a Representative and submitted by him as constituting an obstacle to the taking of the decision in question.

5. Chairmanship

(70) A. The Chair at the inaugural and closing meetings of the first stage of the Conference shall be taken by the Minister for Foreign Affairs of the host country. The Chair at other meetings shall be taken on a basis of rotation, as follows:

(a) The Chair at each meeting shall be taken by the Minister for Foreign Affairs of a different participating State, in an order established in accordance with a list selected by lot country by country before the end of the Helsinki Consultations;
(b) If the Conference should meet both in the morning and in the afternoon of the same day, the two meetings shall be regarded as constituting two distinct meetings;
(c) In the interval between meetings of the Conference, the functions of the Chair shall be exercised by that Minister for Foreign Affairs who presided over the immediately preceding meeting of the Conference;
(d) Should a Minister for Foreign Affairs be prevented from taking the Chair, it shall be taken by the Minister for Foreign Affairs of the country next in the order established.

(71) B. The Chair at the inaugural meetings of the working bodies of the Conference shall be taken by the Representative of the host country. Thereafter, the office of Chairman shall be filled as follows:

(a) The Chairman of the Co-ordinating Committee and the Chairmen of the Committees shall be designated on a basis of daily rotation, in French alphabetical order, starting from a letter drawn by lot;

(b) The Chairman of Sub-Committees and of other subsidiary bodies of the Conference shall be designated on a basis of rotation in accordance with practical arrangements to be established at the appropriate time by the bodies in question.

(72) Where necessary, a rapporteur shall be designated by consensus.

(73) C. The provisions laid down for the meetings of the first stage shall be applicable *mutatis mutandis* to the meetings of the third stage of the Conference. They may be further defined by the Co--ordinating Committee.

(74) 6. The Executive Secretary for technical matters at each stage of the Conference shall be a national of the corresponding host country. He is designated by the host country subject to agreement by the participating States.

(75) In organizing the services, the Executive Secretary of each stage will be responsible for the recruitment of his staff and assured of the collaboration of the Secretariats of the other stages.

(76) The Executive Secretaries will work under the authority of the Conference and report on their activities to the appropriate body of each stage of the Conference, especially on financial matters.

(77) 7. Official verbatim records shall be taken at the meetings of the first and third stages of the Conference.

(78) Proposals on matters of substance and amendments thereto shall be submitted in writing to the Chairman and circulated to all participants. The proposals adopted shall be registered by the Executive Secretary and circulated among the participants.

(79) Representatives of States participating in the Conference may ask for their formal reservations or interpretative statements concerning given decisions to be duly registered by the Executive Secretary and circulated to the participating States. Such statements must be submitted in writing to the Executive Secretary.

(80) 8. The inaugural and closing sessions of the first stage of the Conference will be open. Other sessions of the first stage may be open if the Ministers so decide. The Co-ordinating Committee, the Committees and the Sub-Committees shall not, as a rule, meet in open sessions, unless the participants decide otherwise. Arrangements for the third stage will be similar to those for the first stage and may be further defined by the Co-ordinating Committee.

(81) 9. The working languages of the Conference and of its working bodies shall be: English, French, German, Italian, Russian and Spanish.

(82) Speeches made in any of the working languages shall be interpreted into the other working languages.

(83) 10. Any Representative may make a statement in a language other than the working languages. In this case, he shall himself provide for interpretation into one of the working languages.

(84) 11. Records and decisions of the Conference shall be issued and circulated to participants in the working languages.

(85) The participants shall decide by consensus whether it is desirable to make public, through the appropriate services of the Conference, certain documents or communiqués on the work of the Conference and if they decide in the affirmative shall specify the contents.

(86) 12. During the discussion of any matter, a Representative may raise a point of order and the Chairman shall give him the floor immediately. A Representative raising a point of order may not speak on the substance of the matter under discussion.

(87) 13. During the meeting the Chairman shall keep a list of speakers and may declare it closed with the consent of the meeting. He shall, however, accord the right of reply to any Representative if a speech after he has declared the list closed makes this desirable.

(88) 14. These procedural arrangements shall be adopted by consensus. Once adopted, they can only be altered by consensus.

ANNEX 2

FINAL ACT: CHAPTER ON FOLLOW-UP TO THE CONFERENCE

The participating States,

Having considered and evaluated the progress made at the Conference on Security and Co-operation in Europe.

Considering further that, within the broader context of the world, the Conference is an important part of the process of improving security and developing co-operation in Europe and that its results will contribute significantly to this process,

Intending to implement the provisions of the Final Act of the Conference in order to give full effect to its results and thus to further the process of improving security and developing co-operation in Europe,

Convinced that, in order to achieve the aims sought by the Conference, they should make further unilateral, bilateral and multilateral efforts and continue, in the appropriate forms set forth below, the multilateral process initiated by the Conference.

1. *Declare their resolve*, in the period following the Conference, to pay due regard to and implement the provisions of the Final Act of the Conference:

(a) unilaterally, in all cases which lend themselves to such action;

(b) bilaterally, by negotiations with other participating States;

(c) multilaterally, by meetings of experts of the participating States, and also within the framework of existing international organizations, such as the United Nations Economic Commission for Europe and UNESCO, with regard to educational, scientific and cultural co-operation;

2. *Declare furthermore their resolve* to continue the multilateral process initiated by the Conference:

(a) by proceeding to a thorough exchange of views both on the implementation of the provisions of the Final Act and of the tasks defined by the Conference, as well as, in the context of the questions dealt with by the latter, on the deepening of their mutual relations, the improvement of security and the development of co-operation in Europe, and the development of the process of détente in the future;

(b) by organizing to these ends meetings among their representatives, beginning with a meeting at the level of representatives appointed by the Ministers of Foreign Affairs. This meeting will define the appropriate modalities for the holding of other meetings which could include further similar meetings and the possibility of a new Conference;

3. The first of the meetings indicated above will be held at Belgrade in 1977. A preparatory meeting to organize this meeting will be held at Belgrade on 15 June 1977. The preparatory meeting will decide on the date, duration, agenda and other modalities of the meeting of representatives appointed by the Ministers of Foreign Affairs;

4. The rules of procedure, the working methods and the scale of distribution for the expenses of the Conference will, *mutatis mutandis*, be applied to the meetings envisaged in paragraphs 1 (c), 2 and 3 above. All the above-mentioned meetings will be held in the participating States in rotation. The services of a technical secretariat will be provided by the host country.

ANNEX 3

THE PURPLE BOOK: DECISIONS

ON THE ORGANIZATION OF THE MADRID MEETING 1980 OF REPRESENTATIVES OF THE PARTICIPATING STATES OF THE CONFERENCE ON SECURITY AND CO-OPERATION IN EUROPE; HELD ON THE BASIS OF THE PROVISIONS OF THE FINAL ACT RELATING TO THE FOLLOW-UP TO THE CONFERENCE

In accordance with the provisions of the Final Act relating to the Follow-up to the Conference on Security and Co-operation in Europe and the relevant provisions of the Concluding Document of the Belgrade Meeting 1977, the representatives of Austria, Belgium, Bulgaria, Canada, Cyprus, Czechoslovakia, Denmark, Finland, France, the German Democratic Republic, the Federal Republic of Germany, Greece, the Holy See, Hungary, Iceland, Ireland, Italy, Liechtenstein, Luxembourg, Malta, Monaco, the Netherlands, Norway, Poland, Portugal, Romania, San Marino, Spain, Sweden, Switzerland, Turkey, the Union of Soviet Socialist Republics, the United Kingdom, the United States of America and Yugoslavia met at Madrid from 9 September to 10 November 1980 to organize the Madrid Meeting 1980 of representatives of the participating States.

During the opening session of the Preparatory Meeting the participants were addressed by H.E. Mr. José Pedro Pérez-Llorca, Minister of Foreign Affairs of Spain.

The following decisions concerning the duration, agenda and other modalities of the Madrid Meeting 1980 were adopted:

I. AGENDA

1. Formal opening of the Meeting;
   Address by a representative of the host country;
   Address the Secretary-General of the United Nations or his representative.

2. Opening statements by the representatives of the participating States.

3. Contributions by:
   (a) the United Nations Economic Commission for Europe (ECE) and UNESCO;
   (b) the non-participating Mediterranean States.

4. Reports of the Meetings of Experts and of the "Scientific Forum", held in accordance with the relevant provisions of the Final Act and of the Concluding Document of Belgrade.

5. A thorough exchange of views both on the implementation of the provisions of the Final Act and of the tasks defined by the Conference, as well as, in the context of the questions dealt with by the latter, on the deepening of their mutual relations, the improvement of security and the development of co-operation in Europe, and the development of the process of détente in the future.

Examination of proposals concerning the above questions.

6. Questions relating to security in the Mediterranean will be discussed, in accordance with the relevant provision contained in the Concluding Document of the Belgrade Meeting, in the Plenary and in the subsidiary working body M, in the context of item 5 of the Agenda.

7. Definition of the appropriate modalities for the holding of other meetings in conformity with all the provisions of the chapter of the Final Act concerning the Follow-up to the Conference.

8. Drafting of a concluding document which will include decisions relating to the above-mentioned items of the Agenda.

9. Adoption of the concluding document.

10. Closing statements by the representatives of the participating States.

11. Formal closure of the Meeting.

II. ORGANIZATIONAL FRAMEWORK, TIME-TABLE AND OTHER MODALITIES OF THE MEETING

1. Agenda items 1, 2, 3(a), 9, 10 and 11 will be dealt with in open plenary meetings.

2. Agenda items 3(b), 4, 5, 6, 7 and 8 will be dealt with in the Plenary, which is the main body of the Meeting, and in the appropriate subsidiary working bodies on:

   Questions relating to Security in Europe
   Co-operation in the Field of Economics, of Science and Technology and of the Environment
   Questions relating to Security and Co-operation in the Mediterranean
   Co-operation in Humanitarian and other Fields
   Follow-up to the Conference.

   Other subsidiary working bodies may be set up by the Plenary to deal with specific questions.

3. The discussion under item 5 of the Agenda will begin with a general debate in the Plenary in the second week of the Meeting, for the purpose of initiating the work of the subsidiary working bodies on all chapters of the Final Act. After the general debate, the Plenary should maintain a balance between the amount of time devoted to each chapter of the Final Act. The subsidiary working bodies shall start their work after the second week after the beginning of the Meeting. Work on item 5 of the Agenda will be carried out on the basis of a balanced and adequate allocation of time and will be completed by 11 February 1981.

   It is recommended that substantive proposals referred to under item 5 of the Agenda should be submitted either in the Plenary or in the subsidiary working bodies not later than during the fifth week after the beginning of the Meeting. Examination of the proposals submitted will be preceded by explanatory statements starting during the sixth week.

4. The appropriate subsidiary working bodies will deal with all aspects of item 5 of the Agenda in an organized way in accordance with all the corresponding provisions of the Final Act. They will be guided in their work by the Plenary. They will conduct the examination of this point of the Agenda in a sequential and structured way according to the Final Act.

   The thorough exchange of views on the implementation of the provisions of the Final Act and of the tasks defined by the Conference will be completed by the end of the sixth week.

   As from 12 February 1981 drafting groups shall replace the subsidiary working bodies in order to assist the Plenary in drafting the concluding document of the Meeting.

5. The reports of the Meetings of Experts and the "Scientific Forum" will be introduced in the Plenary. The results of these meetings shall be taken into account, as appropriate, in the Plenary as well as in the subsidiary working bodies.

6. The non-participating Mediterranean States will be invited to make their contributions in the Plenary and in the appropriate subsidiary working body, in the context of the relevant provisions of the Final Act with respect to the realization of the objectives set out in the chapter concerning Security and Co-operation in the Mediterranean. This body will consider inviting these States to make further contributions during the course of the Meeting. The Executive Secretary shall transmit invitations to these States and, after consultation with them, propose to the Plenary dates for their contributions, preferably during the third week of the Meeting.

7. The ECE and UNESCO will be invited to make their contributions in open plenary at the end of the opening statements. The content of these contributions will be dealt with in the appropriate working bodies. The Plenary may also decide to invite these two organizations to make contributions in the appropriate subsidiary working bodies. The Executive Secretary shall transmit invitations to these organizations and, after consultation with them, propose to the Plenary the date for their contributions.

8. Meetings of the Plenary and the subsidiary working bodies will be held during the first six weeks according to the working programme attached to this document as an annex. Subsequent working programmes will be adopted by the Plenary.

9. The rules of procedure, the working methods and the scale of distribution for the expenses of the Conference will, *mutatis mutandis* be applied to the Meeting.

10. In conformity with the rules of procedure, the Government of Spain has designated the Executive Secretary and this designation has been agreed to by the participating States.

11. The opening statements under Agenda item 2 will be made in the following order: Belgium, Netherlands, Canada, Ireland, Switzerland, Norway, Sweden, United Kingdom, Luxembourg, Holy See, Federal Republic of Germany, Malta, Denmark, Hungary, United States of America, Czechoslovakia, Monaco, USSR, Iceland, Yugoslavia, German Democratic Republic, Finland, Turkey, Greece, Poland, Romania, Italy, France, San Marino, Cyprus, Portugal, Spain, Bulgaria, Liechtenstein, Austria.

    The statements, as a rule, should not exceed 30 minutes per speaker.

12. The closing statements under Agenda item 10 will be made in the following order: Switzerland, Canada, Portugal, Holy See, Liechtenstein, France, Federal Republic of Germany, Spain, Czechoslovakia, Poland, German Democratic Republic, USSR, Bulgaria, Cyprus, Turkey, Hungary, Austria, Yugoslavia, United Kingdom, Iceland, Romania, Belgium, Netherlands, Ireland, Denmark, Monaco, Italy, Finland, Greece, Norway, United States of America, Luxembourg, Sweden, Malta, San Marino.

    The statements, as a rule, should not exceed 20 minutes per speaker.

13. The Chair at the opening and closing plenary meetings shall be taken by the representative of Spain. After the opening meeting the Chair shall be taken in daily rotation, in French alphabetical order, starting with the representative of Belgium.

14. The Meeting was opened on 11 November 1980. After a break as from 20 December 1980 the Meeting will resume on 27 January 1981. Every effort should be made to agree on the concluding document not later than 5 March 1981; the date for the closure of the Meeting will be decided by the Meeting itself.

15. Nothing in these decisions can prejudice the principle of consensus.

Madrid, 14 November 1980

WORKING PROGRAMME

Meetings of the Plenary and the subsidiary working bodies will be held according to the following working programme:

- From 11 to 14 November 1980 the Plenary will meet in seven open sessions.
- From 17 November to 19 December 1980 the Plenary will meet in twenty-three closed sessions.
- Preferably during the period from 24 to 28 November 1980, the Plenary will receive contributions from the non-participating Mediterranean States and will take into account the reports of the Meetings of Experts and the "Scientific Forum".
- From 24 November to 19 December 1980 the subsidiary working body S will meet in twenty-four sessions.
- From 24 November to 19 December 1980 the subsidiary working bodies E and H will meet in twenty sessions each.

- From 1 to 19 December 1980 the subsidiary working bodies M and F will, as a rule, average between them five sessions every week.

  Subsequent working programmes will be drawn up by the Plenary.

Explanatory note on the symbols used in the working programme

PL Plenary

S Subsidiary working body on: Questions relating to Security in Europe

E Subsidiary working body on: Co-operation in the Field of Economics, of Science and Technology and of the Environment

M Subsidiary working body on: Questions relating to Security and Co-operation in the Mediterranean

H Subsidiary working body on: Co-operation in Humanitarian and other Fields

F Subsidiary working body on: Follow-up to the Conference.

WORKING PROGRAMME

11 November - 19 December 1980

FIRST WEEK	Monday 10 Nov.	Tuesday 11 Nov.	Wednesday 12 Nov.	Thursday 13 Nov.	Friday 14 Nov.
Morning	-	-	PL	PL	PL
Afternoon	-	PL	PL	PL	PL

SECOND WEEK	Monday 17 Nov.	Tuesday 18 Nov.	Wednesday 19 Nov.	Thursday 20 Nov.	Friday 21 Nov.
Morning	PL	PL	PL	PL	PL
Afternoon	PL	PL	PL	PL	PL

THIRD WEEK	Monday 24 Nov.	Tuesday 25 Nov.	Wednesday 26 Nov.	Thursday 27 Nov.	Friday 28 Nov.
Morning	PL	PL	S E	PL	PL
Afternoon	S E H	S E H	S H	S E H	S E H

FOURTH WEEK	Monday 1 Dec.	Tuesday 2 Dec.	Wednesday 3 Dec.	Thursday 4 Dec.	Friday 5 Dec.
Morning	PL E	S F E	PL	E M	PL
Afternoon	S M H	S M H	S E H	S F H	S E H

FIFTH WEEK	Monday 8 Dec.	Tuesday 9 Dec.	Wednesday 10 Dec.	Thursday 11 Dec.	Friday 12 Dec.
Morning	PL	S E M	PL E	S F	PL
Afternoon	S E H	S F H	S F H	E M H	S E H

SIXTH WEEK	Monday 15 Dec.	Tuesday 16 Dec.	Wednesday 17 Dec.	Thursday 18 Dec.	Friday 19 Dec.
Morning	PL E	S E F	PL	S F	S E H
Afternoon	S H M	S H M	S E H	E M H	PL

Statements by the Chairman

- concerning item 5 of the Agenda:

On the occasion of the registration of item 5 of the Agenda the Chairman noted the general understanding of the Meeting that this item of the Agenda contains two distinct elements.

- concerning item 7 of the Agenda:

On the occasion of the registration of item 7 of the Agenda the Chairman noted the general understanding of the Meeting that the definition in the concluding document of the appropriate modalities for the holding of other Meetings includes setting the date and place of the next Meeting similar to the present one.

ANNEX 4

CONCLUDING DOCUMENT

OF THE MADRID MEETING 1980 OF REPRESENTATIVES OF THE PARTICIPATING STATES OF THE CONFERENCE ON SECURITY AND CO-OPERATION IN EUROPE, HELD ON THE BASIS OF THE PROVISIONS OF THE FINAL ACT RELATING TO THE FOLLOW-UP TO THE CONFERENCE

(1) The representatives of the participating States of the Conference on Security and Co-operation in Europe met in Madrid from 11 November 1980 to 9 September 1983 in accordance with the provisions of the Final Act relating to the Follow-up to the Conference, as well as on the basis of the other relevant documents adopted during the process of the CSCE.

(2) The participants were addressed on 12 November 1980 by the Spanish Prime Minister.

(3) Opening statements were made by all Heads of Delegations among whom were Ministers and Deputy Ministers of Foreign Affairs of a number of participating States. Some Ministers of Foreign Affairs addressed the Meeting also at later stages.

(4) Contributions were made by representatives of the United Nations Economic Commission for Europe (ECE) and UNESCO.

Contributions were also made by the following non-participating Mediterranean States: Algeria, Egypt, Israel, Morocco and Tunisia.

(5) The representatives of the participating States stressed the high political significance of the Conference on Security and Co-operation in Europe and of the process initiated by it as well as of the ways and means it provides for States to further their efforts to increase security, develop co-operation and enhance mutual understanding in Europe. They therefore reaffirmed their commitment to the process of the CSCE and emphasized the importance of the implementation of all the provisions and the respect for all the principles of the Final Act by each of them as being essential for the development of this process. Furthermore, they stressed the importance they attach to security and genuine detente, while deploring the deterioration of the international situation since the Belgrade Meeting 1977.

Accordingly, the participating States agreed that renewed efforts should be made to give full effect to the Final Act through concrete action, unilateral, bilateral and multilateral, in order to restore trust and confidence between the participating States which would permit a substantial improvement in their mutual relations. They considered that the future of the CSCE process required balanced progress in all sections of the Final Act.

(6) In accordance with the mandate provided for in the Final Act and the Agenda of the Madrid Meeting, the representatives of the participating States held a thorough exchange of views both on the implementation of the provisions of the Final Act and of the tasks defined by the Conference, as well as, in the context of the questions

dealt with by the latter, on the deepening of their mutual relations, the improvement of security and the development of co-operation in Europe, and the development of the process of detente in the future.

(7) It was confirmed that the thorough exchange of views constitutes in itself a valuable contribution towards the achievement of the aims set by the CSCE. In this context, it was agreed that these aims can only be attained by continuous implementation, unilaterally, bilaterally and multilaterally, of all the provisions and by respect for all the principles of the Final Act.

(8) During this exchange of views, different and at times contradictory opinions were expressed as to the degree of implementation of the Final Act reached so far by participating States. While certain progress was noted, concern was expressed at the serious deficiencies in the implementation of this document.

(9) Critical assessments from different viewpoints were given as to the application of and respect for the principles of the Final Act. Serious violations of a number of these principles were deplored during these assessments. Therefore, the participating States, at times represented at a higher level, considered it necessary to state, at various stages of the Meeting, that strict application of and respect for these principles, in all their aspects, are essential for the improvement of mutual relations between the participating States.

The necessity was also stressed that the relations of the participating States with all other States should be conducted in the spirit of these principles.

(10) Concern was expressed about the continued lack of confidence among participating States.

Concern was also expressed as to the spread of terrorism.

(11) The implementation of the provisions of the Final Act concerning Confidence-Building Measures, Co-operation in the field of Economics, of Science and Technology and of Environment, as well as Co-operation in Humanitarian and other fields was thoroughly discussed. It was considered that the numerous possibilities offered by the Final Act had not been sufficiently utilized. Questions relating to Security and Co-operation in the Mediterranean were also discussed.

(12) The participating States reaffirmed their commitment to the to the continuation of the CSCE process as agreed to in the chapter on the Follow-up to the Conference contained in the Final Act.

(13) The representatives of the participating States took note of the reports of the meetings of experts and of the "Scientific Forum", and in the course of their deliberations took the results of these meetings into account.

(14) The representatives of the participating States examined all the proposals submitted concerning the above questions and agreed on the following:

QUESTIONS RELATING TO SECURITY IN EUROPE

The participating States express their determination

- to exert new efforts to make detente an effective, as well as continuing increasingly viable and comprehensive process, universal in scope, as undertaken under the Final Act;
- to seek solutions to outstanding problems through peaceful means;
- to fulfil consistently all the provisions under the Final Act, and in particular, strictly and unreservedly to respect and put into practice all the ten principles contained in the Declaration on Principles Guiding Relations between Participating States, irrespective of their political, economic or social systems, as well as of their size, geographical location or level of economic development, including their commitment to conduct their relations with all other States in the spirit of these principles;
- to develop relations of mutual co-operation, friendship and confidence, refraining from any action which, being contrary to the Final Act, might impair such relations;
- to encourage genuine efforts to implement the Final Act;
- to exert genuine efforts towards containing an increasing arms build-up as well as towards strengthening confidence and security and promoting disarmament.

Principles

(1) They reaffirm their determination fully to respect and apply these principles and accordingly, to promote by all means, both in law and practice, their increased effectiveness. They consider that one such means could be to give legislative expression - in forms appropriate to practices and procedures specific to each country - to the ten principles set forth in the Final Act.

(2) They recognize it as important that treaties and agreements concluded by participating States reflect and be consonant with the relevant principles and, where appropriate, refer to them.

(3) The participating States reaffirm the need that refraining from the threat or use of force, as a norm of international life, should be strictly and effectively observed. To this end they stress their duty, under the relevant provisions of the Final Act, to act accordingly.

(4) The participating States condemn terrorism, including terrorism in international relations, as endangering or taking innocent human lives or otherwise jeopardizing human rights and fundamental freedoms, and emphasize the necessity to take resolute measures to combat it. They express their determination to take effective measures for the prevention and suppression of acts of terrorism, both at the national level and through international co-operation including appropriate bilateral and multilateral agreements, and accordingly to broaden and reinforce mutual co-operation to combat such acts. They agree to do so in conformity with the Charter of the United

Nations, the United Nations Declaration on Principles of International Law concerning Friendly Relations and Co-operation among States and the Helsinki Final Act.

(5) In the context of the combat against acts of terrorism, they will take all appropriate measures in preventing their respective territories from being used for the preparation, organization or commission of terrorist activities, including those directed against other participating States and their citizens. This also includes measures to prohibit on their territories illegal activities of persons, groups and organizations that instigate, organize or engage in the perpetration of acts of terrorism.

(6) The participating States confirm that they will refrain from direct or indirect assistance to terrorist activities or to subversive or other activities directed towards the violent overthrow of the regime of another participating State. Accordingly, they will refrain, *inter alia*, from financing, encouraging, fomenting or tolerating any such activities.

(7) They express their determination to do their utmost to assure necessary security to all official representatives and persons who participate on their territories in activities within the scope of diplomatic, consular or other official relations.

(8) They emphasize that all the participating States recognize in the Final Act the universal significance of human rights and fundamental freedoms, respect for which is an essential factor for the peace, justice and well-being necessary to ensure the development of friendly relations and co-operation among themselves, as among all States.

(9) The participating States stress their determination to promote and encourage the effective exercise of human rights and fundamental freedoms, all of which derive from the inherent dignity of the human person and are essential for his free and full development, and to assure constant and tangible progress in accordance with the Final Act, aiming at further and steady development in this field in all participating States, irrespective of their political, economic and social systems.

They similarly stress their determination to develop their laws and regulations in the field of civil, political, economic, social, cultural and other human rights and fundamental freedoms; they also emphasize their determination to ensure the effective exercise of these rights and freedoms.

They recall the right of the individual to know and act upon his rights and duties in the field of human rights and fundamental freedoms, as embodied in the Final Act, and will take the necessary action in their respective countries to effectively ensure this right.

(10) The participating States reaffirm that they will recognize, respect and furthermore agree to take the action necessary to ensure the freedom of the individual to profess and practise, alone or in community with others, religion or belief acting in accordance with the dictates of his own conscience.

In this context, they will consult, whenever necessary, the religious faiths, institutions and organizations, which act within the constitutional framework of their respective countries.

They will favourably consider applications by religious communities of believers practising or prepared to practise their faith within the constitutional framework of their States, to be granted the status provided for in their respective countries for religious faiths, institutions and organizations.

(11) They stress also the importance of constant progress in ensuring the respect for and actual enjoyment of the rights of persons belonging to national minorities as well as protecting their legitimate interests as provided for in the Final Act.

(12) They stress the importance of ensuring equal rights of men and women; accordingly, they agree to take all actions necessary to promote equally effective participation of men and women in political, economic, social and cultural life.

(13) The participating States will ensure the right of workers freely to establish and join trade unions, the right of trade unions freely to exercise their activities and other rights as laid down in relevant international instruments. They note that these rights will be exercised in compliance with the law of the State and in conformity with the State's obligations under international law. They will encourage, as appropriate, direct contacts and communication among such trade unions and their representatives.

(14) They reaffirm that governments, institutions, organizations and persons have a relevant and positive role to play in contributing toward the achievement of the above-mentioned aims of their co-operation.

(15) They reaffirm the particular significance of the Universal Declaration of Human Rights, the International Covenants on Human Rights and other relevant international instruments of their joint and separate efforts to stimulate and develop universal respect for human rights and fundamental freedoms; they call on all participating States to act in conformity with those international instruments and on those participating States, which have not yet done so, to consider the possibility of acceding to the covenants.

(16) They agree to give favourable consideration to the use of bilateral round-table meetings, held on a voluntary basis, between delegations composed by each participating State to discuss issues of human rights and fundamental freedoms in accordance with an agreed agenda in a spirit of mutual respect with a view to achieving greater understanding and co-operation based on the provisions of the Final Act.

(17) They decide to convene a meeting of experts of the participating States on questions concerning respect, in their States, for human rights and fundamental freedoms, in all their aspects, as embodied in the Final Act.

Upon invitation of the Government of Canada, the meeting of experts will be held in Ottawa, beginning on 7 May 1985. It will draw up conclusions and recommendations to be submitted to the governments of all participating States.

The meeting will be preceded by a preparatory meeting which will be held in Ottawa upon the invitation of the Government of Canada, starting on 23 April 1985.

(18) In conformity with the recommendation contained in the Report of the Montreux Meeting of Experts, another meeting of experts of the participating States will be convened, at the invitation of the Government of Greece. It will take place in Athens and will commence on 21 March 1984, with the purpose of pursuing, on the basis of the Final Act, the examination of a generally acceptable method for the peaceful settlement of disputes aimed at complementing existing methods. The meeting will take into account the common approach set forth in the above-mentioned report.

(19) Recalling the right of any participating State to belong or not to belong to international organizations, to be or not to be a party to bilateral or multilateral treaties including the right to be or not to be a party to treaties of alliance, and also the right to neutrality, the participating States take note of the declaration of the Government of the Republic of Malta in which it stated that, as an effective contribution to detente, peace and security in the Mediterranean region, the Republic of Malta is a neutral State adhering to a policy of non-alignment. They call upon all States to respect that declaration.

Conference on Confidence- and Security-building Measures and Disarmament in Europe

The participating States,

Recalling the provisions of the Final Act according to which they recognize the interest of all of them in efforts aimed at lessening military confrontation and promoting disarmament,

Have agreed to convene a Conference on Confidence- and Security--building Measures and Disarmament in Europe.

(1) The aim of the Conference is, as a substantial and integral part of the multilateral process initiated by the Conference on Security and Co-operation in Europe, with the participation of all the States signatories of the Final Act, to undertake in stages, new, effective and concrete actions designed to make progress in strengthening confidence and security and in achieving disarmament, so as to give effect and expression to the duty of States to refrain from the threat or use of force in their mutual relations.

(2) Thus the Conference will begin a process of which the first stage will be devoted to the negotiation and adoption of a set of mutually complementary confidence- and security-building measures designed to reduce the risk of military confrontation in Europe.

(3) The first stage of the Conference will be held in Stockholm commencing on 17 January 1984.

(4) On the basis of equality of rights, balance and reciprocity, equal respect for the security interests of all CSCE participating States, and of their respective obligations concerning confidence- and security-building measures and disarmament in Europe, these confidence- and security-building measures will cover the whole of

Europe as well as the adjoining sea area* and air space. They will be of military significance and politically binding and will be provided with adequate forms of verification which correspond to their content.

As far as the adjoining sea area* and air space is concerned, the measures will be applicable to the military activities of all the participating States taking place there whenever these activities affect security in Europe as well as constitute a part of activities taking place within the whole of Europe as referred to above, which they will agree to notify. Necessary specifications will be made, through the negotiations on the confidence- and security-building measures at the Conference.

Nothing in the definition of the zone given above will diminish obligations already undertaken under the Final Act. The confidence- and security-building measures to be agreed upon at the Conference will also be applicable in all areas covered by any of the provisions in the Final Act relating to confidence-building measures and certain aspects of security and disarmament.

The provisions established by the negotiators will come into force in the forms and according to the procedure to be agreed upon by the Conference.

(5) Taking into account the above-mentioned aim of the Conference, the next follow-up meeting of the participating States of the CSCE, to be held in Vienna, commencing on 4 November 1986, will assess the progress achieved during the first stage of the Conference.

(6) Taking into account the relevant provisions of the Final Act, and having reviewed the results achieved by the first stage of the Conference, and also in the light of other relevant negotiations on security and disarmament affecting Europe, a future CSCE follow-up meeting will consider ways and appropriate means for the participating States to continue their efforts for security and disarmament in Europe, including the question of supplementing the present mandate for the next stage of the Conference on Confidence- and Security-building Measures and Disarmament in Europe.

(7) A preparatory meeting, charged with establishing the agenda, time-table and other organizational modalities for the first stage of the Conference, will be held in Helsinki, commencing on 25 October 1983. Its duration shall not exceed three weeks.

(8) The rules of procedure, the working methods and the scale of distribution for the expenses valid for the CSCE will, *mutatis mutandis*, be applied to the Conference and to the preparatory meeting referred to in the preceding paragraph. The services of a technical secretariat will be provided by the host country.

CO-OPERATION IN THE FIELD OF ECONOMICS, OF SCIENCE AND TECHNOLOGY AND OF THE ENVIRONMENT

(1) The participating States consider that the implementation of all

* In this context, the notion of adjoining sea area is understood to refer also to ocean areas adjoining Europe.

provisions of the Final Act and full respect for the principles guiding relations among them set out therein are an essential basis for the development of co-operation among them in the field of economics, of science and technology and of the environment. At the same time they reaffirm their conviction that co-operation in these fields contributes to the reinforcement of peace and security in Europe and in the world as a whole. In this spirit they reiterate their resolve to pursue and intensify such co-operation between one another, irrespective of their economic and social systems.

(2) The participating States confirm their interest in promoting adequate, favourable conditions in order further to develop trade and industrial co-operation among them, in particular by fully implementing all provisions of the second chapter of the Final Act, so as to make greater use of the possibilities created by their economic, scientific and technical potential. In this context and taking into consideration the efforts already made unilaterally, bilaterally and multilaterally in order to overcome all kinds of obstacles to trade, they reaffirm their intention to make further efforts aimed at reducing or progressively eliminating all kinds of obstacles to the development of trade.

Taking account of the activities of the United Nations Economic Commission for Europe (ECE) already carried out in the field of all kinds of obstacles to trade, they recommend that further work on this subject be directed in particular towards identifying these obstacles and examining them with a view to finding means for their reduction or progressive elimination, in order to contribute to harmonious development of their economic relations.

(3) On the basis of the provisions of the Final Act concerning business contacts and facilities the participating States declare their intention to make efforts to enable business negotiations and activities to be carried out more efficiently and expeditiously and further to create conditions facilitating closer contacts between representatives and experts of seller firms on the one hand and buyer as well as user firms on the other at all stages of transaction. They will also further other forms of operational contacts between sellers and users such as the holding of technical symposia and demonstrations and after-sales training or requalification courses for technical staff of user firms and organizations.

They also agree to take measures further to develop and improve facilities and working conditions for representatives of foreign firms and organizations on their territory, including telecommunications facilities for representatives of such firms and organizations, as well as to develop these and other amenities for temporarily resident staff including particularly site personnel. They will endeavour further to take measures to speed up as far as possible procedures for the registration of foreign firms' representations and offices as well as for granting entry visas to business representatives.

(4) The participating States declare their intention to ensure the regular publication and dissemination, as rapidly as possible, of economic and commercial information compiled in such a way as to facilitate the appreciation of market opportunities and thus to contribute effectively to the process of developing international

trade and industrial co-operation.

To this end and in order to make further progress in achieving the aims laid down in the relevant provisions of the Final Act they intend to intensify their efforts to improve the comparability, comprehensiveness and clarity of their economic and commercial statistics, in particular by adopting where necessary the following measures: by accompanying their economic and trade statistics by adequately defined summary indices based wherever possible on constant values; by publishing their interim statistics whenever technically possible at least on a quarterly basis; by publishing their statistical compilations in sufficient detail to achieve the aims referred to above, in particular by using for their foreign trade statistics a product breakdown permitting the identification of particular products for purposes of market analysis; by striving to have their economic and trade statistics no less comprehensive than those previously published by the State concerned.

They further express their willingness to co-operate towards the early completion of work in the appropriate United Nations bodies on the harmonization and alignment of statistical nomenclatures.

The participating States further recognize the usefulness of making economic and commercial information existing in other participating States readily available to enterprises and firms in their countries through appropriate channels.

(5) The participating States, conscious of the need further to improve the conditions conducive to a more efficient functioning of institutions and firms acting in the field of marketing, will promote a more active exchange of knowledge and techniques required for effective marketing, and will encourage more intensive relations among such institutions and firms. They agree to make full use of the possibilities offered by the ECE to further their co-operation in this field.

(6) The participating States note the increasing frequency in their economic relations of compensation transactions in all their forms. They recognize that a useful role can be played by such transactions, concluded on a mutually acceptable basis. At the same time they recognize that problems can be created by the linkage in such transactions between purchases and sales.

Taking account of the studies of the ECE already carried out in this field, they recommend that further work on this subject be directed in particular towards identifying such problems and examining ways of solving them in order to contribute to a harmonious development of their economic relations.

(7) The participating States recognize that the expansion of industrial co-operation, on the basis of their mutual interest and motivated by economic considerations, can contribute to the further development and diversification of their economic relations and to a wider utilization of modern technology.

They note the useful role bilateral agreements on economic, industrial and technical co-operation, including where appropriate, those of a long-term nature can play. They also express their willingness to promote favourable conditions for the development of industrial co-operation among competent organizations, enterprises and firms. To this end and with a view to facilitating the identification of new possibilities for industrial co-operation projects they recognize the desirability of further developing and improving the conditions for business activities and the exchange of economic and commercial information among competent organizations, enterprises and firms including small and medium-sized enterprises.

They also note that, if it is in the mutual interest of potential partners, new forms of industrial co-operation can be envisaged, including those with organizations, institutions and firms of third countries.

They recommend that the ECE pursue and continue to pay particular attention to its activities in the field of industrial co-operation, *inter alia* by further directing its efforts towards examining ways of promoting favourable conditions for the development of co-operation in this field, including the organization of symposia and seminars.

(8) The participating States declare their readiness to continue their efforts aiming at a wider participation by small and medium-size enterprises in trade and industrial co-operation. Aware of the problems particularly affecting such enterprises, the participating States will endeavour further to improve the conditions dealt with in the preceding paragraphs in order to facilitate the operations of these enterprises in the above-mentioned fields. The participating States further recommend that the ECE develop its special studies pertaining to these problems.

(9) The participating States recognize the increasing importance of co-operation in the field of energy, *inter alia* that of a long-term nature, on both a bilateral and multilateral basis. Welcoming the results so far achieved through such endeavours and in particular the work carried out by the ECE they express their support for continuing the co-operation pursued by the Senior Advisers to ECE Governments on Energy aiming at the fulfilment of all parts of their mandate.

(10) The participating States reaffirm their interest in reducing and preventing technical barriers to trade and welcome the increased co-operation in this field, *inter alia* the work of the Government Officials Responsible for Standardization Policies in the ECE. They will encourage the conclusion of international certification arrangements covering where appropriate the mutual acceptance of certification systems providing mutually satisfactory guarantees.

(11) The participating States recommend that appropriate action be taken in order to facilitate the use and enlarge the scope of arbitration as an instrument for settling disputes in international trade and industrial co-operation. They recommend in particular the application of the provisions of the United Nations Convention on Recognition and Enforcement of Foreign Arbitral Awards of 1958 as well as a wider recourse to the arbitration rules elaborated by the United Nations Commission on International Trade Law. They also advocate that parties should, on the basis of the provisions of the Final Act, be allowed freedom in the choice of arbitrators and the place of arbitration, including the choice of arbitrators and the place of arbitration in a third country.

(12) The participating States recognize the important role of scientific and technical progress in the economic and social development of all countries in particular those which are developing from an economic point of view. Taking into account the objectives which countries or institutions concerned pursue in their bilateral and multilateral relations they underline the importance of further developing, on the basis of reciprocal advantage and on the basis of mutual agreement and other arrangements, the forms and methods of co-operation in the field of science and technology provided for in the Final Act, for instance international programmes and co-operative projects, while utilizing also various forms of contacts, including direct and individual contacts among scientists and specialists as well as contacts and communications among interested organizations, scientific and technological institutions and enterprises.

In this context they recognize the value of an improved exchange and dissemination of information concerning scientific and technical developments as a means of facilitating, on the basis of mutual advantage, the study and the transfer of, as well as access to scientific and technical achievements in fields of co-operation agreed between interested parties.

The participating States recommend that in the field of science and technology the ECE should give due attention, through appropriate ways and means, to the elaboration of studies and practical projects for the development of co-operation among member countries.

Furthermore, the participating States, aware of the relevant part of the Report of the "Scientific Forum", agree to encourage the development of scientific co-operation in the field of agriculture at bilateral, multilateral and sub-regional levels, with the aim, *inter alia*, of improving livestock and plant breeding and ensuring optimum use and conservation of water resources. To this end, they will promote further co-operation among research institutions and centres in their countries, through the exchange of information, the joint implementation of research programmes, the organization of meetings among scientists and specialists, and other methods.

The participating States invite the ECE and other competent international organizations to support the implementation of these activities and to examine the possibilities of providing a wider exchange of scientific and technological information in the field of agriculture.

(13) The participating States welcome with satisfaction the important steps taken to strengthen co-operation within the framework of the ECE in the field of the environment, including the High-Level Meeting on the Protection of the Environment (13-16 November 1979). Taking due account of work undertaken or envisaged in other competent international organizations, they recommend the continuation of efforts in this field, including, *inter alia*,

- giving priority to the effective implementation of the provisions of the Resolution on Long-Range Transboundary Air Pollution adopted at the High-Level Meeting,

- the early ratification of the Convention on Long-Range Transboundary Air Pollution signed at the High-Level Meeting,

- implementation of the Recommendations contained in the Declaration on Low and Non-Waste Technology and Reutilization and Recycling of Wastes,
- implementation of Decisions B and C of the thirty-fifth session of the ECE concerning the Declaration of Policy on Prevention and Control of Water Pollution, including transboundary pollution,
- support in carrying out the programme of work of the ECE concerning the protection of the environment, including, *inter alia*, the work under way in the field of the protection of flora and fauna.

(14) In the context of the provisions of the Final Act concerning migrant labour in Europe, the participating States note that recent developments in the world economy have affected the situation of migrant workers. In this connection, the participating States express their wish that host countries and countries of origin, guided by a spirit of mutual interest and co-operation, intensify their contacts with a view to improving further the general situation of migrant workers and their families, *inter alia* the protection of their human rights including their economic, social and cultural rights while taking particularly into account the special problems of second generation migrants. They will also endeavour to provide or promote, where reasonable demand exists, adequate teaching of the language and culture of the countries of origin.

The participating States recommend that, among other measures for facilitating the social and economic reintegration of returning migrant labour, the payment of pensions as acquired or established under the social security system to which such workers have been admitted in the host country should be ensured by appropriate legislative means or reciprocal agreements.

(15) The participating States further recognize the importance for their economic development of promoting the exchange of information and experience on training for management staff. To this end they recommend the organization, in an appropriate existing framework and with the help of interested organizations such as, for example, the ECE and the International Labour Organisation, of a symposium of persons responsible for services and institutions specializing in management training for administrations and enterprises with a view to exchanging information on training problems and methods, comparing experiences and encouraging the development of relations among the centres concerned.

(16) The participating States welcome the valuable contribution made by the ECE to the multilateral implementation of the provisions of the Final Act pertaining to co-operation in the fields of economics, of science and technology and of the environment. Aware of the potential of the ECE for intensifying co-operation in these fields, they recommend the fullest use of the existing mechanisms and resources in order to continue and consolidate the implementation of the relevant provisions of the Final Act in the interest of its member countries, including those within the ECE region which are developing from an economic point of view.

(17) The participating States, bearing in mind their will expressed in the provisions of the Final Act, reiterate the determination of each

of them to promote stable and equitable international economic relations in the mutual interest of all States and, in this spirit, to participate equitably in promoting and strengthening economic co-operation with the developing countries in particular the least developed among them. They also note the usefulness, *inter alia*, of identifying and executing, in co-operation with developing countries, concrete projects, with a view to contributing to economic development in these countries.

They also declare their readiness to contribute to common efforts towards the establishment of a new international economic order and the implementation of the Strategy for the Third United Nations Development Decade, as adopted. They recognize the importance of the launching of mutually beneficial and adequately prepared global negotiations relating to international economic co-operation for development.

QUESTIONS RELATING TO SECURITY AND CO-OPERATION IN THE MEDITERRANEAN

(1) The participating States, bearing in mind that security in Europe, considered in the broader context of world security, is closely linked to security in the Mediterranean area as a whole, reaffirm their intention to contribute to peace, security and justice in the Mediterranean region.

(2) They further express their will

- to take positive steps towards lessening tensions and strengthening stability, security and peace in the Mediterranean and, to this end, to intensify efforts towards finding just, viable and lasting solutions, through peaceful means, to outstanding crucial problems, without resort to force or other means incompatible with the Principles of the Final Act, so as to promote confidence and security and make peace prevail in the region;
- to take measures designed to increase confidence and security;
- to develop good neighbourly relations with all States in the region, with due regard to reciprocity, and in the spirit of the principles contained in the Declaration on Principles Guiding Relations between Participating States of the Final Act;
- to study further the possibility of *ad hoc* meetings of Mediterranean States aimed at strengthening security and intensifying co-operation in the Mediterranean.

(3) In addition the participating States will, within the framework of the implementation of the Valletta report, consider the possibilities offered by new transport infrastructure developments to facilitate new commercial and industrial exchanges, as well as by the improvement of existing transport networks, and by a wider co-ordination of transport investments between interested parties. In this context they recommend that a study be undertaken, within the framework of the ECE, in order to establish the current and potential transport flows in the Mediterranean involving the participating States and other States of this region taking account of the current

work in this field. They will further consider the question of introducing or extending, in accordance with the existing IMO regulations, the use of suitable techniques for aids to maritime navigation, principally in straits.

(4) They further note with satisfaction the results of the Meeting of Experts held in Valletta on the subject of economic, scientific and cultural co-operation within the framework of the Mediterranean Chapter of the Final Act. They reaffirm the conclusions and recommendations of the report of this Meeting and agree that they will be guided accordingly. They also take note of efforts under way aiming at implementing them as appropriate. To this end, the participating States agree to convene from 16 to 26 October 1984 a seminar to be held at Venice at the invitation of the Government of Italy, to review the initiatives already undertaken, or envisaged, in all the sectors outlined in the report of the Valletta Meeting and stimulate, where necessary, broader developments in these sectors.

Representatives of the competent international organizations and representatives of the non-participating Mediterranean States will be invited to this Seminar in accordance with the rules and practices adopted at the Valletta Meeting*.

CO-OPERATION IN HUMANITARIAN AND OTHER FIELDS

The participating States,

Recalling the introductory sections of the Chapter on Co-operation in Humanitarian and other Fields of the Final Act including those concerning the development of mutual understanding between them and détente and those concerning progress in cultural and educational exchanges, broader dissemination of information, contacts between people and the solution of humanitarian problems,

Resolving to pursue and expand co-operation in these fields and to achieve a fuller utilization of the possibilities offered by the Final Act,

Agree now to implement the following:

Human Contacts

(1) The participating States will favourably deal with applications relating to contacts and regular meetings on the basis of family ties, reunification of families and marriage between citizens of different States and will decide upon them in the same spirit.

(2) They will decide upon these applications in emergency cases for family meetings as expeditiously as possible, for family reunification and for marriage between citizens of different States in normal practice within six months and for other family meetings within gradually decreasing time limits.

---

* The organization of the Venice Seminar is set forth in the Chairman's statement of 6 September 1983 (see Annex I).

(3) They confirm that the presentation or renewal of applications in these cases will not modify the rights and obligations of the applicants or of members of their families concerning *inter alia* employment, housing, residence status, family support, access to social, economic or educational benefits, as well as any other rights and obligations flowing from the laws and regulations of the respective participating State.

(4) The participating States will provide the necessary information on the procedures to be followed by the applicants in these cases and on the regulations to be observed, as well as, upon the applicant's request, provide the relevant forms.

(5) They will, where necessary, gradually reduce fees charged in connection with these applications, including those for visas and passports, in order to bring them to a moderate level in relation to the average monthly income in the respective participating State.

(6) Applicants will be informed as expeditiously as possible of the decision that has been reached. In case of refusal applicants will also be informed of their right to renew applications after reasonably short intervals.

(7) The participating States reaffirm their commitment fully to implement the provisions regarding diplomatic and other official missions and consular posts of other participating States contained in relevant multilateral or bilateral conventions, and to facilitate the normal functioning of those missions. Access by visitors to these missions will be assured with due regard to the necessary requirements of security of these missions.

(8) They also reaffirm their willingness to take, within their competence, reasonable steps, including necessary security measures, when appropriate, to ensure satisfactory conditions for activities within the framework of mutual co-operation on their territory, such as sporting and cultural events, in which citizens of other participating States take part.

(9) The participating States will endeavour, where appropriate, to improve the conditions relating to legal, consular and medical assistance for citizens of other participating States temporarily on their territory for personal or professional reasons, taking due account of relevant multilateral or bilateral conventions or agreements.

(10) They will further implement the relevant provisions of the Final Act, so that religious faiths, institutions, organizations and their representatives can, in the field of their activity, develop contacts and meetings among themselves and exchange information.

(11) The participating States will encourage contacts and exchanges among young people and foster the broadening of co-operation among their youth organizations. They will favour the holding among young people and youth organizations of educational, cultural and other comparable events and activities. They will also favour the study of problems relating to the younger generation. The participating States will further the development of individual or collective youth tourism, when necessary on the basis of arrangements, *inter alia* by encouraging the granting of suitable facilities by the transport

authorities and tourist organizations of the participating States or such facilities as those offered by the railway authorities participating in the "Inter-Rail" system.

Information

(1) The participating States will further encourage the freer and wider dissemination of printed matter, periodical and non-periodical, imported from other participating States, as well as an increase in the number of places where these publications are on public sale. These publications will also be accessible in reading rooms in large public libraries and similar institutions.

(2) In particular, to facilitate the improvement of dissemination of printed information, the participating States will encourage contacts and negotiations between their competent firms and organizations with a view to concluding long-term agreements and contracts designed to increase the quantities and number of titles of newspapers and other publications imported from other participating States. They consider it desirable that the retail prices of foreign publications are not excessive in relation to prices in their country of origin.

(3) They confirm their intention, according to the relevant provisions of the Final Act, to further extend the possibilities for the public to take out subscriptions.

(4) They will favour the further expansion of co-operation among mass media and their representatives, especially between the editorial staffs of press agencies, newspapers, radio and television organizations as well as film companies. They will encourage a more regular exchange of news, articles, supplements and broadcasts as well as the exchange of editorial staff for better knowledge of respective practices. On the basis of reciprocity, they will improve the material and technical facilities provided for permanently or temporarily accredited television and radio reporters. Moreover, they will facilitate direct contacts among journalists as well as contacts within the framework of professional organizations.

(5) They will decide without undue delay upon visa applications from journalists and re-examine within a reasonable time frame applications which have been refused. Moreover, journalists wishing to travel for personal reasons and not for the purpose of reporting shall enjoy the same treatment as other visitors from their country of origin.

(6) They will grant permanent correspondents and members of their families living with them multiple entry and exit visas valid for one year.

(7) The participating States will examine the possibility of granting, where necessary on the basis of bilateral arrangements, accreditation and related facilities to journalists from other participating States who are permanently accredited in third countries.

(8) They will facilitate travel by journalists from other participating States within their territories, *inter alia* by taking concrete measures where necessary, to afford them opportunities to travel more extensively, with the exception of areas closed for security reasons. They will inform journalists in advance, whenever possible, if new

areas are closed for security reasons.

(9) They will further increase the possibilities and, when necessary, improve the conditions for journalists from other participating States to establish and maintain personal contacts and communication with their sources.

(10) They will, as a rule, authorize radio and television journalists, at their request, to be accompanied by their own sound and film technicians and to use their own equipment.

Similarly, journalists may carry with them reference material, including personal notes and files, to be used strictly for their professional purposes*.

(11) The participating States will, where necessary, facilitate the establishment and operation, in their capitals, of press centres or institutions performing the same functions, open to the national and foreign press with suitable working facilities for the latter.

They will also consider further ways and means to assist journalists from other participating States and thus to enable them to resolve practical problems they may encounter.

Co-operation and Exchanges in the Field of Culture

(1) They will endeavour, by taking appropriate steps, to make the relevant information concerning possibilities offered by bilateral cultural agreements and programmes available to interested persons, institutions and non-governmental organizations, thus facilitating their effective implementation.

(2) The participating States will further encourage wider dissemination of and access to books, films and other forms and means of cultural expression from other participating States, to this end improving by appropriate means, on bilateral and multilateral bases, the conditions for international commercial and non-commercial exchange of their cultural goods, *inter alia* by gradually lowering customs duties on these items.

(3) The participating States will endeavour to encourage the translation, publication and dissemination of works in the sphere of literature and other fields of cultural activity from other participating States, especially those produced in less widely spoken languages, by facilitating co-operation between publishing houses, in particular through the exchange of lists of books which might be translated as well as of other relevant information.

(4) They will contribute to the development of contacts, co-operation and joint projects among the participating States regarding the protection, preservation and recording of historical heritage and monuments and the relationship between man, environment and this heritage; they express their interest in the possibility of convening

* In this context it is understood that import of printed matter may be subject to local regulations which will be applied with due regard to the journalists' need for adequate working material.

an inter-governmental conference on these matters within the framework of UNESCO.

(5) The participating States will encourage their radio and television organizations to continue developing the presentation of the cultural and artistic achievements of other participating States on the basis of bilateral and multilateral arrangements between these organizations, providing *inter alia* for exchanges of information on productions, for the broadcasting of shows and programmes from other participating States, for co-productions, for the invitation of guest conductors and directors, as well as for the provision of mutual assistance to cultural film teams.

(6) At the invitation of the Government of Hungary a "Cultural Forum" will take place in Budapest, commencing on 15 October 1985. It will be attended by leading personalities in the field of culture from the participating States. The "Forum" will discuss interrelated problems concerning creation, dissemination and co-operation, including the promotion and expansion of contacts and exchanges in the different fields of culture. A representative of UNESCO will be invited to present to the "Forum" the views of that organization. The "Forum" will be prepared by a meeting of experts, the duration of which will not exceed two weeks and which will be held upon the invitation of the Government of Hungary in Budapest, commencing 21 November 1984.

Co-operation and Exchanges in the Field of Education

(1) The participating States will promote the establishment of governmental and non-governmental arrangements and agreements in education and science, to be carried out with the participation of educational or other competent institutions.

(2) The participating States will contribute to the further improvement of exchanges of students, teachers and scholars and their access to each other's educational, cultural and scientific institutions, and also their access to open information material in accordance with the laws and regulations prevailing in each country. In this context, they will facilitate travel by scholars, teachers and students within the receiving State, the establishment by them of contacts with their colleagues, and will also encourage libraries, higher education establishments and similar institutions in their territories to make catalogues and lists of open archival material available to scholars, teachers and students from other participating States.

(3) They will encourage a more regular exchange of information about scientific training programmes, courses and seminars for young scientists and facilitate a wider participation in these activities of young scientists from different participating States. They will call upon the appropriate national and international organizations and institutions to give support, where appropriate, to the realization of these training activities.

(4) The representatives of the participating States noted the use-

fulness of the work done during the "Scientific Forum" held in Hamburg, Federal Republic of Germany, from 18 February to 3 March 1980. Taking into account the results of the "Scientific Forum", the participating States invited international organizations as well as the scientific organizations and scientists of the participating States to give due consideration to its conclusions and recommendations.

(5) The participating States will favour widening the possibilities of teaching and studying less widely spread or studied European languages. They will, to this end, stimulate, within their competence, the organization of and attendance at summer university and other courses, the granting of scholarships for translators and the reinforcement of linguistic faculties including, in case of need, the provision of new facilities for studying these languages.

(6) The participating States express their readiness to intensify the exchange, among them and within competent international organizations, of teaching materials, school textbooks, maps, bibliographies and other educational material, in order to promote better mutual knowledge and facilitate a fuller presentation of their respective countries.

FOLLOW-UP TO THE CONFERENCE

(1) In conformity with the relevant provisions of the Final Act and with their resolve and commitment to continue the multilateral process initiated by the CSCE, the participating States will hold further meetings regularly among their representatives.

The third of these meetings will be held in Vienna commencing on 4 November 1986.

(2) The agenda, working programme and modalities of the main Madrid Meeting will be applied *mutatis mutandis* to the main Vienna Meeting, unless other decisions on these questions are taken by the preparatory meeting mentioned below.

For the purpose of making the adjustments to the agenda, working programme and modalities of the main Madrid Meeting, a preparatory meeting will be held in Vienna commencing on 23 September 1986. It is understood that in this context adjustments concern those items requiring change as a result of the change in date and place, the drawing of lots, and the mention of the other meetings held in conformity with the decisions of the Madrid Meeting 1980. The duration of the preparatory meeting shall not exceed two weeks.

(3) The participating States further decide that in 1985, the tenth Anniversary of the signature of the Final Act of the CSCE will be duly commemorated in Helsinki.

(4) The duration of the meetings mentioned in this document, unless otherwise agreed, should not exceed six weeks. The results of these meetings will be taken into account, as appropriate, at the Vienna Follow-up Meeting.

(5) All the above-mentioned meetings will be held in conformity with Paragraph 4 of the Chapter on "Follow-up to the Conference" of the

Final Act.

(6) The Government of Spain is requested to transmit the present document to the Secretary-General of the United Nations, to the Director-General of UNESCO and to the Executive Secretary of the United Nations Economic Commission for Europe. The Government of Spain is also requested to transmit the present document to the Governments of the non-participating Mediterranean States.

(7) The text of this document will be published in each participating State, which will disseminate it and make it known as widely as possible.

(8) The representatives of the participating States express their profound gratitude to the people and Government of Spain for the excellent organization of the Madrid Meeting and warm hospitality extended to the delegations which participated in the Meeting.

Madrid, 6 September 1983

CHAIRMAN'S STATEMENT

VENICE SEMINAR ON ECONOMIC, SCIENTIFIC AND CULTURAL CO-OPERATION IN THE MEDITERRANEAN WITHIN THE FRAMEWORK OF THE RESULTS OF THE VALLETTA MEETING OF EXPERTS

(1) The Seminar will open on Tuesday, 16 October 1984 at 10 a.m. in Venice, Italy. It will close on Friday, 26 October 1984.

(2) The work of the Seminar, guided by a Co-ordinating Committee composed of the delegations of the participating States, will be divided among three Study Groups devoted to Economics, Science and Culture respectively.

(3) The first three days of the Seminar will be devoted to six sessions of the Committee.

(4) The first session of the Committee will be public and will be devoted to the opening of the Seminar, to be followed by an address by a representative of the host country.

(5) The second session of the Committee will decide whether to hold further sessions of the participating States to guide the work of the Study Groups and to take any other decisions necessary for the Seminar.

(6) The following four sessions of the Committee will be public and will be devoted to introductory statements by the representatives of the participating States which so desire (in an order selected by lot in advance) and to introductory statements by the representatives of the non-participating Mediterranean States and the international organizations invited. The statements should not exceed 10 minutes per delegation.

(7) Beginning on the fourth day and for the following three and a half working days, simultaneous meetings of the three Study Groups will be held.

(8) The last one and a half days will be devoted to three sessions of

the Committee. Two sessions will decide upon the most appropriate use for the documentation presented in the course of the work concerning the specific sectors indicated in the Valletta Report, such as publication of the introductory statements and distribution of the studies to the relevant international organizations, and will take any other necessary decisions.

The final session of the Committee will be public and will be devoted to the official closing of the Seminar with an address by a representative of the host country.

(9) The Chair at the opening and closing sessions of both the Committee and the Study Groups will be taken by a representative from the delegation of the host country. Selection of the successive chairmen by lot will then ensure daily rotation of the Chair, in French alphabetical order, among the representatives of the participating States.

(10) Participation in the work of the Seminar by the non-participating Mediterranean States (Algeria, Egypt, Israel, Lebanon, Libya, Morocco, Syria and Tunisia) and the international organizations (UNESCO, ECE, UNEP, WHO, ITU) invited will follow the rules and practices adopted at Valletta. This means, *inter alia*, that they will take part in the work of the three Study Groups and of the four sessions of the Committee on the second and third day as well as its opening and closing sessions.

(11) Contributions, on the subjects for consideration in one or more of the working languages of the CSCE, may be sent through the proper channels - preferably not later than three months before the opening of the Seminar - to the Executive Secretary, who will circulate them to the other participating States, and to the non-participating Mediterranean States and to the international organizations which have notified their intention of taking part.

(12) The Italian Government will designate the Executive Secretary of the Seminar. This designation should be agreed to by the participating States. The services of a technical secretariat will be provided by the host country.

(13) Other rules of procedure, working methods and the scale of distribution for the expenses of the CSCE will, *mutatis mutandis*, be applied to the Seminar.

(14) The arrangements outlined above will not constitute a precedent for any other CSCE forum.

Madrid, 6 September 1983

CHAIRMAN'S STATEMENT

BERN MEETING OF EXPERTS ON HUMAN CONTACTS

The Chairman notes the absence of objection to the declaration made by the representative of Switzerland on 15 July 1983 extending an invitation by the Swiss Government to hold a meeting of experts on human contacts. Consequently, the Chairman notes that there is agreement to convene such a meeting to discuss the development of contacts among persons, institutions and organizations, with due account for the introductory part of the Chapter of the Final Act entitled *Co-operation in Humanitarian and Other Fields* and for the introductory part of section one (Human Contacts) of that Chapter, which reads *inter alia* as follows:

"The participating States,

Considering the development of contacts to be an important element in the strengthening of friendly relations and trust among peoples,

Affirming, in relation to their present effort to improve conditions in this area, the importance they attach to humanitarian considerations,

Desiring in this spirit to develop, with the continuance of détente, further efforts to achieve continuing progress in this field; ...."

The meeting will be convened in Bern, on 15 April 1986. Its duration will not exceed six weeks. The meeting will be preceded by preparatory consultations, which will be held in Bern commencing on 2 April 1986. The results of the meeting will be taken into account, as appropriate, at the Vienna Follow-up Meeting.

The Swiss Government will designate the Executive Secretary of the meeting. This designation should be agreed to by the participating States. The services of a technical secretariat will be provided by the host country.

Other rules of procedure, working methods and the scale of distribution for the expenses of the CSCE will be applied *mutatis mutandis* to the Bern meeting.

The Chairman notes further that this statement will be an annex to the concluding document of the Madrid Meeting and will be published with it.

Madrid, 6 September 1983

ANNEX 5

MANNING TABLE OF THE EXECUTIVE SECRETARIAT [a)]
(From 9 September 1980 through 9 September 1983)

(Source: Executive Secretariat, Madrid)

	Prepar. Meeting	Main Meeting						
	Period 9-9/ 10-11-80	Periods 11-11/ 19-12-80 27-1/ 10-4-81	Period 5-5/ 28-7-81	Period 27-10/ 18-12-81	Period 9-2/ 12-3-82	Period 9-11/ 17-12-82	Period 8-2/ 25-3-83	Period 19-4/ 9-9-83 b)
Office of the Executive Secretary and Diplomatic Secretariat								
Executive Secretary	1	1	1	1	1	1	1	1
Deputy Executive Secretary c)	1	1	1	1	1	1	1	1
Special Advisor d)	1	1	1	1	1	1	1	1
Diplomatic Advisor(s) c)	3	3	2	2	2	1	1	1
Special Assistant to Executive Secretary	1	-	-	-	-	-	-	-
Assistant for Conference services and co-ordinator of locally recruited staff	1	1	1	1	1	1	1	1
Clerk/Secretaries	4	4	4	4	4	5	5	4
Messenger	1	-	-	-	-	-	-	-
Sub-total	13	11	10	10	10	10	10	9

a) Not including Temporary Assistance, Overtime and Gratifications, as required.
b) Not including a small number of staff remaining on duty for short periods of time after the closing of the Madrid Meeting.
c) Acting as Committee Secretaries, as required.
d) During certain periods of the Meeting.

	Prepar. Meeting	Main Meeting						
	Period 9-9/ 10-11-80	Periods 11-11/ 19-12-80 27-1/ 10-4-81	Period 5-5/ 28-7-81	Period 27-10/ 18-12-81	Period 9-2/ 12-3-82	Period 9-11/ 17-12-82	Period 8-2/ 25-3-83	Period 19-4/ 9-9-83
Protocol and Security								
Chief of Section	1	1	1	- b)	- b)	- b)	- b)	- b)
Security Assistant	1	1	1	1	1	1	1	1
Protocol Assistant a)	1	1	-	1	1	-	-	-
Protocol and Security Attendants c)	24	20	17	15	14	12	12	10
Secretaries d)	4	5	5	4	3	3	3	3
Sub-total	31	28	24	21	19	16	16	14
Administrative and Financial Services								
Chief of Section	1	1	1	1	1	1	1	1
Financial Assistant	1	1	1	1	1	1	1	1
Personnel Assistant	1	1	1	1	1	-	-	-
Finance/personal Clerk/Secretaries	2	4	4	3	3	3	3	3
Sub-total	5	7	7	6	6	5	5	5

a) For short periods of Ministerial attendance, if required; staff of the Information Service are also called upon to assist as required.
b) Functions assumed by the Deputy Executive Secretary.
c) Not including four hostesses of the Center nor occasional short-term re-inforcements.
d) Of which two for the Duty-free Commissary

- 3rd. page -

	Prepar. Meeting	Main Meeting						
	Period 9-9/ 10-11-80	Periods 11-11/ 19-12-80 27-1/ 10-4-81	Period 5-5/ 28-7-81	Period 27-10/ 18-12-81	Period 9-2/ 12-3-82	Period 9-11/ 17-12-82	Period 8-2/ 25-3-83	Period 19-4/ 9-9-83
<u>Information Service</u>								
Chief	1	1	1	1	1	- a)	- a)	- a)
Deputy	1	1	1	1	1	1 b)	1 b)	1 b)
Assistant	1	1	1	-	-	1 c)	1 c)	1 c)
Secretary	1	1	1	1	1	1	1	1
Sub-total	4	4	4	3	3	3	3	3
Total non-language	53	50	45	40	38	34	34	31

a) Special advisor for short periods, as required.
b) Officer-in-charge.
c) May also be assigned to Protocol, Liaison and Committee functions, as required.

- 4th. page -

	Prepar. Meeting	Main Meeting							
	Period 9-9/ 10-11-80	Periods 11-11/ 19-12-81 27-1/ 10-4-81	Period 5-5/ 28-7-81	Period 27-10/ 18-12-81		Period 9-2/ 12-3-82	Period 9-11/ 17-12-82	Period 8-2/ 25-3-83	Period 19-4/ 9-9-83
<u>Language and Documentation Services</u>				Up to 16-11/	From 16-11				
Chief of Services	1	1	1	1	1	1	1	1	1
Assistants to the Chief	2	2	2	2	2	2	2	2	2
Administrative Secretary	1	1	1	1	1	1	1	1	1
Assistants to Committee Secretaries	1	3	3	3	3	1	1	1	1
Interpreters	18	42	36	24	24	18	18	18	18*
Translators	18	24	17	12	18	6	6	6	6
Typists	18	24	19	12	18	8	8	8	8
Documents registration	2	2	1	2	2	2	2	2	1
Documents reproduction supervisor	1	1	1	1	1	1	1	1	1
Documents reproduction supporting local staff	2	7	6	3	3	4	4	4	4
Documents distribution supervisor	1	1	1	1	1	1	1	1	1
Documents distribution supporting local staff	5	6	6	5	5	5	5	5	5
Total language staff	70	114	94	67	79	50	50	50	49
Grand Total	123	164	139	107	119	88	84	84	80

* This number was reduced to 12 during weeks of lower activity in this period but increased to 24 to cover the closing statements during the three last days of the Meeting.

9 September 1983

SELECTED BIBLIOGRAPHY

Aćimović, Ljubivoje. Problems of Security and Co-operation in Europe. Alphen aan den Rijn: Sijthoff & Noordhoff, 1981.

Alting von Geusau, F.A.M. (ed.). NATO and Security in the Seventies. Leyden: A.W. Sijthoff, 1971.

Basket Three: Implementation of the Helsinki Accords. Hearings before the Commission on Security and Co-operation in Europe, vols. I-XV. Washington, D.C.: US Government Printing Office, 1977-1981.

Baturin, L. "Détente in Europe and Its Opponents". International Affairs, no. 7, 1982.

Birnbaum, Karl E. Peace in Europe; East-West Relations 1966-1968 and the Prospects for a European Settlement. London: Oxford University Press, 1970.

Blishchenko, I. and Shavrov, V. "US hypocritical Human Rights Policies". International Affairs, no. 4, 1981.

Brzezinski, Zbigniew. "The Framework of East-West Reconciliation". Foreign Affairs, vol. 46, no. 2, January 1968.

________________. "America and Europe". Foreign Affairs, vol. 49, no. 1, October 1970.

Buzan Barry. "Negotiating by Consensus: Developments in Technique at the United Nations Conference on The Law of The Sea". American Journal of International Law, vol. 75, no. 2, April 1981.

Chalidze, Valery. "The Humanitarian Provisions of the Helsinki Accord: A Critique of Their Significance". Vanderbilt Journal of Transnational Law, vol. 13, nos. 2-3, Spring-Summer 1980.

Claude Jr., Inis L. Swords into Plowshares; The Problems and Progress of International Organization, 4th edition. New York: Random House Inc., 1971.

Commentary on Canada's Implementation of the Final Act of the CSCE. Madrid, October 1980.

Conference on European Security, Hearings before the Subcommittee on Europe of the Committee on Foreign Affairs, House of Representatives, Ninety-Second Congress, Second Session. Washington, D.C.: US Government Printing Office, 1972.

Conferentie over Veiligheid en Samenwerking in Europa; Helsinki-Genève-Helsinki 1973-1975 [Conference on Security and Co-operation in Europe; Helsinki-Geneva-Helsinki, 1973-1975]. Publication No. 115 of the Ministry of Foreign Affairs of the Netherlands. The Hague: Staatsuitgeverij, 1976.

Cox, Robert W. and Jacobson, Harold K. et. al. The Anatomy of Influence; Decision Making in International Organization. New Haven and London:

Yale University Press, 1974.

"Declaration of the Warsaw Treaty States". New Times, no. 21, May 1980.

Druckman, Daniel. Human Factors in International Negotiations: Social Psychological Aspects of International Conflict. Beverly Hills: Sage Publications, 1973.

__________ (ed.). Negotiations: Social-Psychological Perspectives. Beverly Hills: Sage Publications, 1977.

Dobrosielski, Marian. "The Conference on Security and Co-operation in Europe: Its Origins-Development-Meaning", Polish Institute of International Affairs. Conference on Security and Co-operation in Europe: A Polish View. Warsaw: PWN-Polish Scientific Publishers, 1976.

"European Security System: Content and Ways of Ensuring It", International Affairs, November, 1971.

Eustis, Robert D. "Procedures and Techniques of Multinational Negotiation: The LOS III Model". Virginia Journal of International Law, vol. 17, no. 2, Winter 1977.

Ferraris, Luigi Vittorio (ed.). Report on a Negotiation, Helsinki-Geneva--Helsinki 1972-1975. Alphen aan den Rijn: Sijthoff & Noordhoff International Publishers B.V., 1979.

Follow-up to the Conference on Security and Co-operation in Europe, Report of Finland. Compiled by a Working Group of the Ministry for Foreign Affairs. Helsinki, 1980.

Fulfilling our Promises: The United States and the Helsinki Final Act. A Status Report Compiled and Edited by the Staff of the Commission on Security and Co-operation in Europe. Washington, D.C.: November 1979.

Galtung, Johan. "Seven Theses on the European Security Conference". Bulletin of Peace Proposals, vol. 1, no. 1, 1970.

__________ (ed.). Co-operation in Europe. New York: Humanities Press Inc., 1970.

Hartley, Anthony. "Europe between the Superpowers". Foreign Affairs, vol. 49, no. 2, January 1971.

Hassner, Pierre. "Remarks on 'Some Institutional Suggestions for a System of Security and Co-operation in Europe'". Bulletin of Peace Proposals, vol. 3, no. 2, 1972.

Hemleben, Sylvester John. Plans for World Peace Through Six Centuries. Chicago: The University of Chicago Press, 1943.

Holsti, K.J. "Bargaining Theory and Diplomatic Reality: The CSCE Negotiations". Review of International Studies, no. 8, 1982.

Implementation of the Final Act of the Conference on Security and Co-

-operation in Europe: Findings and Recommendations Two Years after Helsinki. Report submitted to the Congress of the United States by the Commission on Security and Co-operation in Europe on September 23, 1977. Washington, D.C.: US Government Printing Office, 1977.

Implementation of the Final Act of the Conference on Security and Co--operation in Europe: Findings and Recommendations Five Years after Helsinki. Report submitted to the Congress of the United States by the Commission on Security and Co-operation in Europe on August 1, 1980. Washington, D.C.: US Government Printing Office, 1980.

Implementation of the Final Act of the Conference on Security and Co--operation in Europe, Findings and Recommendations Seven Years after Helsinki. Report submitted to the Congress of the United States by the Commission on Security and Co-operation in Europe, November 1982. Washington, D.C.: US Government Printing Office, 1980.

Implementation of Helsinki Final Act. Thirteen Semiannual Reports by the President to the Commission on Security and Co-operation in Europe on the Implementation of the Helsinki Final Act. Washington, D.C.: United States Department of State, Bureau of Public Affairs. June 1, 1976 - November 30, 1982.

Jacobsen, Hans-Adolf; Mallmann, Wolfgang; and Meier Christian (eds.). Sicherheit und Zusammenarbeit in Europe (KSZE); Analyse und Dokumentation [Security and Co-operation in Europe (CSCE); Analysis and Documentation]. Cologne: Verlag Wissenschaft und Politik, 1973.

__________ (eds.). Sicherheit und Zusammenarbeit in Europe (KSZE); Analyse und Dokumentation 1973-1978 [Security and Co-operation in Europe (CSCE); Analysis und Documentation 1973-1978]. Cologne: Verlag Wissenschaft und Politik, 1978.

Jacobson, Harold K. Networks of Interdependence; International Organizations and the Global Political System. New York: Alfred A. Knopf, 1979.

Javorski, Mihajlo. "Yugoslavia and the CSCE". Review of International Affairs, no. 732, October 5, 1980.

Jenks, C. Wilfred. "Unanimity, The Veto, Weighted Voting, Special and Simple Majorities and Consensus as Modes of Decision in International Organizations". Cambridge Essays in International Law, Essays in Honour of Lord McNair. London: Stevens & Sons, 1965.

Kaufmann, Johan. Conference Diplomacy. Leyden: A.W. Sijthoff, 1970.

Kowaljow, Anatoli. ABC der Diplomatie. [ABC of Diplomacy]. Berlin: Staatsverlag der DDR, 1980.

Kravtsov, Valentin. "Towards the Madrid Meeting". New Times, no. 36, September, 1980.

Lall, Arthur. Modern International Negotiation: Principles and Practice. New York: Columbia University Press, 1966.

Laux, Jeanne and Palmer, Michael. "A Rejoinder to 'Some Institutional Suggestions for a System of Security and Co-operation in Europe'". Bulletin of Peace Proposals, vol. 3, no. 2, 1972.

McWhinney, Edward. The International Law of Détente, Arms Control, European Security, and East-West Co-operation. Alphen a/d Rijn: Sijthoff & Noordhoff International Publishers, 1978.

Miles, Edward. "The Structure and Effects of the Decision Process in the Seabed Committee and the Third United Nations Conference on The Law of the Sea". The volume "Restructuring Ocean Regimes" of International Organization, vol. 31, no. 2, Spring 1977.

Milestones of Soviet Foreign Policy, 1917-1967. Moscow: Progress Publishers, 1967.

Mitrović, Tomislav. "Institutionalization of European Security and Co--operation". Review of International Affairs, no. 501, February 20, 1971.

"Negotiating with the Soviets in Madrid". World Affairs, vol. 144, no. 4, Spring 1982.

Neuhold, Hanspeter. "Die neutralen Staaten Europas und die Konferenz über Sicherheit und Zusammenarbeit in Europa". [The Neutral States of Europe and the Conference on Security and Co-operation in Europe]. Europa Archiv, 13/1973.

Newcombe, Hanna. "United Nations Regional Security Commissions: A Proposal". Bulletin of Peace Proposals, vol. 3, no. 3, 1972.

Newhouse, John. Cold Dawn; The Story of SALT. New York: Holt, Rinehart and Winston, 1973.

Nowak, Jerzy M. "All-European Co-operation in the Field of Culture, Education and Human Contacts", Polish Institute of International Affairs. Conference on Security and Co-operation in Europe: A Polish View. Warsaw: PWN-Polish Scientific Publishers, 1967.

"Organization of Security and Co-operation in Europe; The Vienna Proceedings". Bulletin of Peace Proposals, vol. 3, no. 2, 1972.

Palmer, Michael. The Prospects for a European Security Conference. London: Chatham House, PEP, 1971.

____________. "A European Security Conference: Preparation and Procedure". The World Today, vol. 28, no. 1, January 1972.

Pedersen, Richard F. "Diplomacy in the United Nations". Mimeographed Paper. Cambridge, Mass.: Center for International Studies, 1960.

Pesić, Milorad. "European Co-operation and Security Pending the Madrid Meeting". Review of International Affairs, no. 728-9, August 5-20, 1980.

Poland and the Implementation of the CSCE Final Act. Studies on International Relations No. 15. Warsaw: Polish Institute of Affairs, 1980.

Rakhmaninov, Y. "The Key Problem of European Security". International Affairs, No. 12, 1982.

Rosenthal, Benjamin S. "America's Move". Foreign Affairs, vol. 51, no. 2, January 1973.

Schwartz, Hans-Peter and Haftendorn, Helga (eds.). Europäische Sicherheitskonferenz [European Security Conference]. Opladen: Leske Verlag, 1970.

Skilling, H. Gordon. "CSCE in Madrid". Problems of Communism, vol. XXX, July-August 1981.

Sohn, Louis B. "Voting Procedures in United Nations Conferences for the Codification of International Law". American Journal of International Law, vol. 69, no. 2, April 1975.

Stanley, Timothy and Whitt, Darnell. Détente Diplomacy: United States and European Security in the 1970's. New York: Dunellen, 1970.

Suy, Eric. "The Meaning of Consensus in Multilateral Diplomacy" in: Robert J. Akkerman et. al. (eds.). Declarations on Principles; A Quest for Universal Peace. Leyden: Sijthoff, 1977.

The Belgrade Follow-up Meeting to the CSCE: A Report and Appraisal. Report transmitted to the Committee on International Relations, US House of Representatives, by the Commission on Security and Co-operation in Europe on May 17, 1978. Washington, D.C.: US Government Printing Office, 1978.

"Twenty-sixth Congress of the CPSU. Report of the CPSU Central Committee and the Current Tasks of the Party in Home and Foreign Policy. Delivered by General Secretary of the Central Committee Comrade L.I. Brezhnev". New Times, no. 9, February 1981.

UN Doc. A/37/163, 28 April 1982. UN Doc. A/Conf. 62/30/Rev. 1, 1974.

Volle, Hermann and Wagner, Wolfgang (eds.). KSZE, Beiträge und Dokumente aus dem Europa Archiv [CSCE, Contributions and Documents from Europa Archiv]. Bonn: Verlag für Internationale Politik GMBH, 1976.

_______________ (eds.) Das Belgrader KSZE-Folgetreffen; Der Fortgang des Entspannungsprozesses in Europa. In Beiträgen und Dokumenten aus dem Europa Archiv [The Belgrade CSCE Follow-up Meeting; The Continuation of the Process of Relaxation in Europe. In Contributions and Documents from Europa Archiv]. Bonn: Verlag für Internationale Politik GMBH, 1978.

Vukadinović, Radovan. "Toward a New Model of European Security and Co-operation". Review of International Affairs, no. 544, December 5, 1972.

Winham, Gilbert R. "International Negotiation in an Age of Transition". International Journal, vol XXV, 1979-1980.

_______________. "Practitioners' Views of International Negotiation". World Politics, vol. XXXII, no. 1, October 1979.

Working Group on European Co-operation and Security. "Some Institutional Suggestions for a System of Security and Co-operation in Europe". Bulletin of Peace Proposals, vol. 3, no. 1, 1972.

Zartman, William. "Negotiations: Theory and Reality". Journal of International Affairs. vol. 29, no. 1, 1975.

Zartman, William and Berman, Maureen. The Practical Negotiator. New Haven: Yale University, Press, 1982.

Zellentin, Gerda. "Institutions for Détente and Co-operation". The World Today, vol. 29, no. 1, January 1973.

NAME INDEX

Abbé de Saint-Pierre on "peace plans" for Europe, 23

Aćimović, Ljubivoje, 46 (n. 3), 73 (n. 3)

Akkerman, Robert J., 48 (n. 18)

Alekseyeva, L., 121

Alting von Geusau, Frans, 47 (n. 10)
on institutional options for a CSCE, 37

Amalrik, Andrey, 121

Andropov, Yuri V., 228
on RM.39 revised, 165

Baturin L., 246 (n. 16)

Beglov, S.I. on institutional options for a CSCE, 35

Bentham, Jeremy on "peace plans" for Europe, 23

Birnbaum, Karl E., 46 (n. 3)

Blishchenko, I. and Shavrov, V., 108 (n. 10)

Brandt, Willy Kiesinger-Brandt government, 31
and *Ostpolitik*, 80

Brezhnev, Leonid, 108 (n. 11), 228
on multilateral preparatory talks, 32
- doctrine, 74 (n. 8)
and Peace Programme, 89, 90, 209, 233
on CBMs, 89, 228, 230
and visit to Bonn (November 1981), 234

Brosio, Manlio on the permanent body of the CSCE, 29

Brzezinski, Zbigniew, 47 (n. 5, 6)
on institutional options for a CSCE, 33, 34

Bukowskiy, V., 121

Buzan, Barry, 48 (n. 22)
on UNCLOS III, 42

Chalidze, Valery, 192 (n. 2)
on human contacts, 178

Claude Jr., Inis L., 48 (n. 19, 20)
on international decision-making, 42, 43

Cox, Robert W. & Jacobson, Harold K., 245 (n. 4)
on role distribution, 223-226.

Dobrosielski, Marian, 192 (n. 4, 5)

Dongen, F. van, 129 (n. 7)

Druckman, Daniel, 130 (n. 11)

Dubinin, USSR embassador to Spain, 129 (n. 2)

Eustis, Robert D., 48 (n. 22)

Ferraris, Luigi Vittorio, 73 (n. 1, 3, 6), 75 (n. 9), 76 (n. 11, 13), 107 (n. 1, 2)
on the introduction of the word basket, 73 (n. 2)

Galtung, Johan, 47 (n. 11), 48 (n. 14).
on institutional options for a CSCE, 38

Genscher, Hans Dietrich on the "Spanish initiative", 166

Gonzales, Felipe and the "Spanish initiative", 165, 166

Gorbanevskaya, N., 121

Grigorenko, Gen. P., 121

Haftendorn, Helga & Schwartz, Hans-Peter, 46 (n. 3)

Hartley, Anthony on Soviet motives for an ESC, 46 (n. 4)

Hassner, Pierre on institutional options for a CSCE, 47 (n. 14)

Hemleben, Sylvester John, 46 (n. 1)

Holsti, K.J., 192 (n. 6)
on the Final Act, 185

Jacobsen, Hans-Adolf, Mallmann, Wolfgang & Meier, Christian, 46 (n. 3)

Jacobson, Harold K., 46 (n. 1), 76, (n. 14)

Javorski, Mihajlo, 108 (n. 12)

Jenks, C. Wilfred, 48 (n. 17)
on the consensus procedure, 41

Johnson, President, 31

Kampelman, Max, 121

Kant, Immanuel on "peace plans" for Europe, 23

Kaufmann, Johan, 73 (n. 5), 130 (n. 18)

Kissinger, Henry and visit to Moscow (September 1972), 32

Kowaljow, Anatoli, 106 (n. 2), 152 (n. 1)
on the Executive Secretariat, 76 (n. 12)
on Soviet diplomacy, 246 (n. 13)

Kravtsov, Valentin, 108 (n. 9)
on the Western objectives in Madrid, 88
on NATO's Ankara Communiqué, 89

Lall, Arthur, 130 (n. 15)
on negotiators, 123

Laux, Jeanne & Palmer, Michael, 47 (n. 14)
on institutional options for a CSCE, 39

Lenin, V.I., 246 (n. 13)

McWhinney, Edward on the Final Act, 192 (n. 1)

Miles, Edward, 48 (n. 2)

Mitrović, Tomislav, 47 (n. 13)
on institutional options for a CSCE, 39

Neuhold, Hanspeter, 47 (n. 9)

Newcombe, Hannah on institutional options for a CSCE, 48 (n. 14)

Newhouse, John on *domandour*, 245 (n. 2)

Nixon, President and visit to Moscow (May 1972), 31

Nowak, Jerzy M., 192 (n. 5)

Palmer, Michael, 46 (n. 3), 48 (n. 15, 16)
on institutional options for a CSCE, 39, 40, 41
on procedural options for a CSCE, 41

Pedersen, Richard, F., 129 (n. 5)
on the degree of control by the foreign office, 115

Penn, William on "peace plans" for Europe, 23

Pesić, Milorad, 108 (n. 13)

Plyushch, L., 121

Quarles van Ufford, Jhr. B.E., 73 (n. 2)

Rakhmaninov, Yuri, N., 129 (n. 2)
on détente, 246 (n. 18)

Rapacki, Polish foreign minister, 25

Reagan, President, 123
and the "Spanish initiative", 166
on arms control, 228, 234
and chemical weapons, 250
and handling of airline leaders' strike, 251

Rosenthal, Benjamin S. on Soviet motives for an ESC, 46 (n. 4), 47 (n. 4)

Rousseau, Jean-Jacques on "peace plans" for Europe, 23

Skilling, H. Gordon, 130 (n. 8)
on the opening of the Madrid conference, 121

Sohn, Louis B., 48 (n. 21)

Stanley, Timothy & Whitt, Darnell, 46 (n. 3)

Suy, Eric, 48 (n. 18)

Volle, Herman & Wagner, Wolfgang, 47 (n. 9)

Winham, Gilbert R., 129 (n. 3), 130 (n. 9, 10, 16, 17)
on interest-group activity and foreign policy, 112, 121, 122
on negotiators, 123, 124
on "issue" and international negotiations, 129 (n. 1)

Winthrop, Brown, 129 (n. 3)

Zartman, William, 245 (n. 6), 246 (n. 12, 14)
on the analysis of the process of negotiation, 227, 230-232, 235, 240, 242
on referents, 231, 246 (n. 10)

Zartman, William & Berman, Maureen, 130 (n. 12, 13, 14), 192 (n. 3), 245 (n. 7, 8, 9), 246 (n. 12, 14, 15)
on negotiators, 123
on the analysis of the process of negotiation, 227, 242
on stalemate and veto, 245 (n. 3)

Zimmerman, Warren, 73 (n. 7)

SUBJECT INDEX*

ad referendum, 113*

Afghanistan
the - question, 85, 86, 107 (n. 6), 189, 228, 249, 251, 254, 275
Soviet view on -, 88, 249

agenda
- items, 23
- options, 24-33
choices for the CSCE -, 50-53
points for consideration on -, 68, 69
of the follow-up meetings, 70
conclusions on -, 266, 267
recommendations on -, 275, 276, 278
see also Blue Book and Purple Book

agregado, 110*

Albania, 39, 77, 78, 270

Algeria, 82, 83, 104, 243

American Congress, 84, 85

Andorra, 77

Ankara
NATO communiqué (June 1980) issued in -, 86-89, 97

Anti-Bolshevik Bloc of Nations, 121

anti-semitism, 83, 251

apartheid, 99, 251, 257

Arab Mediterranean States, 58, 82, 83

arms control, 23, 37, 38, 89, 228, 234, 237

arms race, 224, 252

associations
37 different - of emigrants, 120

Athens
Expert meeting on the Peaceful Settlement of Disputes (1984) in -, 258, 261

Atlanta
the murders of negro children in -, 251

Australia, 120

Austria, 37, 67, 129 (n. 7), 210
and proposals, 92, 97, 103, 258
and working programmes in Geneva and Belgrade, 147
as co-ordinator, 157
and draft concluding documents, 161, 219
and appeal of April 1983, 164
as a traditional neutral country, 169
and Purple Book, 197
and Blue Book, 200, 201
and interpretative statement to a chairman's statement, 264, 265

Baltic peoples, 249

Baltic states, 62, 63, 121

basket(-s), 52*
introduction of the word -, 73 (n. 2)
and proposals, 91-106, 170
and SWBs, 147-149
and contact groups, 153, 157
and coffee groups, 161
and EC caucus, 170-172
- discussions, 251-253
and Madrid Concluding Document
first basket, 183, 255-258, 263
second basket, 258, 259
third basket, 218, 255-258
fourth basket (Follow-up), 259-261

BBC, 180, 253

Belgium, 169, 172
and proposals, 92, 93, 96
"Belgian Helsinki Committee", 120
and EC presidency, 198, 205

Belgrade
CSCE Follow-up Meeting (1977-1978) in -, 17, 54

---

* Pages which present the definition of a central concept are marked with an asterisk.

and (use of) formal reservations and interpretative statements, 60-62
and mini-groups, 63
and chairmanship, 64, 206
and Plenary, 65, 66
and informal discussions, 65, 161
and contributions of Mediterranean states, 82
and implementation discussions, 87, 133, 137, 247
and contact groups, 150, 156
and proposals, 179, 230
and opening of the Madrid Meeting, 194, 196, 204, 209, 273
and drafting technique, 216, 217
and chairman's statement, 262
and Expert meeting, 279

Belgrade Concluding Document, 17, 18, 59, 134, 179, 216, 232

Berlin, 38
(four-Power) talks about -, 28, 31, 80
four-Power Conference (1954) on -, 36

Bern
Expert meeting on Human Contacts (1986) in -, 255, 261, 263

Bilderberg meetings, 34

Blue Book, 50*
and CSCE agenda, 50-53
and CSCE follow-up system, 53-56
and CSCE rules of procedure, 56-60, 141, 198-201, 206, 261, 262, 268, 269, 271, 281, 282
on observer, 78
on non-participating states, 81, 82
on sessions, 118
on right of reply, 143, 144
on Committees and Sub-committees, 145
recommendation on -, 278
see also Annex 1

Bonn
NATO communiqué (May 1972) issued in -, 30, 32
NATO Document on arms control and disarmament (June 1982) issued in -, 237, 246 (n. 17)

Brussels
NATO declaration (December 1969) issued in -, 27, 28
NATO communiqué (December 1970) issued in -, 31

Bucharest
WP declaration (July 1966) issued in -, 25, 26, 50, 78, 79

Budapest
WP declaration (June 1970) issued in -, 25, 28, 29, 32, 80
- Appeal (March 1969), 26, 79, 80
Cultural Forum (October 1985) in -, 189, 261

Bulgaria, 168
and proposals, 92, 98, 100, 141, 187
- delegation and instructions, 115, 116

Bulletin of Peace Proposals, 38, 39

Canada, 121, 172
and participation in the CSCE, 51, 77-81
and interpretative statement, 74 (n. 8)
and proposals, 85, 95, 106, 260
and implementation of the Final Act, 107 (n. 7)
and members of the delegation, 110
and members of parliament, 110, 111
interest groups in -, 120
and the Polish chairman (9 February 1982), 198

caucus(-es), 167*-174
as most important decision-making organs, 153, 273
Nordic -, 167, 168
WP -, 168
EC -, 169-172
NATO -, 172, 173
of non-state trading countries, 173
of 34 delegations, 243

CDE, 262

censorship, 99, 224, 252, 257

CES, 51

chairman
and the role which the - is expected to play, 64
in the Plenary, 143, 151
conclusion on -, 274

chairmanship
the principle of rotating the -, 49, 56, 57, 163, 208
Blue Book on -, 63*-65
points of consideration on -, 71
and political use, 193
and the "night of silences" (5 March 1982), 206, 207
conclusions on -, 268, 269
recommendations on -, 281, 282

chairman's statements
in Geneva, 63, 75 (n. 8), 262
and Purple Book, 133, 137, 140, 141, 243
to the Madrid Concluding Document, 255, 262-265
recommendations on -, 276, 279-282

chef-de-file system, 125, 171*-173, 215

Chile, 250

Chinese People's Republic, 36, 46 (n. 4)

church
Estonian Evangelical Lutheran Church, 120
Russian Orthodox church, 121

civil rights, 178

CMEA, 34

coffee break, 159, 160*
and the "stopped clock" (11 November 1980), 195, 196
and the Polish chairman (9 February 1982), 202
in the "night of silences" (5 March 1982), 205-207

coffee groups, 132, 153, 155, 159*-161, 272
from - to sherry group, 162
expert -, 214

"Cold War", 24

collective security system, 25, 35*, 36, 78

Commission on Security and Co-operation in Europe (US), 84, 85, 129 (n. 2)

communiqué dialogue, 24, 25, 52, 53, 266

Communist parties
European Communist and Workers' Parties, 25, 79
Communist Party of the Soviet Union (CPSU)
24th congress (1971), 89
25th congress (1976), 89
26th congress (1981), 89, 108 (n. 11), 228

concluding document
and the idea of balance ("substantial and balanced"), 85, 212, 230, 231, 246 (n. 11), 274, 276
drafting of -, 112, 138, 229, 232-234, 269
"bottom-up approach" of -, 65*, 71, 145, 282
Purple book on -, 134-136, 149, 205
conclusions on -, 271, 272
recommendations on -, 280, 281

Conference of the Committee of Disarmament, 37

Conference on Confidence-and-Security-Building Measures and Disarmament in Europe, 234, 237
Madrid Concluding Document on -, 186, 260, 262
see also Stockholm; European Disarmament Conference

Conference on Military Détente and Disarmament in Europe, 230, 233

Conference on Security and Co-operation in Europe (CSCE)
and the idea of balance ("co-operation and security"), 51, 52
and legal competence, 60
as an open book (as propaganda forum), 68, 269, 284
unwritten rule of -, 136, 184
NATO on -, 237
"CSCE-Mark 2", 243
and détente, 275

ad hoc - meeting, 277, 283

Confidence Building Measures (CBMs), 30, 81, 83
- interpretative statement on -, 74 (n. 8)
- proposals on -, 86, 97, 100-104, 258
- Brezhnev on -, 89, 228, 230
- extension of the - regime as common objective of the NNA countries, 90, 91
- Madrid Concluding Document on -, 186
- *see also* Final Act, Chapter I

consejero, 110*

consensus
- - procedure in international decision-making, 41*-45
- rule of - in CSCE, 56, 63, 65, 208, 212, 223, 225, 255, 262, 267, 276
  - Blue Book on -, 57*-60
  - mitigation of the consequences of -, 60, 61, 268, 269
  - points of consideration on -, 70, 71
  - Purple Book on -, 141-143, 151
  - and Madrid Concluding Document, 166, 183, 185, 186, 188, 220, 265
  - and Final Act, 176, 177, 179, 182, 185
  - and political use, 193
  - and the "stopped clock" (11 November 1980), 195-197
  - and the Polish chairman (9 February 1982), 200-203
  - and the "night of silences" (5 March 1982), 204, 206, 207
  - conclusions on -, 268, 269, 272, 273, 280
- "consensus of 34", 220, 270, 273
- on sanctions against non-fulfilment of the Final Act, 268

"conspiracy of silence", 162, 204, 236

contact groups, 132, 150, 151, 153*-159, 272
- from - to coffee group, 159, 160
- expert -, 162, 213-215

Co-ordinating Committee, 53, 64

"Co-ordination Committee of War Veterans and Victims of Seyne-sur--Mer", 120

co-ordinators, 153, 155, 157*-160, 169, 218, 269, 281, 283

Council of Europe, 34, 40

credentials, 109, 271

CSBM, 260, 262

CSCE Digest, 84

Cuba
- missile crisis (1962) in -, 24

Cultural Forum
- proposals on -, 93, 96, 105, 189
- Madrid Concluding Document on -, 189, 260, 261

culture, 171, 249
- proposals on -, 95, 186, 225, 254, 257
- Final Act on -, 254
- Madrid Concluding Document on -, 258

"cut-off", 138*

Cyprus
- and Turkey, 62, 129 (n. 1), 261, 262, 271
- and interpretative statements, 74 (n. 8)
- and clause, 75 (n. 8)
- and proposal, 103
- and members of the delegation, 110
- and appeal of April 1983, 164
- as member of the Non-aligned movement, 169
- and Purple Book, 197

Czechoslovakia, 130 (n. 7), 168
- in Geneva on the follow-up system, 53
- and proposals, 98, 99
- exiles from -, 120
- and the "night of silences" (5 March 1982), 204, 206-208

decision
- types of -, 69, 70, 267

delegates; *see* negotiators

delegations
- size of -, 110, 117, 148
- national -, 126-128
- *see also* heads of delegation

demandeur, 194, 212, 220*-225, 241

Denmark, 167-169, 172
in Geneva on the follow-up system, 54
and proposals, 85, 93, 96, 106

détente
NATO on -, 26, 27
Final Act on -, 55
proposal on -, 105, 258
and implementation, 253-255

developing nations
Group of 77 -, 156

die Deutsche Welle, 180, 253

diplomats
personal security of -, 99

disarmament conference, 140, 141, 161, 166, 209, 222, 230-237, 239, 240, 246 (n. 18)
proposals on -, 88, 97, 100, 101, 103-105, 133, 186, 256
Madrid Concluding Document on -, 186, 256
contact group on -, 217, 218
see also Stockholm; European Disarmament Conference

dissidents, 94, 119, 121, 188, 228, 250
new measures against -, 138, 248
and détente, 249, 254

draft concluding document
first NNA -, 218, 229, 232, 234, 246 (n. 11)
second NNA - (RM.39), 161, 162, 213, 214, 219, 229, 235-240
third NNA - (RM.39 revised), 163-165, 175 (n. 1), 219, 229, 240, 241, 262
see also concluding document

Draft Standard Rules of Procedure for United Nations Conferences, 44

Drafting Groups, 153, 155
from SWBs to -, 142, 143, 145, 149, 215, 249
Purple Book on -, 149*, 150
DG-M, 149, 282
DG-P, 151
and contact groups, 156, 157, 160, 161, 249
and sherry groups, 162
and mini-groups, 163
and the "night of silences" (5 March 1982), 203-206, 208

drafting techniques, 212, 216-220

Eastern Europe
and the rule of consensus, 58
and implementation of the Final Act, 84
and Western accusations of domestic policies, 87, 184, 185, 250, 251
- objectives, 88-90
and proposals, 92, 97-102, 133, 158, 186, 187, 194, 215, 224, 225, 257-259, 276
- delegations
and CSCE experience, 111, 112
and instructions, 116, 117
violation of human rights in -, 119, 184, 244, 249-251
associations of emigrants from -, 120
and peace marches in Western Europe, 122
and review of implementation, 137, 138, 248-255
and follow-up to Madrid, 140, 141
and contact groups, 157-159, 215
and mini-groups, 163
and SU, 168
and dissemination of information, 180, 181
and the "stopped clock" (11 November 1980), 194, 196
and Purple Book, 197
and the Polish chairman (9 February 1982), 202
and the "night of silences" (5 March 1982), 205, 206, 208, 210
as *demandeur*, 221-225
and Western amendments to RM.39 (revised), 238, 239, 241

East-West dialogue, 56, 90, 159, 237, 248

East-West Standing Commission, 39, 40

economic boycott, 98, 184, 275

Economic Commission for Europe (ECE) (UN), 28, 34, 38, 40, 55, 134, 259
proposals on -, 94, 98, 100, 102, 103, 105, 106

Madrid Concluding Document on -, 280

economic co-operation, 111, 173, 249
proposals on -, 87, 94-98, 98-100, 186, 213, 225, 258, 259
Madrid Concluding Document on -, 186, 191, 258, 259
see also Final Act, Chapter II

education
proposals on -, 95, 101, 186, 225, 257
Madrid Concluding Document on -, 186, 258

EEC, 34
see also European Communities (EC)

El Salvador, 250

Egypt, 82, 83, 104, 243

energy, 252
proposals on -, 98, 103, 224, 259
Madrid Concluding Document on -, 259

equality
the principle of sovereign -, 153, 163, 207, 268, 269, 281
Blue Book on -, 56*, 57

escape clause(-s), 60, 180-182, 190, 191

Estonia, 62, 120

Executive Branch commissioners, 84

Executive Secretariat, 66, 67, 69, 109, 110, 163, 175 (n. 1)
and SU, 76 (n. 12)
see also Annex 5

Executive Secretary, 82, 109, 143, 155, 202, 207, 215, 271
and formal reservations and interpretative statements, 61, 62, 261
Blue Book on -, 66, 67
points for consideration on -, 71, 72
conclusions on -, 268, 269, 276
recommendations on -, 278, 282, 283

Expert meetings
Final Act on -, 54
on human rights, 85, 96, 189, 238, 256, 260, 261
on the peaceful settlement of disputes, 103, 258, 260, 261, 279
on human contacts, 165, 219, 238, 256, 260, 261, 263
Purple Book on -, 134, 135
recommendation on -, 279

European Commission (EC), 94, 171, 213

European Communities (EC)
- objectives, 85, 86, 233
and proposals, 86, 92-95, 97, 106, 170, 213, 214, 259
members of the -, 93, 169, 170
- presidency, 93, 94, 124, 144, 157, 169-171, 173, 195, 198, 205, 213, 233
- foreign ministers on the developments in Poland, 197-199, 228, 233, 236
and *"Groupe ad hoc CSCE"* (CSCE work group), 213, 238
and adjournment of the conference, 232, 233
and restrictions on trading, 252
see also caucus(-es)

European Council (EC), 166

European Disarmament Conference (1984), 241-243, 258, 261

European Inter-rail System of the UIC, 95

European Political Co-operation (EPC) (EC), 85, 86, 93, 171, 228
and *"Sous-Comité CSCE"*, 213

European Security Conference (ESC), 46, 51, 80

European security organizations, 23

family reunification, 83, 171
proposals on -, 85, 96, 116
Final Act on -, 179, 182

fascism, 102, 187, 224, 257

Federal Republic of Germany (FRG), 67, 80, 169, 172
and negotiations with SU and Poland, 31
in Belgrade, 64
and interpretative statement, 74

(n. 8)
and Albania, 77
and WP declarations, 79
and proposals, 93, 95, 96
- delegations and instructions, 115, 116
interest groups in -, 120
and the "Spanish initiative", 166
and Human Contacts, 171
West German-Soviet communiqué (November 1981), 234
and European Disarmament Conference, 241
see also Germany

Final Act
signature of -, 17, 53, 54
- items, 23, 68, 69
and the idea of balance ("co-operation and security"), 51, 52
Chapters of -, 51-53, 91
I "Ten Principles", 27, 28, 30, 51, 52, 81, 74 (n. 8), 176, 249, 257
"CBMs", 27, 28, 30, 52, 74 (n. 8), 90, 91, 251, 252
II "Economics", 27, 51, 52, 81, 82
"Mediterranean", 52, 82, 177, 178
III "Humanitarian", 51, 52, 84, 183, 238, 255
IV "Follow-up", 17, 29, 52, 53, 56, 70, 86, 87, 134, 135, 136, 140; *see also* Annex 2
on distinction between conference and meetings, 54, 73 (n. 4)
and obligation of the participating states to fulfil the - provisions, 60
limits of -, 176, 183
maximum results, 177-179
minimum results, 179, 180
ambiguity, 180-183, 185
as referent principle of the CSCE process, 231
and comparison with Madrid Concluding Document, 265

Final Recommendations of the Helsinki Consultations, 49, 50, 262, 266, 267
see also Blue Book

Finland, 32, 37
and the CSCE in Helsinki, 49, 56, 67, 77, 80, 260
and proposals, 90, 92, 93, 103, 104, 106, 258
and implementation of the Final Act, 107 (n. 7), 108 (n. 7)
Finnish "League for human rights and freedoms", 120
and working programmes in Geneva and Belgrade, 147
as co-ordinator, 157
and informal bilateral talks, 161
and appeal of April 1983, 164
as a traditional neutral country, 169
and European Disarmament Conference, 235

follow-up
choices for the CSCE -, 53*-56
points for consideration on the - system, 69, 70
proposals on -, 96, 102
Purple Book on -, 140, 141
- to Madrid, 259-261
conclusions on -, 267, 268
recommendations on -, 276-280
see also Final Act, Chapter IV

formal reservations, 73 (n. 7)
Blue Book on -, 60*-63
and journals, 68, 284
points for consideration on -, 71
to the Madrid Concluding Document, 261, 262
conclusions on -, 269
recommendation on -, 281

Foreign Affairs, 33, 34

France, 67, 169, 172, 264
and Andorra, 77
and proposals, 86, 92, 93, 96, 97, 100, 101, 105, 189, 234
interest groups in -, 120
and Culture, 171
and Military Aspects of Security, 171, 172
and the Polish chairman (9 February), 202

freer movement of people, ideas and information, 17, 27-30, 183, 246 (n. 17)

Fulfilling our Promises, 85

GATT, 34

Geneva
  second stage of the CSCE (1973-1975) in -
    and (use of) reservations and interpretative statements, 60-63, 74 (n. 8), 75 (n. 8)
    and mini-groups, 63, 156
    and chairmanship, 64
    and Committees, 65, 66, 153, 156
    and Executive Secretariat, 66
    and contributions of Mediterranean states, 82, 83
    and drafting technique, 216, 217

German Democratic Republic (GDR), 38, 67, 129 (n. 7), 256
  first multilateral recognition of -, 80
  and proposals, 92, 98, 100, 187
  and the "night of silences" (5 March 1982), 205-208
  see also Germany

Germany, 28, 31, 33, 36, 38, 40

Gesellschaft für Menschenrechte [Association for Human Rights], 121

government-to-government approach/-appeals, 132, 153, 164*-166, 272

"Grand Coalition" (FRG), 31

Great Britain; *see* United Kingdom (UK)

Greece, 172
  and Turkey on Cyprus, 62
  and interpretative statement, 74 (n. 8)
  and proposals, 85, 93, 96
  - delegation and instructions, 116
  and EC, 169

Harmel Report, 26

heads of delegation, 119, 127, 128, 145, 146, 162, 167-170
  informal - meeting, 132, 142, 151*

Helsinki
  CSCE (1973-1975) in -
    commemoration of the tenth anniversary of the conclusion of -, 17, 260, 261, 279
    three stages of -, 54, 141, 153
    see also Geneva, second stage of the CSCE

Helsinki Consultations (1972-1973), 24, 33, 35, 53, 57, 61, 67, 77, 109, 145
  and rules of procedure, 49, 56, 63, 268
  and Malta and the closure of -, 58, 59, 82, 242
  and working bodies, 65
  and proposals, 73 (n. 2)

Holy See, 61, 67, 78
  and proposals, 92, 104, 258
  as co-ordinator, 157
  - delegate, 169
  and UN, 280

House of Representatives (US), 84, 85

human contacts, 73, 149, 171, 203, 221
  chairman's statement on -, 75 (n. 8)
  proposals on -, 87, 95, 158, 222, 256
  Final Act on -, 178, 179, 182, 183, 254, 255
  Madrid Concluding Document on -, 187, 255, 256
  Meeting of Experts on -, 165, 219, 238, 241, 255, 256, 260, 261, 263

human rights, 17, 27, 51, 57, 83, 116, 172, 221, 233, 275
  interpretative statement on -, 74 (n. 8)
  proposals on -, 85, 87, 94, 96, 158, 188, 222, 256, 257
  Meeting of Experts on -, 85, 96, 189, 238, 256, 260, 261
  organizations on -, 120, 121
  violation of -
    in Eastern Europe, 119, 184, 244, 249-251
    in SU, 237, 249
    in the West, 250
  Madrid Concluding Document on -, 189, 190, 256
  NATO Declaration (June 1982) on -, 246 (n. 17)

and détente, 254

Hungary, 129 (n. 7), 168
and proposals, 92, 93, 98-100, 106, 190
on fulfilment of the Final Act provisions, 192 (n. 7)
and the "stopped clock" (11 November 1980), 194-196, 206
and the Polish chairman (9 February 1982), 198

Iceland, 167, 172
and proposals, 92, 93, 106
and members of the delegation, 110, 148

ICNT, 44

IMF, 34

implementation
(review) of - of the Final Act provisions
Final Act on -, 55, 136, 137
Purple Book on -, 134-138, 247, 248
limits of -, 184, 185
- themes, 248-253
and détente, 253-255
Madrid Concluding Document on -, 216, 217
conclusion on -, 274

Implementation of the Helsinki Final Act, 84

India, 123

Indonesia, 120

Informal Single Negotiating Texts (ISNTs), 44, 280-282

information, 117, 149, 203
proposals on -, 87, 95, 97, 103, 158, 222, 224, 257, 258
Final Act on -, 254, 257
Madrid Concluding Document on -, 183, 184, 256-258

institutional framework
options for -
and alliance-based approach, 33-35
and UN linked approach, 36-38
and independent approach, 39-41
conclusions on -, 267, 268
see also follow-up

institutionalization, 41, 53
- of conference and follow-up meetings
points for consideration on the -, 69
proposal on -, 103, 104
conclusions on -, 267-269

instructions, 112-117

Intermediate range Nuclear Forces (INF), 166, 228, 234, 237, 240, 241

International Affairs, 35

International Atomic Energy Agency, 37, 38

International Convenant on Civil and Political Rights, 75 (n. 8)

International Convenant on Human Rights, 98

international decision-making
competing elements in shaping the approach to -, 42

International Herald Tribune, 210

international law, 57, 74 (n. 8), 111, 181

international legal systems, 39

interpretative statement(-s)
Blue Book on -, 60*-63
and journals, 68, 284
points for consideration on -, 71
in Geneva, 74 (n. 8), 75 (n. 8)
to the Madrid Concluding Document, 262
to a chairman's statement, 264, 265
recommendation on -, 281

Interreligious Task Force on Soviet Jewry, 121

IRA, 251

Ireland, 130 (n. 7), 167, 174
and EC, 86, 93, 169
and NATO, 173
and the "stopped clock" (11 November 1980), 195, 196

Iron Curtain, 27

"Islamic Council of Europe", 120

Israel, 82, 104, 120, 243
and SU, 83, 250

Italy, 25, 67, 129 (n. 7), 169, 172
and interpretative statement, 74 (n. 8)
and proposals, 92, 93, 95-97

Jamaica, 120

Jews, 83, 121, 237, 249, 251
as hostages to détente, 254

journalists, 183, 196, 258
and publicity on the CSCE, 68, 72
and CSCE-delegates, 117-119
freedom of movement for -, 203, 252
proposals on -, 95, 103, 256
Madrid Concluding Document on -, 218, 257
responsibility of -
proposals on -, 99, 187, 224, 257

journal(-s), 61, 62, 68, 75 (n. 8)
points of consideration on -, 72
example of -, 129 (n. 7), 130 (n. 7)
Madrid -, 200, 201, 210, 261-264, 284

Karlovy Vary
Declaration on European Peace and Security (April 1967) issued in -, 25, 79

languages
less widely-spread or studied -
proposal on -, 93, 106

Latvia, 62, 120, 121

Lebanon, 82, 104, 243

Le Monde, 121

Libya, 104, 243

Liechtenstein, 32, 67, 78, 130 (n. 7), 169, 174
and interpretative statement, 75 (n. 8)
and proposal, 103
and Purple Book, 197

Lithuania, 62

loophole(-s), 180-182, 190, 191, 264

Luxemburg, 130 (n. 7), 195

and proposals, 93, 96
and EC presidency, 93, 213

Madrid
"counterconference" in -, 121, 122
CSCE Follow-up Meeting (1980-1983) in -, 17, 18
"Madrid never again", 18, 276
and only item fixed before the beginning of -, 59
as propaganda forum, 117
final closing date of -, 139, 140
as reflexion of political reality, 211
and drafting techniques, 217, 218
functions of -, 227, 234, 238

Madrid Concluding Document, 91, 104, 113, 125, 234, 273, 275, 276, 282, 283
adoption of -, 18, 229, 261
as catalogue of contemporary problems, 18, 265, 274
and rule of consensus, 166, 255, 265
limits of -, 185-191
ambiguity, 183, 184, 188-190
maximum results, 186, 187
minimum results, 187, 188
and drafting techniques, 218, 219
as referent principle of the CSCE process, 231
and baskets, 255-260
see also Annex 4

Malta, 32, 91, 103, 129 (n. 7), 148, 161, 174, 235
and the closure of the Helsinki Consultations, 58, 59, 82, 242
and proposals, 92, 97, 104, 242, 258
- delegate and instructions, 116
Malta weeks/phase, 136, 240, 242-244, 270, 273
and mini-groups, 163
and consensus on concluding documents, 166, 220, 241, 242, 270
as member of the Non-aligned movement, 169

and the "stopped clock" (11 November 1980), 195, 196
and the Polish chairman (9 February 1982), 202
and the "night of silences" (5 March 1982), 205, 206
and role distribution, 225
and chairman's statement, 264

mass media
responsibility of -
proposals on -, 99, 187, 224, 257

Mediterranean
security and co-operation in -, 59, 116, 173, 270, 279
proposals on -, 97, 104, 242, 243
Purple Book on -, 134, 135
Drafting Group (DG-M) on -, 149, 282
Madrid Concluding Document on -, 187, 258, 260, 261, 263, 264
see also Final Act, Chapter "Mediterranean"

Meeting(-s) of Experts; *see* Expert meeting(-s)

Middle East, 59, 83

miembro de la delegación, 109, 110*

migrant workers, 83, 252
proposals on -, 96, 97, 103, 105, 259

military détente; *see* détente

military exercises
prior notification of -, 252
see also military manoevres

military manoevres
prior notification of -
interpretative statements on -, 74 (n. 8), 75 (n. 8)
proposal on -, 103
Final Act on -, 181, 252

mini-groups, 132, 153, 156, 163*, 164, 169, 219, 272, 273
and RM.39, 239, 240

MPT, 49
see also Helsinki Consultations

Monaco, 32, 77, 78, 169, 273
and members of the delegation, 110, 148
- delegation and instructions, 115, 116

monitor groups, 84, 94, 120, 121, 188, 237, 238, 249, 251

Montreux
Expert meeting on the Peaceful Settlement of Disputes (1978) in -, 103

Morocco, 82, 83, 104, 243

Moscow - Human Rights Group, 178, 237

Mutual and Balanced Force Reductions (MBFR), 25, 234, 237
and CSCE, 31-33, 181

negotiation(-s)
tactics of -, 63, 114, 115
and instructions, 112-117
and the rule of consensus, 220
aspects of -
demandeur, 220-223
role distribution, 223-226
turning points in -, 227*, 229, 231, 232, 235, 240
phases in (Madrid) -, 226, 244

negotiators
actual -, 110, 111
and instructions, 112-117, 122
and press, 117-119
and pressure groups, 119-122
and personality and power, 123-126, 245 (n. 5)

Netherlands, 73 (n. 2), 119, 129 (n. 7), 169, 172
and proposals, 93, 96
and the "stopped clock" (11 November 1980), 195
and the Polish chairman (9 February 1982), 197-199
and EC presidency, 233

"Neue Ostpolitik" [New East Policy], 31, 80

Neutral countries
and developments in Poland (1981-1982), 130 (n. 7), 136, 188, 189, 197, 209
and the Afghanistan question, 189
and political prisoners in Turkey, 248

Neutral and Non-Aligned (NNA)

countries
- and NATO declaration (May 1970), 25
- in Geneva on the follow-up system, 53, 54, 56
- and informal discussions in Belgrade, 65
- - objectives, 90, 91
- and proposals, 91, 92, 102-105, 186, 225, 258, 259
- as co-ordinators in contact groups; *see* co-ordinators
- as go-between in mini-groups, 163
- and draft concluding documents, 169; *see also* draft concluding documents
- and appeal of April 1983, 164, 165
- and Preamble of the Madrid Concluding Document, 188, 189
- and Purple Book, 197
- and the Polish chairman (9 February 1982), 201-203
- and the "night of silences" (5 March 1982), 206-208, 248
- as *demandeur*, 221, 222
- and role distribution, 225, 226, 272
- and adjournment of the conference, 232
- and collective declaration (February 1983), 239

Non-aligned movement, 169

New International Economic Order, 105

New Times, 88

"non-papers", 215*, 218, 219, 232

Non-Participating Mediterranean States, 58, 59, 104, 243, 264
- Blue Book on -, 81-83
- Purple Book on -, 134, 135
- influence of -, 270

North Atlantic Treaty Organization (NATO)
- and declarations and communiqué's
  - Reykjavik, Brussels, Rome, Bonn (1968-1972), 24-32, 51-53, 81
  - Ankara (1980), 86-89, 97
  - Bonn (1982), 237, 246 (n. 17)
- and meetings
  - Washington (1969), 26
  - Paris (1983), 165
- decision-making in -, 44, 45
- and the rule of consensus, 58
- members of -, 86, 172
- - objectives, 86, 87
- and the "stopped clock" (11 November 1980), 194, 195
- and the Polish chairman (9 February 1982), 197-199, 202, 203
- - foreign ministers on the developments in Poland (1981-1982), 197-199, 202, 203, 236
- "-scenario", 203, 209, 210
- and the "night of silences" (5 March 1982), 204
- - two-track decision (December 1979) on INF missiles, 228, 239-241
- differences of opinion in - on RM.39, 237, 238

Nordic countries
- and proposals, 92, 98, 99, 106
- - delegations and instructions, 116
- *see also* caucus(-es)

Northern Ireland, 250, 251

Norway, 167-169, 172
- and proposals, 85, 96, 106
- and the Polish chairman (9 February 1982), 201

observer status, 78*, 270

observers at military exercises
- exchange of -, 177

OECD, 34

Olympic Games in Moscow (1980)
- boycott of -, 253, 254

order of speakers, 144

organizational framework; *see* institutional framework

Ottawa
- Expert meeting on Human Rights (1985) in -, 238, 261

package deal, 177*, 208, 235

Paris
- NATO meeting (June 1983) in -, 165

parliament
members of -, 110, 111, 270

participating states, 77-81
objectives of -, 84-91
proposals of -, 91-106

peace marches
in Western Europe, 122, 228, 234

peace movements, 120

"peace plans", 23

peaceful coexistence, 30, 35

peaceful settlement of disputes, 35, 38
proposal on -, 103
Meeting of Experts on -, 103, 258, 260, 261, 279

Plenary
and SWBs, 65, 66, 143, 146, 147, 269
and proposals, 91
attendance at -, 110, 111, 145
Purple Book on -, 143-146, 150, 151, 201, 271, 282
and right to speak, 202
and fixing of the grid, 208
and implementation discussions, 249
conclusion on the power of decision-making of -, 271
recommendations on the functioning of -, 282, 284

PLO, 83

Poland
and "collective security system", 78
developments (1981-1982) in -, 90, 107 (n. 6), 130 (n. 7), 136, 138, 162, 188, 189, 201, 204, 208, 211, 228, 233, 236-238, 241, 248, 250, 256, 275
and Western criticism of -, 184, 185, 203, 209, 210
and proposals, 92, 98-101, 190
on fulfilment of the Final Act provisions, 107 (n. 7), 108 (n. 7), 185
exiles from -, 121
and dissemination of information, 180
and chairmanship on 9 February 1982, 193, 197-203, 208-210, 229, 273
as "second Afghanistan", 249

policy
declared -, 21
- formulation and - execution, 122

political parties, 120

Portugal, 129 (n. 7), 172
and interpretative statement, 74 (n. 8)
and proposals, 95-97

Prague
WP Declaration (October 1969) issued in -, 26, 27, 28, 80
WP "Declaration on Peace, Security and Co-operation in Europe" (January 1972) issued in -, 30

Preamble
to the draft concluding documents, 142, 151
to the Madrid Concluding Document, 188, 189, 263, 264

Preparatory Committee, 194-197

Preparatory Meeting
Belgrade -, 54, 55
Madrid -, 131, 133, 137, 140, 194, 221, 229, 245 (n. 1), 247, 261, 277
Vienna -, 261, 276

press, 117-119
official press conferences, 119, 121
freedom of -, 187, 251, 257

pressure groups, 119-122

(Ten) Principles Guiding Relations
Principle I, 183, 184
Principle IV, 62
Principle VI, 74 (n. 8), 87, 184
Principle VII, 74 (n. 8), 94, 179, 180
Principle VIII, 184
Principle IX, 57
Principle X, 74 (n. 8), 183
see also Final Act, Chapter I

psychiatric science
misuse of -, 249, 252

public opinion, 121, 122

Purple Book, 50, 55, 65, 131*-133, 197, 206, 229
and agenda, 133-136, 244
and "optical divison", 136-138, 245 (n. 1)
and time schedule, 138-140, 279
and follow-up, 140, 141, 283
and consensus, 141, 143, 151
and Plenary, 143-145, 146, 150, 151, 201, 271, 282
and SWBs, 145-150
and Drafting Groups, 149, 150, 205, 271
chairman's statement to the -, 262
and implementation, 247, 274
recommendation on -, 278
see also Annex 3

racism, 102, 187, 224, 250, 251, 257

Radio Free Europe, 99, 118, 180, 253, 257

Radio Liberty, 99, 118, 257

radio transmissions (-broadcasts)
jamming of foreign (-Western) -, 95, 180, 181, 188, 224, 238, 241, 252, 253, 256, 257

referent principle(-s), 231, 246 (n. 10)*

religious freedom
proposal on -, 104, 258
Madrid Concluding Document on -, 191, 258, 263

religious minorities, 249

religious organizations, 120

representatives; *see* negotiators

reunification of families; *see* family reunification

Reykjavik
NATO Declaration (June 1968) issued in -, 25, 26, 31

Review of International Affairs, 39

right of reply, 143*-145

RM.39; RM.39 revised; *see* draft concluding documents

Romania
in Geneva on the follow-up system, 53
in Helsinki on equality of the participating states, 56-58, 63
and interpretative statements, 74 (n. 8)
and proposals, 92, 93, 101, 102, 187, 257
- delegation and instructions, 115, 116
Community of Romanians in France, 120
exiles from -, 121
and SU, 157
and mini-groups, 163
and RM.39 revised, 165, 241
and caucus of 34 delegations, 243
and emigration measures, 247

role distribution, 223-226, 245 (n. 5)

Rome
NATO declaration (May 1970) issued in -, 24, 25, 28, 29, 31
Treaty of -, 171, 213

RSNT, 44

rules of procedure
options for -, 41-45
choices for the CSCE -, 56-58
points for consideration on -, 70-72
and British law, 201
conclusions on -, 268, 269
recommendations on -, 278, 280-284
see also Blue Book and Purple Book

SALT, 31, 112, 234, 237

samizdat, 121

San Marino, 67, 78, 129 (n. 7), 148, 169, 174
and appeal of April 1983, 164
and Purple Book, 197

SCE, 39, 48 (n. 14)

Scientific Forum (1980), 95, 134, 279

seating arrangements
of the contact groups, 153, 156, 157

sherry groups, 132, 153, 161*, 219, 272, 273
from - to mini-groups, 163

Solidarity union movement, 210, 228, 237

South Africa, 250

South Korea
  and the shooting down of a Boeing-747 airliner over the Russian island Sachalin (September 1983), 21, 244

Soviet Committee on Security and Co-operation, 129 (n. 2)

Soviet Union (SU)
  and USA, 24, 34, 62, 88, 90, 124, 125, 237, 250-252
  - aims, 29, 46 (n. 4), 47 (n. 4), 239; *see also* Eastern Europe-objectives
  and FRG, 31
  and link between MBFR and CSCE, 32, 33
  in Helsinki on the principle of equality, 56
  in Geneva on the rule of consensus, 58
  and interpretative statements, 75 (n. 8)
  and (collaborators in the) Executive Secretariat, 76 (n. 12)
  and collective security system, 78
  and Israel, 83, 250
  and Britain, 88
  and disarmament conference, 140, 141, 222, 230, 231, 233, 234, 237, 239, 241, 242
  and Western accusations on domestic policies, 88, 140, 249, 250
  and proposals, 92, 98-100, 102, 187
  - delegation
    members of -, 110, 129 (n. 2)
    and press relations, 119
  and peace marches in Western Europe, 122, 234
  and contact groups, 156, 157
  and Romania, 157
  and (Western amendments to) RM.39 revised, 165, 166, 240, 241
  and developments in Poland (1981-1982), 136, 184, 185, 203, 204, 236, 248, 250
  and Principle VII, 179, 180
  and the opening of the Madrid Meeting, 194, 195, 209, 221, 230
  and Purple Book, 197
  and the "night of silences" (5 March 1982), 203-208, 211
  and drafting techniques, 217
  as *demandeur*, 221, 222, 241, 242
  as vetoer, 225
  as controller, 226
  West German-Soviet communiqué (November 1981), 234
  and human rights, 237, 249
  and boycott of 1980 Olympic Games, 253
  and review of implementation and détente, 253-255
  and chairman's statement, 263, 264
  and political influence, 273

Spain, 67, 129 (n. 7)
  and Andorra, 77
  and interpretative statement, 74 (n. 8)
  and proposals, 85, 92, 95-97, 103, 258
  and NATO, 103, 157, 172
  and members of the delegation, 110
  and the Preparatory Meeting, 133, 137
  and compromise on RM.39 revised ("Spanish Initiative"), 165, 166, 219, 229, 242, 243
  and the "stopped clock" (11 November 1980), 194-197
  and the Polish chairman (9 February 1982), 200

standing commission on East-West relations (SCEWER), 29, 33

Standing European Conference, 37

START, 234, 237

status quo in central Europe
  international recognition of -, 221

Stockholm
  European Disarmament Conference (1984) in -, 241-243, 258, 261

Structured Informal Negotiations, 132, 153, 161

Sub-Committees, 64, 65, 145

subject to confirmation, 113*

Subsidiary Working Bodies (SWBs), 132, 142
  and proposals, 91, 104, 150, 215
  Purple Book on -, 145*-149, 150
  discussion (-themes) in -, 159, 249, 251-253
  conclusion on -, 269

Syria, 82, 104, 243

Sweden, 37, 129 (n. 7), 167
  and interpretative statement, 74 (n. 8)
  and proposals, 92, 103-106
  and working programmes in Geneva and Belgrade, 147
  as co-ordinator, 157
  and appeal of April 1983, 164
  as a traditional neutral country, 169
  and Purple Book, 197
  and chairman's statement on Malta's proposals, 244
  and SU, 245 (n. 1)

Switzerland, 37, 67, 73 (n. 2), 129 (n. 7), 165
  and proposals, 97, 103, 106, 179, 180, 258
  and working programmes in Geneva, Belgrade and Madrid, 147
  as co-ordinator, 157
  and informal bilateral talks, 161
  as a traditional neutral country, 169
  as go-between in the Preparatory Committee, 196
  and the "night of silences" (5 March 1982), 204
  and the UN, 280

Tartars, 249

terrorism
  combatting of -
    proposal on -, 96, 97, 186

The Practical Negotiator, 227

Third World, 83

time schedule (-table)
  Purple Book on -, 138-140, 279

trade union(-s), 120, 183, 251, 267
  proposal on -, 238, 256

Tunesia, 82, 83, 104, 243

Turkey, 172
  and Cyprus, 62, 73 (n. 7), 75 (n. 8), 129 (n. 1), 261, 262, 271
  and proposal, 95, 96
  - delegation and instructions, 116
  associations of exiles from -, 120
  on fulfilment of the Final Act provisions, 185
  and the "night of silences" (5 March 1982), 206, 207
  and political prisoners, 248
  and interpretative statement to the Madrid Concluding Document, 262

UIC, 95

Ukrain, 120, 121, 249

Ukrainian Helsinki Group, 107 (n. 6)

UNESCO, 38, 55, 96, 100, 134, 280

United Kingdom, 67, 169
  and SCEWER, 29, 33
  and proposals, 85, 93, 95, 96
  and SU, 88
  and Human Rights, 172
  British law, 201
  and the "night of silences" (5 March 1982), 207

United Nations, 33, 44, 47 (n. 14), 48 (n. 14), 67, 115, 156
  - General Assembly, 25, 37, 42, 43
  - Security Council, 36-40, 42, 48 (n. 14)
  - Conventions, 74 (n. 8)
  - Friendly Relations Declaration, 75 (n. 8)
  - Charter, 36-40, 42, 75 (n. 8), 249
  - (Deputy) Secretary General, 134, 135
  and CSCE, 267, 279, 280

(Third) United Nations Conference on the Law of the Sea (UNCLOS III),

43, 44, 71, 281

United States (US)
and SU, 24, 34, 62, 88, 90, 124, 125, 237, 250-252
and link between MBFR and CSCE, 32
and participation in the CSCE, 51, 77-81
and reservation, 62, 63, 73 (n. 7)
and interpretative statements, 74 (n. 8), 75 (n. 8)
and WP declarations, 79
- delegation, 84, 85, 270
members of -, 110, 111, 129 (n. 2)
and instructions, 115, 116
and the Afghanistan question, 85
and implementation of the Final Act, 85, 107 (n. 7)
and proposals, 85, 96, 260
and pressure groups, 112, 120
"US Helsinki Watch Committee", 120
and the "stopped clock" (11 November 1980), 195
and the Polish chairman (9 February 1982), 198
as controller, 226
- tariffs, 252
and political influence, 273

"Uniting for Peace" resolution (1950), 42

Universal Declaration (of Human Rights, 1948), 74 (n. 8)

Venice
Seminar on Co-operation in the Mediterranean (October 1984) in -, 97, 260, 261, 263

Venlo (the Netherlands)
EPC meeting on Poland (May 1981) in -, 228, 233

Vienna
CSCE Follow-up Meeting (1986) in -, 22, 259-261, 268, 276-278

Voice of America, 180, 253

Warsaw
Treaty of - (May 1955), 35
WP declaration (May 1980) issued in -, 88

Warsaw Pact (WP)
and declarations and communiqué's
Budapest, Bucharest, Prague (1966-1972), 24-32, 50, 52, 53, 78-80
Warsaw (1980), 88
Consultative Committee of -, 25
and collective security system, 34, 35, 78
and US, 79, 80, 88
and implementation, 88, 267
and disarmament conference, 88
and "Spanish Initiative", 166
and the Polish chairman (9 February 1982), 198-200, 210
and the "night of silences" (5 March 1982), 204, 207

Washington
NATO meeting (April 1969) in -, 26

West, the
and possible voting procedures in the CSCE, 57, 58
in Helsinki on working methods, 65
- objectives, 84-88, 108 (n. 10), 247, 255
and "Non-intervention in internal affairs", 87
and proposals, 87, 88, 94-99, 158, 162, 168, 172, 186-188, 214, 215, 224, 225, 230, 231, 234, 238, 239, 255-260, 276
- delegations
and CSCE experience, 111, 112
and press relations, 118, 119
two most considerable Western political powers, 124
and developments in Poland (1981-1982), 130 (n. 7), 136, 162, 188, 189, 197, 209, 210, 241, 249, 273
and review of implementation, 86-88, 133, 136-139, 184, 248-255, 273, 278
and follow-up meeting to Madrid, 140, 141
and contact groups, 157-159, 215
and mini-groups, 163
and amendments to drafting concluding documents
RM.39, 229, 238, 239
RM.39 revised, 165, 219, 229, 240-242

and dissemination of information, 180, 181
and the Afghanistan question, 189, 249, 251
as *demandeur*, 194, 221, 222, 241
and the "stopped clock" (11 November 1980), 114, 194-196, 208, 209, 273
and Purple Book, 197
and the Polish chairman (9 February 1982), 198, 199, 201-203, 210, 273
and the "night of silences" (5 March 1982), 203, 205-208, 210, 211, 248, 273
and disarmament conference, 217, 218, 230, 231, 234
and (violation of) human rights in Eastern Europe, 244, 250
and détente, 249, 253-255
and East European accusations, 251

Westphalia
Peace of - (1648), 23

WEU, 40

working bodies; *see* Subsidiary Working Bodies (SWBs)

Working Group on European Co--operation and Security, 39, 46 (n. 2), 47 (n. 12)

working groups, 57
Blue Book on -, 65, 66
Purple Book on -, 131, 201

working languages, 66, 148, 165, 175 (n. 1), 215, 269
Blue Book on -, 67
points for consideration on -, 72
English, 67, 72, 75 (n. 8), 166, 175 (n. 1) , 263, 269, 284
French, 64, 67, 73 (n. 4), 75 (n. 10), 197, 263, 264, 269, 284
German, 67, 73 (n. 4), 269, 284
Italian, 67, 73 (n. 4), 269, 284
Spanish, 67, 269, 284
Russian, 67, 75 (n. 8), 166, 168, 175 (n. 1), 263, 269, 284
recommendations on -, 283, 284

working methods
Blue Book on -, 65, 66
Purple Book on -, 143
conclusions on -, 269

"World Congress of Free Ukrainians", 120, 121

"World Federation of Free Latvians", 120

"World Parliament of the Peoples for Peace", 120

"World Veterans Federation", 120

Yellow Book, 50*, 55, 64, 65, 137, 139, 141, 145, 262

young people
proposals on -, 99-102
Final Act on -, 178
Madrid Concluding Document on -, 115, 116, 187

"Youth Committee for Peace", 120

Yugoslavia, 37, 39
and CSCE Follow-up Meeting in Belgrade, 64
- objectives, 90
and proposals, 92, 93, 103, 105, 258
- delegation and instructions, 116
as co-ordinator, 157
and informal bilateral talks, 161
and mini-groups, 163
and appeal of April 1983, 164
as member of the Non-aligned movement, 169
and Purple Book, 197
as *demandeur*, 225